REASON OF STATE

This historically embedded treatment of theoretical debates about prerogative and reason of state spans over four centuries of constitutional development. Commencing with the English Civil War and the constitutional theories of Hobbes and the Republicans, it moves through eighteenth-century arguments over jealousy of trade and commercial reason of state to early imperial concerns and the nineteenth-century debate on the legislative empire, to martial law and twentieth-century articulations of the state at the end of empire. It concludes with reflections on the contemporary post-imperial security state.

The book synthesizes a wealth of theoretical and empirical literature that allows a link to be made between the development of constitutional ideas and global *realpolitik*. It exposes the relationship between internal and external pressures and designs in the making of the modern constitutional polity and explores the relationship between law, politics and economics in a way that remains rare in constitutional scholarship.

THOMAS POOLE is Professor of Law at the London School of Economics and Political Science.

CAMBRIDGE STUDIES IN CONSTITUTIONAL LAW

The aim of this series is to produce leading monographs in constitutional law. All areas of constitutional law and public law fall within the ambit of the series, including human rights and civil liberties law, administrative law, as well as constitutional theory and the history of constitutional law. A wide variety of scholarly approaches is encouraged, with the governing criterion being simply that the work is of interest to an international audience. Thus, works concerned with only one jurisdiction will be included in the series as appropriate, while, at the same time, the series will include works which are explicitly comparative or theoretical - or both. The series editors likewise welcome proposals that work at the intersection of constitutional and international law, or that seek to bridge the gaps between civil law systems, the US, and the common law jurisdictions of the Commonwealth.

Books in the series

Reason of State: Law, Prerogative and Empire
Thomas Poole

Bills of Rights in the Common Law
Robert Leckey

The Guardian of the Constitution: Hans Kelsen and Carl Schmitt on the Limits of Constitutional Law
Translated by Lars Vinx, with an introduction and notes by Lars Vinx

Parliamentary Bills of Rights: The Experiences of New Zealand and the United Kingdom Experiences
Janet L. Hiebert and James B. Kelly

Lawyering for the Rule of Law: Government Lawyers and the Rise of Judicial Power in Israel
Yoav Dotan

Balancing Constitutional Rights: The Origins and Meanings of Postwar Legal Discourse
Jacco Bomhoff

Judges on Trial: The Independence and Accountability of the English Judiciary
Shimon Shetreet and Sophie Turenne

Proportionality and Constitutional Culture
Moshe Cohen-Eliya and Iddo Porat

The Politics of Principle: The First South African Constitutional Court, 1995–2005
Theunis Roux

The New Commonwealth Model of Constitutionalism, Theory and Practice
Stephen Gardbaum

Searching for the State in British Legal Thought, Competing Conceptions of the Public Sphere
Janet McLean

Judging Social Rights
Jeff King

Proportionality, Constitutional Rights and Their Limitations
Aharon Barak

Parliamentary Sovereignty, Contemporary Debates
Jeffrey Goldsworthy

REASON OF STATE

Law, Prerogative and Empire

THOMAS POOLE

CAMBRIDGE
UNIVERSITY PRESS

CAMBRIDGE
UNIVERSITY PRESS

University Printing House, Cambridge CB2 8BS, United Kingdom

One Liberty Plaza, 20th Floor, New York, NY 10006, USA

477 Williamstown Road, Port Melbourne, VIC 3207, Australia

314-321, 3rd Floor, Plot 3, Splendor Forum, Jasola District Centre, New Delhi - 110025, India

79 Anson Road, #06-04/06, Singapore 079906

Cambridge University Press is part of the University of Cambridge.

It furthers the University's mission by disseminating knowledge in the pursuit of education, learning and research at the highest international levels of excellence.

www.cambridge.org
Information on this title: www.cambridge.org/9781107461741

First published 2015
First paperback edition 2018

A catalogue record for this publication is available from the British Library

Library of Congress Cataloging in Publication data
Poole, Thomas (Thomas M.), author.
Reason of state : law, prerogative and empire / Thomas Poole.
pages cm. – (Cambridge studies in constitutional law ; 14)
Includes bibliographical references and index.
ISBN 978-1-107-08989-1 (hardback)
1. Reason of state. 2. Economic policy. 3. Imperialism. I. Title.
K3169.P667 2015
340′.11–dc23
2015005647

ISBN 978-1-107-08989-1 Hardback
ISBN 978-1-107-46174-1 Paperback

For my mother, Anne, and in memory of my father, Michael.

Novis orbis victus vos vicit
(The New World, conquered by you, has conquered you in its turn)

Lipsius

CONTENTS

ACKNOWLEDGEMENTS

I have enjoyed writing this book immensely. I hope this comes across. The idea sprang from a series of conversations with the Cambridge Studies in Constitutional Law series editors, David Dyzenhaus and Adam Tomkins, the first with David in New York when we realized that there was no modern treatise on prerogative. Since then, David has been instrumental in getting two events organized at the London School of Economics (LSE) off the ground, one on Hobbes and the other on the twentieth-century theorists Schmitt, Hayek and Oakeshott, which advanced my thinking in areas of central importance to this book. I would like to thank both David and Adam for their support.

Over the past few years or so, I presented papers that made their way in one guise or other into the book. I would like to thank the organizers and participants in those seminars, given at Law Schools in Cambridge, Durham and Glasgow; the University of Melbourne and the University of New South Wales; Paris II Panthéon-Assas and the European University Institute; Harvard, Toronto and Yale; the Law and Public Affairs Program at Princeton and an ASIL workshop in Washington.

Parts of Chapter 2 appeared in a somewhat different form in my contribution to David Dyzenhaus and Thomas Poole (eds.), *Hobbes and the Law* (Cambridge, 2012), and a version of Chapter 7 appears in David Dyzenhaus and Thomas Poole (eds.), *Law, Liberty and State: Schmitt, Hayek and Oakeshott on the Rule of Law* (Cambridge, 2015).

I would like to mention here the LSE Legal & Political Theory Forum and thank Philip Cook, who set the Forum up with me, and Chandran Kukathas, who now hosts it with me. Without the Forum it would simply not have been possible for me to write a book of this sort, and its imprint can be found on almost every page.

I would particularly like to thank Neil Duxbury, Conor Gearty, Michael Lobban and Adrian Vermeule, who read and provided detailed and insightful comments on most if not all the book in draft form. Martin Loughlin commented on the chapters and has been a formative influence on me. David Kershaw not only read all the draft chapters – presumably having little real interest in any of it – but also made sure that I saw the wood for the trees. I would also like to thank Mark Aronson, Nehal Bhuta, Sean Brennan, Megan Donaldson, Carol Harlow, Tom Hickman, Bernard Keenan, Karen Knop, Nico Krisch, John McCormick, Sankar Muthu, Paul McHugh, Sangeeta Shah, Gerry Simpson, Samuel Tschorne, Neil Walker, Grégoire Webber, Mike Wilkinson and Lea Ypi for their help and advice.

Above all, though, I would like to thank Devika, Xavier and Lulu, who are everything to me.

London

1

The safety of the people: from prerogative to reason of state

The safety of the people is the supreme law. This deceptively simple maxim seems to have been coined by Cicero.[1] Certainly the phrase *salus populi suprema lex esto* appears in *The Laws* as part of an ideal constitution embodying the principles of the uncorrupted Republic. When faced with a violent threat to the security of the republic, the Senate was to designate the consuls as supreme military commanders and authorize them to take any measures they thought necessary to counter the threat. In such a situation, Cicero argued, a procedure was needed through which the consuls might be permitted to use force against fellow citizens without concerning themselves too much with the strict legality of what they did. A legal process was required that would allow the subversion of normal legal guarantees in extraordinary moments for the purposes of safeguarding the legal order as a whole.

The process Cicero described was a stylized version of the so-called 'last decree' (*senatus consultum ultimum*)[2] increasingly used in the late Republic as the widening empire began to put intolerable strain on existing political structures.[3] As consul in 63 BC, Cicero himself had been the recipient of a last decree, and drew on its authority to crush the Catiline conspiracy before persuading a reluctant Senate to agree the extra-legal execution of the defeated conspirators.[4] Cicero argued

[1] Marcus Tullius Cicero, *The Laws* (Oxford: Oxford University Press, trans. Niall Rudd, 1998), Book 3.8, 152.

[2] Andrew Lintott, *The Constitution of the Roman Republic* (Oxford: Oxford University Press, 1999), 89–90. Lintott notes that the term *senatus consultum ultimum* was not used in antiquity and that a more precise title would be the *senatus consultum de re publica defendenda*.

[3] Michael Crawford, *The Roman Republic* (London: Fontana, 2nd edn., 1992), 94–170.

[4] Sallust, *Catiline's Conspiracy* (Oxford: Oxford University Press, ed. William W. Batstone, 2010). After the Second Punic War (218–201 BC), the office of dictator largely fell into disuse, although it did resurface when the *Lex Valeria* named Sulla dictator in 82 BC and again in 49 BC when Caesar (soon to become *dictator perpetuo*) was nominated by Lepidus after a similar law. These later uses revived the institution in a stronger and more

before the Senate that when the law was impotent, extra-legal action was necessary and that by taking action against the state the conspirators had in any case become enemies of the state (*hostes*) and so relinquished their rights as citizens.[5] This stance came back to haunt him. The persistent use of the last decree did absolutely nothing to halt the collapse of the Republic he cherished.[6] And Cicero himself was proscribed as an enemy of state under the Second Triumvirate of Mark Antony, Lepidus and Octavian (soon to become Emperor Augustus), to be killed shortly afterwards.[7]

The type of power invoked by Cicero, which in turn brought about his demise, was expressed at a later stage in European history in the idiom of 'reason of state'. The term entered the political vocabulary shortly after the death of Machiavelli, that great student of republican constitutional politics, and can be linked to the revolution in thinking about politics that he instigated.[8] In his analysis of the concept's subsequent development, Philip Bobbitt shows how changes in the nature of reason of state connect to epochal shifts in state form.[9] So, the Italian origins of *ragione di stato* reflect the genesis of the concept in the idea of the princely state that Machiavelli[10] and his fellow Florentine Guicciardini[11] formulated

authoritarian form as the Republic collapsed into anarchy. Crawford, *Roman Republic*, 151; Lintott, *Constitution of the Roman Republic*, 109–113.

5 Marcus Tullius Cicero, '*In Catilinam ("Against Catiline") I*' in *Cicero Political Speeches* (Oxford: Oxford University Press, ed. D. H. Berry, 2006). Julius Caesar made a famous speech in dissent. He argued, presciently as it turned out, that the illegal repression of the conspirators would set a dangerous precedent for future proscriptions.

6 On Cicero's role in articulating the disintegration that accompanied the collapse of political authority in the late Republic, see Andrew Wallace-Hardrill, *Rome's Cultural Revolution* (Cambridge: Cambridge University Press, 2008), chapter 5.

7 Kathryn Tempest, *Cicero: Politics and Persuasion in Ancient Rome* (London: Continuum, 2011), chapter 16.

8 Maurizio Viroli, *From Politics to Reason of State: The Acquisition and Transformation of the Language of Politics 1250–1600* (Cambridge: Cambridge University Press, 1992).

9 Philip Bobbitt, *The Shield of Achilles: War, Peace, and the Course of History* (New York: Alfred A. Knopf, 2002), 87, 108, 135–136.

10 On Machiavelli and the reason of state tradition see Friedrich Meinecke, *Machiavellism: The Doctrine of Raison d'État and Its Place in Modern History* (New Brunswick: Transaction Publishers, ed. Werner Stark, 1998).

11 It seems that it was Francesco Guicciardini who introduced the actual expression *ragione di stato* (reason of state) into political discourse. Guicciardini enjoined the reader of his *Dialogo del reggimento di Firenze* (1526) to think in terms of the reason and customs of the states ('*secondo la ragione e uso degli stati*') rather than the imperatives of moral conscience when considering the preservation of states. Viroli, *From Politics to Reason of State*, 178.

in the sixteenth century.[12] The proliferation in the seventeenth century of the term in its French form *raison d'état* reflects the emergence of the kingly state, exemplified by the state-building machinations of Richelieu.[13] The German cognate *Staats raison* is more appropriate once the eighteenth-century territorial state emerges, Bobbitt argues, since that stage is best reflected in the designs of Frederick the Great. At each of these historical phases the meaning of reason of state subtly changes in accordance with emerging beliefs about the state and the relationship between government and governed. Among the Italian princely states, '*ragione di stato* simply stood for a rational, unprincipled justification for the self-aggrandizement of the State; whereas *raison d'état* achieved a parallel justification through the personification of the state, and leveraged the imperatives of this justification to impose obligations on the dynastic ruler'. *Staats raison*, by contrast, represented 'a rationale given on behalf of the State, and imperative that compels its strategic designs' but which 'identifies the state with the country, the land'.[14]

The point of introducing Bobbitt's stylized historical reconstruction[15] is to illustrate the value of reason of state as a lens through which to examine constitutional change. Reason of state presupposes a situation in which state action moves from one register, based on law and right, to another, based on interest and might.[16] The condition for such a shift is normally

12 The concept soon spread elsewhere in the Italian peninsula. Perhaps the most famous work in this genre is that of the Piemontese Giovanni Botero, *Della Ragion di Stato* (Venice, 1589).

13 On Richelieu, reason of state and the kingly state, see William F. Church, *Richelieu and Reason of State* (Princeton: Princeton University Press, 1972) which provides extensive treatment of the professional writers Guez de Balzac and Jean de Silhon, the jurist Cadin Le Bret, the diplomat Philippe de Béthune, and, perhaps most important of all, Henri, duc de Rohan. See also J. H. Elliott, *Richelieu and Olivares* (Cambridge: Cambridge University Press, 1984), 121–129; Martti Koskenniemi, 'International Law and *Raison d'État:* Rethinking the Prehistory of International Law' in Benedict Kingsbury and Benjamin Straumann (eds.), *The Roman Foundations of the Law of Nations: Alberico Gentili and the Justice of Empire* (Oxford: Oxford University Press, 2010), 305–314.

14 Bobbitt, *Shield of Achilles*, 87, 108, 135–136.

15 For a nuanced historical exploration of the connection of *raison d'état* and the 'new humanism' infused with Tacitean scepticism, see Richard Tuck, *Philosophy and Government 1572–1651* (Cambridge: Cambridge University Press, 1993). Tuck points to the central importance of two thinkers, one Dutch, Justus Lipsius, the other the Frenchman Michel de Montaigne, and notes the way in which in the Netherlands and France in particular the Wars of Religion made manifest the concept's core idea, the legitimacy of violent and immoral means in the service of higher ends.

16 Carl Joachim Friedrich, *Constitutional Reason of State* (Providence: Brown University Press, 1957).

the assertion that the state's vital interests are at stake. In the course of acting in its own interest, the state might face the prospect of violating moral and legal norms in protecting its overriding interests or security.[17] Understood in these terms, reason of state offers a number of advantages for the constitutional theorist. First, it is a juridical concept that operates not only in the interstices of law and politics – as many other concepts do, including 'sovereignty' and 'rights' – but also, and in particular, at the intersection between political norms and state action. Second, reason of state is a relative constant, having been in continuous use since Machiavelli's time. Third, it connects to the relationship between government and governed – between the agents of government to whom the 'reason' of reason of state refers and the 'people' with whose well-being the *salus populi* principle is concerned. Fourth, it is associated with hard strategic choices and difficult political and moral decisions. Concentrating on this dimension of constitutional politics is rather like focusing on hard cases in the study of law.[18] We expect a hard case to reveal not just something about itself but also something important about the wider context of which it forms a problematic part. Likewise, reason of state has the potential to illuminate disproportionately the deep structure of a constitution and the principles that inform it.

Reason of state describes a category familiar enough in practice, including in our own time where recourse is often made to exceptional powers to deal with crises or emergencies. Courts today frequently hear arguments about necessity and legal exceptionalism, and the constitutional politics of security and secrecy is now a feature of public debate. Writers on law looking to contribute to this debate have typically worked within one of three conceptual frameworks. While each offers insight, none is entirely successful. One such framework is 'emergency powers'.[19] It is increasingly clear, however, that we are not really talking about emergencies – or at least not *just* about emergencies. Some of the juridical developments that we want to discuss are not really about emergencies. Moreover, many laws

[17] Gianfranco Poggi, *The State: Its Nature, Development and Prospects* (Cambridge: Polity, 1990), 84.

[18] Ronald Dworkin, 'Hard Cases' (1975) 88 *Harvard Law Review* 1057.

[19] See, e.g., Bruce Ackerman, *Before the Next Attack: Preserving Civil Liberties in an Age of Terrorism* (New Haven: Yale University Press, 2006); Oren Gross and Fionnuala Ní Aoláin, *Law in Times of Crisis: Emergency Powers in Theory and Practice* (Cambridge: Cambridge University Press, 2006); Eric A. Posner and Adrian Vermeule, *Terror in the Balance: Security, Liberty, and the Courts* (New York: Oxford University Press, 2007).

initially justified as emergency measures stay on the books after the emergency is over.[20] They end up as part of the normal legal framework. This is a familiar pattern – indeed we see it at work in a later chapter when considering martial law in the *fin-de-siècle* British empire[21] – but it underscores the limited capacity of the emergency powers' framework to capture what is often most important about this area of state action.

A second framework works from the idea of the 'state of exception'.[22] There are some parallels between this framework and the approach taken in this book. But it needs to be handled with great care. One of its strengths is that it allows the commentator to rise above the level of legal specifics. But the synoptic view comes at a price. The language of exception seems all but impossible to disentangle from the work of the constitutional theorist (and sometime Nazi jurist) Carl Schmitt and other Weimar era 'crisis' theorists.[23] This body of work is undoubtedly important and stimulating, and I discuss it in a later chapter. But it is of limited relevance to our current situation – are we really living in a state of near anarchy? Worse, the vocabulary associated with this framework is tarnished. It is the language of grandiloquence, of *Sturm und Drang*, and it tends to trap commentators in an unfruitful binary opposition between 'norm' and 'exception', dragging them into problematic – and often existential – directions.[24] Working in this framework makes otherwise sane writers sound almost hysterical. Above all, exceptionalism tends to make one think of fundamental and existential moments – the birth and death of a constitution, for instance. But reason of state usually operates on a slightly less dramatic plane – war, diplomacy, safety, security – and in ways that are often rather quotidian. In fact, rather than being something exceptional that reaches outside legal orders for inspiration, reason of

[20] See, e.g., Conor Gearty, *Can Human Rights Survive?* (Cambridge: Cambridge University Press, 2006), chapter 4.

[21] See Chapter 6.

[22] See, e.g., Giorgio Agamben, *State of Exception* (Chicago: University of Chicago Press, trans. Kevin Attell, 2005); Giorgio Agamben, *Homo Sacer: Sovereign Power and Bare Life* (Stanford: Stanford University Press, trans. Daniel Heller-Roazen, 1998); Oren Gross, 'The Normless and Exceptionless Exception: Carl Schmitt's Theory of Emergency Powers and the "Norm-Exception" Dichotomy' (2000) 21 *Cardozo Law Review* 1825; Nomi Claire Lazar, *States of Emergency in Liberal Democracy* (New York: Cambridge University Press, 2009).

[23] See, e.g., David Dyzenhaus, *Legality and Legitimacy: Carl Schmitt, Hans Kelsen and Hermann Heller in Weimar* (Oxford: Oxford University Press, 1999); Arthur J. Jacobson and Bernhard Schlink (eds.), *Weimar: A Jurisprudence of Crisis* (Berkeley: University of California Press, 2000).

[24] I explore this propensity in Schmitt's thought in Chapter 7.

state is generally built into the institutional structures and deeply embedded within the everyday working life of the modern state.

A third framework uses the language of 'prerogative'.[25] One advantage of this term is that it immediately connects our present concerns back to old debates about the abuse of power by unruly kings. It is familiar to Anglophone lawyers in particular and can certainly pack a polemical punch. Prerogative is usually used to express the writer's view that we are living under a government that is exercising powers arbitrarily. The tyranny of Stuart kings provides an implicit echo.[26] I have no doubt about the value of studying historical debates about law and the limits of legitimate authority. But this book, while immersed in the historical record, largely avoids the language of prerogative. One reason for this is that the historical parallel that the contemporary use of prerogative trades on is inaccurate. Fundamental changes in state and government have made prerogative in its original sense much less relevant as both an explanatory and a legal category. This is an important argument in the book and is sustained over its first chapters. But the prerogative is also too narrow for our purposes. It refers to a specific type of executive power, exercised in Britain in the name of the Crown and not requiring parliamentary consent. But many of the state actions that commentators now want to group together do not derive from this source – in fact, the vast majority take statutory form.

This book takes a different path. It uses reason of state as a conceptual category with which to frame British debates about law, constitution and empire between roughly 1650 and the present day. It follows William Church's injunction that 'the only valid method of studying the history of reason of state is to examine the manner in which the problem was handled in a given period'.[27] The book does not track precisely the use of the phrase 'reason of state' across time – although we discover that a surprising number of the authors who play a central role in the book did in fact use that precise term or one of its cognates. Instead its standard method is to select key texts – Hobbes's *Leviathan* in Chapter 2, Harrington's *Oceana* and other major republican works in Chapter 3, Hume's political essays in Chapter 4, Smith's *Wealth of Nations* alongside Burke's speeches on India in Chapter 5, and so on. These texts, read in conjunction with relevant legal developments, court judgments and legal treatises, elucidate the dynamics

[25] See, e.g., Clement Fatovic, *Outside the Law: Emergency and Executive Power* (Baltimore: Johns Hopkins University Press, 2009).

[26] See, e.g., Judith Butler, *Precarious Life: The Powers of Mourning and Violence* (London: Verso, 2004).

[27] Church, *Richelieu and Reason of State*, 4.

of reason of state in a given era. The book can be said to adopt a contextual approach to its subject that is not altogether dissimilar from the method of the Cambridge historians of ideas.[28] Texts are read here against the constitutional background that gives them meaning. So read, they in turn illuminate the constitutional landscape to which they relate.

This method is grounded in a view that the best way to understand a constitutional concept is often through an elaboration of the way it evolved over time. But the historical method has additional benefits here. It reinforces the now familiar connection between political theory and public law,[29] while spotlighting the juridical elements of central works in British political theory. Moreover, in tracing a continuous tradition of reflection on reason of state within British constitutional thought,[30] it exposes the inaccuracy of those critics of liberalism, like Carl Schmitt, who claim that liberal theory had a blind spot as far as reason of state is concerned.[31] Unearthing such a tradition helps us to identify resources internal to liberal constitutional theory capable of handling the reason of state questions that face us today.

* * *

Reason of state raises the issue of state agency. The concept presupposes the idea of a state which functions as a group agent capable of making choices and acting in ways it determines itself.[32] The 'reason' in question

[28] See, e.g., Quentin Skinner, 'Interpretation, Rationality and Truth' in his *Visions of Politics I: Method* (Cambridge: Cambridge University Press, 2002), 47. See also Quentin Skinner, *Liberty Before Liberalism* (Cambridge: Cambridge University Press, 1998), 103: the task of the historian of ideas is to conduct a 'wide-ranging investigation of the changing political languages in which societies talk to themselves'. For discussion of this method see my 'What's God Got to Do With It? Waldron on Equality' (2004) 31 *Journal of Law and Society* 387, 394–397.

[29] See, e.g., Martin Loughlin, *Public Law and Political Theory* (Oxford: Oxford University Press, 1992); T. R. S. Allan, *The Sovereignty of Law: Freedom, Constitution and Common Law* (Oxford: Oxford University Press, 2013), 18–20.

[30] For reasons of elegance and simplicity I have for the most part avoided the awkward but more accurate label 'Anglo-British' to describe this tradition. The use of the word 'English' would be particularly problematic given the importance of Scottish thinkers to the analysis.

[31] Carl Schmitt, *Political Theology: Four Chapters on the Concept of Sovereignty* (Chicago: University of Chicago Press, trans. George Schwab, 2005), 11–14; Carl Schmitt, *The Crisis of Parliamentary Democracy* (Cambridge, Mass.: MIT Press, trans. Ellen Kennedy, 1985), 37–38.

[32] Christian List and Philip Pettit, *Group Agency: The Possibility, Design, and Status of Corporate Agents* (Oxford: Oxford University Press, 2011). List and Pettit's theory is drawn upon extensively in Chapter 8.

is, then, neither that of the people nor identical quite with that of the rulers. Reason of state thus raises the tricky question of the relationship between the active state – the state as decider – and the liberal constitution, not least because the latter tends to be predicated on the ideal of a depersonalized politics in which rules and procedures are relied upon to institutionalize politics and reduce the human factor to a minimum in the hope of taming the excesses that arise from the practice of politics.[33] This is a question that jurists today on the whole tend to avoid.[34] But the relationship between liberal principles and the active state deciding matters of necessity and security is a major reason why contemporary cases about national security and the politics of secrecy are so difficult. Older styles of constitutional theory were not so reticent. Constitutional theorists of the past recognized that reason of state related to an area of state action where the goals or *telos* of a political community and the norms and principles of its constitution were especially likely to collide. As the German historian Friedrich Meinecke observed in his treatise on the subject, reason of state reflects the balance each constitution strikes between *Kratos* and *Ethos*, between action prompted by the power impulse and action prompted by moral responsibility.[35] The reconciliation effected between power and right that occurs within the framework of reason of state contributes in no small measure to defining what one of the greatest of the old writers called the *spirit* of the constitution.[36]

The book seeks to recapture some of the flavour and ambition of those older theories. One element that sets them apart from modern accounts is their sensitivity towards *both* the inner and outer membranes of the constitution,[37] which they saw as internally related. A constitution, to adapt Hume, can be understood as an institutional and normative arrangement that reflects the balance a political community has struck between

[33] Sheldon Wolin, *Politics and Vision: Continuity and Innovation in Western Political Thought* (Princeton: Princeton University Press, expanded ed., 2004), 349–351.

[34] But see, e.g., Philip Bobbitt, *The Garments of Court and Palace: Machiavelli and the World That He Made* (London: Atlantic Books, 2013), which talks in terms of the relationship between law and strategy.

[35] Meinecke, *Machiavellism: The Doctrine of Raison d'État and Its Place in Modern History*, 5.

[36] Charles de Secondat, Baron de Montesquieu, *The Spirit of the Laws* (Cambridge: Cambridge University Press, trans. and eds. Anne M. Cohler, Basia Carolyn Miller and Harold Samuel Stone, 1989).

[37] Bobbitt, *The Garments of Court and Palace*, 70.

authority and liberty.[38] But the old theorists realized that this balance was not purely the product of internal or endogenous growth. Constitutions face outwards as well as inwards, they recognized, and these two faces are related to the extent that the way in which a state engages with the world outside it feeds back into the way it constructs itself internally. This idea of the double-facing constitution has been largely lost from our discourse, due in no small measure to the specialization of the academic profession. The external dimension of constitutions tends now to be left to international relations theorists and international lawyers. But there are good reasons to recapture it for the study of public law too, not least because one of the few more obvious effects of contemporary trends, including globalization, the increased penetration of domestic legal orders by international law, and the pervasiveness of constitutionalism and rights as governance techniques, has been to undermine the image of a national constitution as a juridically sealed container.[39]

Reason of state has been an important part of the external dimension of constitutions since the birth of the state in its modern form. I have indicated already how it might be said to mediate between law and power, right and might. But reason of state is a limit concept in a second sense, in that it navigates the borders between the national and international, between the internal construction of the state and its external actions. One aim of this book is to illustrate the reflexive nature of reason of state, an objective realized largely through an exploration of the legal and constitutional debates over trade and empire. This focus is inevitable in a sense given the extent to which the British debate on reason of state is bound up with the history of (commercial) empire. But it has more general implications for public law scholarship. British public lawyers these days tend to think very much in national terms. For them, public law is essentially an island story. They tend to accept what has become the standard history in which principles and concepts developed largely as a result of autochthonous

[38] David Hume, 'Of the Origin of Government' in Hume, *Essays: Political, Moral and Literary* (Indianapolis: Liberty Fund, ed. Eugene J. Miller, 1985), 40. Hume is discussed at length in Chapter 4.

[39] Karen Knop, 'Here and There: International Law in Domestic Courts' (2000) 32 *New York University Journal of International Law and Politics* 501; Nico Krisch, *Beyond Constitutionalism: The Pluralist Structure of Postnational Law* (Oxford: Oxford University Press, 2010); Neil Walker, 'Postnational Constitutionalism and Postnational Public Law: A Tale of Two Neologisms' (2012) 3 *Transnational Legal Theory* 61; Jean Cohen, *Globalization and Sovereignty: Rethinking Legality, Legitimacy and Constitutionalism* (Cambridge: Cambridge University Press, 2012).

pressures. (Honourable exceptions being made for fairly recent additions stemming from the UK's membership of the European Union and involvement in the European human rights system.[40])

Two prominent and contrasting examples might suffice to illustrate the point. Martin Loughlin's classic *Public Law and Political Theory* examines traditions of thought within British public law.[41] But the book makes the lawyers and theorists it discusses talk and write as though the empire never happened. By contrast, the analysis developed in this book suggests that reading great public law authors such as Dicey or Bagehot – let alone constitutional theorists such as Burke or Mill – without also trying to understand the external and imperial dimensions of their work leads at best to a partial understanding of their constitutional thought. T. R. S. Allan's great work on the common law constitution *Law, Liberty, and Justice* proceeds in a similar manner to Loughlin.[42] Its narrative is a British – indeed a very English – one. If it pays any attention to the external dimension of the constitution at all, it assumes that being an essential part of a juridical web that stretched rather haphazardly around the globe had no impact on the common law's essential nature. This account in my view diminishes the common law, not least in terms of its global significance and the range and complexity of the jurisdictional questions it handled.[43] It also blinds us to the fact that the common law is an imperial law in at least two senses. First by virtue of its origins: it extended the writ of the Crown throughout English domains, helping to consolidate Norman/Angevin holdings in England.[44] Second by virtue of its

[40] There was also a significant strand within public law thought which sought to draw upon American principles and the US experience more generally: see, e.g., Paul Craig, *Public Law and Democracy in the United Kingdom and the United States of America* (Oxford: Oxford University Press, 1991). This trend seems to have all but disappeared.

[41] Martin Loughlin, *Public Law and Political Theory* (Oxford: Oxford University Press, 1992). More recently, it is only fair to say, Loughlin has explored the development of British public law in the context of more general trends within European state theory: see his *Foundations of Public Law* (Oxford: Oxford University Press, 2010).

[42] T. R. S. Allan, *Law, Liberty, and Justice: The Legal Foundations of British Constitutionalism* (Oxford: Oxford University Press, 1994). See also J. W. F. Allison, *The English Historical Constitution: Continuity, Change and European Effects* (Cambridge: Cambridge University Press, 2007).

[43] One excellent example of this is the 'Great Writ' of habeas corpus: see Paul D. Halliday, *Habeas Corpus: From England to Empire* (Cambridge, Mass.: Harvard University Press, 2012).

[44] S. F. C. Milsom, *Historical Foundations of the Common Law* (Oxford: Oxford University Press, 2nd ed., 1981); Paul Brand, 'Judges and Judging 1176–1307' in Paul Brand and Joshua Getlzer (eds.), *Judges and Judging in the History of the Common Law and Civil Law* (Cambridge: Cambridge University Press, 2012).

early-modern transformation: as the great judge-jurists of the period Edward Coke and Matthew Hale were quick to realize,[45] the common law would change as England expanded. The historic common law was an institutional normative structure that enabled people to invoke the King's authority in the (King's) common law courts. As the realm expanded significantly, the pressing question became: who now counts as the people as far as the common law is concerned? The process of legal expansion and fragmentation that accompanied colonization and empire raised the prospect of a common law less tied to its ancient institutional roots in the courts at Westminster and the Inns of Court[46] and becoming more clearly and centrally a body of doctrine, even a jurisprudence of principles.[47] The pressures of colonization and empire thus conspired with other trends to induce a shift from a predominantly jurisdictional to a more substantive understanding of the common law.[48]

I am not centrally concerned in this book with the common law, not least because I do not think the British constitution really is a common law constitution.[49] But the book does seek to challenge the island story of the development of the British constitution, in particular by observing the extensive overlap, even symbiosis, between debates about the constitution and debates about empire. The study draws in this respect on a vast, diverse and rich body of scholarship on Britain and the empire, a subject on which historians and historians of political thought have expended considerable energy in recent times. It seeks to bring this material to the attention of public lawyers and in so doing asks whether it might be time

[45] See in particular Sir Matthew Hale's seminal *The Prerogatives of the King* (London: Selden Society, 1976). Coke's hugely important judgment in *Calvin's Case* ('The Case of the Post-Nati') 7 Coke Rep. 1a, 77 ER 377 (1608) is discussed in a later chapter.

[46] On the importance of the Inns of Court in the education of common lawyers and the development of common law doctrine, see J. H. Baker, 'Why the History of English Law Has Not Been Finished' (2000) 59 *Cambridge Law Journal* 62, 80–83.

[47] David Lieberman, *The Province of Legislation Determined: Legal Theory in Eighteenth Century Britain* (Cambridge: Cambridge University Press, 2002). An early version of this process of reflection on the scope and nature of the common law in the imperial setting occurred in Ireland: see Hans Pawlisch, *Sir John Davies and the Conquest of Ireland: A Study in Legal Imperialism* (Cambridge: Cambridge University Press, 2002).

[48] Daniel J. Hulsebosch, *Constituting Empire: New York and the Transformation of Constitutionalism in the Atlantic World, 1664–1830* (Chapel Hill: University of North Carolina Press, 2005); Paul McHugh, *Aboriginal Societies and the Common Law: A History of Sovereignty, Status, and Self-Determination* (Oxford: Oxford University Press, 2004).

[49] See my 'Dogmatic Liberalism? T.R.S. Allan and Common Law Constitutionalism' (2002) 65 *Modern Law Review* 463.

for public law scholarship to make a similar 'imperial turn'.[50] The case I press in this book is that conceptual development within British public law is bound up with the constitutional discourse of empire.

The book opens with the great early seventeenth-century prerogative cases. Some of them remain familiar to public lawyers. But they play an unconventional role in my narrative, representing something like a pre-history of the concept of reason of state in England. The history proper begins with the seventeenth-century state theorists. Their response to the collapse of authority in the English polity as a result of the crisis over prerogative was to imagine the state as an autonomous juridical entity. The central figure is Thomas Hobbes. The bulk of Chapter 2 considers how Hobbes sought to escape the problems associated with prerogative by subsuming it within a conception of the state as an architectonic structure of legal rule ('Leviathan'). I argue that his theory not only represents an attempt to escape contemporary problems surrounding prerogative but also contained a more ambitious programme of transcending the whole notion of *raison d'état* through the application of principles derived from what Hobbes called 'civil science'. Hobbes concentrated largely on the internal part of the constitution. But his argument on the external aspect of the state, while sketchy, parallels this wider ambition. The state looks distrustfully at the world around it. But the sovereign is expected to act in foreign affairs as it operates in the domestic sphere – rationally – and with the same goal in mind – peace. Such an approach provides the germs of a vision of a non-expansionary constitution operating in a world where states are inclined to make covenants and treaties with other states, creating in so doing passable conditions of peace.

Chapter 3 explores the work of the republican state theorists, Hobbes's contemporaries. It concentrates on three writers: Marchamont Nedham above all for his writings on law, Algernon Sidney on war and James Harrington on empire. Public lawyers often overlook these writers.[51] That is a mistake, not only because of their influence on the US Constitution and thus on the archetype of the modern constitution but also because of the connection they made between liberty and overseas expansion ('Oceana'). They joined with Hobbes in calling for a state built on strong

[50] David Armitage, *Foundations of Modern International Thought* (Cambridge: Cambridge University Press, 2013), 17.

[51] An exception is Adam Tomkins, *Our Republican Constitution* (Oxford: Hart Publishing, 2005).

rule of law lines. Unlike Hobbes, though, they sought to ensure that the state so constructed remained properly the instrument of its people. A major feature of their model constitution was thus an intensely creative conceptual and institutional programme designed to stop the declension of the public reason of state into the private reason of a governing elite. The differences between our three writers are substantial, in temperament as well as in substance. Nonetheless, they agreed – conciliatory Harrington as much as mercurial Nedham and bellicose Sidney – that the ideal republic ought to take the course of Rome. Channelling Machiavelli, they argued that the survival of the republic required citizens to be armed and ready to fight. Not only that, but the free state had the right and duty to liberate non-free states, with force if need be. Thus would the word of liberty (and God) spread across the globe. While their dreams were not realized in the republicans' own time, the relationship between liberty and empire that they did so much to frame became perhaps the dominant theme within British constitutional discourse over the next three centuries.[52]

The book may have seventeenth-century foundations, but its centre of gravity lies in the eighteenth century. With J. G. A. Pocock it argues that the British constitution grew out of an alliance between Leviathan and Oceana – an informal reconciliation of Hobbes's theory of the state as a distinct and juridical union of a people on the one hand and the advent of commercial society on the other.[53] The year 1688 may have witnessed what later came to be seen as a pivotal constitutional moment. But the process of constitutionalization was largely an eighteenth-century affair. That century is often a 'flyover' period for British public lawyers, who tend to be attracted to the drama and seismic shifts of seventeenth-century constitutional politics and then to the development of the state in a more recognizably modern form from roughly the 1830s onwards.[54] But as

[52] See, e.g., David Armitage, *The Ideological Origins of the British Empire* (Cambridge: Cambridge University Press, 2000).

[53] J. G. A. Pocock, *The Machiavellian Moment: Florentine Political Thought and the Atlantic Republican Tradition* (Princeton: Princeton University Press, 2nd ed., 2003), 474–475. See also Istvan Hont, *Jealousy of Trade: International Competition and the Nation-State in Comparative Perspective* (Cambridge, Mass.: Harvard University Press, 2005), 21.

[54] I make this criticism of J. A. G. Griffith, doyen of political constitutionalists, in 'The Elegiac Tradition: Public Law and Memory' [2014] *Public Law* 68. I have previously made similar criticisms of the use of history by common law constitutionalists in 'Back to the Future? Unearthing the Theory of Common Law Constitutionalism' (2003) 23 *Oxford Journal of Legal Studies* 435. Another, particularly clear, example is Tomkins *Our Republican Constitution*. The book starts with a detailed history of legal and constitutional events in the first half of the seventeenth century in particular, then shoots over to

foreign commentators perceived most clearly,[55] the eighteenth century saw the consolidation and regularization of a distinctive system of rule in which government was understood to be firmly under the rule of law and subject to the popular will as represented through Parliament.[56] Chapter 4 looks at this process through the work of the leading political philosopher of the period, David Hume. The 'new' British constitution appears through his eyes as a self-consciously, if somewhat accidental, modern creation. He thought its civilizing features were in harmony with broader currents within European politics – commerce and Enlightenment, above all – that inclined the constitution to evolve in a direction in which its powers and forces were balanced and prerogative naturalized and tamed. In contrast to Blackstone, who thought there was room for *both* an omnipotent Parliament and a very expansive royal prerogative, Hume saw the prerogative as a relic, something that a mature and civilized government would all but grow out of. Hume's writings on the external aspects of the constitution, however, disturb the equanimity of this picture. Dark clouds sit on the horizon. Hume became increasingly concerned about the effects of commercial reason of state and the attendant 'jealousy of trade' politics of European states. He worried that reason of state policies played out in the arena of overseas trade and empire would infect the body politic and unbalance the domestic constitution, and that the massive scale of the debt incurred in financing overseas adventures would rob future generations of even the possibility of living under a free constitution.

This discourse carries into Chapter 5, which has as a focal point the East India Company, a key subject of constitutional debate in the period. We read Adam Smith's *Wealth of Nations* as a disquisition on reason of state in the context of commercial empire before turning to Edmund Burke's philippics against British rule in India and the French revolutionary republic. While moving in the terrain mapped out by Hume and Smith, Burke was uniquely capable of recasting those arguments in juridical form. He saw clearly how the 'internal' dimension of the constitution, the sphere of law and liberty, could be affected by what happens in the

late twentieth and early twenty-first century concerns about parliamentary government and the role of the Crown.

[55] See, e.g., Montesquieu, *Spirit of the Laws*, Pt 2, Book 10, chapter 6, 156–166; Voltaire, *Letters on England (Lettres Philosophiques)* (1734) (London: Penguin, trans. Leonard Tancock, 2005), Letters 8–10.

[56] On the eighteenth-century British state-building process more generally see, Linda Colley, *Britons: Forging a Nation 1707–1837* (London: Pimlico, 1992).

'external' dimension, not least because he understood them as being really two parts of the same thing. He was obsessed by the idea of the *regression* of moral sentiments and developed a compelling account of the feedback loops and possibilities of contagion that activity in the external sphere might have on the other. Deploying this framework, he understood the rapacious behaviour of Company officials in India not as an esoteric or purely humanitarian matter but as a clear and present threat to the British constitution. His case for all-out war with revolutionary France rested on a similar understanding. With the continent's most powerful country in the hands of ideologically motivated zealots, reason of state thinking threatened to become the new norm and the new basis for inter-state relations in Europe. A war to bring about regime change, while in violation of accepted standards of the European legal order, was necessary precisely because that same legal order was threatened by the continued existence of the revolutionary regime.

Moving into the nineteenth century, Chapter 6 retains the focus on the constitutional debate over empire in general and India in particular. Two characteristically modern governance techniques, legislation and bureaucracy, are explored by examining how Benthamite liberals engaged with colonial matters. The chapter discusses James Mill, author of the *History of British India*, who spent many years as a senior East India Company official. But the main focus falls on his son, John Stuart Mill, the greatest English political philosopher of the Victorian period, who also worked as a Company official for most of his life. On reading his writings on politics, liberty and international relations, we see how the attack on what Burke called 'geographical morality' morphed in nineteenth-century liberalism into a paternalistic concern to cultivate and educate non-civilized peoples.[57] The sphere of liberty so eloquently articulated by Mill rested on a distinction between progressive (free) and non-progressive (unfree) societies. But this apparently clear-cut distinction between norm and exception turns out to be rather slippery. Reading Walter Bagehot's *English Constitution*, still a standard text, in light of this analysis, we see the deployment of the same distinction applied by Mill in the imperial context but now to the *internal* structures of the British constitution. Developing the point, the chapter looks at the Victorian and Edwardian debates on martial law. The great constitutional jurist Dicey figures here, but his laudable attempt to circumscribe martial law ends inconclusively. True,

[57] Jennifer Pitts, *A Turn to Empire: The Rise of Imperialism in Britain and France* (Princeton: Princeton University Press, 2006).

many of his arguments in this area came to be accepted by the courts. But his position turned on the 'common law versus prerogative' binary that became increasingly redundant as government officials started to do in this area what they had done in many others: that is, they legislated and created administrative structures to realize the new regulatory framework thereby created. Martial law also illustrates the feedback effects of colonial lawmaking, because those contexts provided a laboratory for the type of emergency legislation whose archetype became the domestic wartime Defence of the Realm Acts.

Ending Chapter 6 in the context of war and emergency powers provides a suitable jumping-off point for the following chapter, devoted to reason of state in the twentieth-century constitutional thought. The analysis focuses in particular on the 'mystery of lawlessness' that seemed to many contemporaries to accompany not only the crisis-ridden first half-century but also and more mundanely the rise of the 'positive' state. The work of three theorists is subject to special treatment – Carl Schmitt, Friedrich Hayek and Michael Oakeshott – all of whom were deeply concerned with the relationship between war, law and the administrative state. Schmitt's presence in a work on the British constitutional tradition is problematic. But his inclusion is nonetheless justified, perhaps even necessary, given the subsequent influence of his work on the exception on Anglo-American constitutional theory. The chapter argues that each thinker represents a characteristic twentieth-century response to reason of state. For Schmitt, reason of state is tied to a substantive politics of belonging and so to the basic political question of who counts as our friend and who the enemy and, as such, offers a possibly redemptive path out of the humdrum realities of the creeping bureaucratic state. Hayek, by contrast, sees reason of state as the antithesis of the constitution of liberty fashioned out of the crooked timber of *nomos*, the evolutionary body of law tied closely to the lived experience of the people. His theoretical ambition is to eradicate reason of state, both normatively and as a matter of institutional design. The attempt fails, not least because the theory allows reason of state to re-emerge as part of an animistic (non-cognitive, de-institutionalized) account of emergency politics. Oakeshott, while sharing Hayek's distrust of the concept, grudgingly recognizes that reason of state lies at the heart of one of two conceptions of politics that vie for prominence within the modern state and is as such built into the institutional structures and pathways of government.

Chapter 8 turns to the present, and takes up the challenge to reason of state presented by mainstream Rawlsian liberals. In Hayekian fashion, they tend to argue for the virtual elimination of reason of state as a concept. It is slippery and dangerous, they say, and should be encompassed within a broader notion of public reason.[58] I argue in the chapter that liberal trends since 1945, including the rise of rights as a cornerstone element of the concept of the modern constitution, may have transformed reason of state but have not led to its demise. On the contrary, they might even be said to have increased its prevalence – if our index is the frequency with which such matters appear before courts, this is most definitely the case. This insight is developed in relation to some important recent cases involving questions of empire, trade, diplomacy and emergency. Building out of these case studies, I argue that it is not the term reason of state that is dangerous but rather some of the action that the term describes. Banishing the term in the hope that doing so will make those things vanish does not help. On the contrary, reason of state remains a useful notion with which to conceptualize this sphere of state action, not least because it allows us to group together actions that take place on a number of different fronts and are not otherwise easy to connect. Treating the matter as a particularly acute problem of group agency, the chapter concludes by outlining a model designed to subject reason of state claims, and especially the increasingly familiar problem of the 'embedded exception', to exceptional scrutiny. Nothing is simple in this sphere of constitutional politics, however. Reason of state is an important part of the constitutional narrative into which constitutional norms must somehow fit.[59] To halt the regression of moral sentiments its misuse can trigger involves developing an understanding that can harmonize *nomos* and narrative, principle and history.

The book is a treatise on reason of state, then, but it is also and equally an essay on the British constitution. As a work on reason of state, if it has any claim to novelty it lies, I have suggested, in the articulation of a liberal reason of state tradition within British constitutional thought whose central figures are Hobbes, Harrington, Hume, Smith, Burke, Mill, Hayek and Oakeshott. As an essay on the British constitution, it draws attention to the constitution's external dimension and the importance of empire and reason of state in constitutional evolution and development. Beyond this,

[58] Wojciech Sadurski, 'Reason of State and Public Reason' (2014) 27 *Ratio Juris* 21

[59] Robert Cover, 'Nomos and Narrative' in Martha Minnow, Michael Ryan and Austin Sarat (eds.), *Narrative, Violence, and the Law: The Essays of Robert Cover* (Ann Arbor: University of Michigan Press, 1995).

it asks us to think seriously about the public law 'canon'. The theorists identified a few lines ago are read in this book as writers on the constitution. In reading them this way, a case is made for including them alongside standard works by Coke, Hale, Blackstone, Bagehot and Dicey – all of whom also appear in these pages – as key texts in the history of our subject.

2

Prerogative in early-modern state theory

The British constitution, at least in its basic elements, is often thought of as a seventeenth-century creation. Out of a period of turmoil and anarchy during which the world was 'turned upside down'[1] arose a settlement that not only survived a long period of colonial expansion but also served as a model of limited and stable rule.[2] What is harder to ascertain is precisely why. The most obvious answer points to the founding 'moment' of 1688.[3] And it is true that this development set in train a process by which princely power became subject to the will of a representative Parliament. It was in this period that power became normalized and authority structures secured. That was certainly how many later commentators came to understand it.[4]

A deeper, if ultimately related, answer points to the constitutional theory of the period of roughly 1640–90, unique within English history in its range and ambition. This turn to theory was a response to the inability of existing governing and ideological structures to manage legal and political conflicts, in particular those that centred on the royal prerogative.[5] England had of course seen significant political turmoil before. What was special about the mid-seventeenth century was that the crisis related not just to the identity of the rulers, as had been the case in the War of the

1 Christopher Hill, *The World Turned Upside Down: Radical Ideas During the English Revolution* (Harmondsworth: Penguin, 1972).

2 This was particularly true of continental European commentators: see, e.g., Voltaire, *Letters on England (Lettres Philosophiques)* (1734) (Harmondsworth: Penguin, trans. Leonard Tancock, 2005), Letters 8 & 9; Charles de Secondat, Baron de Montesquieu, *The Spirit of the Laws (De L'Esprit des Lois)* (1748) (Cambridge: Cambridge University Press, 1989) Pt 2, Book 10, chapter 6.

3 The case for understanding the events of 1688–9 as a constitutional revolution has been made most cogently by Steve Pincus, *1688: The First Modern Revolution* (New Haven: Yale University Press, 2009).

4 See in particular Chapter 4.

5 See, e.g., Chris Thornhill, *A Sociology of Constitutions: Constitutions and State Legitimacy in Historical-Constitutional Perspective* (Cambridge: Cambridge University Press, 2011), 139–153.

Roses,[6] but also to the root of existing structures of authority. Given this context, the theoretical task was an unusually complicated form of intellectual alchemy. Inherited ideas and practices had to be rethought almost entirely, recast and remade anew, to suit modern conditions.[7] This meant, perhaps above all, devising a constitutional theory that accommodated modern man. As Michael Oakeshott wrote, 'the emergent human character of western Europe in the seventeenth century was one in which a feeling for individuality was becoming preeminent – the independent, enterprising man out to seek his intellectual or material fortune'.[8] It is in this period that we first see emerging recognizably modern ideas about state, constitution and law.[9]

This may well be true of all constitutions, but the development of what became the British constitution was something of a bootstrapping exercise, assuming at the outset a structure and authority that it would only later gain. As much retrospective acknowledgment as contemporaneous construction, we might say that while the British constitution may have been a creature of the eighteenth century, its foundations were laid with as much hope as expectation in the previous century.[10] This is certainly the position that is developed in the following chapters. Naturally, the narrative has a number of overlapping layers. The focus throughout this book is on an aspect of that history which was fundamental at the time and vital more generally for an understanding of the dynamic operation of public law, namely the concept of reason of state, for which the prerogative was the main manifestation in the law and constitutional politics of the period.

The major figure in this chapter is Thomas Hobbes. Hobbes sought to answer the central political questions of his age. How do you secure a

[6] The term 'War of the Roses' is anachronistic, only coming into common use after the nineteenth-century novelist Walter Scott used it in *Anne of Geierstein, or the Maiden of the Mist* (1829).

[7] See, e.g., Quentin Skinner, 'The State' in Terence Ball, James Farr and Russell Hanson (eds.), *Political Innovations and Conceptual Change* (Cambridge: Cambridge University Press, 1989), 91–112; Joseph R. Strayer, *On the Medieval Origins of the Modern State* (Princeton: Princeton University Press, 2005).

[8] Michael Oakeshott, 'The Moral Life in the Writings of Thomas Hobbes' in Oakeshott, *Hobbes on Civil Association* (Indianapolis: Liberty Press, 1975), 83.

[9] Quentin Skinner, *Foundations of Modern Political Thought, Vol. 2: The Age of Reformation* (Cambridge: Cambridge University Press, 1978).

[10] For an argument about the benefits of approaching the study of the seventeenth century from the perspective of the eighteenth, see J. C. D. Clark, *Revolution and Rebellion: State and Society in the Seventeenth and Eighteenth Centuries* (Cambridge: Cambridge University Press, 1986).

political unity out of (post-Reformation) disunity? How do you secure obedience to authority at a time when men were increasingly inclined to conceive of themselves as individuals, with a right to independent thought and judgement even on profound questions of morality and politics? Hobbes developed a 'civil science' designed to answer these questions with geometric precision.[11] He was the first to speak 'systematically and unapologetically in the abstract and unmodulated tones of the modern theorist of the sovereign state'.[12] Building on Bodin and Grotius,[13] he identified the state as an architectonic structure of rule, an enclosed and entirely man-made system of laws and offices that has no purpose beyond sustaining itself and in so doing making possible the meaningful life of individual subjects. The state, so constructed, offered something akin to a lifeboat for modern men – the only suitable vessel, given what we know about the human condition, to escape existential conflict over religion and politics and thus the only hope for sustained and peaceful coexistence.

'Ordinary' and 'absolute' prerogative

Note that the escape route Hobbes identified is through law. We may be able to agree substantively on very little. But at least we might all be able to cling on to a system of laws. We must be shown that the only sensible thing to believe in is the need for almost complete obedience[14] to a structure of collective authority whose power is massive and whose mouthpiece is law, and that the reason for doing so lies in the fact that only this combination can secure our collective and individual security and

[11] Noel Malcolm, 'Hobbes's Science of Politics and His Theory of Science' in Malcolm, *Aspects of Hobbes* (Oxford: Oxford University Press, 2002), 146–155.

[12] Quentin Skinner, 'From the State of Princes to the Person of the State' in Skinner, *Visions of Politics, Vol. II: Renaissance Virtues* (Cambridge: Cambridge University Press, 2002), 413.

[13] Richard Tuck, *Philosophy and Government 1572–1651* (Cambridge: Cambridge University Press, 1993), chapters 5 and 7. Larry May also points to the influence of Richard Hooker's covenant-based rulership and late sixteenth-century developments within the common law of contract on Hobbes's model of the social contract: see *Limiting Leviathan: Hobbes on Law and International Affairs* (Oxford: Oxford University Press, 2013), 21–25. Daniel Lee makes a compelling reevaluation of the influence of civil law ideas on Hobbes's thought in 'Hobbes and the Civil Law: The Use of Roman Law in Hobbes's Civil Science' in David Dyzenhaus and Thomas Poole (eds.), *Hobbes and the Law* (Cambridge: Cambridge University Press, 2012), 210-35.

[14] On the limits of obedience in Hobbes's political theory, see Suzanne Sreedhar, *Hobbes on Resistance: Defying the Leviathan* (Cambridge: Cambridge University Press, 2010).

well-being. Leviathan operates – or should operate – on juridical principles.[15] Medieval ideas about the prerogative powers of the prince are to be sublimated within the modern structure of the 'artificial man', the state. The attachment to law inherent within this vision of the state entailed the conceptual subjugation of prerogative, as we shall see. And the theory really *had* to contain some sort of answer to the problem of prerogative power that had been the bane of seventeenth-century constitutional politics. It was 'around the issues of the scope, nature and limits of royal prerogative that the most significant political debates and disagreements of Jacobean political theory' cohered.[16] Many of the prerogative cases decided in this period are familiar to lawyers today, at least through the glosses on them made by later generations of jurists and judges. The context that animated these cases is less familiar. We turn first to these cases in order to illuminate the juridical problems to which Hobbes's theory responded.

The Latin *praerogativa* not only referred to the tribe that voted first in the Roman Republican *Comitia* (and, by extension, a prior preference, privilege or claim) but also meant a token or omen. The English derivate *prerogative* took on the more particular meaning: a special right or privilege possessed by an individual or group, or an inherent advantage or privilege. But the otherworldly element of the idea did not altogether disappear, at least in the context we are discussing, where it was bound up with the idea of *majesty*. The king's prerogative originally denoted those rights and privileges due to the monarch by virtue of his position as feudal overlord. This bundle of kingly rights related almost entirely to landholding. 'The process of seizing land and granting livery of it was a profound expression of lordship, and the exercise of prerogative lordship was an equally profound expression of kingship.'[17] These traditional rights were presented in a text called *Prerogativa Regis*, a statute (if such it was – contemporaries were uncertain as to whether it was a statute or not) passed probably in the late thirteenth or early fourteenth century.[18] These feudal rights, although increasingly anachronistic, were exploited more

[15] David Dyzenhaus, 'Hobbes on the Authority of Law' in Dyzenhaus and Poole, *Hobbes and the Law*.

[16] Glenn Burgess, *The Politics of the Ancient Constitution: An Introduction to English Political Thought, 1603–1642* (London: Macmillan, 1992), 139.

[17] Margaret McGlynn, *The Royal Prerogative and the Learning of the Inns of Court* (Cambridge: Cambridge University Press, 2003), 248.

[18] McGlynn, *Royal Prerogative*, 8. Compare E. E. Henderson, 'The Date of "Prerogativa Regis"' (1890) 5 *English Historical Review* 753, arguing for an earlier date in the reign of Henry III.

systematically during the years of the 'New Monarchy' (from the restoration of Edward IV to the death of Henry VIII), not only to obtain money for the Crown, a necessary obsession of the kings of this period, but also to curb noble power. The prerogative was, then, 'a means of inculcating a healthy fear of royal power',[19] and it played an important role in the move from the early Lancastrian idea of the king as first among equals to the Tudor conception of the king as a lonely being elevated above even the greatest of his lords.[20]

Two cases tend to come up when lawyers today refer to the seventeenth-century prerogative: *Prohibitions del Roy* and the *Case of Proclamations*.[21] The former now stands for the proposition that 'the King in his own person cannot adjudge any case' (Sir Edward Coke); the latter for the better known proposition that 'the King hath no prerogative, but that which the law of the land allows him' (Coke again). Let's leave to one side the fact that the reports of the cases were Coke's own and were published some years after the events they report and look at each case. The *Case of Proclamations* was more of a legal consultation than a judgment in the more familiar sense. Coke, at that time Chief Justice of the Common Pleas, was summoned to the king's council to give a legal opinion on the legality of two royal proclamations, the first of which prohibited new buildings in London and the second the making of starch from wheat. Pressed to give a favourable answer, Coke stalled for time, insisting that he needed to consult first with his fellow judges. Having consulted with three judges, he answered that the king cannot by his prerogative create any new offence.[22] This is certainly consistent with the use modern lawyers make of the case. The problem is that the judicial opinion seems to have had very little impact on subsequent practice. As Maitland observed, 'though James I had the opinion of his judges against him, still he went on issuing proclamations'.[23] In total, 267 proclamations were issued in James's reign,[24] enforced by the Court of Star Chamber. The case can be

[19] McGlynn, *Royal Prerogative*, 248.

[20] David Starkey, *The English Court: From the Wars of the Roses to the Civil War* (London: Longman, 1987), 3.

[21] See, e.g., P. P. Craig, 'Prerogative, Precedent and Power' in Christopher Forsyth and Ivan Hare (eds.), *The Golden Metwand and the Crooked Cord* (Oxford: Oxford University Press, 1998), 67.

[22] *The Case of Proclamations* (PC 1611), 12 *Co. Rep.* 74.

[23] F.W. Maitland, *The Constitutional History of England* (Oxford: Oxford University Press, ed. H. A. L. Fisher, 1963), 257–258.

[24] Christopher W. Brooks, *Law, Politics and Society in Early Modern England* (Cambridge: Cambridge University Press, 2008), 408.

seen as an assertion or reassertion[25] of the principle that the king had no capacity to interfere in the course of ordinary cases, save perhaps where such action might be justified by necessity. The principle arising from the case can perhaps best be read as an advisory opinion to the effect that adherence to a formal structure of rule was the best way to ensure the legitimacy of the system as a whole[26] which, as we have seen, the government overrode, perhaps ultimately to its detriment. In essence, *Proclamations* was a kind of seventeenth-century declaration of incompatibility – a ruling, in as much as it was one, delineating a principle which the king felt legally entitled to ignore.

Prohibitions was even less of a real case than *Proclamations*.[27] As Adam Tomkins observes, it was in fact 'more like a meeting (or a series of meetings) between the king and his political, legal and ecclesiastical advisers'.[28] The matter arose from a jurisdictional conflict at a time when courts relied on litigation fees for revenue. The Archbishop of Canterbury, Richard Bancroft, had complained to the king about the growing practice of the common law courts of issuing prohibitions in the king's name forbidding the ecclesiastical courts from entertaining cases that the common lawyers said belonged to lay courts. The case shows Coke's propensity to articulate the jurisdictional superiority of the common law in the teeth of political pressure and even in opposition to the king.[29] But his position did not necessarily replace the equally plausible view that 'as all jurisdictions emanate from the King, so he is the great reconciler, determining what are their boundaries'.[30] Indeed, the very context in which

[25] In Mary's reign the judges had said that 'no proclamation can make a new law, but only confirm and ratify an ancient one': Maitland, *Constitutional History*, 258.

[26] See, e.g., this passage: 'the King hath his Court, viz. in the Upper House of Parliament, in which he with his Lords is the supreme Judge over all other Judges; for if error be in the Common Pleas, that may be reversed in the King's Bench; and if the Court of King's Bench err, that may be reversed in the Upper House of Parliament, by the King, with the assent of the Lords Spiritual and Temporal, without the Commons: and in this respect the King is called the Chief Justice'.

[27] *The Case of Prohibitions del Roy* (CP 1608), 12 *Co. Rep.* 63. For commentary see W. Epstein, 'Issues of Principle and Expediency in the Controversy over Prohibitions to Ecclesiastical Courts in England' (1980) 1 *Journal of Legal History* 211.

[28] Adam Tomkins, *Our Republican Constitution* (Oxford: Hart, 2005), 70.

[29] If nothing else, Coke was an indefatigable asserter of the jurisdictional rights of the common law. Coke was embroiled at one time or another in jurisdictional conflict with not only the bishops' courts but also the court of High Commission, commissioners of sewers, and the councils of the North and of the Marches. See Alan Cromartie, *The Constitutionalist Revolution: An Essay on the History of England, 1450–1642* (Cambridge: Cambridge University Press, 2006), 211.

[30] William Harrison Moore, *Act of State in English Law* (London: John Murray, 1906), 11.

Prohibitions took place – formal meetings convened by the king to resolve jurisdictional conflict between his courts – rather supports this latter reading of events. The 'powers of Courts are a delicate subject, coming very near to the mystery part of prerogative', William Harrison Moore wrote in his treatise *Act of State in English Law*, paraphrasing James I, and to dispute the authority of a tribunal set up by the king was seen as presumptuous.[31] This can be illustrated by events in the proceedings against James Whitelocke,[32] who was imprisoned briefly after falling foul of king and council. Lord Chancellor Ellesmere reacted angrily to a challenge to the Earl Marshall's jurisdiction over the plaintiff's claim, declaring that it was too great a question for a (Coke-led) common law court. James I's position on the relationship between the common law and prerogative more generally is revealing.[33] He did not deny Coke's claim that the common law is a system of artificial reason and that the common lawyers are its appropriate guardians.[34] But he insisted that the results produced by the workings of this system should not run too far contrary to natural reason itself. Questions concerning prerogative should not be dealt with too rashly in the courts, but should be resolved through consultation between king, council and judges, 'so may you [not] wound the King through the sides of a private person' (that is, through ordinary litigation at common law).[35]

One complicating factor in studying the prerogative in this period is that the assertions of common lawyers cannot simply be assumed to reflect contemporary practice. Coke's remark in *Bagg's Case* that 'no wrong or injury, either public or private, can be done but that it shall be here reformed or punished by due course of law'[36] is described as a 'staggering assertion' by a leading historian.[37] Ellesmere's reaction at the time was more acerbic: 'in giving excess of authority to the King's Bench he [Coke] doth as much as insinuate that this court is all sufficient in itself

[31] Moore, *Act of State in English Law*, 10. This was not an unusual position for the period. Louis XIII, in a short speech to the Parlement of Paris in 1636, written for him by Cardinal Richelieu, said firmly: 'it is not for you to meddle in the affairs of my state'. See J. H. Elliott, *Richelieu and Olivares* (Cambridge: Cambridge University Press, 1984), 46.

[32] 1613, 2 *State Trials* 765.

[33] On which see J. H. Baker, 'The Common Lawyers and the Chancery: 1616' 4 *The Irish Jurist* 368, 383–385.

[34] Cromartie refers to this as an argument based on 'the wisdom of a guild': *Constitutionalist Revolution*, 215.

[35] James I, 'Speech in the Stare-Chamber', *Works*, 556.

[36] *James Bagg's Case* (KB, 1615), 11 *Co. Rep.* (1615).

[37] Cromartie, *Constitutionalist Revolution*, 212.

to manage the state'.[38] The common lawyers were also far less successful than we tend to assume. *Proclamations* and *Prohibitions* were by no means insignificant cases, especially the former, although neither led to what could be described as a full or complete victory for the common law position. But these cases are dwarfed by other prerogative cases of the period: *Bate's Case*; the *Five Knights Case* and *Ship Money*. These cases concerned the extra-parliamentary taxing powers of the king, a defining constitutional issue of the age. In all of them the courts gave the king the victory he sought or else evaded or narrowed the issue in a way that allowed him to claim victory.

Bate's Case, sometimes called the *Case of Impositions*, concerned the legality of a retaliatory duty (impositions) on the import of currants via Venice. This was by no means a trivial matter. Imported currants from the Mediterranean were beginning to find a mass market. The Venetian ambassador claimed that the English were so addicted to currants that they had been known to hang themselves when they could not afford to buy them.[39] The race to satisfy consumer cravings of this sort was leading to the creation of relatively large-scale trading companies. The East India Company, which became the largest of these operations, is an important character in later chapters of this book. Many of the great prerogative cases involved the relationship between these companies and the monopoly powers of the Crown exercised through royal prerogative.[40] *Bate's Case* can be seen, then, as one of the earlier skirmishes in this larger constitutional battle. The case reached the court of Exchequer in 1606, where it was settled in favour of the government. Bate's counsel accepted that there were some secrets of state, such as making war and peace, that were determinable according to the royal prerogative and not subject to ordinary law, but argued that taxes and customs fell within the prerogative that was under the law. 'And in our kingdom', as opposed to (Catholic) France

[38] Louis A. Knafla, *Law and Politics in Jacobean England: The Tracts of Lord Chancellor Ellesmere* (Cambridge: Cambridge University Press, 1977), 307.

[39] David Scott, *Leviathan: The Rise of Britain as a World Power* (London: Harper Press, 2013), 126.

[40] See also *Darcy v Allen* (*Case of Monopolies*), 77 Eng. Rep. 1260 (K.B. 1602), where the King's Bench narrowly construed a royal monopoly to vindicate the right of a subject to practise his trade, which was the manufacture of playing cards. There was no judicial opinion in the case, and the meaning of the judgment was in considerable doubt at the time. However, Coke's report of the case – in which he was not a judge – contained broader language and the case was subsequently viewed as the seminal statement of the common law policy against restraints of trade. See Jacob I. Corré, 'The Argument, Decision, and Reports of *Darcy v. Allen*' (1996) 45 *Emory Law Journal* 1261.

or Spain, 'our princes have at all times ruled by the golden letter of the law'. In his influential lead judgment, Sir Thomas Fleming declared that the royal prerogative had a two-fold nature, ordinary and absolute. The ordinary prerogative, which included the administration of justice in private law, was for the benefit of individual people, and was subject to the court's jurisdiction. The absolute prerogative, however, applied to the general benefit of the people and was not controlled by the common law or bound by 'respect for private right'. Its exercise was justified by *salus populi* and was properly 'named Pollicy and Government'. As matters of state varied, 'so varieth this absolute law, according to the wisdom of the king, for the common good'.[41]

Fleming's judgment helped to establish the 'duplex theory' of prerogative, which shaped the conventional early Stuart understanding of the royal prerogative.[42] The theory holds that within its own sphere the common law was self-sufficient and arguably supreme. This fits Coke's opinion in *Proclamations* and, perhaps, *Prohibitions* but not his seemingly aberrant remarks in *Bagg's Case*. But not all matters did fall within the jurisdiction of the common law.[43] 'Thus kings could claim to be acting *outside* the common law – in which case their actions could be defended using political languages other than that of the common law.'[44] Although the theory tries to make sense of two underlying values of the age, that law protects property and personal liberty, and the idea of legitimate kingly rule, it does leave open two crucial questions, namely what were the boundaries of common law and who gets to decide when those boundaries have been crossed.[45]

[41] State Trials, II, cols. 389–90. See also Brooks, *Law, Politics and Society in Early Modern England*, 136–138.

[42] Burgess, *Politics of the Ancient Constitution*, 139.

[43] See, e.g., James I's communication to the judges in the *Case of Commendams* (1616): 'His Majesty had a double prerogative, whereof the one was ordinary, and had relation to his private interest, which might be, and was every day disputed in Westminster Hall; the other was of a higher nature, referring to his supreme and imperial power and sovereignty, which ought not to be disputed or handled in vulgar argument'.

[44] Burgess, *Politics of the Ancient Constitution*, 89.

[45] The major set-piece debate in the House of Commons in 1610 was triggered by *Bate's Case* and focused on the limits of the common law theory of prerogative. The debate shows how legalism was a property common to all branches of the Stuart state and was a language in which all politically active men were fluent. James Whitelocke, soon to fall foul with the king, argued that sovereignty lay in the king in parliament not the king acting alone. Sir John Davies argued to the contrary that the law of nations proves that monarchs enjoy extensive prerogative powers. Davies was a major proponent of

Five Knights Case and the *Case of Ship Money* are two of the most significant cases ever decided by English courts. They were flashpoints within a crisis of legitimacy that led to civil war. *Five Knights Case* concerned a forced loan levied in order to finance wars against both France and Spain. Unable to raise money through Parliament, a divided privy council agreed a plan for raising money through a series of assessed loans. The scheme, despite the opposition it provoked, eventually released an enormous sum of money (which meant that there was no realistic prospect of repayment). In the expectation of public opposition, the judges were called before the privy council in October 1626. Charles I outlined his plan for the loan and ordered the judges to pass on the news to lawyers, hoping that in doing so they would provide a lead to the rest of the country. When asked two weeks later for a declaration that the loan was legal, the judges refused. The government subsequently tried to avoid proceeding against those who refused to pay, but in the autumn of 1627 the imprisonment of five squires on the king's orders without charges being specified following their refusal to pay the loan triggered a *habeas corpus* action in King's Bench.[46] In anticipation of the case, the government stated that the detention of the five knights was 'by his majesty's special commandment' a form of words which was designed to shift the attention of a court away from the forced loan and on to the stronger ground of the king's prerogative.[47]

In fact, the brief decision that ensued was not in one sense a decision at all. In a vain attempt to limit the impact of their decision,[48] the judges chose not to issue a judgment but instead made a judicial order. The court refrained from taking steps to free the plaintiffs, but stopped short of endorsing the government's right to imprison them. Chief Justice Hyde said that the precedents showed that the practice was to send the prisoner back into detention to await further developments. If no cause of imprisonment was specified, the court would presume that the lack of

ancient constitutionalism. His position in the debate shows how that theory was compatible with extensive princely power. See Hans S. Pawlisch, *Sir John Davies and the Conquest of Ireland: A Study in Legal Imperialism* (Cambridge: Cambridge University Press, 2002).

46 See Paul D. Halliday, *Habeas Corpus: From England to Empire* (Cambridge, MA: Harvard University Press, 2010), 137–139.

47 J. A. Guy, 'The Origins of the Petition of Right Reconsidered' (1982) 25 *Historical Journal* 289, 291.

48 If such was the judges' hope, then it was not to be realized. Release rates on *habeas corpus* plunged during the reign of Charles I until the start of the Civil War in 1642: see Halliday, *Habeas Corpus*, 160.

specification amounted to a matter of state, 'which we cannot take notice of'. 'We are too wise, nay, we are too foolish in undertaking to examine matters of State to which we are not born.'[49] The case settled no more than that the defendants were refused bail. They were to be remanded pending the filing, hearing and judgment of substantive charges – charges that the king had no intention of bringing. The case is still more complicated in that as a 'rule of court' it was not at all the same thing as a final judgment: 'Quite categorically an entry in a rule book – being on paper not parchment – was not "on record" and could not subsequently be cited as a source of legal knowledge' – which meant that technically the king could not rely on the *Five Knights Case* as a precedent.[50]

As it happened, the loan refusers were released at the end of December 1627, and the king conceded a month or so later that a parliament was the proper way to supply a war. But the case showed cracks in the duplex theory, beaming 'a searchlight on to a minor loophole, which had become a political weapon in the hands of Charles I'.[51] *Five Knights Case* led to fierce debates within Parliament on discretionary imprisonment and the prerogative. The Lords' position encapsulated the 'just meridian' that most contemporaries thought existed between liberty and prerogative, a position summarized by Ashley during the debate:

> If the subject prevail, [he gains] liberty but loses the benefit of that state government without which a monarchy may too soon become an anarchy; or, if the state prevail, it gains absolute sovereignty but loses the subjects, not their subjection (for obedience we must yield, though nothing be left us but prayers and tears); but it loses the best part of them, which is their affections, whereby sovereignty is established and the crown firmly fixed on his royal head.[52]

Note here not just the surface image of balance, with more than a hint of the mixed constitution, but also how the language of service and related sentiments ('affections', with its connection to ideas of loving allegiance) that permeate the text connect to notions of legality and legitimacy. But MPs remained intransigent in their denial of Charles's right to imprison for unknown causes, all the more so once they discovered Attorney General Heath's illegal attempt to pervert the record of the King's Bench. Charles

[49] *Five Knight Case* or *Darnel's Case*, 3 How. St. Tr. 1, (KB, 1627). See also Moore, *Act of State in English Law*, 13.

[50] Guy, 'Origins of the Petition of Right', 295.

[51] Guy, 'Origins of the Petition of Right', 294.

[52] Brooks, *Law, Politics and Society in Early Modern England*, 175.

tried to defuse the situation by making the issue a question of trust, and by promising to govern according to the laws of England. The Commons were not placated – after all, the king had done nothing to show that his *interpretation* of English law corresponded to theirs. Running out of time and unable to secure the support of the Lords, the Commons passed the Petition of Right (initiated by Coke), the provisions of which read almost like a direct commentary on and response to the events surrounding the *Five Knights Case*.[53]

The *Case of Ship Money* (*R v Hampden*) concerned the same combination of war, tax and prerogative.[54] The underlying cause of the case was the pressure to create a specialized navy. Existing legal arrangements were designed for a type of 'private enterprise' warfare that was fast disappearing. By the 1630s, only regular king's ships could keep up with the growing French and Dutch fleets. The trigger for the gathering arms race was the collapse of the long Spanish hegemony within Europe, causing an epochal shift in 'global' politics.[55] A more proximate cause was the utter dysfunction of the English system of governance and its inability to innovate. The law 'still allowed the King to conscript private ships, but did not allow to raise money to fit out his own. It allowed him to do what he did not need to do, but did not allow him to do what he did need to'.[56] The problem of Ship Money stemmed from an inability to update public law, a problem that owed as much to the obtuse traditionalism and legalism of the era as to the political ineptitude of the king and his advisers.[57]

[53] Provisions include: taxation without Parliament's consent, forced loans, arbitrary arrest, imprisonment contrary to Magna Carta, arbitrary interference with property rights, lack of enforcement of *habeas corpus*, forced billeting of troops, imposition of martial law, exemption of officials from due process. Interestingly, perhaps, the text makes no mention of the word 'prerogative'.

[54] Edmund Burke was later to note the way in which the issue of tax served as the anvil on which English freedom was defined and articulated: 'Speech on Conciliation with America' in Burke, *Pre-Revolutionary Writings* (Cambridge: Cambridge University Press, ed. Ian Harris, 1993), 222.

[55] J. H. Elliott, *Spain, Europe and the Wider World 1500–1800* (New Haven: Yale University Press, 2009), chapters 8–10; Brendan Simms, *Europe: The Struggle for Supremacy 1453 to the Present* (London: Allen Lane, 2013), 40–41.

[56] Conrad Russell, *The Causes of the English Civil War* (Oxford: Oxford University Press, 1990), 183.

[57] Daniel J. Hulsebosch, *Constituting Empire: New York and the Transformation of Constitutionalism in the Atlantic World, 1664–1830* (Chapel Hill: University of North Carolina Press, 2005), 35: 'Common-law constitutionalism contributed to the English Civil War in the 1640s.'

Ship money was strictly speaking merely a cash payment in lieu of the provision of a vessel. It was uncontroversial that the king could make levies on coastal towns to provide ships for naval warfare. The payments of the 1630s were innovatory, first, because they covered the cost of merchant ships levied for royal service (ship levy money) rather than to build ships (ship money) and, second, because inland counties were also asked to contribute. Old notions of service were evoked alongside more cutting-edged justifications based on the language of necessity and reason of state.[58] The arguments were not necessarily far-fetched, as prerogative was seen as a legitimate resource to supplement the common law in cases where the common law did not apply, such as emergency conditions. On the other hand, critics saw the levy as an attempt to expand the range of actions that fell within the bounds of prerogative. They denied the crisis-related arguments offered in its defence and worried that if implausible arguments could be deployed to extend prerogative powers over property then property was no longer safe.[59]

Five Knights was a short case, made under pressure in which the judges just about managed to avoid articulating a definitive position on constitutional fundamentals. *Ship Money*, by contrast, was one of the longest hearings in early-modern legal history and forced the judges to spell out exactly where they stood with regard to the king's claims on the property of his subjects. It was described as 'one of the greatest cases that ever came before the judges of the law' by a judge in the case. Before the case was heard, the king had canvassed the judges twice (in December 1635 and February 1637) in a bid to ascertain their receptiveness to reason of state arguments. The judges agreed, albeit after internal wrangling, that when the kingdom was in danger the king could command all subjects to furnish and supply ships for the defence of the kingdom and that the king was 'sole judge both of the danger, and when and how the same is to be prevented and avoided'.[60]

The case proper took place according to an established procedure for dealing with points of exceptional difficulty before an extraordinary bench of twelve judges in the Exchequer Chamber. The judges decided seven to five for the king. It is unclear the extent to which external

[58] Crown lawyers also made use of arguments drawn from the great jurist and polymath John Selden's *Mare Clausum* (1636), completely rewritten at the request of Charles's government: Tuck, *Philosophy and Government*, 212. For an account of Selden's anti-royal sentiments, for which he was twice imprisoned, see Anthony Arlidge and Igor Judge, *Magna Carta Uncovered* (Oxford: Hart Publishing, 2014), chapter 19.

[59] Michael J. Braddick, *State Formation in Early Modern England c.1550–1700* (Cambridge: Cambridge University Press, 2000), 243.

[60] 'The King's Case laid before the Judges, with the Answer' (Feb 7, 1637, Rushworth, ii. 355).

pressure weighed on the outcome.[61] The majority accepted the king's view that Ship Money was not a tax but a service owed to the king in an emergency to enable him to carry out his duty to defend the realm. One majority judge, Crawley, opined, 'You cannot have a king without these royal rights'. Finch, in a ruling that became particularly controversial, thought that it was not the role of the court to judge whether an emergency existed and said that he wished that Parliament had not encouraged 'private humours' to create discontent in the commonwealth. It is 'a dangerous tenet', he said, 'a kind of judaizing opinion, to hold that the weal public must be exposed to peril of utter ruin or subversion, rather than such a charge as this, which may secure the commonwealth, may be imposed by the King upon the subject, without common consent in Parliament'.[62] The laws know 'no king-yoking policy'. In dissent, two judges argued on technical grounds: a failure to specify in the writs to whom the money was to be paid rendered them invalid. The other dissenters were more forthright. Croke argued that the levy was against 'the common law of the land' by which a man is given a freedom in his property that cannot be taken away without parliamentary approval and that 'no necessity nor danger can allow a charge which is in breach of the laws'. Hutton drew a distinction between ancient and modern forms of kingship and argued that the lack of convincing evidence that there was a danger to the realm meant that necessity could not override property rights.

There is much, then, that divided the court. But all the judges showed considerable discomfort at being asked to handle the matter. 'They did not appreciate', Burgess writes, 'being made to give legal shape to the king's absolute prerogative – particularly when it was being employed on specious grounds that they were bound to ignore'.[63] Reaction to the case in the first session of the Long Parliament in 1640 was extreme, and 'a torrent of abuse … swept down upon the judges'.[64] What the case seemed to reveal was that the common law was no barrier against an unruly king. Hyde, a Royalist in the Civil War and Lord Chancellor after the Restoration, called the judges 'delinquents'. The people, he said:

[61] For a discussion, see R. L. Noble, 'Lions or Jackals? The Independence of the Judges in Rex v. Hampden' (1962) 14 *Stanford Law Review* 711.

[62] J. P. Kenyon, *The Stuart Constitution* (Cambridge: Cambridge University Press, 1966), 112.

[63] Burgess, *Politics of the Ancient Constitution*, 209.

[64] Noble, 'Independence of the Judges in Rex v Hampden', 711.

> when they saw in a court of law … apophthegms of state urged as elements of law; judges as sharp-sighted as Secretaries of State and in the mysteries of state; judgment of law grounded upon matter of fact of which there was neither inquiry or proof; and no reason given for the payment of the thirty shillings in question but what concluded the estates of all the standers-by; they had no reason to hope that that doctrine or the preachers of it would be contained within any bounds.[65]

Hyde's invective against the *Ship Money* judges may seem straightforward enough, but the rhetoric conceals a basic ambiguity, since it is unclear whether his complaint is with the judgment itself or the fact that the case went before a court.[66] Juridical confusion in the context of political passions is reflective of the wider debate on prerogative in this era. But we should be careful not to overstate the degree of disagreement at the level of principle. There were important matters relating to law and prerogative on which most could agree. At the general level, political culture was shaped by an attachment to the idea of the ancient constitution, the belief in an immemorial law being 'the nearly universal belief' of contemporaries.[67] The Stuart kings might make more than some of their predecessors did on the mystical claims of royal blood,[68] but the view that rule 'by will' (*arbitrium*) was unacceptable still held sway.[69] While the belief in the existence of an ancient constitution operating as fundamental law can appear vague, even mystical, it allowed for the elaboration of a reasonably coherent set of principles, including the idea that legitimate rule, including the king's prerogative, had to have legal expression. Almost no one claimed that the king could operate *above* the law, but it could plausibly be claimed that he had the capacity in the exercise of his 'absolute' prerogative to operate *outside* the *common* law. No one seriously doubted that the king was or should be bound by law in some

[65] Quoted in Cromartie, *Constitutionalist Revolution*, 237.

[66] Cromartie, *Constitutionalist Revolution*, 237.

[67] J. G. A. Pocock, *The Ancient Constitution and the Feudal Law: A Study of English Historical Thought in the Seventeenth Century* (Cambridge: Cambridge University Press, 2nd ed., 1987).

[68] See, e.g., James I's poem 'The wiper of the peoples teares' (1622–3) which includes the lines 'Kings walke the heavenly milky-way,/ But you in by-paths goe astray./ God and King doe pace together,/ But vulgars wander light as feather …/ Hold you the publick beaten way,/ Wonder at Kings and them obey./ For under god they are to chuse,/ Whats rights to take and what refuse': quoted in Scott, *Leviathan: The Rise of Britain as a World Power*, 104.

[69] Glenn Burgess, *Absolute Monarchy and the Stuart Constitution* (New Haven: Yale University Press, 1996), 135.

sense or another (natural law)[70] but that in certain circumstances this special type of lawful action fell outside the jurisdiction of the courts. On Hale's analysis later in the century, when operating under the prerogative the king was outside the 'coercive' power of the law, meaning the remedial jurisdiction of his courts, but he remained subject to the law's 'directive' power.[71] It was a common theme, moreover, that the king's powers were in principle individually specified and policed by law: 'the king, properly speaking, had in the eyes of the lawyer prerogatives, not a prerogative'.[72] This understanding of the relationship between law and prerogative was underpinned by a near unshakable belief in legal *form*, a sentiment that if anything hardened after *Five Knights Case* and *Ship Money*. Englishmen had come to believe in a thorough and complete legalism, that 'correct political behaviour could be dictated by a list of rules; conversely, they were easily persuaded that any loophole in such rules presented an intolerable menace'.[73]

The dominant image for the state remained that of the king's two bodies.[74] One way in which this conception was manifested in practice related to the legal construction of what we would now call citizenship. *Calvin's Case*, also known as the *Case of the Post-Nati*,[75] was decided early in the reign of James I of England (who was already James VI of Scotland) and concerned the legal status of Scots born after James had acceded to the English throne. The court held that allegiance follows the king. As Hale wrote, the case decided that the status of subjects of the king of England is not only confined to those that are born in England and within the territories and dominions of the Crown of England but extends 'to those that are born under the same king, though in separate and independent territories'.[76] The strength of the personal element within contemporary notions of authority can also be seen in the ideas of service used in

[70] In his report on *Calvin's Case*, Coke argued that natural law was 'Part of the Law of England' (195). Note also the connection between common law and religious beliefs. Cromartie, *Constitutionalist Revolution*, 208–209: 'the common law was part of the foundations of English structures of authority, in part because it could be seen as nature's law for England.'

[71] Hulsebosch, *Constituting Empire*, 37.

[72] Burgess, *Absolute Monarchy and the Stuart Constitution*, 141. The classic expression of this position is Hale, *Prerogatives of the King*.

[73] Cromartie, *Constitutionalist Revolution*, 204.

[74] Ernst Kantorowicz, *The King's Two Bodies: A Study in Medieval Political Theology* (Princeton: Princeton University Press, 1998).

[75] 7 Co. Rep. 1a (1608).

[76] Hale, *Prerogatives of the King*, 54.

defence of Ship Money.[77] The prerogative acted as a nodal point between personal and official conceptions of authority. Ideally these two conceptions were complementary. The king's power could in one sense be seen as unbounded ('absolute prerogative') but at the same time bounded ('the King hath no prerogative, but that which the law of the land allows him'). However comprehensible the theory may have appeared to those who developed it, the ambiguities of the law relating to the prerogative did not remain hidden. The early Stuart prerogative cases revealed these ambiguities and the jurisdictional conflict that they produced to all but the most stolid of contemporaries. As political relations became increasingly strained, arguments based on trust and custom became less convincing. This, in turn, pushed people to seek clearer answers to fundamental questions concerning prerogative power. These were not forthcoming.

'Champions of anarchy'

This was the juridical situation that Hobbes encountered, two features of which are particularly worth noting. First, a fundamental tension at the level of basic principles, especially in relation to whether sovereign authority was personal (service) or official (law), and a corresponding lack of clarity concerning legal jurisdictions. Second, the deeply legalist way in which contemporaries thought about political authority. We turn now to consider Hobbes's solution to the problems of authority and obligation. In general terms, Hobbes retained the legalism of early-modern politics but rerouted it through an integrated state structure which exists as though newly constructed rather than as the container for perhaps contradictory and conflicting habits and customs. Transforming medieval ideas of personal authority[78] into the authority that is invested in the state understood as a legal personality (*persona*) – the move, that is, from the state of princes to the person of the state[79] – Hobbes's intention was to transcend the conflict between legal and personal aspects of authoritative rule.

The theory starts with conflict. Our natural condition, Hobbes argues, is one of inescapable and systemic disagreement, the source of which lies in our natural freedom. Each of us has a natural right to use our power to

[77] A theme developed in Thomas Poole, 'Judicial Review at the Margins: Law, Power, and Prerogative' (2010) 60 *University of Toronto Law Journal* 81, 96–101.

[78] See, e.g., Paul Kléber Monod, *The Power of Kings: Monarchy and Religion in Europe, 1589–1715* (New Haven: Yale University Press, 2000).

[79] Skinner, 'From the State of Princes to the Person of the State'.

stay alive and a natural right to be 'judge himself of the necessity of the means, and of the greatness of the danger'.[80] It is not that we have no guide as to how best to exercise this right. Principles of natural law, which are general rules or theorems of reason conducive to our preservation, are available to us. But such laws even if self-evident are not self-applying.[81] Since 'men are by nature provided of notable multiplying glasses, (that is their Passions and Selfe-love,) through which, every little payment appeareth a great grievance',[82] the natural state is characterised by partial judgements supporting self-interested actions.

Conflict is endemic in Hobbes's world. But it arises not so much from man's antisocial character as from the 'self-destructive character of judgement'.[83] Conflict in the natural state is not purely contingent or factual, the kind that might not exist if people were less irascible or competitive. It is a result also of a 'necessary jural conflict between people whose *rights* overlap or conflict in some sense with one another until they have been renounced'.[84] Such disagreement produces conflict which leads to disorder; disorder induces fear; fear in turn leads to more disagreement. While this condition lasts, 'there can be no Propriety, no Dominion, no Mine and Thine distinct: but onely that to be every mans, that he can get it; and for so long, as he can keep it'.[85] It is the ineluctably conflict-ridden condition of the natural state, and the exceptionally dour consequences attendant to it, that motivates people to form the commonwealth, even though this means signing away one of the core rights of natural personhood, the right to judge for myself what is best for me. Within the commonwealth, the plurality of voices is reduced to the single, authoritative voice of the sovereign, turning the disordered Babel of the natural state into a 'commonwealth of ordered words',[86] and the multiplicity of

[80] Thomas Hobbes, *Elements of Law* (Oxford: Oxford University Press, ed. J. G. A. Gaskin, 1994) ('EL'), 79; also *Leviathan* (Cambridge: Cambridge University Press, ed. Richard Tuck, 1991) ('L'), 91.

[81] Thomas Hobbes, *On the Citizen* (Cambridge: Cambridge University Press, ed. Richard Tuck and Michael Silverthorne, 1998) ('DC'), 69: 'the natural laws do not guarantee their own observance as soon as they are known'.

[82] L, 129. [83] Tuck, *Philosophy and Government*, 307.

[84] Noel Malcolm, 'Hobbes and Spinoza' in J. H. Burns and Mark Goldie (eds.), *The Cambridge History of Political Thought, 1450–1700* (Cambridge: Cambridge University Press, 1991), 535.

[85] L, 90.

[86] Philip Pettit, *Made With Words: Hobbes on Language, Mind, and Politics* (Princeton: Princeton University Press, 2008), chapter 8.

overlapping individual judgements about rights is replaced by a single, authoritative jurisdiction.

The commonwealth, then, vastly reduces the complexities that otherwise beset the interpretation of any body of law, whether written or unwritten. It resolves a fundamental coordination problem that can only be solved by the introduction of an all-powerful sovereign.[87] That solution involves elements of both law and power, the sword and scales of sovereign capacity. The sovereign can impose a solution on the 'necessary jural conflict' that grows out of natural rights not just because he is supreme judge or ultimate source of legal authority but also because he has the power to impose his interpretation of the laws if necessary through the threat or use of overwhelming force. As Hobbes writes in *Leviathan*, for the sovereign alone there 'can not be any knot in the Law, insoluble; either by finding out the ends, to undoe it by; or else by making what ends he will, (as *Alexander* did with his sword in the Gordian knot,) by the legislative power; which no other Interpreter can doe'.[88]

'Man's tongue is a trumpet to war and sedition'

A finer-grained understanding of Hobbes's theory of law can be gained by turning to his late book on the English Civil War, *Behemoth*. Writing 'as from the Devil's Mountain',[89] Hobbes supplies in this work an anatomy of disorder a crucial feature of which is the claim that the proliferation of private judgements at the expense of the public judgement of the sovereign leads to civil strife.

Behemoth is a litany of blame, holding group after group responsible for the collapse of social order. It begins with a parade of 'seducers'[90] who corrupted the kingdom. At the top of the list come religious groups: Presbyterians, Papists, and various non-conformist sects. It also includes the educated who were led astray by classical authors, those 'champions of Anarchy',[91] into espousing 'democratical principles'. The universities that educated them are chastised for producing deliberately obfuscatory works on religion and politics on behalf of their paymaster the Pope.[92] Parliament is also criticised,[93] as are the independent-minded

[87] Pasquale Pasquino, 'Hobbes, Religion, and Rational Choice: Hobbes's Two Leviathans and the Fool' (2001) 82 *Pacific Philosophical Quarterly* 406.

[88] L, 191.

[89] Thomas Hobbes, *Behemoth or the Long Parliament* (Chicago: University of Chicago Press, ed. Stephen Holmes, 1990) ('B'), 1.

[90] B, 3. [91] DC, 133. [92] B, 17. [93] B, 109.

mercantile cities.[94] In each case, blame stems from the same source: encouraging the false belief that each individual should see himself as judge of matters of religion and politics eroded habits of obedience and led to the ruin of the commonwealth. In the constitutional-legal sphere, this attitude translated into a hardline opposition to the exercise by the king, on grounds of national security, of prerogative powers to raise revenue. Each 'thought himself to be so much master of whatsoever he possessed, that it could not be taken from him upon any pretence of common safety without his own consent'.[95]

It is not that the king's side escapes blame altogether. But here the reason for criticism is almost the opposite – not too much assertive independent-mindedness but rather too little. The king's party fell into strategic and conceptual error when, through their 'love with mixarchy', they threw away the chance of decisive military victory by pursuing a negotiated settlement.[96] In allowing public authority to become diluted they enabled private voices to proliferate. Discussing the Earl of Strafford's impeachment and attainder, a crucial moment in the lead-up to Civil War, Hobbes offers a version of the Hydra myth:

> B. You have read, that when Hercules fighting with the Hydra, had cut off any one of his many heads, there still arose two other heads in its place; and yet at last he cut them off all.
>
> A. The story is false. For Hercules at first did not cut off those heads, but bought them off; and afterwards, when he saw it did him no good, then he cut them off, and got the victory.[97]

This sardonic telling of the tale points not just to what Hobbes takes to have been a crucial tactical mistake on the King's part – trying to buy off the opposition instead of taking it on. It also reveals Hobbes's view of the causes of decline. Just as the Hydra's heads multiply, so the multiplicity of voices in the public realm causes the commonwealth to spin out of control. Decisive force, well applied, is the one thing that can stop it.[98]

Behemoth shows how a ragbag of factions spouting fictions brought down a commonwealth. Disagreement, Hobbes suggests, has a tendency to *cascade*.[99] Theological questions seep into questions of political

[94] B, 3–4. [95] B, 4.
[96] B, 116–117. [97] B, 72.
[98] Interestingly, Oliver Cromwell comes out pretty well in *Behemoth*. One reason for this was that Cromwell was precisely the kind of decisive leader that Hobbes found attractive.
[99] It may be possible to model Hobbes's conception of the state of nature in similar terms. The war of all against all results, that is, from a fear-driven cascade: the anticipation of

authority. What universities teach impacts on Parliament. Elite behaviour is copied by the people. Such cascades are neither predictable nor easily controlled. Situations of confusion make perfect breeding grounds for manipulation. Hobbes often uses the language of seduction to capture this phenomenon. As we saw, he first calls those who led the commonwealth astray the 'seducers'. Seduction is a two-way relationship. And Hobbes finds both seducer and seduced guilty – one for manipulating the other, the other for not resisting; one for being corrupt, the other for being so weak. *Behemoth* is full of such dangerous liaisons. Universities seduce the impressionable. Classical authors lead young gentlemen astray. Orators lure the populace from its duty.

Once political speech moves beyond public control and becomes a matter of private enterprise and private judgement, as happened in the 1640s,[100] the demise of sovereign authority and the collapse of social order is imminent. This specific pathology of the death of the English body politic is of a piece with Hobbes's more general fascination with the dangers of language: 'man's tongue is a trumpet to war and sedition', as he put it in *De Cive*.[101] Disorder is not caused, as the Greeks taught, by the re-emergence of the beast in man. Rather it results from 'the unruliness of the world-made mind'.[102] Ideas and the words used to convey them matter profoundly to us as they are the stuff that we use to construct the worlds in which we live. But the human mind, as well as being a source of ingenuity, is at the same time tragically limited and as such a source of great danger. This is why Hobbes keeps returning to the failings of the universities. Within a mind-constructed world these institutions, quintessential centres of ideas, have immense influence, not least on the

one man being attacked causes them to attack the other because the first considers it a better option than waiting to be attacked.

100 See David Zaret, *Origins of Democratic Culture: Printing, Petitions, and the Public Sphere in Early-Modern England* (Princeton: Princeton University Press, 2000). This was a Europe-wide phenomenon. See, e.g., Noel Malcolm, *Reason of State, Propaganda, and the Thirty Years' War: An Unknown Translation by Thomas Hobbes* (Oxford: Oxford University Press, 2007), 30: 'Since the outbreak of the Thirty Years' War in 1618, a flood of pamphlets, newsletters, and broadsheets, both informative and polemical, had poured from the presses … [C]onsiderable efforts were made by rulers and political leaders both to control the flow of such publications and to insert into it works supportive of their own policies.'

101 DC, 71. This is a direct echo of something James I wrote. See also DC, 4 (discussing the Latin maxims 'Man is a God to man, and Man is a wolf to Man'): 'men have a natural tendency to use rapacity as a term of abuse against each other, seeing their own actions reflected in others as in a mirror where left becomes right and right becomes left'.

102 Pettit, *Made With Words*, 99.

key subject of religion. Hobbes places 'consistent emphasis on the public function of the universities as the places where the blank paper of the ruling classes' minds was imprinted with civil doctrine'.[103] They are, as we might say, a source of considerable soft power. But the 'Schoole-men' tend, so Hobbes claims, to use that power irresponsibly at best, treasonously at worst. 'When men write whole volumes of such stuffe, are they not Mad, or intend to make others so?'[104] These remarks, while aimed at the universities, have a wider significance. The proliferation of political tracts, penned by individuals for their own private ends, is either madness in itself or else designed to induce madness in others. Either way, to allow for such a plurality of competing voices means that the authoritative voice of sovereign command will be drowned out. With the loss of the public voice goes the commonwealth's standard of right reason. Also lost is the idea of a single judge and with it the possibility of justice. We are back in the state of nature, or something very much like it.

The problem posed by the resurgent 'sovereign' subject is discussed in *Leviathan* where the 'poyson of seditious doctrines' comes very high on the list of things that weaken a commonwealth. First among such doctrines is the idea that '*every private man is Judge of Good and Evill actions*'. The central error here is that it mistakes the civil for the natural condition: 'This is true in the condition of meer Nature, where there are no Civill Lawes; and also under Civil Government, in such cases as are not determined by the Law. But otherwise, it is manifest, that the measure of Good and Evil actions, is the Civill Law.'[105] The lengths to which the civil authorities should go in order to stamp out behaviour of this sort is evident in the way Hobbes suggests Presbyterian ministers should have been dealt with before the Civil War. Since their sedition was in his view a primary cause of civil war and the deaths of perhaps 100,000 people, would it not have been better had 'those seditious ministers, which were not perhaps 1000, had been killed before they had preached? It had been (I confess) a great massacre; but the killing of 100,000 is greater'.[106]

Killings of this (presumably extra-legal) sort are exceptional. In normal times, Hobbes envisages a structure in which the propagation of ideas is tightly controlled. It is essential that the commonwealth speak with one voice. This entails the absence of any division or restriction in

[103] R. W. Serjeantson, '"Vaine Philosophy": Thomas Hobbes and the Philosophy of the Schools' in Conal Condren, Stephen Gaukroger and Ian Hunter (eds.), *The Philosopher in Early Modern Europe* (Cambridge: Cambridge University Press, 2006), 118.

[104] L, 59. [105] L, 223. [106] B, 95.

the constitution of government.[107] It also means that the multiplicity of private wills must be subordinated to the sovereign's determination of the public interest.[108] This injunction plays out most strongly in respect of two institutions, the church and the universities, where ideas proliferate most readily. For the church, Hobbes espouses a statist ecclesiology according to which the 'sovereign would act as absolute lord of the commonwealth's spiritual life, an archbishop with his dominion as his diocese'.[109] The universities must likewise 'bend and direct their studies to ... the teaching of absolute obedience to the laws of the King'.[110] Common to both is the imposition of the public interest as determined by the sovereign over private interests.

'By the laws, I mean, laws living and armed'

We can now more clearly specify the mischief that civil law is designed to cure. Stability, let alone peace, is impossible in the natural condition where rights-holding and self-adjudicating individuals are free to do as they please. Law provides a systematic structure of rule that enables authority to be concentrated in the hands of the sovereign. Law gives the commonwealth its standard of right and measure of justice.[111] All laws need interpretation and enforcement, but the radical pluralism of the natural condition makes authoritative determination impossible. The advent of civil law ends this polyphonic confusion. Enabling the commonwealth to speak in one voice enables truly concerted action, action as a political community (*civitas*) rather than as disjointed groups of individuals (*multitudo*).[112]

Law circumscribes the ambit of the subject's duty of obedience. 'The virtue of a subject is comprehended wholly in obedience to the laws of the commonwealth.'[113] Liberty begins where the laws run out.[114] There are a few exceptional cases where Hobbes allows the subject to disobey a law

[107] EL, 166–167.

[108] At least in public. Hobbes distinguished carefully between forbidding teaching and forbidding men to believe what they were taught: 'But what (may some object) if a King, or a Senate, or other Soveraign Person forbid us to believe in Christ? To this I answer, that such forbidding is of no effect; because Beleef, and Unbeleef never follow mens Commands.' (L, 343)

[109] Jeffrey R. Collins, *The Allegiance of Thomas Hobbes* (Oxford: Oxford University Press, 2008), 26.

[110] B, 56. [111] DC, 79. [112] DC, 75–76. [113] B, 44.

[114] This is consistent with his more general position on freedom. See Thomas Hobbes, *Treatise 'Of Liberty and Necessity'* in Vere Chappel (ed.), *Hobbes and Bramhall on Liberty and Necessity* (Cambridge: Cambridge University Press, 1999), 38: 'I conceive liberty to be rightly defined in this manner: Liberty is the absence of all the impediments to action that are not contained in the nature and intrinsical quality of the agent.'

without injustice, for instance where a man is commanded to harm or kill himself. But in general, liberties 'depend on the Silence of the Law. In cases where the Soveraign has prescribed no rule, there the Subject hath the Liberty to do, or forbeare, according to his own discretion'.[115] Since civil authority, the regulation of human conduct by law, does not and cannot prescribe the whole of man's conduct, Hobbes can argue that the purpose of laws is not to stop people from doing all that they want, but to prevent them from doing harm through rashness or their impetuous desires. Laws are 'as Hedges are set, not to stop Travellers, but to keep them in the way'.[116]

Hobbes's account of law's function is reflected in his analytical jurisprudence. Law (*lex*) is to be distinguished from right (*ius*), he insists, since 'right is that liberty which the law leaveth us'.[117] Nor should law be confused with covenant, which only binds in relation to the promise specifically covenanted for.[118] Nor is law counsel, which carries no obligation.[119] Rather, 'CIVIL LAWS (to define them) are nothing other than commands about the citizens' future actions from the one who is endowed with sovereign authority'.[120] This succinct definition comes from *De Cive*. I will probe the more elaborate definitions he provided in later works shortly. But note here how the ability to enforce law is built into law's very definition: 'By the Laws, I mean, Laws living and Armed.'[121] Laws, if they are to count as such, must be effective.[122] The subject has no duty to obey a putative authority that does not operate a system of laws that provides for the subject's safety and protection.

The functional dimensions of law, as Hobbes sees them, are also realized in the systematic way he clears the jurisdictional terrain of other

115 L, 151–152. 116 L, 239–240.

117 EL, 179; also L, 200; D, 35.

118 EL, 178. Also EL, 166: 'law implieth a command; covenant is but a promise.' See also EL, 139: 'A Lawe bindeth, by a promise of obedience in general'.

119 EL, 178. The parallel passages in DC, chapter 14 distinguish laws from advice (*consilium*) and agreement (*pactum*).

120 DC, 79. See also EL, 76: 'when the command is a sufficient reason to move us to the action [commanded], then is that command called a LAW.'

121 Thomas Hobbes, *A Dialogue Between a Philosopher and a Student, of the Common Laws of England* in Thomas Hobbes, *Writings on Common Law and Hereditary Right* (Oxford: Oxford University Press, ed. Alan Cromartie and Quentin Skinner, 2008) ('D'), 59.

122 Stephen Holmes, 'Hobbes's Irrational Man' in Stephen Holmes, *Passions and Constraint: On the Theory of Liberal Democracy* (Chicago: University of Chicago Press, 1995), 79. See also D, 14: "Tis not therefore the word of a Law, but the Power of a Man that has the strength of the Nation, that makes the Laws effectual.'

sources and systems of law. The notion of fundamental law is dismissed, unless it refers to either the sovereignty principle or the safety of the people. There is no 'fundamental law to a King', he wrote, 'but *salus populi*, the safety and well-being of his people'.[123] Custom is not a valid source of law unless it receives the imprimatur of the sovereign.[124] Natural laws are not laws properly so called so much as theorems of reason conducive to self-preservation.[125] As such they are counsel not command.[126] They are only laws if the sovereign wills it. 'One can be obliged to follow the dictates of the laws of nature only in the context of a political society firmly ruled by a sovereign who will enforce them as *legal* laws.'[127]

Hobbes systematically downgrades forms of law other than civil law, then, and reserves the word 'law' for the public commands of the sovereign. This imperial quality of Hobbes's jurisprudence, with its seemingly insatiable harmonizing drive, flows directly from the polity-stabilising functions that he ascribes to law. Authority is funnelled into a single channel – the civil law. The sovereign provides a single public voice for the commonwealth. His commands are the standards of right in relation to which the subjects are to organise their lives and resolve their conflicts. The dangers of allowing that public standard of right to become confused or challenged are so significant that no interference with those transmission cables of authority, the 'Artificiall Chains' of laws that link sovereign and subject, can be permitted: 'all Judicature is essentially annexed to the Soveraignty; and therefore all other Judges are but Ministers of him, or them that have the Soveraign Power'.[128]

The same centralizing instinct is evident in Hobbes's late work, the *Dialogue Between a Philosopher and a Student, of the Common Laws of*

[123] B, 67–68. See also L, 199: 'There is another distinction of Laws, into *Fundamentall*, and *not Fundamentall*: but I could never see in any Author, what a Fundamentall Law signifieth.'

[124] L, 184.

[125] L, 185. See also L, 111: 'These dictates of Reason, men use to call by the name of Lawes, but improperly: for they are but Conclusions, or Theoremes concerning what conduceth to the conservation and defence of themselves; whereas Law, properly is the word of him, that by right hath command over others.'

[126] We might say that natural laws are divine commandments. But even then, divine commands are binding in the commonwealth only insofar as the sovereign says that they are. S. A. Lloyd talks about the 'self-effacing' quality of the natural law in Hobbes: 'Hobbes's Self-Effacing Natural Law Theory' (2001) 82 *Pacific Philosophical Quarterly* 285.

[127] Russell Hardin, 'Hobbesian Political Order' (1991) 19 *Political Theory* 156, 162. See also Perez Zagorin, *Hobbes and the Law of Nature* (Princeton: Princeton University Press, 2009), 49.

[128] L, 168.

England, a central feature of which is its attack on the common lawyers. Throughout, Hobbes asserts the power of modern, scientific reason[129] over the medieval 'reason of the guild'.[130] He took aim at their claim to be stewards of a separate, near autonomous system of justice that some of them took to embody a fundamental constitution to which king and parliament were subject.[131] This independent-mindedness could lead to instability in the operation of the laws, as events leading to Civil War proved.[132] Hobbes, who at the time of writing the *Dialogue* feared he might be charged with heresy,[133] also disliked the shrillness of the lawyers and the tendency to populist updrift in sentencing policy (especially for heresy) when they gave themselves freedom to manoeuvre beyond statute. So, when the Student, representing the common lawyers, tries the standard lawyer's move of opening up a space between the common law and statute, the Philosopher (Hobbes's alter ego) closes him down:

Law. You speak of the Statute Law, and I speak of the Common Law.
Ph. I speak generally of Law.[134]

The Philosopher then steals Sir Edward Coke's line about the common law being supreme reason to subvert Coke's message. Law is reason, agreed. Yet it receives its highest expression not in the pronouncements of judges but in the commands of the sovereign: 'the Kings Reason, when it is publickly upon Advice, and Deliberation declar'd, is that *Anima*

[129] D, 13: '*Ph.* See you Lawyers how much you are beholding to a Philosopher, and 'tis but reason, for the General and Noble Science, and Law of all the World is true Philosophy, of which the Common Law of *England* is a very little part.' Jean Bodin in *Iuris universi distributio* (1580) similarly argued that jurisprudence must be a science, for it permits men to distinguish the true from the false.

[130] Cromartie, *Constitutionalist Revolution*, 215. Donald R. Kelley refers to the 'guild sense' of the common lawyers in his *History, Law and the Human Sciences* (London: Variorum Reprints, 1984).

[131] The final pages of the final volume of Coke's Reports (on *Bagg's Case*) contain the assertion that 'no wrong or injury, either public or private, can be done but that it shall be here reformed or punished by due course of law.' (Coke, *Eleventh Reports*, 98a). See also Pocock, *The Ancient Constitution and the Feudal Law*; Cromartie, *Constitutionalist Revolution*, ch 7.

[132] Alan Cromartie, 'General Introduction' in Hobbes, *Writings on Common Law and Hereditary Right*, xxxv: 'Though common lawyers ranked behind the presbyterian clergy in Hobbes's private demonology, he was consistent in his fear of them and in his diagnosis of the ultimate source of the mischief.'

[133] John Parkin, *Taming the Leviathan: The Reception of the Political and Religious Ideas of Thomas Hobbes in England 1640–1700* (Cambridge: Cambridge University Press, 2007), 240.

[134] D, 10.

Legis, and that *Summa Ratio*, and that Equity which all agree to be the Law of Reason, is all that is, or ever was Law in *England*'.[135] What is true for making laws should also be true for adjudicating on the basis of those laws: 'since therefore the King is sole Legislator, I think it also Reason he should be sole Supream Judge'.[136] This has to be the case given that our goal is the instantiation of the public reason of the sovereign and the eradication of 'any private Reason' of the type offered by the common lawyers. To do otherwise would mean that 'there would be as much contradiction in the Lawes, as there is in the Schooles'.[137]

Law as command 'publickly and plainly declar'd'

Law, when allied to sovereign power, is the solution to instability and insecurity. Since law itself is open to disagreement, particularly in its interpretation, it is essential that the structure of legal command is kept as clear as possible: 'all Judicature is essentially annexed to the Soveraignty'.[138] This applies both to legislation and adjudication. In 'all Courts of Justice, the Soveraign (which is the Person of the Common-wealth,) is he that Judgeth'.[139] The sovereign, then, has virtually unlimited legal capacity. He is endowed with plenipotentiary authority, the open-ended power 'to legislate, potentially on any aspect of life, for the whole community.'[140] But this does not mean that the sovereign has licence to do what he wills. The commonwealth of laws, as well as framing the exercise of enormous power, also provides obstacles to the misuse of power.

There can be no legal limits to the sovereign's authority.[141] Yet law can provide some sort of brake on sovereign power. We can start to unravel this apparent paradox by exploring the notion of civil law as public

[135] D, 19. [136] D, 27.

[137] L, 187. Hobbes's specification of the king's reason as *summa ratio* has a religious dimension or quality. In *Leviathan* chapter 37, discussing miracles and their use, he says that the question of whether the report of a miracle is true or a lie is not one for 'our own private Reason, or Conscience, but the Publique Reason, that is, the reason of Gods Supreme Lieutenant, Judge; and indeed we have made him Judge already, if wee have given him a Soveraign power'. (L, 306)

[138] L, 168. [139] L, 187.

[140] Noel Malcolm, 'Hobbes's Theory of International Relations' in Malcolm, *Aspects of Hobbes*, 432, 443.

[141] L, 184: 'The Soveraign of a Common-wealth ... is not Subject to the Civill Lawes. For having the power to make, and repeale Lawes, he may when he pleaseth, free himselfe from that subjection, by repealing those Lawes that trouble him, and making of new; and consequently he was free before.'

command. That those commands need to be clear is elementary; otherwise they would be incapable of performing the stabilising function that Hobbes envisages. This is evident even in the pithy definition of law Hobbes gives in his earlier writings. In *De Cive*, as we saw, law is defined as the sovereign's public commands concerning future actions of the citizen, a formulation that contains implicit limits. The category 'law' would not seem to include the sovereign's non-public commands ('Will no one rid me of this turbulent priest?'). Nor can the term 'law' apply to sovereign acts relating to past behaviour. The subject is presumably free from retrospective criminalising of his conduct.

Later definitions expand on the publicity requirement. The formulation in *Leviathan* is as follows: 'CIVILL LAW, Is to every Subject, those Rules, which the Common-wealth hath Commanded him, by Word, Writing, or other sufficient Sign of the Will, to make use of, for the Distinction of Right and Wrong; that is to say, of what is contrary, and what is not contrary to the Rule.'[142] Admittedly the limits here seem pretty trivial. All the more so as Hobbes in the same passage indicates that laws need not be general,[143] thereby seeming to accept for instance the legality of bills of attainder (the measure that did for Strafford). But there is still a requirement that the sovereign intends to create legal obligations and of some agreed public formality to signify that intention. The point is elaborated in the *Dialogue*. Law is defined as such 'when it is *publickly upon Advice, and Deliberation declar'd*'.[144] This statement, while suggestive, is ambiguous since it is not clear whether the two conditions – publicity and advice – are essential elements of law or whether they are aspirational or prudential, qualities that a good law should possess. The Philosopher's second attempt at a definition clarifies matters:

> *Ph.* Thus; A Law is the Command of him, or them that have the Soveraign Power, given to those that be his or their Subjects, declaring Publickly, and plainly what every of them may do, and what they must forbear to do.[145]

The advice requirement has now been dropped to the realm of prudence. This is consistent with the way advice is treated elsewhere in the work. The Student describes at one point the sovereign's failure to consult before making decisions about war and peace as a 'sin' – not, that is, something that renders his actions unlawful. The publicity requirement, by contrast,

[142] L, 183. [143] L, 183.
[144] D, 19 (emphasis added). [145] D, 31.

seems now to be firmly embedded within the concept of law. If anything, it has been strengthened. To count as a law the command must be declared both publicly and plainly. And the Philosopher indeed reasserts the requirement against opposition from the Student, who says 'whereas you make it *of the Essence of a Law* to be Publickly and plainly declar'd to the People, I see no necessity for that'.[146] The Philosopher then spells out what the publicity requirement might entail. When new statutes are passed, he says:

> the Knights of the Shires should be bound to furnish People with a sufficient Number of Copies (at the Peoples Charge) of the Acts of Parliament at their return to the Country; that every man may resort to them, and by themselves, or Friends take notice of what they are obliged to; for otherwise it were Impossible they should be obeyed: And that no Man is bound to a thing Impossible is one of Sir *Edw. Cokes* Maxims at the Common-Law.[147]

The content of the duty to promulgate reflects what Hobbes says elsewhere. 'Knowledge of the laws depends on the legislator, who has a duty to promulgate them', he writes in *De Cive*, 'for otherwise they are not laws.'[148] It is also consistent with his theory of political obligation. Unlike Machiavelli's Prince who manipulates allegiance personally in the interests of securing his estate, through his alertness, decisiveness and forcefulness as a ruler,[149] Hobbes's sovereign is a public and formal creation, a piece of legal artifice, albeit on the grandest scale. Subject to what I have to say later on prerogative power, the sovereign exists and exercises power through law. It speaks through the civil laws.[150] The Prince governs in his own interest; the Sovereign exists for the security and well-being of the commonwealth. Hobbes's ideal is a state that provides a stable framework of laws in which people can seek the satisfaction of their desires, whatever those desires may be.[151] But if that ideal is to be realized those subject to the laws must be clear about the legal boundaries in which they are meant

[146] D, 32 (emphasis added). [147] D, 32.

[148] DC, 160. See also DC, 172 'a ruler's *precepts* are laws for the ruled. But they are not *laws* unless they are promulgated clearly, so that there can be no excuse for ignorance'.

[149] Cornelia Navari, 'Hobbes and the "Hobbesian Tradition" in International Thought' (1982) 11 *Millennium: Journal of International Studies* 203, 210–212.

[150] See DC, 161: 'By *written* law I mean law which requires the voice or some other sign of the will of the legislator to become law … the requisite of *written law* is not *writing* but vocal expression [*vox*] … *Unwritten law* is law which needs no promulgation but the voice of nature, or natural reason, such as are *natural laws*.'

[151] Malcolm, 'Hobbes's Theory of International Relations', 440.

to operate. If you want certainty about the laws, you want it all the way down. You cannot assume, as the Student does, that people should have knowledge of the laws that bind them.[152] You must do all that you can to make sure that they know. Only then can you engender certainty about the operation of the system of laws as a whole. Absent this and insecurity and lack of trust sneak back in, leading to precisely the problems Hobbes's commonwealth was set up to resolve.

But how is the publicity requirement supposed to be enforced in a context where sovereignty is 'power unlimited'?[153] Hobbes insists, after all, that there are no legal controls over the sovereign[154] and that the sovereign is not subject to the civil laws.[155] And yet it would seem that Hobbes expects the sovereign's judges when faced with a putative law that was not properly promulgated to decline to enforce it. So hostile to the questioning of sovereign authority in other quarters,[156] Hobbes is surprisingly open to legal challenges to the exercise of sovereign power. As he writes in *Leviathan*:

> If a Subject have a controversie with his Soveraigne, of debt, or of right of possession of land or goods, or concerning any service required at his hands, or concerning any penalty, corporall, or pecuniary, grounded on a precedent Law: he hath the same Liberty to sue for his right, as if it were against a Subject; and before such Judges, as are appointed by the Soveraign. For seeing the Soveraign demandeth by force of a former Law, and not by vertue of his Power; he declareth thereby, that he requireth no more, than shall appear to be due by that Law. The sute therefore is not contrary to the will of the Soveraign.[157]

This passage indicates not just that litigation against the sovereign is possible, but that the category of possible suits is in fact very wide. It includes the types of action a subject might bring against another subject (property, contract, tort, employment etc.). But it goes further by allowing a series of actions in public law ('concerning any penalty, corporall, or pecuniary, grounded on a precedent Law'). If we read this passage alongside what Hobbes says about the duty to promulgate, then the subject

[152] There is another dimension to the argument against the Student, namely that in the monarchical commonwealth Hobbes favours, Parliament cannot consent to new laws on behalf of the people because it is not their representative.

[153] L, 155. [154] L, 222; D, 76. [155] L, 224.

[156] Holmes, 'Hobbes Irrational Man', 69: 'Thomas Hobbes apotheosized unquestionable authority as the only practicable alternative to anarchy and disparaged political liberty in almost all its forms.'

[157] L, 153.

ought to be able to argue in court that the 'precedent Law' under which you are charged is in fact no law at all.[158]

Hobbes also says that this type of action is not a challenge to the sovereign. But how can this be true if, in public law cases, the court will sometimes limit the sovereign's capacity to act? An answer might be found if we pay closer attention to the different types of limits that law can impose. Law can limit *substantively*. It can restrict the range of possible options open to a decision-maker. Constitutional law does this when it disallows action contrary to basic rights (e.g. imprison without cause). Hobbes rejects this kind of limit on the basis that sovereignty is plenitude of power. There is no law more fundamental than the idea of absolute sovereignty. Law can limit *institutionally*. One institution's room for action may be limited or checked by another institution (e.g. tax without the consent of Parliament). Again, Hobbes explicitly rejects any such separation of powers arrangement.[159] But law can also limit in a way that is internal to itself. In this case, the limit stems from law's *form*. Law has enormous coordinating potential, but only if it has certain qualities. Only if law is publicly and plainly made known is it able to specify in advance the behaviour required of subjects. Clarity is vital here because what is at stake is the public command of the sovereign. Without such clarity there can be no real stability or security, and subjects would not be able to shape their lives sure in the knowledge of what the law expects of them.

The benefits that stem from the effective operation of the laws are considerable – peace, order and good government. These benefits come, though, at a price. And that price is paid to the integrity of the legal form. Sovereignty flows through legal channels. But the value of such channels diminishes if the sovereign neglects or bypasses them. The importance

[158] Comparing the following passage from *De Cive*, 85: 'There are indeed many things permitted to citizens by the commonwealth, and legal action may sometimes be taken against the holder of *sovereign power*; but such action is not a matter of *civil law* but of *natural equity*; and the question is not what the holder of *sovereign power may* rightly do, but what he willed; hence he himself will be the judge, as if he could not give an unfair judgement, when equity is taken into account.' This is a problematic passage, not least because its meaning is not especially clear. It resembles the passage from *Leviathan* in that it allows legal challenges to the sovereign. It appears to differ in that it would require suits to be made in equity rather than (as the *Leviathan* passage suggests) at law ('he hath the same Liberty to sue for his right, as if it were against a Subject'; 'the Subject has the Liberty to demand the hearing of his Cause; and sentence, according to that Law'). I suspect the difference Hobbes imagines is primarily jurisdictional. Cases against the sovereign (in *De Cive*) should go through something like the Court of Chancery. Such cases (in *Leviathan*) should go through something like the common law courts.

[159] See L, 225; EL, 166–167.

of form to legal order explains the need to police the formal integrity of laws through a body charged with that task. This is the scenario that Hobbes raises with the prospect of public law actions against the sovereign. These actions do limit sovereign power. They do so, however, in a way that is internal to the formal structure of law and for reasons relating to the integrity of the system of laws. The judges who decide these cases unquestionably owe allegiance to the sovereign. But they fulfil their office by ensuring that the system of public command at the apex of which is the sovereign functions in the way that it should.

That Hobbes took legal form seriously is evident from the care he took to distinguish the private acts of the king in his natural capacity from the public commands of the king as sovereign. The difference marks the boundary between public command (law) and private wish (counsel), only the first of which carries an obligation. Those acts, he writes in the *Dialogue*, 'which are done by the King previously to the passing of them under the Great Seal of *England*, either by word of Mouth, or warrant under his Signet, or privy Seal, are done in his natural Capacity; but when they have past the Seal of *England*, they are to be taken as done in his politick Capacity'.[160] This is a particularly good example of the attention Hobbes paid to the public/private divide – and the especial importance of identifying and isolating the category of 'the public'. In this instance, the vital moment of transition from private to public is utterly formal and appears almost trivial. But it makes all the difference when it comes to specifying the duties of the subject. (No court, we are to presume, would enforce a mere wish, however kingly, as opposed to a proper legal command.) Why should form count for so much? We should not ignore the element of performance here. There is a theatricality of sorts at play here, after all, and Hobbes was always attuned to the role-playing dimensions of public life. But what is most at stake is clarity and publicity. All relevant actors – king, officials, judges, subjects – know that when something is done under the Great Seal it counts as law. It doesn't matter much what the proper form is, so long as it is generally accepted and sufficiently public. Reason of state writers of Hobbes's time revelled in the claim that political truths are always shrouded in mystery.[161] Hobbes insisted to the contrary that subjects should know the laws of the commonwealth and the reason why it exercises authority over them. The commonwealth, as he wrote in *De Cive*, 'does not want to take anything away from the citizen

[160] D, 139. [161] Malcolm, *Reason of State*, 122.

in underhanded ways, and yet is willing to take everything from him in an open fashion'.[162]

'By vertue of his power': the sovereign and the prerogative

But perhaps we have been a little hasty. So far, we have a reasonably benevolent, if rather austere, theory of rule through law. Yet Hobbes says repeatedly that the sovereign is not bound by civil law but only by the law of God. Does that mean that the sovereign can act outside the law? Is there anything (at least of this world) that prevents him from doing so? Even the passages I drew upon that envisage litigation against the sovereign seem to assume that the sovereign can act in this way. Hobbes tells us that such litigation is in order 'seeing the Soveraign demandeth by force of a former law, and not by vertue of his Power'. This seems to presuppose that the sovereign has a choice between exercising power in two ways, the legal and the extra-legal. This reading is supported by a later part of the same passage: 'But if he [the sovereign] demand, or take any thing by pretence of his Power; there lyeth, in that case, no action of Law'.[163] If the sovereign has free rein when it comes to acting in accordance with the law and its formal constraints, what becomes of the rule of law commonwealth that Hobbes has so painstakingly constructed?

There is no doubt that Hobbes was exercised by such legal questions. He wrote *The Elements of Law* as a response to one of the last pre-Civil War crisis points involving prerogative power, and one of his ambitions in writing it was 'to resist and push aside the full weight' of the various competing traditions of constitutional thought that his age had inherited.[164] The burden of his theory was to defeat the tendentious claims of constitutionalists and believers in fundamental law and divided rule. It is strange, then, that in none of his major works on political theory is the prerogative a feature.[165] Compare Locke's *Second Treatise of Government*. As is well known, that slender work contains a chapter dedicated to king's

162 DC, 86. 163 L, 153.

164 Quentin Skinner, *Hobbes and Republican Liberty* (Cambridge: Cambridge University Press, 2008), 16–17, 72.

165 One possible reason for this silence is that Hobbes was trying to avoid saying too much too directly about contemporary flashpoints. DC, 6: 'I have paid careful attention through the whole length of my discourse not to say anything of the civil laws of any nation, i.e. not to approach shores which are sometimes dangerous because of rocks, sometimes because of current storms.'

prerogative.[166] The burden of Locke's theory lies in its insistence that the powers of government 'ought to be exercised by established and promulgated laws'.[167] But Locke explicitly permits the executive (the king) to exercise extraordinary discretionary powers in times of crisis or emergency. These powers are said to operate *extra et contra legem* – they take their shape *against* the normal system of civil law – and there is no doubt that prerogative power is invested here in the *person* as well as the *office*.[168] The prerogative only fits with the underlying state theory in the sense that it provides an exception to it – and a potentially very significant one at that. Justified by necessity, grounded in notions of personal rule, legitimated on the basis of whether or not it works, Locke's theory in this respect carries vestiges of the pre-modern order over into the modern constitution.[169] As such, it goes against the grain of the dominant narrative that I trace in these chapters. That is, from the personal to the official and from the exceptional to the normal.

Hobbes's silence on prerogative in his theoretical works does not mean that his position on the subject is unclear. His consistent assertion that the sovereign is not subject to the civil law – indeed, that it is the merest confusion to suggest that any genuine sovereign can ever be limited by the law of the land[170] – aligned him politically with the most intransigent proponents of the divine right of kings.[171] Elsewhere in his output, there is a little more to point. In *Behemoth*, as we have seen, Hobbes raises the option of killing a few thousand Presbyterian ministers – presumably an exceptional act outside the domain of normal law – to avoid the bigger slaughter that followed. Questions concerning the existence and scope of various prerogative powers crop up more frequently in the *Dialogue*, which deals directly with contemporary legal and political issues. When

[166] John Locke, 'The Second Treatise of Government', chapter XIV 'Of Prerogative' in Locke, *Two Treatises of Government* (Cambridge: Cambridge University Press, ed. Peter Laslett, 1988), 374–80.

[167] *Second Treatise*, II, s. 137.

[168] See, e.g., Clement Fatovic, *Outside the Law: Emergency and Executive Power* (Baltimore: Johns Hopkins University Press, 2009), 65.

[169] For further elaboration, see Thomas Poole, 'Constitutionalism Exceptionalism and the Common Law' (2009) 7 *International Journal of Constitutional Law* 247.

[170] EL, 166: 'It is an error therefore to think: that the power which is virtually the whole power of the commonwealth, and which in whomsoever it resideth, is usually called supreme or sovereign, can be subject to any law but that of God Almighty.' L, 224: 'while it is true that the sovereign is subject to the law of nature, it is 'repugnant to the nature of the Common-wealth' to imagine that '*he that hath the Soveraign Power, is subject to the Civill Lawes*.'

[171] Skinner, *Hobbes and Republican Liberty*, 80.

they do, Hobbes persistently advocates giving the king the widest degree of latitude in the exercise of those powers. His defence is often strident and derisive of supposed legal limits. On the subject of the king's power to levy soldiers and the money needed to pay for them without Parliament's consent, Hobbes writes: 'You may therefore think it good Law, for all your Books; that the King of *England* may at all times, that he thinks in his Conscience it will be necessary for the defence of his People, Levy as many Souldiers, and as much Money as he please, and that himself is Judge of the Necessity.'[172] The position entails that the king is entitled to ignore even Acts of Parliament that purport to limit his prerogative.[173]

The same type of argument recurs in relation to other prerogatives – the capacity to do justice in individual cases (equity),[174] the power to punish,[175] and the power to pardon (mercy).[176] In each case, Hobbes stakes a position at the far 'royalist' reaches of the spectrum of contemporary opinion. This is true even of the most significant of absolute prerogatives, the so-called dispensing power. At issue here was whether the sovereign had the power to override or ignore (dispense with) existing law.[177] Hobbes is clear that it does. The safety and well-being of the people, as determined by the sovereign, must trump ordinary legal rules.[178] While there is nothing to stop a king agreeing to pass statutes that restrict his power, those grants are always subject to the more fundamental duty to protect his subjects. A prudent king will consult before dispensing with such a law. But Hobbes leaves us in no doubt that this is exclusively the province of the sovereign:

> But if a King find that by such a Grant he be disabled to protect his Subjects if he maintain his Grant, he sins: and therefore may, and ought to take no Notice of the said Grant: For such Grants as by Error, or false Suggestion are gotten from him, are as the Lawyers do Confess, Void and of no Effect, and ought to be recalled.[179]

Hobbes's analysis of prerogative often sees him slipping from the institutional plane (the institution of sovereign authority) to the individual

172 D, 22. 173 D, 18. 174 D, 55.

175 D, 91: where Hobbes suggests that in respect of exceptional acts that are sins, even where there is no law in place, 'surely the King has power to Punish him (on this side of Life or Member) as he please; and with the Assent of Parliament (if not without) to make the Crime for the future Capital'.

176 D, 127–129.

177 Kenneth Pennington, *The Prince and the Law, 1200–1600* (Berkeley: University of California Press, 1993).

178 Malcolm, *Reason of State*, 117. 179 D, 20.

(the prerogatives of the king). Indeed, it is hard to escape the conclusion, on reading passages like this one, that we have moved from the realm of stable and public laws into a world once more beset by private judgement. Hobbes would deny this. In the body of the king, private interest and public interest are almost entirely coextensive.[180] Even if we accept this, the prerogative introduces a destabilizing, anti-formal element into a theory that is otherwise rigorous in its insistence on form and formality in lawmaking. We are left with something of a puzzle. The sovereign is legally constituted, but sovereign capacity is not exhausted by law nor is sovereign power constrained by law. Existing law can be ignored if the sovereign thinks that it needs to be.[181]

The prerogative opens up a fissure within Hobbes's theory that is not easily closed. One approach that might help us is to pay attention to the theory's self-description as a science of politics. The commonwealth should apply Hobbes's principles for the 'well governing of men's Actions' if it seeks peace and good order.[182] 'Sovereigns act, and the science on the basis of which they act is Hobbesian civil science.'[183] Civil science must be able to explain two things in respect of the prerogative. First, why in principle you need so much of this type of power (as per the *Dialogue*). Second, why in practice you expect prerogative powers – or at least the more serious of them – to be used very rarely (as per *Leviathan*). Answering the first question is straightforward. Sovereignty requires plenitude of power – power needs to be united in the hands of one authority.[184] Absent which a stable and well-ordered commonwealth is impossible: it takes Leviathan to subdue Behemoth. This position requires a sovereign with a

180 L, 131.

181 Hobbes's broad interpretation of what counts as the safety of the public serves merely to heighten the tensions here. See, e.g., EL, 172: '*Salus populi suprema lex*; by which must be understood, not the mere preservation of their lives, but generally their benefit and good.'

182 See the Dedicatory Letter to *De Cive*. DC, 4. See also Thomas Hobbes, 'The Verse Life: A Contemporary Translation (Anonymous)' in *Human Nature and De Corpore Politico*, 257: To Various Matter and Various Motion brings/ Me, and the different Species of Things./ Man's inward Motions and his Thoughts to know,/ The good of Government, and Justice too,/ These were my Studies then, and in these three/ Consists the whole course of Philosophy:/ Man, Body, Citizen'.

183 Ross Harrison, *Hobbes, Locke and Confusion's Masterpiece: An Examination of Seventeenth-Century Political Philosophy* (Cambridge: Cambridge University Press, 2002), 59.

184 Denis Baranger, *Écrire la Constitution Non-Écrite: Une Introduction au Droit Politique Britannique* (Paris: Presses Universitaires de France, 2008), 228.

capacity unlimited by other institutions or by existing laws for the sovereign to do what he thinks is necessary to preserve order.

The answer to the second question is more complicated. We can accept that Hobbes's project is a normalizing one that favours ordinary law over extraordinary prerogative. But it is still not clear what basis we have for thinking that the sovereign, given the option of going outside the laws, would choose to remain within them. Why choose law, with its formal and institutional constraints, when you could enjoy the much freer style of rule through prerogative? The sovereign, then, seems to have a 'commitment' problem that persists so long as he can break the legal fetters whenever he chooses. Russell Hardin's reading of Hobbes as a proto-game theorist might offer a way forward.[185] The whole point for Hobbes of artificial virtues like law and justice, Hardin argues, is strategic. 'They are valued not per se but rather for their beneficial regulation of social interaction.'[186] If civil and political relations could be modelled as a series of one-off games between sovereign and his subjects, then we might well expect the sovereign to opt for the prerogative. The prerogative has less baggage (fewer formalities and constraints) and so lets him get what he wants done with a minimum of fuss. But Hobbes rightly sees the civil condition as an ongoing affair. And in repeated games law is to be preferred. I remarked earlier on the enormous coordinating capacity of law. Prerogative gives you no such pay-off over the long run, since it is anti-formal and unpredictable. The more recourse the sovereign makes to its prerogatives, the more it will undermine law's capacity to act as a stable framework for political and social obligations. The result is less efficiency in the operation of rule. And, since it would be less clear what the real obligations of the subjects are (and even less clear what they are likely to be in future), it would also result in less trust and less loyalty. Subjects would begin to see the sovereign as incapable of providing the benefits of efficient rule by law (order and security) and begin to treat him as a terribly powerful private enemy.

The sovereign chooses law because reason tells it to. Does that mean that we can ignore prerogative power, or at least relegate it to a box marked 'only in case of dire need'? I don't think so. Although he is not terribly

[185] See also John Finnis, 'Law's Authority and Social Theory's Predicament' in John Finnis, *Philosophy of Law: Collected Essays, Vol. IV* (Oxford: Oxford University Press, 2011), 55: 'Some theorists, like Hobbes, have thought to explain the point of legal regulation in terms of one of the paradigm games in game theory: the Prisoners' Dilemma', referring in particular to Hobbes's state of nature.

[186] Hardin, 'Hobbesian Political Order', 163.

clear on this, Hobbes's insight may be that the prerogative is one of the operating conditions of effective law. Sovereign authority flows through law but prerogative power is needed to institute law. The sovereign must have at his disposal a spectrum of special legal and extra-legal capacities up to and including the power to dispense with particular laws and the power to act ruthlessly (the killing of Presbyterian ministers) where the public interest demands it. On this reading, prerogative acts as something like the dark matter of Hobbes's constitutional universe.[187] Rarely visible, its residual presence holds together the more prominent and in the normal course of events more important stuff of political life. The civil laws in particular cannot properly be understood without it. Law's stabilizing and harmonizing functions can only take effect in the shadow of this only partly legal framework of power. The possibility of overwhelming force, concentrated in the hands of the supreme lawmaker, is what allows law to be law. Odd though it may seem, if our goal is peace, this concentration of force and law is essential. The availability of force on this scale, behind the operation of normal law, makes the sovereign feel secure and so more likely to exercise power through normal legal channels.[188] Beyond the specific (and presumptively reasonable) sanctions that individual laws may carry, it also inclines subjects towards obedience.

'In the posture of gladiators': Leviathan abroad

One remaining aspect of Hobbes's theory that needs to be addressed is what the new state theory entails for what we would now call international law and international relations. The reason for tackling this subject becomes clearer in the following chapters, particularly when we set Hobbes's theory of state against more belligerent and expansionist republican theories. Mention was made earlier of the 'imperial quality' of Hobbes's jurisprudential theory. To what extent does this imperializing

[187] In astronomy, dark matter is a currently undetermined type of matter which accounts for a large part of the mass of the universe (thought to be 83% of the mass in the universe and 23% of the mass-energy) but neither emits nor scatters light or other electromagnetic radiation and so cannot be directly seen with telescopes. Its existence is inferred from its effects on visible matter. Dark matter is what created the structure of the universe and is essentially what holds it together.

[188] Compare David Hume, 'Of Passive Obedience' in David Hume, *Essays – Moral, Political and Literary* (Indianapolis: Liberty Fund, ed. Eugene F. Miller, 1987), 492: 'Where the king is an absolute sovereign, he has little temptation to commit such enormous tyranny as may justly provoke rebellion: But where he is limited, his imprudent ambition, without any great vices, may run him into that perillous situation.'

tendency stop at the borders of the state? Moreover, in this context, especially where there is war or the threat of war, the tension in that theory between the more visible juristic conception and the generally more occluded moral or personalized conception of the state comes to the fore.[189]

International lawyers and international relations scholars associate Hobbes with a 'realist' position according to which states exist in the same ways as men in the natural condition, in a perpetual state of war. 'Within the conventional typologies of international relations theory', David Armitage writes, 'Hobbes stands between Hugo Grotius and Immanuel Kant as the presiding genius of one of three major theoretical traditions.'[190] Charles Beitz, for instance, claims that today's 'international sceptics' who picture international relations as a state of nature and deny the possibility of effective regulative principles for the conduct of nations adopt a 'Hobbesian conception of international relations'.[191] In a recent paper, Johan Olsthoorn calls Hobbes's doctrine that justice and injustice are non-existent outside the state Justicial Statism, construing it as an extra-political (international) version of the pre-political (domestic) state of nature.[192]

There is textual support for this reading. The issue is raised only in the last paragraph of the *Elements of Law*: 'As for the law of nations, it is the same with the law of nature. For that which is the law of nature between man and man, before the constitution of commonwealth, is the law of nations between sovereign and sovereign, thereafter.'[193] In *De Cive*, Hobbes makes the connection between the law of nature, 'the natural law of *men*', and the law of nations, 'the natural law of *commonwealths*' – that is, between the pre-political and the extra-political. 'The precepts of both are the same: but because commonwealths once instituted take on the personal qualities of men, what we call a *natural law* in speaking of the duties of individual men is called the *right of Nations*, when applied to whole commonwealths, peoples or nations.'[194] He also says at

189 See David Runciman, *Pluralism and the Personality of the State* (Cambridge: Cambridge University Press, 1997), 17–18.

190 David Armitage, *Foundations of Modern International Thought* (Cambridge: Cambridge University Press, 2013), 59–60.

191 Charles R. Beitz, *Political Theory and International Relations* (Princeton: Princeton University Press, 1999), 28–33.

192 John Olsthoorn, 'Why Justice and Injustice Have No Place Outside the Hobbesian State' (2015) 14 *European Journal of Political Theory*, 19.

193 EL, 182. 194 DC, 156.

the start of the book that '*Man is a God to man*, and *Man is a wolf to Man*. The former is true of the relations of citizens with each other, the latter of relations between commonwealths.'[195] Once constituted, it would appear that the artificial person of the state took on the characteristics of the fearful and defensive individuals who instituted it.[196] The position is elaborated in *Leviathan*, where Hobbes writes that 'in all times, Kings and Persons of Soveraigne authority, because of their independency, are in continuall jealousies, and in the state and posture of Gladiators; having their weapons pointing, and their eyes fixed on one another; that is, their Forts, Garrisons, and Guns upon the Frontiers of their Kingdomes; and continuall Spyes upon their neighbours, which is the posture of War'.[197] The Latin *Leviathan* (1668) goes still further, adding to the passage just quoted by asserting that 'whatever a particular man could do before commonwealths were constituted, a commonwealth can do according to the *ius gentium*'.[198]

But as so often with Hobbes, what at first appears straightforward turns out to be anything but. As Ross Harrison puts it, 'in Hobbes, as in other philosophers, there's the bit where you say it and the bit where you take it back'.[199] For one thing, although Hobbes consistently draws an analogy between man in the natural condition and the relations between sovereign states, it is clear that he doesn't intend the analogy to be exact. True, the world is populated by fearful and competitive actors. But states are not nearly as vulnerable as men in the state of nature. It is a simpler proposition for them to make treaties and establish leagues – and in so doing make justice, however provisionally, govern international relations. In addition, the state is not like an individual in that it is expected to act rationally and in the public interest.[200] To explain why, we can use the same logic that helped us make sense of the conundrum that otherwise bedevilled Hobbes's conception of law and prerogative (reserve power). There, we said that while the sovereign in principle is free to act as it wills, the sovereign is a rational entity that works in furtherance of the

[195] DC, 3–4.

[196] Armitage, *Foundations of Modern International Thought*, 64.

[197] L, 90.

[198] Thomas Hobbes, *Leviathan* (Oxford: Oxford University Press, ed. Noel Malcolm, 2012), II, 553: '*Quod potuit fieri ante Civitates constitutas, a quolibet homine, idem fieri potest per Ius Gentium a qualibet Civitate*'.

[199] Ross Harrison, 'The Equal Extent of Natural and Civil Law' in Dyzenhaus and Poole, *Hobbes and the Law*, 45.

[200] See also Tom Sorell, 'The Burdensome Freedom of Sovereigns' in Tom Sorell and Luc Foisneau (eds.), *Leviathan After 350 Years* (Oxford: Oxford University Press, 2004), 184.

long-term public interest (peace). In its inter-state relations, then, we would expect the sovereign to act in the same manner (rationally) and with the same goal in mind (peace). Under normal conditions this means making covenants and treaties with other states, converting if only in a piecemeal fashion the conditions of anarchy that otherwise prevail into passable conditions of peace.

In Hobbes's theory, *salus populi*, the safety and benefit of the people, is the aim of the sovereign's foreign (as well as domestic) policy. 'Unlike the caricature version of the Hobbesian position', Noel Malcolm argues, 'such a theory can give a prominent place to the pursuit of prosperity through international trade, and of other advantages that flow from international cooperation.'[201] The Hobbesian state is not crudely Machiavellian – it does not act in a moral vacuum[202] – and Hobbes was not much of a warmonger nor an enthusiastic imperialist.[203] There would be no point in trying to escape from the destructive cynicism of *raison d'état* politics at the domestic level only for it to re-enter via the back door through the sovereign's foreign engagements.[204] As the Philosopher observes in the *Dialogue*, it is important to create a juridical scenario that is good for both King and People, 'as creating some kind of Difficulty for such Kings as for the Glory of Conquest might spend one part of their Subjects Lives and Estates, in Molesting other Nations, and leave the rest to Destroy themselves at Home by Factions'.[205] It may well be that the stable and peaceful vision of the state in its domestic context is only sustainable if it adopts a cautious international pose.[206] It is precisely the sovereign's job to avoid what Locke

201 Malcolm, 'Hobbes's Theory of International Relations', 448.

202 Malcolm, 'Hobbes's Theory of International Relations', 437: 'Hobbes clearly does not mean that the law of nature is whatever the sovereign wills it to be.'

203 But see *Leviathan*, 239. The last line of the quote is particularly chilling: 'The multitude of poor, and yet strong people still encreasing, they are to be transplanted into Countries not sufficiently inhabited: where neverthelesse, they are not to exterminate those they find there; but constrain them to inhabit closer together, and not range a great deal of ground, to snatch what they find; but to court each little Plot with art and labour, to give them their sustenance in due season. And when all the world is overcharged with Inhabitants, then the last remedy of all is Warre; which provideth for every man, by Victory, or Death.' See also Richard Tuck, *The Rights of War and Peace: Political Thought and the International Order from Grotius to Kant* (Oxford: Oxford University Press, 1999), 138.

204 See, e.g., Martti Koskenniemi, 'International Law and *Raison d'État*: Rethinking the Prehistory of International Law' in Benedict Kingsbury and Benjamin Straumann (eds.), *The Roman Foundations of the Law of Nations: Alberico Gentili and the Justice of Empire* (Oxford: Oxford University Press, 2010), 297–339.

205 D, 21.

206 Larry May, *Limiting Leviathan: Hobbes on Law and International Affairs* (Oxford: Oxford University Press, 2013), 225.

called 'the goblins of warre and bloud'. The more active the sovereign is in the international realm, the more concerned it is with enlarging its territories through war and conquest, the more likely that the apparatus of government will become co-opted by the private interests of the rulers rather than function in the interest of the public as a whole.

Coda

This chapter has charted the first and foundational moves in the transformation of prerogative into reason of state. Seen in these terms, the great seventeenth-century prerogative cases examined in the first half of the chapter represent something like a pre-history of reason of state. It is true that these cases failed to stabilize the legal situation that existed at the time. But in so doing they revealed the juridical and jurisdictional difficulties inherent in trying to reconcile what were ultimately competing conceptions of lawful authority, one based in the notion of service, the other in the idea of office. The second half of the chapter considered the constitutional theory of the greatest of the early-modern state theorists, Thomas Hobbes. We have spent so long in his company because he articulated more clearly than anyone else the basic operating framework of the state understood as an autonomous juridical structure (lex) that has its own logic and its own internal sense of justice (ius). As such, his theory marks perhaps the first systematic attempt to transcend the prerogative by folding it into a complete and integrated structure of legal rule. The next chapter examines a similar enterprise, albeit one animated by very different goals. The republican writers from mid-century onwards offered plans for redefining reason of state that went beyond Hobbes in certain respects, especially in terms of institutional design. But whereas Hobbes conceived the state in defensive terms as a safe harbour in a hostile world, the republicans intended to harness the energies of the now united state to spread the gospel of liberty abroad.

3

Republican principles of state and empire

'I will make the name of Englishman to be as much feared as ever was the name of *civis Romanus*.' So said Oliver Cromwell on hearing the news that an English sailor had been beaten up for insulting a Spanish religious procession in the New World.[1] The incident symbolized the failure of Cromwell's 'Western Design' of 1654–5, an attempt to interrupt Spanish operations in the Caribbean.[2] As his first foreign-policy reversal, it sowed doubt about what Cromwell took to be his providential mission. The policy was driven by the assumption that the English revolution, and the Protestantism that underpinned it, was providentially intended for universal exportation against the forces of Catholic Spain.[3] Cromwell's outburst contains the germs of a more assertive outlook, Spain being still the dominant imperial power with pretensions to world hegemony, of lordship over the world.[4] Alluding to ancient Rome and expressed in the new language of republicanism, it suggests a vision of England assuming the mantle of the just Roman *imperium* against the present reality of domination at the hands of the heretical and bullying Spanish.

1 The outburst, at least on Gilbert Burnet's recounting of the event, probably occurred in the summer of 1656: Wilbur Cortez Abbott, *The Writings and Speeches of Oliver Cromwell* (4 vols., Cambridge, MA: Harvard University Press, 1937–47), vol. III, 759 (quoted in David Armitage, 'The Cromwellian Protectorate and the Languages of Empire' (1992) 35 *Historical Journal* 531, 537).

2 The Western Design represented the first deployment of the military resources of the British state in the interests of transoceanic, as opposed to Irish, colonization: Nicolas Canny, 'The Origins of Empire: An Introduction' in Canny (ed.), *The Origins of Empire* (Oxford: Oxford University Press, 1998), 20.

3 Blair Worden, 'Providence and Politics in Cromwellian England' (1985) 59 *Past and Present* 55.

4 Anthony Pagden, *Lords of All the World: Ideologies of Empire in Spain, Britain and France c.1500-c.1800* (New Haven: Yale University Press, 1995).

The failure of the Western Design and the Protector's reaction to it induced a period of deep reflection within the young commonwealth.[5] Combining the English state's first real forays into the world of imperial politics[6] and the possibility of a radical reordering the commonwealth, this was at once a republican and an imperial moment unique in English history.[7] '[N]o other period of comparable brevity', Zagorin observes, 'has borne so splendid a harvest' for English political philosophy as these revolutionary decades.[8] This chapter examines a group of writers whose response to the situation was to argue that England should recast its constitution on republican principles.[9] This was not simply a matter of reworking Machiavelli to fit English conditions.[10] As well as looking backwards to the classical republics of Rome and Athens, it meant looking outwards to contemporary republics, above all the example of the United Provinces.[11] It also meant pursuing Machiavelli's insight linking

[5] Cromwell himself came out of the crisis with a militant speech to Parliament in which he confronted MPs with the seriousness of the nation's predicament: 'truly your great enemy is the Spaniard. He is. He is a naturall Enemy', not least for his design for universal empire. Abbott, IV, 260; 261–262; 264; 269 (quoted in Armitage, 'The Cromwellian Protectorate', 548).

[6] Michael J. Braddick, 'The English Government, War, Trade, and Settlement, 1625–1688' in Canny, Origins of Empire, 3–5: 'Before 1649 all forms of colonial government were varieties of government by licence, whether company or proprietary charter, or self-government under a royal Governor. After 1649 this "contractual empire" began to give way to the "legislative empire".'

[7] Matters of empire were, however, much in vogue after the succession of James I of England raised the question of the union of England and Scotland into a greater Britain. This question formed the context of legal argument in *Calvin's Case* (1608), discussed in Chapter 2. On English imperial aspirations in this period, see Thomas James Dandelet, *The Renaissance of Empire in Early Modern Europe* (New York: Cambridge University Press, 2014), 259–274.

[8] Perez Zagorin, *A History of Political Thought in the English Revolution* (London: Routledge & Kegan Paul, 1954), 1.

[9] Richard Tuck, *Philosophy and Government 1572–1651* (Cambridge: Cambridge University Press, 1993), 225: 'the most important fact about the English civil war was that this constitutionalism gave way to a wholly different mode of discourse'. See also Blair Worden, 'English Republicanism' in J. H. Burns and M. Goldie (eds.), *The Cambridge History of Political Thought 1450–1700* (Cambridge: Cambridge University Press, 1991).

[10] J. G. A. Pocock, *The Machiavellian Moment: Florentine Political Thought and the Atlantic Republican Tradition* (Princeton: Princeton University Press, 2nd ed., 2003). On the impact of Machiavelli on sixteenth-century English political thought, especially in discussions of Ireland, see Markku Peltonen, *Classical Humanism and Republicanism in English Political Thought 1570–1640* (Cambridge: Cambridge University Press, 1995), 73–102.

[11] Jonathan Scott, 'Classical Republicanism in Seventeenth-Century England and the Netherlands' in Martin van Gelderen and Quentin Skinner (eds.), *Republicanism: A Shared European Heritage, Vol. I: Republicanism and Constitutionalism in Early Modern Europe* (Cambridge: Cambridge University Press, 2002).

the strength of internal institutions to the pressures of external policy.[12] This entailed, in turn, that thinking about the current state of England involved both an internal (domestic) and external (foreign) dimension. 'The republican experience became a prism, receiving the broadest rays of antiquity and the Renaissance and refracting them for the use of modern Europe and America. Among their number the republican writers included some of the most innovative and influential of a century exceptionally endowed with both.'[13] This chapter pays close attention to the way that three of these writers rethought the relationship between liberty and reason of state. They are chosen not just because of the influence they had on later generations of republican theorists and politicians, but also because each makes a distinctive contribution to one of three central themes. So, Nedham is particularly important on the subject of law, Sidney on war and Harrington on empire.

Constituting the free state

Republican ideas may have proliferated in the earlier part of the seventeenth century,[14] but a fully fledged republican account had to wait until after the Civil War. The English commonwealth was not the result of some insurrectionary plan but emerged from a period of problematic legalism and the failure to secure a political settlement.[15] Few of the revolutionaries planned to execute the king and fewer still planned to turn England into a commonwealth. They 'did not execute the king in order to change the constitution. Rather their determination to execute the king swept constitutional calculation aside. The abolition of monarchy was not a motive for the regicide but a practical consequence of it.'[16] The writers

[12] David Armitage, 'Empire and Liberty: A Republican Dilemma' in Martin van Gelderen and Quentin Skinner (eds.), *Republicanism: A Shared European Heritage, Vol. II: The Values of Republicanism in Early Modern Europe* (Cambridge: Cambridge University Press, 2002), 34.

[13] Jonathan Scott, 'The Rapture of Motion: James Harrington's Republicanism' in Nicholas Phillipson and Quentin Skinner (eds.), *Political Discourse in Early Modern Britain* (Cambridge: Cambridge University Press, 1993), 139–140.

[14] Peltonen, *Classical Humanism and Republicanism in English Political Thought*; Quentin Skinner, 'Classical Liberty, Renaissance Translation and the English Civil War' in Skinner (ed.), *Visions of Politics II: Renaissance Virtues* (Cambridge: Cambridge University Press, 2002).

[15] Thomas N. Corns, 'Milton and the Characteristics of a Free Commonwealth' in David Armitage, Armand Himy and Quentin Skinner (eds.), *Milton and Republicanism* (Cambridge: Cambridge University Press, 1995), 27.

[16] Blair Worden, 'Republicanism, Regicide and Republic: The English Experience' in van Gelderen and Skinner, *Republicanism: A Shared European Heritage, Vol. I*, 315.

examined in this chapter were responding to a series of emergencies that raised fundamental constitutional and political questions.

The republic (or commonwealth) was formally declared on 7 February 1649, eight days after the king's death. In March, Parliament passed an Act for the abolishing of the kingly office. The Act observes how 'regal power and prerogative' has been used 'to oppress and impoverish and enslave the subject' and links the office of the king with servitude. Kings are inclined to set up 'their own will and power above the laws, that so they might enslave these kingdoms to their own lust'.[17] It trawls through republics both ancient and modern to show how free states were better off in 'Riches, Freedom, Peace, and all Happiness'. In May, Parliament passed another act declaring 'the people of England' a 'Commonwealth and Free State' to be governed 'by the supreme authority of this nation, the representatives of the people in parliament', now shorn of 'any king or house of Lords'.

The word 'king' was removed from all legal documents and replaced by the phrase 'Keepers of the Liberties of England'. But an ambiguity surrounded the constitution of the new state that was never successfully resolved,[18] proving the republican point that it 'would be one thing to kill the king. It would be another to kill kingship, and tyranny, in every English soul.'[19] With the Levellers crushed by the leaders of the new regime in the spring and summer of 1649,[20] the republicans provided a source of internal opposition to the commonwealth regime during the 1650s. They managed to shine 'through the window of this brief break with political custom ... an intense ideological light.'[21] While much

[17] 'An Act for the abolishing of the kingly office in England and Ireland, and the dominions thereunto belonging, 17 March 1649' in J. P. Kenyon, *The Stuart Constitution 1603–1688: Documents and Commentary* (Cambridge: Cambridge University Press, 1966), 340.

[18] Worden, 'Republicanism, Regicide and Republic', 323.

[19] Jonathan Scott, *Commonwealth Principles: Republican Writings of the English Revolution* (Cambridge: Cambridge University Press, 2004), 254.

[20] Pocock talks about the Levellers at Putney representing a 'Savonarolan moment' of 'freedom triumphing over necessity', where 'the illuminists of liberty had come to an apocalyptic moment, at which their swords and spirits appeared at the point of remodeling the laws and reinstituting freedom': *Machiavellian Moment*, 375. Andrew Sharp writes in his introduction to *The English Levellers* (Cambridge: Cambridge University Press, 1998) that the Levellers 'take their place as minor figures in the canon of the history of western political thought as precursors of Locke'. See also Zagorin, *Political Thought in the English Revolution*, chapters 2 and 3. On the influence (or rather lack of it) on later English constitutional thought, see Martin Loughlin, 'The Constitutional Thought of the Levellers' (2007) 60 *Current Legal Problems* 1.

[21] Scott, 'The Rapture of Motion', 139.

separates republican authors, they do tend to agree on certain fundamentals, often building from a series of binary opposites – liberty and slavery, virtue and corruption, law and prerogative – that they took from Roman law,[22] classical authors such as Tacitus and Livy, and from the republican discourse of Machiavelli. And they share the belief that English politics could only be purified or reformed if the nation's leaders were willing to draw on the wisdom and political architecture of ancient republics.[23]

Our inquiry begins with Marchamont Nedham, turncoat, scurrilous journalist and master propagandist. He was the first English republican writer[24] and probably the one closest to the Levellers.[25] As Editor of *Mercurius Politicus*, the new government's weekly newspaper, under Milton's apparently light-touch supervision,[26] Nedham wrote a series of editorials aimed at inculcating commonwealth principles. These editorials 'add up to the first sustained English exposition of republican democracy in classical and Machiavellian terms'.[27] Nedham developed a consistent republican line not just in the brief 'season of liberty'[28] following Charles I's execution but later as commonwealth turned into protectorate and became increasingly autocratic.[29] The editorials were collected and re-published as *The Excellencie of a Free State* (1656), after the Instrument of Government 1653 had restored a monarchical element to the constitution and immediately after the failure of the Western Design. The new text constituted 'a bold, comprehensive case for genuinely popular

[22] On the importance of Roman law in articulating these binary opposites – free/slave, law/prerogative – see Quentin Skinner, 'John Milton and the Politics of Slavery' in Skinner, *Visions of Politics, Vol. II.*

[23] Blair Worden, 'Marchamont Nedham and English Republicanism' in David Wootton (ed.), *Republicanism, Liberty, and Commercial Society, 1649–1776* (Stanford: Stanford University Press, 1994), 46.

[24] An accolade he shares perhaps with Milton, who was writing political tracts at the same time. See, e.g., John Milton, *The Tenure of Kings and Magistrates* (1650) in *Milton: Political Writings* (Cambridge: Cambridge University Press, ed. Martin Dzelzainis, 1991) and *Defence of the People of England* (1651) in *Areopagitica and Other Political Writings of John Milton* (Indianapolis, IN: Liberty Press, ed. John Alvis, 1999). See also Christopher Hill, *Milton and the English Revolution* (London: Faber, 1977); Zagorin, *Political Thought in the English Revolution*, chapter 9. Milton wrote primarily for a European, and Nedham for a domestic, audience.

[25] Worden, 'Marchamont Nedham and English Republicanism', 66.

[26] Blair Worden, 'Milton and Marchamont Nedham' in Armitage *et al.*, *Milton and Republicanism.*

[27] Pocock, *Machiavellian Moment*, 382.

[28] *Mecurius Politicus*, 5 June 1651, 832.

[29] Zagorin, *Political Thought in the English Revolution*, 78: 'The republic which was erected on the monarchy's ruins was a military dictatorship.'

government in lieu of kingly or senatorial rule'.[30] If in their original form Nedham's Machiavellian populism had chided Parliament to secure the genuinely free state, their re-publication in a different political climate amounted to 'an act of radical opposition'.[31]

The Excellencie begins with the question: since 'Liberty is the most previous Jewel under the sun', how best to preserve it? Is it best to commit it to a 'standing Power' or to place it in the 'hands of the People, in a constant succession of their supreme Assembly'? For there is a great difference, Nedham insists, between being called free and actually *being* free. The Romans called themselves free after getting rid of their kings. But really they lived under 'a meer shadow and pretence of liberty'. Only when the people wrestled political control from the ruling class and secured their rights and privileges through the office of the tribune were they 'free indeed'.[32] What is essential is the existence of a constitution that ensures that republics are oriented towards the common good rather than particular private interests – normally the pleasure of the Prince.[33] Private interest corrupts the polity, which explains why monarchies are so prone to corruption and instability. Free states are much better placed to harness the energies of the people.[34]

To achieve true freedom, a free state needs to expunge 'not onely the Name of King, but the Thing King'.[35] Oppression is not really about the temper or designs of particular individuals so much as the prevalence or possibility of standing power, whatever the form. The maintenance of freedom requires, then, 'a due and orderly Succession of the Supreme Assemblies'.[36] The people are always the best keepers of their own liberties. They do not seek to usurp other men's rights, as do kings and 'grandees'.[37] So it should be the people who call and dissolve the assemblies, elect deputies and enact laws.[38] Succession or rotation in the body politic is like motion in natural bodies in that it prevents corruption or disease.

[30] Eric Nelson, *The Greek Tradition in Republican Thought* (Cambridge: Cambridge University Press, 2004), 91.

[31] Scott, *Commonwealth Principles*, 283.

[32] Machamont Nedham, *The Excellencie of a Free-State or, the Right Constitution of a Commonwealth* (Indianapolis: Liberty Fund, ed. Blair Worden, 2011), 11 ('*Excellencie*').

[33] *Excellencie*, 17. [34] *Excellencie*, 16. [35] *Excellencie*, 13.

[36] *Excellencie*, 19. See also *Excellencie*, 124: 'Since it appears, then, that the right, liberty, welfare, and safety of a people, consists in a due succession of their supreme Assemblies: surely then, the right constitution and orderly motion of them, is of the greatest consequence that can be, there being so much imbarqued in this Vessel, that if it should miscarry, all is irreparably lost, unless it can be recovered again out of the Sea of confusion.'

[37] *Excellencie*, 20. [38] *Excellencie*, 10.

It takes time to further factional interests. So it is in the interest of the state to prevent any party gaining control of government for any length of time.[39]

Political equality is fundamental to the freestate.[40] '[N]o Load shall be laid upon any, but what is common to all, and that always be common consent; not to serve the Lusts of any, but onely to supply the Necessities of their Country.'[41] The people must know what laws they are to obey, and penalties are to be applied only for breach of known laws.[42] Nedham cites the Tudor monarchs for their abuse of arbitrary power, where prerogatives became 'Snares ... (like a grand Catch-pole) to pill, poll, and geld the Purses of the People'.[43] But the problem is structural to monarchical and oligarchic constitutions rather than a problem of bad princes. All standing powers, left to their own devices, will tend to make and execute laws in their own interests.

The remedy is to ensure that 'no Laws or Nominations whatsoever should be made, but by the Peoples Consent and Election'.[44] This injunction is institutionalized partly through a separation of powers. The freestate cannot permit the legislative and executive powers of a state to rest in the same hands, except perhaps in emergencies.[45] Executive power must be subordinate to legislative power. And all power is exercised on trust for the people. It is not that Nedham anticipates the eradication of special executive powers but rather a different institutional arrangement of those powers designed to prevent abuse. Early on in *The Excellencie* he draws a distinction between 'state affairs' that require wisdom and experience and ordinary laws and law-making powers that do not. This distinction connects to an institutional division between a standing counsel or senate and Grand Assemblies.[46] The discussion is augmented later in the text where we are told that there are two elements of government, 'Acts of State' (*Acta Imperii*) and 'Secrets of State' (*Arcana Imperii*). The former equates to ordinary legislative authority concerning matters of general importance. These matters are amenable to common sense and so ought to be handled in the Assemblies, as the people 'best know where

[39] *Excellencie*, 21–22.

[40] Nedham makes clear that his is not a programme for social levelling. See *Excellencie*, 42, where he distinguishes 'not an Equality (which were irrational and odious)' from 'an Equability of Condition among all Members'. For a discussion of Nedham's vacillations on the subject of agrarian laws, see Nelson, *Greek Tradition in Republican Thought*, 90–93.

[41] *Excellencie*, 25. [42] *Excellencie*, 36.

[43] *Excellencie*, 37. [44] *Excellencie*, 38.

[45] *Excellencie*, 109.

[46] *Excellencie*, 15. This arrangement is based on the constitution of the Roman republic.

the shooe pinches them'. The latter equates to executive authority on matters requiring 'prudence, time, and experience, to fit men for management'. Such affairs should be handled by 'Peoples Trustees' accountable to the Assemblies, ideally on a temporary and ad hoc basis. (Nedham's inspiration was the *Areopagus* in democratic Athens 'to whom all their Secrets of State were committed'.[47]) The Peoples Trustees do not constitute a standing senate: their authority continues, 'of right, no longer than meer Necessity requires, for their [the people's] own redress and safety; which being provided for, they [the Trustees] are to return into a condition of Subjection and Obedience, with the rest of the people, to such Laws and Government as themselves have erected'.[48]

This is tribunitian politics.[49] The people cannot be complacent about the political system but must always be active in their oversight of those in positions of power. Secrecy in government is a particular concern. It is wrong to keep 'the people ignorant of those ways and means that are essentially necessary for the preservation of their Liberty; for, implicite Faith, and blind Obedience, hath hitherto passed currant, and been equally pressed and practised by Grandees, both Spirituall and Temporal, upon the People'.[50] Keeping the people in ignorance, hiding matters of state from them, is how elites capture power. Knowledge is twinned with reason and the common good; secrecy and ignorance are equated with passion, private interest government and corruption.[51] But Nedham was prepared to push these insights further in the direction of democracy than most republicans. His relentless mistrust of aristocracy fuelled his insistence on curbs to executive power. 'Nedham articulated the fear of central government that runs through seventeenth-century English history and that becomes, after the Restoration, one of the animating forces of English republicanism.'[52] He read Roman history from a 'militantly plebeian' standpoint[53] and rejected models of Sparta and Venice as far too prone to capture by elites.[54] Very unusually, he took Athens as his

[47] *Excellencie*, 56. [48] *Excellencie*, 55–56.

[49] Scott, *Commonwealth Principles*, 241. See also Worden, 'Marchamont Nedham and English Republicanism', 68.

[50] *Excellencie*, 82.

[51] Scott, 'Classical Republicanism in Seventeenth-Century England and the Netherlands'.

[52] Worden, 'Marchamont Nedham and English Republicanism', 70.

[53] Pocock, *Machiavellian Moment*, 382.

[54] The 'serene republic', Nedham sneered, was 'rather a Juncta than a Common-weal', whose subjects preferred the 'Pagan Tyranny' of the 'Turk' to their own government: *Mercurius Politicus*, no. 86, 1368.

constitutional model since, as the antithesis of 'grandee government', it offered the least chance of capture by powerful factions.[55]

Nedham stuck to Machiavellian orthodoxy on the link between freedom and a citizen-army. 'The Sword, and Soveraignty, ever walk hand in hand together.'[56] It is hard to oppress the people when the people are the army. And republican armies outperform monarchies because republican citizens have a direct stake in what they fight for. Nedham's republic, then, is a martial republic. Citizens of a free state are on a permanent war footing – the model here being the Romans, 'trained up perpetually in Arms, and the whole Common-weal, by this means became one formal Militia, a generall Exercise of the best part of the people in the use of Arms, was the onely Bulwark of their Liberty'.[57] As well as being the best way to preserve liberty at home, a warlike posture helps deflect threats from abroad. Nedham believed, with Machiavelli, that the healthiest free state is a 'commonwealth for expansion'.[58] He was proud of English military successes in the early years of the republic, which he thought were enough to 'match [the achievements of] any of the ancients'.[59] And he compared the foreign policy of the new republics, 'the valiant Swisses, the Hollanders, and also our own Nation', favourably with the degenerate monarchies of Spain and France.[60] Republics were more active when it came to commerce too.[61] The ability of free states to tap the energy of the people gives them a comparative advantage.[62] Their very success makes it more likely that people in other states will throw off the yoke of tyranny as the English had done already.[63] That it might not be inappropriate for the free English to lend

[55] Scott, *Commonwealth Principles*, 137. As we see in Chapter 6, it was not really until the mid-nineteenth century that Athenian democracy became a popular constitutional model.

[56] *Excellencie*, 90. [57] *Excellencie*, 90.

[58] Worden, 'Machiavelli and English Republicanism', 71.

[59] MP, 22 January 1652, 1352.

[60] *Mercurius Politicus*, 18–25 January 1652, 1349–1352.

[61] David Armitage, *The Ideological Origins of the British Empire* (Cambridge: Cambridge University Press, 2000) 119: the engraving accompanying Nedham's translation of Selden's *Mare Clausum* was the first representation of Britannia as the ruler of the waves.

[62] *Excellencie*, 16. 'Nor is it onely a meer Gallantry of spirit that excites men to the love of Freedom; experience assures it to be the most commodious and profitable way of Government, conducing every way to the enlarging a people in Wealth and Dominion.'

[63] Marchamont Nedham, *The Case Stated Between England and the United Provinces, In This Present Juncture* (1652) (Chalottesville, VA: University of Virginia Press, ed. Philip A. Knachel, 1969), 53: 'we of this Nation of *England*, do believe that there is such a Cause of God this day amongst us, that wil take off the *Burthen and the Yoak, and cause Justice to be administred equally to all, and establish Reighteousnesse and Judgement in the Earth*'.

Providence a helping hand is clear from Nedham's position on England's relationship with the United Provinces. Writing at a point when a possible union between the two countries had transmuted into war, Nedham claimed that since it was the 'Cause of God this day amongst us ... to shake off the exorbitant and wicked lusts of Kings and great ones, whether in *Monarchies* or [Free-]*States*' then if the Dutch republic would not unite with the English peacefully it might have to be done by force.'[64]

But how well do such expansionary objectives match up with Nedham's constitutional prescriptions, particularly those concerning limits to executive power? Foreign policy and questions of war and peace fall within his category of secrets of state, *arcana imperii*, and are as such matters for the magistrates, suitably accountable, rather than the assembly. One might expect that the more common and important matters of trade and foreign warfare become, the more pressure we would expect to see on the limitations to the magistrates' power. A deeper point relates to reason of state, the discourse that dominated international affairs at the time,[65] which is discussed late on in *The Excellencie*. Nedham takes care to specify what he means by the term: 'that reason of state, which is the states mans reason, or rather his will and lust, when he admits Ambition to be a reason, Preferment, Power, Profit, Revenge, and Opportunity, to be a reason, sufficient to put him upon any designe of Action that may tend to the present advantage'. This 'strange *Pocus*' which 'the *Italians* call *Raggione distato*' (*ragione di stato*) is a 'sandy Foundation of Policy'. 'It can rant as a Souldier, complement as a Monsieur, trick it as a Juggler, strut it as a States man, and is changable as the Moon, in the variety of her appearances.'[66] The juxtaposition here is between a strategic, changeable and interest-based approach to foreign policy ('Italian' reason of state) and a honest and principled approach, grounded in public reason and the common good: '*viz.* a simple reliance upon God in the vigorous and present actings of all Righteousness, exprest by honest men, in plain language, to this effect: *Fiat justitia, & fractus illabatur Orbis*; Deal uprightly, walke close and real to your promises, and principles, though the Fabrick of Heaven and earth should fall, yet God is able to support'.

Reason of state, on this account, is subject to a number of failings. As it is a 'principle of Humane Invention' to use it as a basis for foreign policy

[64] Nedham, *The Case Stated*, 53.

[65] Martti Koskenniemi, 'International Law and *Raison D'Etat*: Rethinking the Prehistory of International Law' in Benedict Kingsbury and Benjamin Straumann (eds.), *The Roman Foundations of the Law of Nations: Alberico Gentili and the Justice of Empire* (Oxford: Oxford University Press, 2010).

[66] *Excellencie*, 105–106.

is to quit 'the Cause of God'. (Most of Nedham's examples here are taken from the Bible rather than secular sources.) Not only is this wrong in itself, it also means in the long run that the nation will do badly since Providence will not be on its side. Reason of state theory shows men being too clever for their own good. Honesty, both to your principles and in the way you engage with other states, is the best policy. Reason of state is deleterious to the nation because it is aimed at the realization of the private interest of princes or their advisers. Associated in English history with the arrival of the Stuart kings,[67] 'wicked Reason of State' is another instrument of servitude.

While the blistering tenor of the critique of reason of state seems to point in only one direction, Nedham's message may be more nuanced. It is true that 'Italian' *ragione di stato*, understood as the foreign-policy manifestation of private-interest government, rests on a hubristic misunderstanding of the human condition. Everything done through that framework is ultimately both morally and spiritually bankrupt. But Nedham does not necessarily mean that the same is true if a properly constituted free state adopted a similar approach to international affairs.[68] What is in the common interest of the republic – for example, to unite with the Dutch, even if they do not want to – is in the universal interest of mankind and thus a dictate of reason. The crucial distinction, then, may not be between reason of state and principled decision-making but between reason of state as private interest and reason of state as public interest where the former represents the policy aspirations of private individuals (princes) who happen to be in control of government, their 'will and lust', and the latter the manifestation of the public reason of the state. 'Reason of state' divorced from the world of princes ceases to be reason of state in the pejorative 'Italian' sense. The interest (reason) of the state as determined by its republican magistrates is aligned with the interest (reason) of the nation as a whole.

Onward Christian soldiers

For all his mercurial brilliance as a polemicist, Nedham's lasting influence was not great.[69] With Algernon Sidney, we turn to a writer central

[67] *Excellencie*, 108–109.

[68] Indeed, as Zagorin wryly observes, Nedham's 'condemnation of Machiavellian reason-of-state is also not credible in so mercenary a writer who had himself engaged in reason-of-state theorizing' (*Political Thought in the English Revolution*, 125).

[69] Although *The Excellencie* was reprinted in France during the revolution and was discussed extensively by John Adams, the second president of the United States.

to the republican canon.[70] Scion of a famous aristocratic family,[71] cavalry officer in the Parliamentary Army, diplomat for the commonwealth, republican martyr – he was executed in 1683 as a political opponent of the Restoration regime largely on the basis of the unpublished manuscript of his *Discourses Concerning Government*[72] – Sidney became a seminal figure in the Whig tradition.[73] He was important to the revolutionary generation in America, where his work was extensively referenced.[74] He was also influential in eighteenth-century France, where he was taken up by Montesquieu, Rousseau and Condorcet.[75]

Sidney's fate reminds us that the republicans were defenders of losing causes. The opportunity presented with Charles I's execution and the birth of the Commonwealth went begging and the republican cause 'betrayed' by Cromwell, who was hated by these writers. The Restoration, with its revivified princely and prerogative-heavy politics,[76] represented

[70] Caroline A. Robbins, *The Eighteenth-Century Commonwealthman* (Cambridge, MA: Harvard Unviersity Press, 1959), chapter 2; J. G. A. Pocock, 'The Varieties of Whiggism from Exclusion to Reform: A History of Ideology and Discourse' in Pocock (ed.), *Virtue, Commerce, and History* (Cambridge: Cambridge University Press, 1985), 232–233. Constructed by John Toland and other eighteenth-century Commonwealthmen to the time of Thomas Hollis, the canon included Harrington, Sidney, Milton, Vane, Marvell, Nevile and Nedham.

[71] He was born of the union of two very old and important families, the Sidneys and the Percys. His great-uncle, Sir Philip Sidney, was a Elizabethan military hero, fighting in defence of international Protestantism against persecution at home and abroad, who died fighting at Zutphen against the papist Spanish armies.

[72] Blair Worden, 'Republicanism and Restoration, 1660–1683' in Wootton, *Republicanism, Liberty, and Commercial Society*, 158: 'the arguments of the *Discourses* are unmistakably directed towards the overthrow of the king and the adoption of a fresh constitution that will prohibit the resurrection of arbitrary rule and establish instead the conditions of republican virtue.' For context see Richard Ashcraft, *Revolutionary Politics and Locke's Two Treatises of Government* (Princeton: Princeton University Press, 1986), chapter 8.

[73] Alan Craig Houston, *Algernon Sidney and the Republican Heritage in England and America* (Princeton: Princeton University Press, 1991); Quentin Skinner, 'Augustan Party Politics and Renaissance Constitutional Thought' in Skinner, *Visions of Politics, Vol. II*.

[74] Bernard Bailyn, *The Ideological Origins of the American Revolution* (Cambridge, MA: Harvard University Press, 1971), 34–35. Compare Donald S. Lutz, 'The Relative Influence of European Writers on Late Eighteenth-Century American Political Thought' (1984) 78 *American Political Science Review* 189.

[75] Jonathan Scott, *Algernon Sidney and the English Republic 1623–1677* (Cambridge: Cambridge University Press, 1988), 5.

[76] See, e.g., Tim Harris, *Restoration: Charles II and His Kingdoms, 1660–1685* (London: Penguin, 2006). Some of the prerogative cases of the period are discussed in Chapter 5.

another defeat – and a return to the threat of popery and arbitrary government against which the rebels had taken up the cause in 1642.[77] And the Glorious Revolution, although it got rid of the Stuarts, was far from a republican victory. Given this record of defeat, it is perhaps not surprising that of Sidney's significant works the *Court Maxims* was written around 1665 in exile on the Continent and was aimed at uniting republicans in an effort to re-establish the commonwealth, and the *Discourses Concerning Government* were probably written between 1681 and 1683, that is, after the instability of 1679–81 when anti-Stuart revolt had at least been a live possibility.

This context may be one reason for the strident quality of Sidney's writing. His is a republicanism of uncompromising militant radicalism. '[H]ands and swords were given to men that they only may be slaves who have no courage.'[78] Its power comes from the 'combination of a high moral tone with the most ruthless and militaristic Machiavellianism of the century'.[79] It combines a sense of the variety and mutability of all earthly things with a belief in a fixed core of changeless and timeless values, anchored in God – in this latter aspect, true to the Platonist spirit of Protestant humanism.[80] Grounded in an extensive range of contemporary and historical source material, it aims to show that republics are better and more natural forms of government. Like most English republicans, Sidney was not especially interested in the niceties of governmental forms and procedures. In this respect, he shared some of the protestant anti-formalism of republicans such as John Milton[81] and Henry Parker[82]

[77] Jonathan Scott, *Algernon Sidney and the Restoration Crisis, 1677–1683* (Cambridge: Cambridge University Press, 2002), 63: 'The second crisis of parliaments (1680–1), and its progress, thus led to a revival of the "old cause", because it *was* the "old cause".'

[78] Algernon Sidney, *Discourses Concerning Government* (Indianapolis: Liberty Press, ed. Thomas G. West, 1990), 523.

[79] Scott, *Algernon Sidney and the English Republic*, 13.

[80] Peltonen, *Classical Humanism and English Republicanism*.

[81] The relationship between the personal and the political is apparent in the opening lines of Milton's *Tenure of Kings and Magistrates*: 'If men within themselves would be govern'd by reason, and not generally give up their understanding to a double tyrannie, of Custom from without, and blind affections within, they would discerne better, what it is to favour and uphold the Tyrant of a Nation. But having been slaves within doors, no wonder that they strive so much to have the public State conformably govern'd to the inward vitious rule, by which they govern themselves. For indeed none can love freedom heartily, but good men; the rest love not freedom, but licence; which never hath more scope or more indulgence than under Tyrants.'

[82] On Parker, see e.g., Tuck, *Philosophy and Government*, 226–235; Quentin Skinner, 'Classical Liberty and the Coming of the English Civil War' in van Gelderen and Skinner, *Republicanism: A Shared European Heritage, Vol. II*, 15–28.

for whom virtuous people rather than virtuous institutions were important. But Sidney was concerned about political architecture and fundamental constitutional questions. On such matters he has important things to say, especially on law, war and freedom.

Change was the key to Sidney's theory.[83] Following Plato's account of the 'second-best constitution' in the *Laws*,[84] Sidney accepts that it would be best if we could constitute a government that would last forever but that this is not an option. Things change in a way that men cannot foresee. *Pace* Harrington, but one model cannot possibly fit all: 'he who would oblige all nations at all times to take the same course, would prove as foolish as a physician who should apply the same medicine to all distempers'.[85] Far from being something that we should fear, change brings with it the possibility of regeneration, an opportunity to build anew on the basis of eternal values and thus a basis for restoring liberty. After all, stability cannot be a good in itself. No one delights in sickness or pain because it is long or incurable. Stability is of value only if it is conducive to the good.[86] What we can say, though, is that some types of government are more prone to instability than others. Virtuous governments have at least a chance of existing for a long while but absolute monarchies are necessarily doomed being 'by principle led unto, or rooted in' corruption and decay.[87]

If the success of a polity does not depend on how long it lasts, then how is it measured? Liberty is what really counts, Sidney insists, above all the freedom to choose the political order we live in: 'all those nations which deserve to be imitated were governed by their own laws'.[88] Authority is conferred on chief magistrates by 'the free consent of a willing people'.[89] In principle, a number of forms of government might be freely chosen.[90]

[83] Scott, *Algernon Sidney and the English Republic*, 17.

[84] Sidney makes extensive and explicit reference to Plato at an early stage in the *Discourses*: D, 82–83.

[85] D, 173. [86] D, 136.

[87] D, 189. See also D, 136: 'if there be any stability in man, it must be in wisdom and virtue, and in those actions that are thereby directed; for in weakness, folly and madness there can be none.'

[88] Algernon Sidney, *Court Maxims* (Cambridge: Cambridge University Press, ed. Hans W. Blom, Eco Haitsma Mulier and Ronald Janse, 1996), ('CM') 13.

[89] D, 189.

[90] Including limited monarchy, D, 140: 'those monarchies only which are mixed and regulated by laws, where diets, parliaments, assemblies of estates or senates, may supply the defects of a prince, restrain him if he prove extravagant, and reject such as are found to be unworthy of their office'.

But the best choice is a mixed[91] form of republican government with a very strong commitment to the rule of law understood as the rule of reason. This bottom-up perspective makes a difference to the way political power is understood. If power comes from the people, then magistrates have 'no other power but what is so conferred upon them by that multitude' and 'are to exercise those powers according to the proportion, and to the ends for which they were given'.[92] Power, being held on trust, is exercisable only for the common good. Magistrates do not govern by virtue of some universal law, as Filmer claimed, 'but by the particular laws of each country; which give to every one so much power, as in the opinion of the givers conduces to the end of their institution, which is the publick good'.[93] The right to choose the constitution of government (constituent power) is an ongoing right. The plurality of existing constitutional and governmental arrangements is the consequence of the exercise of this right.[94] The exercise of the right, whether through constitutional means or extra-constitutional (i.e. rebellion),[95] is often vital to secure freedom. 'All human constitutions are subject to corruption, and must perish, unless they are timely renewed, and reduced to their first principles.'[96]

A republic is a much truer instantiation of this constitutional model than is a monarchy, which Sidney sees as an unstable and irrational political form dependent on the lottery mechanism of inheritance. A good prince might be followed by a madman or drunkard. For government to be based on the will of an individual is against reason and nature, reason being man's God-given faculty to determine what is good for him. Republics can operate, if need be, as efficiently as any monarchy.[97] They are much more likely to operate in the public interest since 'in commonwealths it is not men but laws, maxims, interest, and constitutions that govern: men die or change, but these remain unalterable.'[98] Republican government is a more rational and natural form of government.[99] As a system in which 'every man's liberty is least restrained, because every man hath an equal part'[100] it is the political form closest to God. Like Milton, Sidney's overarching goal is to bring man closer to God, narrowing the

[91] D, 166: 'there never was a good government in the world, that did not consist of the three simply species of monarchy, aristocracy and democracy'.

[92] D, 99. [93] D, 113. [94] D, 113.

[95] D, 227: 'Extrajudicial proceedings by sedition, tumult, or war, must take place, when the persons concern'd are of such power, that they cannot be brought under the judicial.' See also D, 339–343.

[96] D, 150. [97] CM, 26. [98] CM, 27. [99] CM, 23.

[100] D, 192. See also CM, 33.

gap opened up by the Fall.[101] Politics for these men was 'the means by which God's creatures used His gift of reason to erect a collective apparatus of self-improvement, in accordance with His wishes.'[102] Liberty, the removal of impediments to improvement, was as much a spiritual as secular priority. Commonwealths are thus 'nurses of virtue',[103] providing the conditions in which the free individual can act in a way that takes him closer to God. '[T]here is no happiness without liberty, and no man more a slave than he that is overmastered by vicious passions, there is neither liberty, nor happiness, where there is not virtue.'[104] The Manichaean perspective of seventeenth-century English republicans is very much apparent here. Liberty, reason and virtue (godliness) are opposed to slavery, subjection to another's will and the passions (ungodliness). Everything is at stake. A monarchy to a free state is like 'death unto life. And as death is *the greatest evil that can befall a person, monarchy is the worst evil that can befall a nation.*'[105] For monarchy is an order of slavery, the people subject to the will of the king and the king a slave to his own passions. This condition is not only unnatural, it is contrary to God. Tyranny is a natural fit with idolatry.[106] No wonder tyrants so often meet with sticky ends. The death of Polycrates, tyrant of Samos, is apt: crucified and then melted by Apollo the sun-god in his own fat, so anointed in his own grease.[107]

There is absolutely nothing monkish about Sidney's republicanism. Indeed, he comes close to making war the overriding measure of political worth: 'all governments whether monarchical or popular, absolute or limited, deserve praise or blame as they are well or ill constituted for making war'.[108] What he most likes about republics is not their capacity to foster harmony among subjects but because they are better at creating wealth and waging war 'with glory and advantage':[109]

> that government is evidently the best, which, not relying upon what it does at first enjoy, seeks to increase the number, strength, and riches of the people; and by the best discipline to bring the power so improved into such order as may be of most use to the publick. This comprehends

[101] William Poole, *Milton and the Fall of Man* (Cambridge: Cambridge University Press, 2005).

[102] Scott, *Algernon Sidney and the Restoration Crisis*, 228: political societies for these men were 'the means by which God's creatures used His gift of reason.

[103] D, 79. [104] CM, 24.

[105] CM, 20. Italics in original.

[106] CM, 48. [107] CM, 43.

[108] D, 212–213. See also the title of D, Chapter Two, Section 23: '*That is the best Government, which best provides for War*'.

[109] D, 79.

> all things conducing to the administration of justice, the preservation of domestic peace, and the increase of commerce, that the people being pleased with their present condition, may be filled with love to their country, encouraged to fight boldly for the publick cause, which is their own[.][110]

Sidney imagines a world in which only the active survive: 'the struggle for liberty between nations as well as within them, had no static middle ground, only two choices: increase or decrease; liberty or slavery; rule or be ruled'.[111] Monarchies tend to be militarily incapable because their rulers are parasites and the people subjugated. Commonwealths are better at deploying their manpower.[112] Their incentive structures are rationally aligned: 'every man is concerned; every one has a part[;] ... the body of the people is the public defence, and every man is armed and disciplined; the advantages of good success are communicated to all, and every one bears a part in the losses'.[113] Running counter to Nedham's levelling instincts, Sidney thinks a strong aristocracy is vital for the war effort. Republics need 'a nobility great in power and credit, full of virtue and gallantry, and exercised in arms that the people might follow them'.[114] There is more than a trace here of nostalgia for the feudal order of knights geared for war.[115] He even has a sneaking admiration for those 'boisterous fighting kings of the Plantagenet race'.[116]

A more systematic analysis can be found in Sidney's handling of Machiavelli's taxonomy of republican models.[117] Rome was set up for

110 D, 209. See also CM, 18.

111 Scott, *Algernon Sidney and the Crisis of the English Republic*, 32.

112 D, 216.

113 D, 216. See also D, 209, discussing the terror in London invoked by the attack by a 'few Dutch ships' on the naval dockyard in Chatham.

114 CM, 67. Sidney argues elsewhere in the *Court Maxims* that a vigorous aristocracy, secure in its landed wealth, is a necessary counterbalance to a monarch. Kings who aspire to absolute rule always 'endeavour to corrupt, ruin, and effeminate the nobility' in order to remove competing sites of power (CM, 78).

115 Worden, 'Republicanism and the Restoration, 1660–1683', 163: 'It was Sidney's achievement to merge classical republicanism with the nostalgic medievalism of the Exclusion Crisis.'

116 CM, 67. See also D, 575–578, where Sidney praises Henry V's government: since Henry's main aim had been the conquest of France, he had been careful not 'to encroach upon the liberties of his subjects'. Since the only way to pursue glory and greatness was 'by the bravery of a free and well-satisfied people', Henry had maintained the 'courage, strength, and love' of his people.

117 Machiavelli, *The Discourses* (Harmondsworth: Penguin, ed. Bernard Crick trans. Leslie J. Walker, 1998), II, 3–4. Machiavelli, in turn, drew inspiration from Sallust's moral account of Roman decline and Polybius's constitutional analysis. For discussion

wars of expansion. Sparta, while equally warlike, was geared for wars of preservation. Athens was devoted to trade so that it was better placed for war. Venice gives itself to trade and seeks to avoid war. (There are also federations of free states, like Switzerland, better given to peaceful co-existence.[118]) It is a 'mortal error', Sidney argues, to follow the course of peace since it makes a state too dependent on foreign powers.[119] The expansionist vigour of Rome is far preferable to the stability and permanence of Venice:

> the best judges of these matters have always given the preference to those constitutions that principally intended war, and make use of trade as assisting to that end: and think it better to aim at conquest, rather than simply to stand up to their own defence; since he that loses all if he be overcome, fights upon very unequal terms; and if he obtain the victory, gains no other advantage, than for the present to repel the danger that threatened him.[120]

Here we find English republicanism, rarely afraid of a fight, at its most bellicose. The best republic is one geared to war and to trade in the interests of war.[121] Offensive wars are to be preferred to defensive wars. Whereas in the *Court Maxims* Sidney at least nodded in the direction of the idea of just war,[122] there is very little but pure interest theory and naked aggression at play in these passages in the *Discourses*. Conquest is painted in

of Machiavelli's analysis see Armitage, 'Empire and Liberty: A Republican Dilemma', 29–36; Quentin Skinner, 'Machiavelli's *Discorsi* and the Pre-humanist Origins of Republican Ideas' in Gisela Bock, Quentin Skinner and Maurizio Viroli (eds), *Machiavelli and Republicanism* (Cambridge: Cambridge University Press, 1990).

[118] D, 206. See also CM, 16.

[119] D, 205–206. Sidney's taxonomy is rather different from Machiavelli's, which distinguishes (i) Rome (republic ordered so that it can master its external environment); (ii) German republics (defensive stability and curbed ambition); (iii) Sparta, Athens or Venice (internal tranquility but only if neither necessity nor greed forces expansion).

[120] DC, 205. Machiavelli's analysis follows a slightly different path. Under perfect conditions, Machiavelli would advise a new republic to be defensive and non-expansionary, for that way it might achieve longevity. But, in the flux of human affairs, such a recommendation would be idealistic. The Roman example should be followed instead, with the risk of tumults as the price of greatness: *Discorsi*, I, 6.

[121] See also John Streater, *Observations Historical, Political and Philosophical, Upon Aristotles First Book of Political Government* (R. Moon, 1654) no. 4, 20–21: a prudent state would provide for increase 'either by sending of Colonies abroad as the Romans and other Cities did formerly, and now as we may do to *Virginia* and other parts of *America*, the planting of which places will bring great Riches to this Commonwealth, or else by increasing and incouraging of Artificers'.

[122] CM, 17: 'States are to consider not only whether such conquests may be useful to them but also whether they have a right of war.'

an almost entirely positive light, as a natural thing that occurs almost as a reward for nations properly constituted: 'when a people multiplies (as they will always do in a good climate under a good government) such an enlargement of territory as is necessary for their subsistence can be acquired only by war'.[123]

This emphasis on military success is of a piece with Sidney's robust position on change in human societies: 'arms are the cutting edge for change'.[124] In the competition for wealth and territory, republics are better placed than monarchies. And some republics are better placed than others. We have already seen why Sidney thinks republics are better than monarchies at fighting. He also thinks they are better at accruing the money needed for war. It is easy for monarchs to ruin trade, since they control it. And it is in their interest too,[125] since they want to keep the people down: 'Princes are never so rich as when their subjects are poor.'[126] The free state releases people from these constraints thereby allowing enterprise to flourish. The emphasis on business and trade connects to the lineage of republican thinking, so tied to city-states and the idea of the city. The victory of Parliament in the Civil War was also a victory for London.[127] Sidney wants London to rise again, to do away with the structure of oppression in the interest of realizing on a nationwide scale the ideal of the free city.

In pointing out one of the major tenets of modern reason of state that trade provided one of the sinews of war, Sidney marks a transition point in the English republican tradition.[128] But what does he mean when he talks about a constitution being geared to war, or to trade and war? For Sidney, it is connected to the rule of law. Republics are ordered through general laws known in advance and equally applicable to all subjects.[129]

[123] D, 210.

[124] Scott, *Algernon Sidney and the Restoration Crisis*, 237.

[125] CM, 73: 'To effect this work of impoverishing and bringing the people low we find it to be the king's interest to destroy trade. For there is no keeping a people low while that continues which increases their number, riches, and strength.'

[126] CM, 77. See also Marchamont Nedham, *Interest Will Not Lie: Or, a View of England's True Interest* (Thomas Newcomb, 1659), 45–46: 'as to … your *Trade*, it is easie to guess what will become of that, when it shall be counted Reason of State to keep you poor and low'.

[127] Scott, *Algernon Sidney and the English Republic*, 202–203.

[128] Armitage, 'Empire and Liberty: A Republican Dilemma', 38–39; Steve Pincus, 'Neither Machiavellian Moment Nor Possessive Individualism: Commercial Society and the Defenders of the English Commonwealth' (1998) 103 *American Historical Review* 705.

[129] CM, 13.

Men do not govern, laws do. Law restrains the lusts of the vicious and the foolish.[130] It eliminates arbitrary power and gives the legal subject (now citizen) both liberty in the present and a reasonable security that liberty will last into the future. This means not only that citizens can plan into the future with some assurance, it also gives them the incentive to invest and to develop enterprises in the expectation that they will keep any profits that accrue. The rule of law thus makes republics inclined towards meritocracy. It is the skilled and enterprising that prosper in this type of society, whereas in monarchies it is the sycophant and the connected that tend to do well.

But the rule of law can only operate if certain conditions are met. Since within a republic it is the law that rules, it follows that there can be no 'private' authority 'outside' the law. This means, first, that magistrates possess no original authority stemming from their position as magistrate. There is 'no such thing as a right universally belonging to a name; but everyone enjoys that which the laws, by which he is, confer upon him. The law that gives the power, regulates it'.[131] It means, second, that magistrates have no authority outside what the law gives them. 'They are under the law, and the law is not under them; their letters or commands are not to be regarded: In the administration of justice, the question is not what pleases them, but what the law declares to be right, which must have its course, whether the king be busy or at leisure, whether he will or not.'[132] If a magistrate purports to exercise a power not given by the law to that extent he acts as a private individual and can be restrained as such.[133]

Much of this analysis turns on the prerogative, so vital an issue for Sidney and his contemporaries, although we might note the difference in the way republicans approached this subject compared with typical Jacobean assumptions.[134] A claim of magisterial entitlement to sovereign power above and outside the law is the sort of claim an occupying force makes of a captive nation, not one a legitimate government makes to its people.[135] To give one man such extravagant powers is irrational: 'vast powers … can reasonably be granted to none, because no man knows what anyone will prove till he be tried'.[136] Prerogative is a danger zone

130 D, 389. 131 D, 225. 132 D, 394. 133 D, 222.
134 See the discussion in Chapter 2.
135 D, 222: 'I know not where to find an example of this sovereign power, enjoy'd without restriction, under better title than occupation.'
136 D, 300.

where arbitrary power – the will (lust) of one individual or body combined with force – can trump the law (reason) that preserves liberty:

> If the laws of God and men are therefore of no effect, when the magistracy is left at liberty to break them; and if the lusts of those who are too strong for the tribunals of justice, cannot be otherwise restrained than by sedition, tumults and war, those seditions, tumults, and wars are justified by the laws of God and man.[137]

Legal restraint is good for the prince.[138] In a discussion that parallels moments in Hobbes's *Leviathan*,[139] analysed in the previous chapter, Sidney juxtaposes rule by force and rule through law. But Sidney's prescription is very different from Hobbes's solution to the same problem. To allow the prince to rule by force is a mistake, not just because of its deleterious effect on civil life but also because it means that there is no choice but to resort to force when the prince oversteps the mark: 'where no provision was made by law against ill-governing princes, [the people] have found no other remedy than to kill them'.[140] The prerogative, then, is a 'dangerous extravagance' and a potential source of corruption. In breaking the legal order by which alone he is king, its exercise 'obliges me to disobey' the king. 'The law errs not, the king may be mad or drunk. Order requires that we obey God rather than men.'[141]

The rule of law requires decent lawyers and independent judges.[142] Monarchies create corrupt lawyers and partial judges.[143] Self-interest lures them into the vortices of private interest government. They then complicate the laws to the disadvantage of the subject.[144] 'The common law is so entangled with statutes and cases often unjustly judged, that no man can be said to understand it. They found the craft of the lawyers useful to

[137] D, 220.

[138] D, 303: 'They therefore who place kings within the power of the law, and the law to be a guide to kings, equally provide for the good of king and people. Whereas they who admit of no participants in power, and acknowledge no rule but their own will, set up an interest in themselves against that of the people, lose their affections, which is their most important treasure, and incur their hatred, from whence results their greatest danger.'

[139] Thomas Hobbes, *Leviathan* (Cambridge: Cambridge University Press, ed. Richard Tuck, 1996) 153.

[140] D, 389. [141] CM, 823.

[142] CM, 115: 'The Scotch Solomon [James I of England], who, having a padlock on his sword, applied himself wholly to kingcraft, used to say: let me create bishops and judges, and I will have what law and gospel I please. Whatsoever the king now desires to do is found to be legal.'

[143] CM, 114.

[144] CM, 118: 'The subtlety of lawyers is far more useful to the king than the violence of soldiers.'

them, and the lawyers found as great advantage by the power of kings.'[145] Worse, English law comes in 'a barbarous gibberish, never spoken by any people, understood only by those of the profession who invented it'.[146] (Law French was used in case reports and legal treatises until almost the end of the century.) Laws that should defend people become snares to trap them.[147] Sidney's solution is to reverse the trend of 'this corrupted age' and return to the purity and simplicity of 'the ancient constitutions of our Northern kingdoms'.[148] Here is a species of ancient constitutionalism at work, albeit one different from that of the common lawyers earlier in the century or from that popularized by Blackstone in the next. Things will improve only if we can recapture the spirit of the good old law, stripped of the corruption that has resulted from kings seeking to rule 'according to lust under pretence of law'.[149]

More fundamentally, law must be good law if it is to be recognized as law at all. 'The essence of the law consists in the justice of it: if it be not just, it is no law. The justice of it depends upon the end: if it conduces not to a good end, it cannot be just.'[150] This theory is best articulated in the *Court Maxims*. All laws ought to aim at the preservation of society and do justice to the individuals that compose it. This entails that: (a) laws should not deprive subjects of anything that belongs to them; (b) penalties should be proportionate to the end of deterring those who might otherwise be inclined to commit offences tending to the dissolution of civil society; (c) since people cannot be deterred from doing something unless they know the law, laws must be plain and clear so that every man can understand them.[151] Sidney does not go into details about the sort of a legal framework capable of realizing these principles. But if we add what appears to be a radically subjective account of what counts as law – it is presumably up to each and every legal subject to determine whether a putative law is good enough to be a law – with his advocacy of disobedience and rebellion when a subject regards the magistrate as acting without legal warrant, it is clear that Sidney presents us with a highly individualist ('protestant') theory of law and one which is highly unstable – precisely the sort of thing, in fact, against which Hobbes so strongly took issue.

Sidney may at first appear a warlike champion of reason, defined against 'Italian' reason of state. Taking the St Bartholomew's Day massacre, a *cause célèbre* for Protestants, as his starting-point for a discussion

[145] CM, 130. [146] CM, 129. [147] CM, 130, 131.
[148] D, 302. See also CM, 129, where Sidney speaks of the 'ancient purist constitutions'.
[149] CM, 143. [150] CM, 122. [151] CM, 122.

of the topic in the *Court Maxims*, he asks 'how many princes in our days have by reason of state been obliged to kill their fathers, wives, or children … As soon as Cromwell came to be a monarch he well understood this Arcanum Imperii.'[152] But his actual position is more complicated. His work is 'an attempt to combine sceptical and politic insight' sourced in Machiavelli 'with the moral and religious high ground; to define a "right" policy, in conformity with "reason" and "truth", but in tune with the special demands of "that science they call Policy" '.[153] The attack on the prerogative is not on the sort of uses it tends to get put to – waging war, control of the army, dealing with emergencies – all of which Sidney enthusiastically embraces. He is happy with the Roman model of dictatorship so long as the power granted for such an occasion lasts no longer than the occasion lasts.[154] Sidney is against prerogative because of the abuse it has had – and *must* have – at the hands of princes, who use it as a device to escape the law in order to act in their own interest at the expense of the people as a whole. Moreover, he is someone who thinks that a government based not on virtue alone, but on virtue and interest, is the best way of promoting the common good.[155] What Sidney is really doing is setting 'monarchical' reason of state against a 'republican' variant. This involves more than a switch of clothes. It means bringing the discourse of reason of state properly into the structure of the state. The reason of the prince becomes the reason of the state, now identified as a commonwealth for the mutual preservation of liberty. This transformation subtly changes the nature of reason of state discourse – or the way it works itself out – and so purifies it. A discourse geared to the furthering of the private interest (will or lust) of an individual or elite becomes the province of a structure necessarily geared towards the public interest (reason) of the nation as a whole.

The Oceanic republic

With James Harrington, we meet the most original political writer of English republicanism.[156] His major work *The Commonwealth of Oceana*

[152] CM, 83.
[153] Scott, *Algernon Sidney and the English Republic*, 188.
[154] CM, 29.
[155] Pincus, 'Neither Machiavellian Moment Nor Possessive Individualism', 731.
[156] David Hume, 'Essay Twenty-Seven: Idea of a Perfect Commonwealth' in Hume, *Political Essays* (Cambridge: Cambridge University Press, ed. Knud Haakonssen, 1994), 221–222: 'All plans of government, which suppose great reformation in the manners of mankind, are plainly imaginary. Of this nature, are the *Republic* of PLATO, and the

(1656) is 'one of those works that transcend their immediate context' and marks 'a paradigmatic breakthrough' in English political thought.[157] But Harrington is far from being a typical republican. Indeed, for Scott, he is 'the most idiosyncratic member of the republican intellectual flock'.[158] He was a gentleman of the bedchamber to the King until shortly before the regicide. He wrote not to justify the fall of the English monarch but to explain it[159] and was more interested in reconciliation, settlement and stability than most republicans. Like other republicans, he inherited from Aristotle and Livy via Machiavelli[160] the belief that 'a commonwealth is an empire of laws and not of men'.[161] But he was not much interested with the moral qualities (virtues) of individual citizens,[162] having instead a 'boffin-like preoccupation' with constitutional machinery.[163] For Harrington, an adequate constitution was the only foundation for peace. Get the constitutional architecture right, or so he thought, and there is no reason why the commonwealth should not flourish for eternity.

Oceana is an account of the founding of a republican constitution for England. Much of the work is given over to a fictional account of a constitutional convention at which a lawgiver[164] guides debate out of which springs a model of the commonwealth contained in a series of basic laws or 'orders'. The semi-fictional portrayal in which England becomes Oceana and where real political figures are given stage names is a bit strange, although it had predecessors in works such as More's *Utopia*[165] and Bacon's *New Atlantis*.[166]

Utopia of Sir THOMAS MORE. The *OCEANA* is the only valuable model of a commonwealth, that has yet been offered to the public.'

157 Pocock, *Machiavellian Moment*, 384.

158 Scott, 'The Rapture of Motion', 141.

159 J. G. A. Pocock, 'Introduction' to Harrington, *The Commonwealth of Oceana and a System of Politics* (Cambridge: Cambridge University Press, 1992), ix.

160 *Oceana*, 30: 'Machiavel, the sole retriever of this ancient prudence'. See also p. 155.

161 *Oceana*, 20.

162 Scott, *Commonwealth Principles*, 141.

163 Blair Worden, 'James Harrington and "The Commonwealth of Oceana", 1656' in Wootton, *Republicanism, Liberty, and Commercial Society*, 99.

164 Ideally, the lawgiver should be one man and the constitution made at one moment. The extraordinary situation requires extraordinary means and 'whereas a book or a building hath not been known to attain perfection, if it had not had a sole author or architect, a commonwealth, as to the fabric of it, is of the like nature' (*Oceana*, 67).

165 *Oceana* also shares *Utopia*'s debt to Greek political theory in general and Plato in particular: see Nelson, *Greek Tradition in Republican Thought*, chapters 1 and 3, especially 102–106.

166 Francis Bacon was important to the English republicans. In his political writings, civic greatness and the idea of the armed citizen assumed a central place for the first time in English humanist thought. It was Bacon 'more than anyone else who familiarized

But it is also appropriate. By the time Harrington wrote the work, the opportunity for structural reform was all but gone.[167] The text stands, then, as a testament to what might have been. It also serves as a rebuke to living politicians, none more than Cromwell whose fictional counterpart in *Oceana*, Lord Archon, who 'does everything for the effective establishment of the nation's liberty' that Cromwell had promised but failed to do, is a virtuous inversion of the bungling Lord Protector.[168]

Oceana begins with a statement of the principles of government. From the start, Harrington is involved in a wrestling match with *Leviathan*,[169] a typical strategy being to accept much of Hobbes's analysis only to harness it to republican ends.[170] Within the first few paragraphs, Harrington establishes an opposition between Machiavelli's republicanism, which aims to distill the wisdom of the ancients, and Hobbes's modern state theory, which seeks to eradicate it.[171] In *Oceana*, Harrington, 'labouring in the mines of ancient prudence, and bringing her hidden treasures unto new life',[172] aims to redeem the former at the expense of the latter.

Politics can be understood in one of two ways: according to the precepts of 'ancient prudence' or through the lens of 'modern prudence'. Ancient prudence is that 'art whereby a civil society of men is instituted and preserved upon the foundation of common right or interest, or (to follow Aristotle and Livy) it is the empire of laws and not of men.'[173] Ancient prudence, on the wane after the fall of the Roman Republic, was lost almost

the English with Machiavellian theory of *grandezza*': Peltonen, *Classical Humanism and Republicanism in English Political Thought*, 196. See also Stephen L. Collins, *From Divine Cosmos to Sovereign State: An Intellectual History of Consciousness and the Idea of Order in Renaissance England* (New York: Oxford University Press, 1989), 143–145.

[167] Blair Worden, 'Harrington's "*Oceana*": Origins and Aftermath, 1651–1660' in Wootton, *Republicanism, Liberty, and Commercial Society*.

[168] Scott, *Commonwealth Principles*, 284. See also Scott, 'Rapture of Motion', 146: '*Oceana* is, in fact, a deliberate subversion of classical republicanism with its roots in a post-humanist rebellion linked to that of Hobbes.'

[169] Jonathan Scott, 'Classical Republicanism in Seventeenth-Century England and the Netherlands' in van Gelderen and Skinner, *Republicanism: A Shared European Heritage, Vol. I*, 72: 'The objective of *Oceana*, as of *Leviathan*, is peace. It is the second great interregnum work of settlement in continuous dialogue and competition with the first.'

[170] Worden, 'Harrington and "The Commonwealth of Oceana"', 91: '*Oceana* seeks to provide a "political architecture" that will accommodate Hobbes's sceptical insights into the functions of the passions and of instinct within the republican language of virtue and reason.'

[171] *Oceana*, 9 (which includes a paragraph quoted from *Leviathan*, 'A Review and Conclusion').

[172] *Oceana*, 68. [173] *Oceana*, 8.

entirely[174] with the collapse of the Roman Empire.[175] Government from that time has been defined by modern prudence, or the 'art whereby some man, or a few men, subject a city or nation, and rule it according unto his or their private interest … an empire of men and not of laws'.[176]

It is immediately apparent that Harrington shares the same binary perspective as other republicans. Liberty is contrasted with slavery; republican government with tyranny; reason with passion or will; law with license and misrule.[177] So: 'the liberty of a commonwealth consisteth in the empire of her laws, the absence whereof would betray her to the lusts of tyrants'.[178] What is interesting is what Harrington means by such terms. Sidney, as we have seen, juxtaposes reason and interest seeing one as categorically different from the other. Reason is connected to virtue, and so to God. Interest is linked to corruption, and so to the Devil. The difference is enough to serve as a basis for favouring one form of government over another. Harrington avoids this sort of metaphysics. He is happy in the first instance to accept Hobbes's equation of reason and self-interest. But he then distinguishes between three types of reason operating within politics:[179] private reason ('the interest of a private man'); 'reason of state' (the interest of the ruler or rulers); and 'that reason which is the interest of mankind or of the whole'. This last kind of reason is better than the other two:

> if reason be nothing else but interest, and the interest of mankind be the right interest, then the reason of mankind must be right reason. Now compute well, for if the interest of popular government come the nearest unto the interest of mankind, then the reason of popular government must come the nearest unto right reason.[180]

Harrington's love of keeping things simple can be seen in the use he makes of an example of two girls dividing a cake. 'Divide', one girl says to the other, 'and I will choose. Or let me divide and you shall choose.'[181] That

[174] The exception is Venice. See *Oceana*, 8: 'Venice, which, escaping the hands of the barbarians by virtue of her impregnable situation, hath had her eye fixed upon ancient prudence and is attained to a perfection even beyond her copy.'

[175] *Oceana*, 8. [176] *Oceana*, 9.

[177] See, e.g., *Oceana*, 19: 'Now government is no other than the soul of a nation or city; wherefore that which was reason in one in the debate of a commonwealth, being brought forth by the result, must be virtue; and for as much as the soul of a city or nation is the sovereign power, her virtue must be law. But the government whose law is virtue, and whose virtue is law, is the same whose empire is authority, and whose authority is empire.'

[178] *Oceana*, 19–20. [179] *Oceana*, 21.

[180] *Oceana*, 22. [181] *Oceana*, 22.

is the only fair way to proceed. Neither dominates. A simple process is agreed upon that gets the girls out of a potentially conflict-laden situation. The same, Harrington argues, should be true of the commonwealth.[182] In specific terms, this means a division between debating ('dividing') and choosing ('resolving') that should map on to an institutional distinction between senate (aristocracy) and assembly (the people). A senate composed of a 'natural aristocracy' of men with experience and talent debates matters and makes proposals for law but have no power to turn those proposals into law. The assembly of representatives of the people chooses, without debate, whether or not such proposals should become law. A third party (magistracy) is needed to execute the laws made by the other two. Outlining a separation of powers structure that predates Montesquieu by almost a century, the commonwealth thus consists 'of the senate proposing, the people resolving, and the magistracy executing, whereby partaking of the aristocracy as in the senate, of the democracy as in the people, and of monarchy as in the magistracy, is it complete'.[183]

Ultimate sovereignty within the constitution of Oceana rests in the people: 'this free-born nation liveth not upon the dole or bounty of one man but, distributing her annual magistracies and honours with her own hand, is herself King People'.[184] Interestingly, Harrington reserves the term 'prerogative', until now associated with princes and kings, with the people.[185] The people become the 'prerogative tribe'[186] and the prerogative power they wield has two parts: the legislative power (the power to decide on what is law) and the power of judicature (the highest court in the commonwealth).[187] It follows that the executive (or magistracy) is under the law, its officers being 'answerable unto the people that his execution be according unto the law; by which Leviathan may see that the hand or sword that executeth the law is in it, not above it'.[188] If the executive

[182] Worden, 'Harrington and "The Commonwealth of Oceana"', 91: 'His elaborate constitutional machinery … is intended to make politics a recurrent enactment of that image.'

[183] *Oceana*, 25.

[184] See also *Oceana*, 171: 'the prerogative tribe … is the supreme judicature and the ultimate appeal in this commonwealth. For the popular government that makes account to be of any standing must make sure in the first place of the appeal unto the people. … Wherefore the right of supreme judicature in the people … is confirmed by the constant practice of all commonwealths'.

[185] When he talks about prerogative in the traditional sense, as he does in *Oceana* p. 35 when discussing the capture of the state by an individual or small group of individuals who then make decisions in their private interest, he refers specifically to 'the prerogative of monarchy'.

[186] *Oceana*, 147. [187] *Oceana*, 166. [188] *Oceana*, 25.

officers were not answerable in this way, then in time the commonwealth will become private interest government and liberty will end.

But for all Harrington's use here of the Hobbesian rhetoric of sovereignty, his real ambition is to fold sovereignty into the constitution of the commonwealth and thereby tame it. This is the more general message he draws from the image of the girls sharing the cake. Sovereign power, like gunpowder for the soldier, is at one and the same time a means of keeping the people safe and a potential source of oppression. The ability to channel power upwards from the people to institutions and agents with the authority to command and the ability to take decisions is an enormous source of strength and can be used to ward off threats at home or abroad. But that same structure of power can be turned on the people themselves in order to deprive them of their liberties, or even their lives. The ideal constitution, then, distributes sovereign power in such a way that it can still be used for beneficial purposes but stops it from being used as an instrument of tyranny.[189] It is no point trying to improve individuals or to get politicians to be more virtuous. Those like Milton or Sidney who emphasize the personal in politics,[190] construing it as a 'war between a party of vice and a party of virtue',[191] make a basic mistake. People are what they are.[192] You will only change behaviour if you change the structures in which and through which people operate. That being the case, if you establish the right institutions and procedures there is no reason why you should not achieve perpetual peace within the commonwealth. 'For neither by reason nor by experience is it impossible that a commonwealth should be immortal, seeing the people, being the materials, never dies, and the form, which is motion, must without opposition be endless.'[193]

The search for order starts with the people, the basic political units. 'For except the people be methodically distributed, they cannot be methodically collected, but the being of a commonwealth consisteth in the methodical collection of a people.'[194] They are ordered into a series of tribes, which are

[189] *Oceana*, 99–100.

[190] Cromwell and his principal ally Ireton took a similar view. Forms of government were secondary issues, 'but dross and dung', as Cromwell put it, 'in comparison of Christ' (quoted in Worden, 'Republicanism, Regicide and Republic', 316).

[191] Worden, 'Republicanism and the Restoration, 1660–1683', 153.

[192] *Oceana*, 163: 'where there is a liquorishness in a popular assembly to debate, it proceedeth not from the constitution of the people, but of the commonwealth'.

[193] *Oceana*, 99. See also p. 158: 'a commonwealth that is internally equal hath no internal cause of commotion, and therefore can have no such effect but from without'.

[194] *Oceana*, 77.

at once political and military units.[195] A republican structure of government is built on top of this foundation with separate assemblies for debating and voting, as we have seen, and a dispersed and rotating executive magistracy. *Oceana* also provides comprehensive instructions about elections to each of these institutions, incorporating the Venetian ballot system.[196] The goal of Harrington's enterprise (like Hobbes's) is perpetual peace, the strategy for achieving that goal is the equal commonwealth, and the tactics balance in government: 'in an equal commonwealth, there can be no more strife than there can be overbalance in equal weights'. But in the process of transforming the people into 'materials' in the greater construction of the commonwealth, Harrington in fact does away with the idea of popular participation in government. Political action is based around the repetition of prescribed rituals that cannot be changed. 'Nobody is autonomous in Oceana, for everyone is enslaved to the state.'[197]

Harrington identifies two basic principles of balance: rotation and the agrarian. The latter, modelled on the troubled practice of republican Rome,[198] is a 'perpetual law' imposing limits of wealth and property holding. The figure Harrington sets is low by contemporary standards, so his agrarian will break up larger estates and widen ownership of land.[199] The

[195] The martial aspect of Oceana should not be overlooked. Subjects are soldier citizens and the commonwealth is arranged almost like a barracks. So, for instance, the account of the ordering of the people (*Oceana*, 147) begins: 'The face or *mine* of the prerogative tribe for the arms, the horses and the discipline, but more especially for the select men, is that of a very noble regiment, or rather of two; the one of horse, divided into three troops (besides that of provinces, which will be shown hereafter), with their captains, cornets, and two tribunes of the horse at the head of them; the other of foot in three companies (besides that of the provinces) with their captains, ensigns, and two tribunes of the foot at the head of them. The first troop is called the Phoenix, the second the Pelican, and the third the Swallow.' See also J. G. A. Pocock, *The Ancient Constitution and the Feudal Law: A Study of English Historical Thought in the Seventeenth Century* (Cambridge: Cambridge University Press, 2nd ed., 1987), 129: 'Harrington, we must keep in mind, was a Machiavellian, and the starting-point of his thought was Machiavelli's perception that in a republic the soldiers must be citizens and the citizens soldiers; if the soldiers follow private men for reward, then the republic cannot survive.'

[196] *Oceana*, 114. [197] Scott, 'The Rapture of Motion', 150–151.

[198] Nelson, *Greek Tradition in Republican Thought*, 49–68. Nelson argues that Harrington's account of Roman land law and the political troubles that surrounded it derive from Plutarch: 'Harrington sees the Roman agrarian laws through the eyes of a Greek' (p. 95).

[199] See also James Harrington, *The Art of Lawgiving* (1659) in David Wootton (ed.), *Divine Right and Democracy* (Harmondsworth: Penguin, 1986), 397–404. The largest estate in Oceana should yield no more than £2,000 which works out to four times the value of a middling English estate in Harrington's time. Restrictions are also placed on inheritances and other gifts. See Andrew Reeve, 'Harrington's Elusive Balance' (1984) 4

point is to prevent individuals or groups from becoming too powerful, 'as exorbitant riches overthrow the balance of a commonwealth, so extreme poverty cannot hold it nor is by any means to be trusted with it'.[200] The balance of property yields the balance of power, so a commonwealth must maintain relatively equal fortunes in order to survive. 'Equal rotation' provides for the frequent succession of office holders on the basis of the 'free election or suffrage of the people'.[201] Harrington also calls for permanent representative bodies with rotating memberships, a third of whose members will be replaced each year. The system avoids the boom and bust problem associated with princes, an excellent one followed by a dud or maniac. Elected officials are only likely to succeed through merit. It also stabilizes the commonwealth, making it less dependent on individual charisma and vainglory.[202] More fundamentally, rotation prevents the stagnation and capture of the republic: 'if you allow not a commonwealth her rotation, in which consists her equality, you reduce her to a party'.[203]

The chaotic situation in which England found itself in the 1650s provided an opportunity from which to build a new republic capable of transcending its existing divisions and enmities, a commonwealth modelled on Venice,[204] which 'being always changing, is forever the same'.[205] Writing in a context contested by royalists of various stripes, apologists for the Protectorate and republicans divided among themselves, Harrington's project was not to align himself with any of those positions against another but rather 'to draw upon all of them in a holistic opposition to disunity itself'.[206] It is characteristic that Harrington does not seek

History of European Ideas 401. Harrington took the substance of his agrarian proposals from Plato's *Laws*: see Nelson, *Greek Tradition in Republican Thought*, 117.

200 *Oceana*, 77. 201 *Oceana*, 33.

202 *Oceana*, 35–36. 203 *Oceana*, 123.

204 *Oceana*, 33. Neo-Harringtonians share this fascination with Venice – and with constitutional detail. See, e.g., Henry Nevile, *Plato Redivivus, or a Dialogue Concerning Government* (1681) in Caroline Robbins (ed.), *Two English Republican Tracts* (Cambridge: Cambridge University Press, 1969), a work which also contains a fascinating proposal for splintering the royal prerogative and exercising it through the king acting through various parliamentary committees (although the king is allowed a free hand with imperial and mercantile concerns). Nevile was Harrington's literary partner and close friend.

205 *Oceana*, 145. Blair Worden, 'James Harrington and "The Commonwealth of Oceana", 1656' in Wootton, *Republicanism, Liberty, and Commercial Society*, 88: 'Harrington, writing in a time of … instability and offering himself as "a lover of antiquity" who could end it, proposed a remedy in which virtuous government would not merely outlast revolutions of the sun but acquire their regularity and permanence.'

206 Scott, *Commonwealth Principles*, 143.

to exclude political opponents from office, unlike his fellow republicans Nedham, Sidney and Milton.[207] What he is after is not outright victory, whether religious or political, but reconciliation:

> But now, when no man is desired to throw up a farthing of his money or a shoveful of his earth, and that all we can do is but to make a virtue of necessity, we are disputing whether we should have peace or war. For peace you cannot have without some government, nor any government without the proper balance; wherefore, if you will not fix this which you have, the rest is blood.[208]

Even Harrington's history is designed to bind wounds rather than reopen them. In the second preliminary, he develops a schematic history of England from the collapse of the Roman Empire right up to the Civil War. The account is based on the historical scholarship of the seventeenth-century polymath John Selden,[209] a major influence on both republicans and monarchists.[210] The history aims to look beneath the surface of events to discover their material causes. It should be possible, Harrington thinks, given our expanding intellectual universe, to identify the laws of political history.[211] The key to those laws lies in the shifting balance of political power to changes in underlying structures of property, especially ownership of land. It is as though Machiavelli is refracted through English feudal forms and English political history.

The ultimate message to be derived from Harrington's history is that 'the dissolution of the late monarchy was as natural as the death of a man'.[212] The political structure on the apex of which stood the Stuart kings, always unstable, had become unworkable. As a work of modern prudence, it was only by happenstance that this 'Gothic constitution' produced good results. The 'Gothic balance' that helped secure liberties was simply the result of the inability of king or nobility to dominate. The

[207] *Oceana*, 62: 'To the commonwealthsman I have no more to say but that if he exclude any party, he is not truly such, nor shall ever found a commonwealth upon the natural principle of the same, which is justice'.

[208] *Oceana*, 113–114.

[209] Pocock, *Ancient Constitution*, 135.

[210] Tuck, *Philosophy and Government*, 205: 'the closest parallel in the whole of Europe to Grotius in his own lifetime [was] the Englishman, John Selden'. Armitage, *The Ideological Origins of the British Empire*, 119: 'Selden's work provided the foundation for later claims to dominion over the seas in the name of a "British Empire".'

[211] Pocock, *Ancient Constitution*, 146. This type of historical method was to become a standard feature of political and constitutional writing in the eighteenth century: see Chapters 4 and 5.

[212] *Oceana*, 62.

ancient constitution, far from being a political masterpiece, was nothing 'other than a wrestling match, wherein the nobility, as they have been stronger, have thrown the king, or the king if he have been the stronger, hath thrown the nobility'.[213] It was a balance of power rather than a balanced constitution, an index of which was the irreconcilable messiness of its public laws: 'the laws were so ambiguous that they might be eternally disputed and never reconciled'.[214]

The Tudors broke this Gothic balance. In an attempt to secure their throne, they took power away from the nobility which opened up a space for the people, a move that was in any case in line with underlying economic trends.[215] It was only a matter of time before politics caught up with material realities and the people started demanding control over government: 'the balance being in the people, the commonwealth (though they do not see it) is already in the nature of them'.[216] In an important passage, Harrington asks whether it is right to use the language of corruption to describe this process. It is possible to do so in an attenuated sense, as when referring to the natural movement ('corruption') from one natural state to another. But from a true normative standpoint, a move from monarchy to popular government is the opposite of corruption since it represents a shift from private interest to public interest government and thus a movement in the direction of justice and right reason. A movement in the other direction would be a different matter, for which the term corruption would be appropriate.[217]

The point of the historical narrative was both to take the sting out of the contemporary affairs by showing how they were subject to historical forces or laws beyond the control of political actors and to signpost the best way forward:

> Governments no longer degenerate because of the operation of tendency inherent in all nature; they do so because man has ignored, for almost two thousand years, part of the logic of the situation in which he finds himself ... the original blunder can be remedied and the degenerative cycle brought to a halt.[218]

But what do these historical laws entail for Oceana's foreign policy? One might have expected the advocate of reconciliation and stability at home to opt for peace abroad. To the contrary, Harrington is every bit as expansionary as Nedham or Sidney and believed just as fervently as they did

[213] *Oceana*, 53. [214] *Oceana*, 62. [215] *Oceana*, 60.
[216] *Oceana*, 60. [217] *Oceana*, 61.
[218] Pocock, *Ancient Constitution*, 145–146.

'that God had singled out England for a critical responsibility at a critical moment in His scheme of history. Her duty is to rid the world of its "sick" and "corrupted" monarchies.'[219] Oceana is ordered as a martial polity where subjects are soldier-citizens on a permanent war footing.[220] Slipping loose from Machiavelli's binaries, Harrington intends Oceana to combine the qualities of *both* Venice and Rome.[221] It was to be a Rome in respect of unlimited expansion but a Venice in respect of perpetual stability, liberty and virtue.[222] Staying true to commonwealth principles in the international arena means aping Cicero's injunction[223] that the Romans should undertake the patronage or protectorate (as opposed to the empire) of the world:

> This is a commonwealth of the fabric that hath an open ear and a public [general] concernment; she is not made for herself only, but given as a magistrate of God unto mankind, for the vindication of common right and the law of nature ... A commonwealth, I say, of this make is a minister of God upon earth, to the end that the world may be governed with righteousness.[224]

Expansion is thus a necessity – the best form of defence – and a moral obligation. Oceana's mission is to rescue nations labouring under the yoke of Gothic Empires existing in a zombie-like state: 'yet tumbling and tossing upon the bed of sickness, they cannot die, nor is there any means of recovery for them but by ancient prudence'.[225] This is not quite the nearly unconstrained belligerence of Sidney's *Discourses*. Harrington is more responsive to the moral core of the case against empire, expressed in Tacitus's famous charge that Roman imperialism 'created a desert and called it peace'.[226] Understood as a tutelary mission, conquest ('patronage') is conditional upon maintaining liberty and justice at home.[227] As

219 Worden, 'Harrington and the "Commonwealth of Oceana"', 101.

220 *Oceana*, 205: 'this commonwealth [is] constituted ... of two elements, arms and councils'.

221 Armitage, 'Empire and Liberty: A Republican Dilemma', 36.

222 Pocock, *Machiavellian Moment*, 393.

223 Pagden, *Lords of All the World*, 127–130.

224 *Oceana*, 221. 225 *Oceana*, 232.

226 Cornelius Tacitus, *Agricola* (Oxford: Oxford University Press, eds. R. M. Ogilvie and Ian Richmond, 1967), c.30: '*Auferre, trucidare, rapere, falsis nominibus imperium; atque, ubi solitudinem faciunt, pacem appellant.*' On the importance of Tacitus and Tacitean scepticism to the 'new' humanism, in part transmitted via *raison d'état* thinkers, see Tuck, *Philosophy and Government.*

227 The parallel with the nineteenth-century liberal justification for empire is striking. See Chapter 6.

such, this part of *Oceana* represents a criticism of the Protectorate's failure to safeguard liberty while asserting its foreign *imperium*.[228] Harrington's image of the English republic as hegemon is also more oceanic than continental.[229] As a theorist who linked political power to land-based wealth, it is not surprising that he saw the proliferation of overseas plantations as central to Oceana's fledging empire.[230]

In Oceana's constitution, liberty and empire are almost two sides of the same coin. The principles that undergird the commonwealth also drive its overseas mission. Similarly, Oceana's foreign exploits spill back into the republic. This goes beyond the familiar Machiavellian point that expansion can often be the best form of defence, with which Harrington agreed: 'If your liberty be not a root that grows, it will be a branch that withers'.[231] What Harrington is suggesting is that only through the act of expansion does the commonwealth fully realize itself. Just as Rome 'in confirming her liberty propagated her empire' so too must Oceana become 'an holy asylum unto the distressed world', acting as 'a minister of God upon earth'.[232] Empire of this sort, far from being a threat to liberty, rather confirms the republic in its liberty – and thus the people in its power. 'Excellent patriots, if the people be sovereign, here is that which establish their prerogative.'[233] The evangelical streak to Harrington's theory of liberal empire is consistent with the overarching objective of political immortality.[234] The reason of the commonwealth, radiating justice around the globe, may become as 'perfect and immortal' as the cosmos itself.[235] It is this perspective, in which glory and peace become one, that makes sense of the apocalyptic Song of Solomon–inspired rhapsody that closes this section of *Oceana*:

> Oceana is as the rose of Sharon; and the lily of the valley ... She is comely as the tents of Kedar, and terrible as an army with banners. Her neck is as the tower of David, builded for an armoury, whereon there hang a thousand bucklers and shields of mighty men ... The south hath dropped and

228 Armitage, *Ideological Origins of the British Empire*, 139.

229 See also John Streater, *Observations* no. 3, 19–26 April 1654, 21: 'it is safer to chuse some remote place or new Plantation, which no State claimeth, for by this means the Commonwealth ... that doth do so, avoideth many wars'.

230 See also Milton, *Paradise Lost*, Book IV, 691–692: where God is praised as 'the sovereign Planter' who 'framed all things to man's delightful use'. On Milton's imperialism compare Armitage, 'John Milton: Poet Against Empire' in Armitage *et al.*, *Milton and Republicanism* and Scott, *Commonwealth Principles*, 213–220.

231 *Oceana*, 223: 232 *Oceana*, 221. 233 *Oceana*, 233.

234 Scott, 'Rapture of Motion', 147.

235 Nelson, *Greek Tradition in Republican Thought*, 124.

> the west is breathing upon the garden of spices. Arise, queen of the earth; arise, holy spouse of Jesus. For lo, the winter is past, the rain is over and gone.[236]

It is passages like this that make *Oceana* 'the supreme contemporary text of the imperial moment in the English republic'.[237] But what does it reveal about reason of state? What Harrington finds objectionable is reason of state understood as the private interest of particular rulers operating through the lens of modern prudence. Once the commonwealth is established in accordance with the principles set down in *Oceana*, that objection no longer applies. The decisions and actions that emanate from the institutions of the new commonwealth will reflect or embody the public reason of the nation. As such, they will get us as close as we are likely to get to universal reason, the triumph of which is also the triumph of God.[238]

This reading also fits the analysis of reason of state developed in Harrington's later work *A System of Politics*. Harrington distinguishes two types of reason of state: 'Administration of government, or reason of state, to such as propose to themselves to play upon the square is one thing; and to such as propose to themselves to pack the cards is another.' The point is a little cryptic but seems to parallel Nedham's distinction between fair play and subterfuge in international affairs. Harrington then systematizes and institutionalizes that distinction. Reason of state operates, he says, in both the domestic and foreign spheres. The latter consists 'in balancing foreign princes and states in such a manner as you may gain upon them', the former is the administration of government 'according to [its] foundation and superstructures'. But in either sphere what really counts is the way the polity is constituted. 'Reason of state, in a democracy which is rightly founded and rightly ordered, is a thing of great facility, whether in a foreign or in a domestic relation.' Domestically, it aims at nothing more than preventing the restoration of monarchy. In foreign relations, because a republic is such a strong form of government, it 'will easily give the balance abroad at its pleasure'.[239] It is the 'aristocratical monarchies' that need to be watched most, as these states operating within 'the true theatre of expedient-mongers and state-empirics, or the deep waters wherein that *Leviathan* the minister of state takes his pastime'.[240] Harrington is clear,

236 *Oceana*, 233.
237 Armitage, 'Cromwellian Protectorate and the Languages of Empire', 552.
238 Worden, 'Harrington and "The Commonwealth of Oceana"', 109.
239 James Harrington, 'A System of Politics' in Harrington, *The Commonwealth of Oceana and a System of Politics*, 291.
240 'System of Politics', 292.

in other words, that reason of state is a function of every state, but will necessarily vary according to its constitution. What is essentially a good thing when practised by a republic is problematic when used by governments geared to private interest, whether anarchy (that is, Athenian-style democracy), oligarchy or tyranny, where 'that which is reason of state with them is directly opposite to that which is truly so'.[241]

'Wherefore, you are to take the course of Rome'

Significant differences separate the republicans whose work has been surveyed in this chapter. Nedham's deploys razor-sharp cynicism about political power[242] to describe a levelling commonwealth modelled on democratic Athens. Sidney produces a republican account based on Rome (and Israel) from the perspective of a death-or-glory aristocratic libertarian. Harrington, prizing peace, looks to Venice and mechanistic philosophy for the pattern of the stable and harmonious commonwealth. Yet there are substantial levels of agreement. All three are deeply militaristic, sieving Machiavelli through the lens of their own experience. This emphasis on arms is of profound political importance, since all three equate political liberty with military strength.[243] The republic is likely to remain free so long as its citizens are prepared to take up arms in its defence. And the citizen derives equal standing within the body polity in large measure on the basis of his willingness to commit to military service. The three writers also agree that the commonwealth should be one of expansion. So, whether committed to the model of Athens, Rome or Venice at the domestic level, all take the course of Rome when it comes to international affairs.

The republican response, then, was very much of a piece with Cromwell's remarks with which this chapter started. They too wanted to make the name of Englishman to be as much feared as ever was the name of *civis Romanus*. But they wanted to do it properly. This meant, at the domestic level, setting the nation up so that it was in a position to wage war effectively. This entailed, above all, the operation of a strong rule of law framework. Not only did the rule of law prevent aristocratic and monarchical oppression, but, in so doing, it also meant that the people were ready and willing to fight. A free people is a strong people. And a

[241] 'System of Politics', 293.
[242] Zagorin, *Political Thought in the English Revolution*, 121.
[243] Scott, 'Motion of Rapture', 145.

state constituted for freedom is a state geared for war. At the level of foreign policy and international affairs, it meant a rethinking of reason of state. The republicans were critical, often witheringly so, about reason of state (*ragione di stato*) as practised by European princes. But their objections are largely washed out once the state is reformed along republican lines. As the interest of the government becomes aligned with the interest of the nation as a whole, 'monarchical' or private interest reason of state is replaced by 'true' or public interest reason of state – or, as another seventeenth-century commentator put it, between 'Pseudo-Policy' and political 'science' built upon 'piety and prudence'.[244]

The difference is not necessarily one of policy, although it might be, but relates to the legitimacy of the state and thus to the question of representation. When can an individual or body justifiably claim the power to act on behalf of the public?[245] Writing at a crucial time in English political and imperial history,[246] the republicans reached by a different route a conclusion not dissimilar to Hobbes's. Hobbes maintained that only their personation by the Leviathan made people (*multitudo*) into a community (*civitas*). Community thus began with the creation of government and sovereignty rested with its authorized powers. The republicans disagreed with many of Hobbes's conclusions. But they agreed with Hobbes about the need for a new covenant between power and right – a systematic reshaping of the old order which centrally involved the elimination of the idea of 'original' power vested in rulers and of 'reason of state' understood in similarly princely terms. They saw that political nature should now reflect the formal structure of the relations between individuals.[247] There was nothing outside or beyond the empire of law since a properly functioning state acts only through law and is presumed to act in the interests of all.

Philip Bobbit in his magisterial book *The Shield of Achilles* makes a similar point about the changing nature of reason of state in the early modern period. For the sake of emphasis, he distinguishes more sharply

[244] William Sandcroft, *Modern Policies, Taken from Machiavel, Borgia, and Other Choice Authors, by an Eye Witnesse* (London, 4th ed., 1653), sig. A12r quoted in Peter N. Miller, *Defining the Common Good: Empire, Religion and Philosophy in Eighteenth-Century Britain* (Cambridge: Cambridge University Press, 1994), 34.

[245] Miller, *Defining the Common Good*, 43–44.

[246] Canny, 'The Origins of Empire', 21: 'While the Cromwellian initiatives produced few lasting gains for Britain, besides the island of Jamaica, they did result in an alteration of foreign-policy priorities that was to have enduring significance.'

[247] Collins, *From Divine Cosmos to Sovereign State*, 163.

than the historical and philological record would strictly allow between (a) *ragione di stato*, which he associates with the Machiavellian reformulation of politics and the creation of the idea of the princely state in the sixteenth century, (b) *raison d'état*, which he connects to the kingly state that emerged in the seventeenth century, most obviously so in the state-building programme of Richelieu in France that reached an apogee in the reign of Louis XIV and (c) *Staats raison*, which he associates with the eighteenth-century territorial state whose dynamics are most visible in the designs of Frederick the Great. On this reading, *ragione di stato*, *raison d'état* and *Staats raison* become principles of the princely, kingly and territorial constitutional orders, respectively. 'Among the Italian princely states, *ragione di stato* simply stood for a rational, unprincipled justification for the self-aggrandizement of the State; whereas *raison d'état* achieved a parallel justification through the personification of the state, and leveraged the imperatives of this justification to impose obligations on the dynastic ruler.' *Staats raison*, by contrast, 'is a rationale given on behalf of the State, and imperative that compels its strategic designs', but which 'identifies the state with the country, the land'.[248] Updating Harrington's account in this model's terms, we might say that seventeenth-century England faced a crisis that resulted from the collapse of the princely state epitomized by Henry VIII or Elizabeth I. England was divided at key moments in the century between advocates of the kingly state – those associated with Charles I and James II especially, who wanted to modernize the English polity in self-conscious imitation of the model of absolutist France – and those who saw the only solution as lying in an embryonic version of the territorial state (Leviathan) accompanied by state-based strategic designs (Oceana) – that is, the designs not of the prince or king but of the collective (*civitas*).

In Bobbit's terms, the call is to transform *ragione di stato* – or what the republicans called 'Italian' reason of state – into *Staats raison*, or 'true' reason of state, at a time when royalists seemed inclined to stake a claim for the absolute monarch's *raison d'état*. Reason of state was to be dethroned and brought in-house, the republicans insisted, made part

[248] Philip Bobbit, *The Shield of Achilles: War, Peace, and the Course of History* (New York: Alfred A. Knopf, 2002), 87, 108, 135–136. On Machiavelli and the reason of state tradition see Friedrich Meinecke, *Machiavellism: The Doctrine of Raison d'État and Its Place in Modern History* (New Brunswick: Transaction Publishers, ed. Werner Stark, 1998). On Richelieu, reason of state and the kingly state, see William F. Church, *Richelieu and Reason of State* (Princeton: Princeton University Press, 1972); J. H. Elliott, *Richelieu and Olivares* (Cambridge: Cambridge University Press, 1984), 121–129.

of the properly constituted state grounded in the notion of public interest. This reordering of the constitution opened the way for republicans to rethink questions of constitutional design so that institutions of government might be aligned more closely with the interests of the public, even in situations of war and emergency (e.g. Nedham's 'Peoples Trustees' to handle *arcana imperii*). And whereas Hobbes, for all the robustness of his rhetoric, favoured a 'safety first' approach to international relations,[249] the English republican theory of state is interwoven with a theory of empire. Not content with reconstituting their own polity, the republicans made themselves evangelists for liberty whose aim was to see commonwealth values conquer on the global stage.

[249] See the discussion in Chapter 2.

4

Jealousy of trade: reason of state and commercial empire

Republican theories of state and empire were always aspirational. Consistently on the losing side, whether in internal opposition to the army-led Cromwellian regime or as opponents of the late Stuarts, the republicans offered something of a minority report. And while the state-building and martial enterprise of the Cromwellian period should not be underestimated,[1] England's imperial pretensions in the later seventeenth century were little more than a pipedream. Nedham envisioned Britannia as ruler of the waves,[2] and Milton rhapsodized about God 'the sovereign planter' framing 'all things for man's delightful use',[3] while Harrington had expansive dreams of a commonwealth for increase built 'upon the mightiest foundation that any hath been laid from the beginning of the world'.[4] But the truth was that the English state remained relatively passive when it came to overseas matters.[5] Even Cromwell's attempt to break the mould achieved little more concrete than the capture of Jamaica from the Spanish.

By the middle of the eighteenth century, all this had changed. Britain (as it now was[6]) had become 'without any doubt the supreme maritime and

[1] David Hume, *The History of England, vol. 6* (Indianapolis: Liberty Fund, 1983), 41: 'Notwithstanding the late wars and bloodshed, and the present factions, the power of England had never, in any period, appeared so formidable to the neighbouring kingdoms as it did in this time, in the hands of the commonwealth.'

[2] Nedham's translation of John Selden's *Mare Clausum* contained as its accompanying engraving the first representation of Britannia as the ruler of the waves: see David Armitage, *The Ideological Origins of the British Empire* (Cambridge: Cambridge University Press, 2000), 119.

[3] John Milton, *Paradise Lost*, Book IV, 691–692.

[4] James Harrington, *The Commonwealth of Oceana and a System of Politics* (Cambridge: Cambridge University Press, 1992) 233.

[5] On the transformation of intercontinental trade in seventeenth-century England, see Nuala Zahedieh, 'Overseas Expansion and Trade in the Seventeenth Century' in Nicholas Canny (ed.), *The Origins of Empire* (Oxford: Oxford University Press, 1988).

[6] The English Parliament, multinational since the conquest of Wales in the 1530s, was formally abolished with the Act of Union with Scotland in 1707, becoming in time

colonial power and hub of global commerce'.[7] It emerged from the Seven Years' War (1756–63), the first global war, as the preeminent European power. Commerce and empire moved from the periphery to the heart of political debate. The central constitutional question was no longer, as it had been for Sidney or Locke, whether a ruler might be resisted for misconduct, 'but whether a regime founded on patronage, public debt, and professionalization of the armed forces did not corrupt both governors and governed'.[8]

This period of state-building and overseas expansion, enterprise and Enlightenment, was of defining importance for the development of the idea of reason of state and for the British constitution more generally. 'Overseas expansion and the English constitution developed simultaneously and reciprocally, each structuring the other.'[9] The chapter concentrates on the work of one of the age's seminal writers, David Hume. A Scot – and, as such, a newcomer to the constitutional history that we are charting – his work contains acute insights into the old English state as well as the new British constitution. 'Hume's philosophical, psychological, and economic analyses of society were as subtle and complex as any his age (or most others) had to offer.'[10] The chapter's central theme is the domestication of power and conflict, so characteristic a feature of the constitutionalism of the period. But it begins by looking backwards from the world in which Hume wrote. How did the middling, strife-torn kingdom become a vibrant trading entrepôt and all-conquering fiscal-military state? Some account of the transformation of the English state in the closing years of the seventeenth century is required before uncovering what Hume thought about trade, empire and reason of state.

a 'pan-British and imperial legislature': David Armitage, *Foundations of Modern International Thought* (Cambridge: Cambridge University Press, 2013), 136. For analysis of the Act see Allan I. Macinnes, *Union and Empire: The Making of the United Kingdom in 1707* (Cambridge: Cambridge University Press, 2007), chapter 11.

[7] Jonathan I. Israel, 'The Emerging Empire: The Continental Perspective, 1650–1713' in Canny, *Origins of Empire*, 423.

[8] J. G. A. Pocock, 'Virtues, Rights, and Manners' in Pocock, *Virtue, Commerce, and History* (Cambridge: Cambridge University Press, 1985), 48.

[9] Daniel J. Hulsebosch, *Constituting Empire: New York and the Transformation of Constitutionalism in the Atlantic World, 1664–1830* (Chapel Hill: University of North Carolina Press, 2005), 15.

[10] J. G. A. Pocock, *The Machiavellian Moment: Florentine Political Thought and the Atlantic Republican Tradition* (Princeton: Princeton University Press, 2nd ed., 2003), 497.

Glorious Revolutions

Hume's contemporaries saw the Glorious Revolution of 1688–9 as a fundamental constitutional moment, righting the polity in a way that secured its liberty, stability and prosperity. Looking back at those events, Hume himself had no doubt they represented 'a new epoch in the constitution'.[11] Fellow Scot John Millar agreed: 'from the era of the revolution we may trace', he wrote, 'a new order of things'.[12] But if the Revolution was a turning point it was as much due to financial and fiscal developments as anything that happened in respect of more formal changes in public law.[13] Indeed, it was possible to argue that the Revolution had changed little on that score. Blackstone – although he had his own (Tory) axe to grind – thought that the 'theoretical perfection' of English public law had been achieved in the period *preceding* the Revolution: 'the constitution of England had arrived to its full vigour, and the true balance between liberty and prerogative was happily established by law, in the reign of Charles the second.'[14] The Revolution itself, he argued, merely 'asserted our liberties in more clear and emphatical terms'.[15] To many republicans – or commonwealthmen as they came to be called[16] – 1688 was a missed opportunity for root and branch reform. The Revolution was more like a 'second Restoration' than a genuine revolution, 'a reconstruction, but at the same

[11] Hume, *History of England, vol.* 6, 329.

[12] John Millar, *An Historical View of the English Government, vol. 4* (London: J. Mawman, 4th ed., 1818), 329.

[13] Although the post-1688 regime was far from idle on this score. The Act of Toleration 1689 provided freedom of worship to Protestant dissenters. The Triennial Act of 1694 and the Act of Settlement of 1701 included important provisions that created constraints on royal prerogative, the former by stipulating that a Parliament had to be called at least once every three years and that no Parliament could sit for more than three years, the latter by prohibiting the Crown from unilaterally removing members of the judiciary, establishing a foundation for judicial independence.

[14] William Blackstone, *Commentaries on the Laws of England* (Chicago: Chicago University Press, ed. Stanley Katz, 1979), IV, 439. Blackstone had in mind three significant developments: the abolition of feudal tenures (12 Car. II, c. 24); the Habeas Corpus Act (31 Car. II, c. 2) and the abolition of the writ *de haeretico comburendo* (29 Car. II, c. 9). See Robert Willman, 'Blackstone and the "Theoretical Perfection" of English Law in the Reign of Charles II' (1983) 26 *Historical Journal* 39.

[15] *Commentaries* IV, 440. For another critical position on post-1688, see William A. Petigrew, 'Free to Enslave: Politics and the Escalation of Britain's Transatlantic Slave Trade, 1688–1714' (2007) 64 *William and Mary Quarterly* 3.

[16] Caroline Robbins, *The Eighteenth-Century Commonwealthman: Studies in the Transmission, Development, and Circumstance of English Liberal Thought from the Restoration of Charles II until the War with the Thirteen Colonies* (Cambridge, MA: Harvard University Press, 1959).

time re-stabilization, of the conditions under which crown, parliament and national church could co-exist'.[17] Political actors worked hard to ensure that there had been no caesura in constitutional time, no moment in which the English state could self-consciously be made anew by its people. A conservative revolution, 1688 was in one sense a victory for the ancient constitution.[18] Continuity had been the order of the day.[19] Ousting James II was justified through the necessity of preserving the constitution in its 'ancient' form. 'In 1689, both William's "conquest" and James's "treason" could have been read as dissolutions of government, but there were unacceptable interpretations, appealing to no more than a handful of radicals and rejected unceremoniously by the Convention and the political nation at large.'[20]

Nowhere is this clearer than in William of Orange's *Declaration* 'of the reasons inducing him to appear in armes in the Kingdome of England'.[21] In an echo of Locke's contemporaneous *Two Treatises on Government*, written in exile in the United Provinces, in which William figures as the 'Great Restorer',[22] the *Declaration* represented the Dutch assault on English

[17] J. G. A. Pocock, 'Empire, State and Confederation: The War of American Independence as a Crisis in Multiple Monarchy' in Pocock, *Discovery of Islands: Essays in British History* (Cambridge: Cambridge University Press, 2005), 140. See also Jonathan Scott, 'Radicalism and Restoration: The Shape of the Stuart Experience' (1988) 31 *Historical Journal* 453.

[18] J. G. A. Pocock, 'The Significance of 1688: Some Reflections on Whig History' in Pocock, *Discovery of Islands*, 119.

[19] Indeed, the fact that much of southern England in 1688 was in the grip of a full-scale Dutch military occupation was very quickly obscured. As Jonathan Israel writes: 'Since the early eighteenth century, a thick wall of silence has descended over the Dutch occupation of London 1688–90. The whole business came to seem so improbable to later generations that by common consent, scholarly and popular, it was simply erased from the record.' ('The Dutch Role in the Glorious Revolution' in Jonathan Israel (ed.), *The Anglo-Dutch Moment: Essays on the Glorious Revolution and Its World Impact* (Cambridge: Cambridge University Press, 1991), 128.)

[20] Howard Nenner, 'The Later Stuart Age' in J. G. A. Pocock (ed.), *The Varieties of British Political Thought, 1500–1800* (Cambridge: Cambridge University Press, 1993), 202.

[21] 10 October 1688. It was intended for an international as well as an English audience. A separate *Declaration* of the Prince for Scotland was also circulated. The main rationale for invasion was strategic. 'There can be no doubt whatever that the Dutch State invaded Britain ... to crush late Stuart absolutism thoroughly, turn England into a parliamentary monarchy and, by so doing, transform Britain into an effective counterweight to the then overwhelming power of France', with which the Dutch were on the verge of war: Israel, 'The Dutch Role', 120.

[22] John Locke, *Two Treatises on Government* (Cambridge: Cambridge University Press, ed. Peter Laslett, 1960), 155: 'These [papers] I hope are sufficient to establish the Throne of our Great Restorer, Our present King William, to make good his Title, in the Consent of the People, which being the only one of all lawful Governments, he has more fully and clearly than any Prince in Christendom: And to justifie to the World, the People of

sovereignty as an entirely reasonable intervention by a well-intentioned party in support of English fundamental rights. 'It is most certain and evident to all men', it began, 'that the publick peace and happiness of any state or kingdom cannot be preserved where the law, liberties, and customs, established by the lawful authority in it, are openly transgressed and annulled; especially where the alteration of religion is endeavoured.' No wonder this version of the intellectual underpinnings of the Glorious Revolution has been embraced by all but specialist historians of the period, Lisa Jardine observes, for here 'is a worthy political manifesto for the dawn of the Age of Reason – the English Enlightenment'.[23] Lauded for having survived both Cromwellian (democratic) and Stuart (monarchical) attempts to subvert it, the constitution was rebranded as the 'balanced' constitution and, as such, almost universally admired.

But for all its conservative elements, the Revolution can still be seen as radically transformative. Steve Pincus argues that it led to substantial change in three central areas of state policy. In foreign policy, England moved from the pro-French position under the late Stuarts to an anti-French alliance with the Dutch. In political economy, a 'Tory' policy favouring land was replaced by a 'Whig' approach that supported manufacturing. And in religious matters, the state moved decisively towards a broader and more tolerant church. Together, these transformations amount to a 'new vision of the English polity'.[24] On this view, 1688–9 marks a decisive point in that it drew England more closely into the European state system, as its Dutch king made immediate use of his new acquisition in his war against France.[25] But this was not the only impact of the Dutch connection. The constitutional politics of 1688 must be connected with the financial and commercial revolution of the period and also the extensive restructuring of the administration. These developments were in response to the war needs of the state.[26] The ejection of James II inaugurated the longest period of British warfare since

England, whose love of their Just and Natural Rights, with their Resolution to preserve them, saved the Nation when it was on the very brink of Slavery and Ruine.'

[23] Lisa Jardine, *Going Dutch: How England Plundered Holland's Glory* (London: Harper Perennial, 2009), 35.

[24] Steve Pincus, *1688: The First Modern Revolution* (New Haven: Yale University Press, 2009), 12.

[25] J. G. A. Pocock, 'Archipelago, Europe and Atlantic after 1688' in Pocock, *Discovery of Islands*, 108.

[26] For a general theory linking the character and development of European states to the needs of war and the availability of capital, see Charles Tilly, *Coercion, Capital, and European States: AD 990–1992* (London: Blackwell, 1990).

the Middle Ages.[27] Prolonged war against the French,[28] now unquestionably Europe's leading power, necessitated a series of major fiscal reforms. These reforms were often modelled on Dutch financial practice, the Netherlands long being considered a leader in the field.[29] The tax system was recast, to the extent that Britain became a heavily taxed nation.[30] The bureaucracy responsible for tax collection expanded, and some of it was revamped on distinctly modern lines. The Excise Office in particular became known for its efficiency.[31] Professionally run and expanding massively throughout the period, it 'more closely approximated to Max Weber's idea of bureaucracy than any other government agency in eighteenth-century Europe'.[32] (And this 150 years before the Northcote-Trevelyan civil service reforms.)

Many of these developments built on reforms instigated in the reigns of Charles II and James II, sometimes earlier.[33] The scale and intensity of change, though, were new – it was with good reason that Defoe called it the 'projecting age'.[34] England also made increasingly aggressive use of new financial techniques.[35] In the 1690s, Parliament moved in the direction

[27] John Brewer, *The Sinews of Power: War, Money and the English State, 1688–1783* (Cambridge, MA: Harvard University Press, 1988), 27.

[28] The Nine Years' War (1689–1697) and the War of the Spanish Succession (1701–1714).

[29] Macinnes, *Union and Empire*, chapter 8.

[30] Brewer, *Sinews of Power*, 88–91.

[31] Indeed, it drew criticism from Blackstone, who questioned whether 'the rigour and arbitrary proceedings of excise-laws' were 'compatible with the temper of a free nation'. Excise proceedings were so fast 'that a man may be convicted in two days time in the penalty of many thousand pounds … to the total exclusion of trial by jury, and disregard of the common law'. *Commentaries* I, 308.

[32] Brewer, *Sinews of Power*, 66–68. In 1690, there were 1,211 full-time Excise officials; by 1782, there were 4,908. See also P. G. M. Dickson, *The Financial Revolution in England: A Study in the Development of Public Credit, 1688–1756* (London: Macmillan, 1967), 42.

[33] Michael J. Braddick, *State Formation in Early Modern England c.1550–1700* (Cambridge: Cambridge University Press, 2000), 265: after 1688, the 'changes in borrowing suggested by the reforms of the 1650s and 1660s, and the institution of the excise, became steadily more important, while the size of the military mobilization was staggering by comparison with what had gone before'.

[34] Daniel Defoe, 'Essay upon Projects' (1697).

[35] The main inspiration may have been Dutch, but not just Dutch techniques were emulated. The government drew from a wide array of European examples. French fiscal policy, developed from Richelieu through Colbert to Sully, was widely admired. Spain provided the model for at least one tax policy. Naples provided the source for the tontine, which had also been used in both the Netherlands and France. See Dickson, *Financial Revolution*, 41, 51; Anne L. Murphy, *The Origins of English Financial Markets: Investment and Speculation before the South Sea Bubble* (Cambridge: Cambridge University Press, 2009), 45–46.

of long-term public borrowing, when it encouraged individuals to loan £1 million to the government in the form of a Tontine (not a great success), life annuities and lotteries (much more so).[36] Long-term loans were cheaper and easier for the government to service. They were also guaranteed by Parliament, which set aside specific revenues to meet interest repayments.[37] These acts constituted a new bargain between Crown and Parliament. 'Perhaps intentionally, perhaps not, the governance reforms of the Glorious Revolution supported a rule of law and constraints on government actions that positively affected English political, military, commercial, and financial success.'[38] The fact that the state now fully endorsed parliamentary review of taxation meant that it could 'generate a high level of social trust in its activities, and this allowed it exponentially to raise its capacity for obtaining revenue.'[39] The Bank of England was created in 1694 and became a major lender to the government as well as a provider of useful financial services.[40]

Cumulatively, the financial innovations of the 1690s marked the establishment of a long-term national debt and in so doing altered over time the relationship between the state and the public.[41] There was an important link between these public finance initiatives and parallel developments in private finance. The success of the various schemes for raising money for the government depended on the availability of capital that could be invested. Thanks to the growth of trade and commerce,[42] there was such a growing pool of capital. A hundred new joint-stock companies were established between 1685 and 1695. With the arrival of these companies came the opportunity to trade in their shares. At the same time, secondary markets grew up for the trading of some of the public funds – for instance, the Million Adventure lottery tickets, drawn in 1694, rapidly

[36] Andrew C. Sobel, *Birth of Hegemony: Crisis, Financial Revolution, and Emerging Global Networks* (Chicago: University of Chicago Press, 2012), 110–114; Murphy, *Origins of English Financial Markets*.

[37] Bruce G. Carruthers, *City of Capital: Politics and Markets in the English Financial Revolution* (Princeton: Princeton University Press, 1996), 73–74.

[38] Sobel, *Birth of Hegemony*, 103.

[39] Chris Thornhill, *A Sociology of Constitutions: Constitutions and State Legitimacy in Historical-Sociological Perspective* (Cambridge: Cambridge University Press, 2011), 149.

[40] D. W. Jones, *War and Economy in the Age of William III and Marlborough* (London: Blackwell, 1988), 18–21.

[41] Murphy, *Origins of English Financial Markets*, 43.

[42] For detailed analysis see Zahedieh, 'Overseas Expansion and Trade in the Seventeenth Century'; Jacob M. Price and P. G. E. Clemens, 'A Revolution of Scale in Overseas Trade: British Firms in the Chesapeake Trade, 1675–1775' (1987) 47 *Journal of Economic History* 1.

generated a vibrant secondary market both for the tickets themselves and in the interest payments attached to them.[43]

Whether, or to what extent, these developments can be linked to the events of 1688, the financial revolution of the 1690s had a profound impact on constitutional politics.[44] The radical increase in taxation, the creation of a (long-term) national debt on an unprecedented scale, and the growth of a sizeable public administration were developments that laid the foundations of Britain's 'fiscal-military' state,[45] a state capable of fighting large wars and raising the resources needed to pay for them. 'The public fisc was the basis for state expansion and empire building.'[46] If there is a revolutionary moment in the course of early-modern British history it is to be found here, Pocock argues, in the creation of a standing army[47] to fight big wars and the institution of a system of public credit capable of maintaining it.[48] The process was nation building (and, in the end, regime stabilizing) in two senses. First, the debt was now recognized as binding the state rather than the Crown.[49] This had the effect of making Parliament increasingly not only the watchdog of government but part of the government itself.[50] For Adam Smith, looking back at this period and always with an eye on the money, this was the crucial feature of the constitutional settlement. The Revolution, he said, 'brought in a new [royal] family which as the royal demesnes were entirely alienated depended wholly upon taxes, and were obliged to court the people for them. Ever since, the kings revenue tho' much greater than it was then depends so much on the concurrence of the Parliament that it never can endanger the liberty of the nation.'[51]

[43] Murphy, *Origins of English Financial Markets*, 58–59; Carruthers, *City of Capital*, 76.

[44] Julian Hoppitt, *A Land of Liberty? England 1689–1727* (Oxford: Oxford University Press, 2000), 123–30.

[45] Brewer, *Sinews of Power*, xvii. See also P. G. M. Dickson, *The Financial Revolution in England: A Study in the Development of Public Credit, 1688–1756* (London: Macmillan, 1967).

[46] Carruthers, *City of Capital*, 83.

[47] Another defeat for the republicans who, following Machiavelli, preferred a citizen army or militia. The creation of a standing army was a hugely controversial issue at the time.

[48] Pocock, 'The Significance of 1688', 123. See also J. G. A. Pocock, 'The Varieties of Whiggism from Exclusion to Reform: A History of Ideology and Discourse' in Pocock, *Virtue, Commerce, and History*, 230, where 1698 is pinpointed as the key 'moment' and William III identified as 'a revolutionary actor in the history of British monarchy' for obliging 'his new kingdoms to reorganize their military, financial, and political structures in order to achieve effective participation in continental and imperial warfare'.

[49] Carruthers, *City of Capital*, 73,

[50] Brewer, *Sinews of Power*, 70, 159; Braddick, *State Formation in Early Modern England*, 266.

[51] Adam Smith, *Lectures on Jurisprudence* (1766 Report), 62 (Indianapolis: Liberty Fund, eds. R. L. Meek, D. D. Raphael and P. G. Stein, 1982).

Second, the government was now in a position to commit credibly to its debt obligations, thereby securing the rights of creditors and encouraging more lending to the government.[52] The existence of public credit on such an unprecedented scale made people the creditors of their government. Large numbers of people subscribed to shares, and the companies loaned their money to the government. Standing to lose personally and directly if the regime failed, the public now literally had a stake in the survival of their government. 'The state's financial system was more than just an extractive machine, an engine of state, because it helped build up a political constituency in support of the post-1688 Protestant regime.'[53]

These fiscal reforms changed the way that government did business. But they also reworked the relationship between state and subject. The post-1689 regimes managed over time to engender a sense of stability.[54] Although this was precarious at times,[55] this success contributed to the process by which political debate became more civilized. The existential sting surrounding seventeenth-century argument was gradually drawn. In time, ultimate questions about sovereignty and legitimacy were replaced by, or subsumed within, second-order questions about money, trade, the army, public debt and corruption. Debate had stopped being fundamental and became constitutional. Contemporaries became less concerned about conceptual matters – the 'hardware' of the state – and more interested in questions of institutional architecture and political culture – the 'software' of government.[56] The pace of commercial change produced a dynamic and fluid society, with little sense of solid foundations and where *sensibility* (towards one's surrounding environment) and *artifice* (relations that were 'more opaque, more mediated, more dependent on representations') were defining features.[57] These were reflected in a new

[52] Douglass C. North and Barry R. Weingast, 'Constitutions and Commitment: The Evolution of Institutions Governing Public Choice in Seventeenth-Century England' (1989) 49 *Journal of Economic History* 803; Ron Harris, 'Could the Crown Credibly Commit to Respecting Its Charters? England, 1558–1640' in D'Maris Coffmann, Adrian Leonard and Larry Neal (eds.), *Questioning Credible Commitment: Perspectives on the Rise of Financial Capitalism* (Cambridge: Cambridge University Press, 2013).

[53] Carruthers, *City of Capital*, 87.

[54] See, e.g., Linda Colley, *Britons: Forging a Nation 1707–1837* (London: Pimlico, 1992).

[55] Particularly so, perhaps, in the early years of William III's reign and during the Jacobite rebellions of 1715, and perhaps also 1745.

[56] Pocock, *Machiavellian Moment*, 401–402: 'During the late seventeenth and the eighteenth centuries ... Western political and social thought passed from its post-medieval to its early modern stage.'

[57] Dror Wahrman, *The Making of the Modern Self: Identity and Culture in Eighteenth-Century England* (New Haven: Yale University Press, 2004), 186, 210.

style of political debate.[58] Britain had entered its coffee house phase[59] and developed a buzzy but well-tempered culture and language of manners.[60] Addison and Steele, writing in new journals like the *Tatler*, *Spectator* and *Guardian*,[61] exemplified the new politics of anti-enthusiasm, of polish and style accompanied by a morality of moderation – the stuff of gentlemanly conversation.[62] They 'preached the virtues of gentility and politeness as an antidote to the vagaries of opinion and the fury of faction'.[63] Shaftesbury elaborated this mode of engagement at the philosophical level, arguing that true politeness entailed the self-conscious cultivation of naturally benevolent sentiments and tracing a vision 'of politics and culture that replaced godly and courtly understandings with a public gentlemanly one'.[64] Satire was one of the new culture's characteristic styles, perfected by Defoe and Swift to express the political values of that new entity 'The Town'.[65] Not that eighteenth-century debate was entirely free from the concerns of the previous era. The self-conscious anti-seventeenth-century nature of this engagement reveals how much that debate took place against the background of seventeenth-century religious and constitutional disturbances. The language of politeness developed as a response to the earlier period's political and religious zealotry.[66] Eighteenth-century

[58] Nicholas Phillipson, 'Politics and Politeness in the Reigns of Anne and the Early Hanoverians' in Pocock, *Varieties of British Political Thought.*

[59] Steve Pincus, '"Coffee Politicians Does Create": Coffeehouses and Restoration Political Culture' (1995) 67 *Journal of Modern History* 807.

[60] 'Manners', Burke was later to write, 'are of more importance than laws … they aid morals, they supply them, or they totally destroy them.' Edmund Burke, *Letters on a Regicide Peace* (1796) quoted in Pocock, 'Virtues, Rights, and Manners', 49.

[61] This was part of a revolution in the press made possible by the government's failure to renew the Licensing Act in 1695.

[62] Iain Hampsher-Monk, 'From Virtue to Politeness' in Martin van Gelderen and Quentin Skinner (eds.), *Republicanism: A Shared European Heritage, Vol. II The Values of Republicanism in Early Modern Europe* (Cambridge: Cambridge University Press, 2002).

[63] Nicholas Phillipson, *David Hume: The Philosopher as Historian* (Harmondsworth: Penguin, 2011), 24.

[64] Lawrence E. Klein, *Shaftesbury and the Culture of Politeness: Moral Discourse and Cultural Politics in Early Eighteenth-Century England* (Cambridge: Cambridge University Press, 1994), 21.

[65] Nicholas Phillipson, 'Propriety, Property and Prudence: David Hume and the Defence of the Revolution' in Nicholas Phillipson and Quentin Skinner (eds.), *Political Discourse in Early Modern Britain* (Cambridge: Cambridge University Press, 1993), 302–312; Roy Porter, *English Society in the 18th Century* (Harmondsworth: Penguin, 1990), 234–235; Pocock, 'The Varieties of Whiggism', 230–239. Hume calls Swift's writings the 'first polite prose we have': 'Of Civil Liberty' in Hume, *Essays Moral, Political and Literary* (Indianapolis: Liberty Fund, ed. Eugene J. Miller, 1985), 91.

[66] Phillipson, *David Hume*, 22.

theories of political freedom and the rule of law took shape, then, under the shadow of the attempts (as contemporaries saw them) at autocracy under Cromwell and James II.[67] As such, this was a local manifestation of a European project of 'inducing Europeans to substitute a culture based on manners and commerce for one given to disputing its religious beliefs and warring over them'.[68]

In a sense, post-1688 developments proved both Hobbes and the republicans right, albeit in ways they did not foresee and for reasons they had not guessed at. 'England was leaving the world of civil and social war and entering that of European reason of state . . . It was the end of Hobbesian politics; or rather, it was the victory of Leviathan.'[69] The state had become (more) sovereign: a juridical entity that brooked no internal competitor and whose structuring dynamics were obedience in return for protection. (A process that the successful defeat of the Jacobite rebellions of 1715 and 1745 helped to cement.) But it had done so (*pace* Hobbes) on the basis of a balance of functionally independent governing institutions (Crown, Parliament, courts) and through the agency of money and war. And despite the absence of a grand constitutional settlement (*pace* the republicans), England had become dynamic and assertive (and more cohesively Protestant), particularly in its foreign policy and commercial strategy. Certainly, both Hobbes and the republicans would have appreciated one significant internal ramification of these developments, namely the increased identification of the people with their state. It was much less far-fetched to imagine that the acts of the state were also (or really) the acts of the public collective. It was not that Hobbes's rulebook for civil rule had been adopted. It was more that the mutual indebtedness of government and governed, in the context of overall stability and success, served over time to induce the necessary sense of political unity. Government bonds had produced – as it was at least part of their intention to – political bonds.[70]

[67] Brewer, *Sinews of Power*, 22.

[68] J. G. A. Pocock, 'European History and the Global Ocean' in Pocock, *Barbarism and Religion, Vol. 4: Barbarians, Savages, and Empires* (Cambridge: Cambridge University Press, 2005).

[69] Pocock, 'The Significance of 1688', 123.

[70] Carruthers, *City of Capital*, chapter 8. See also Charles de Secondat, Baron de Montesquieu, *The Spirit of the Laws* (1748) (Cambridge: Cambridge University Press, eds. Anne M. Cohler, Basia C. Miller and Harold S. Stone, 1989), 327: 'This nation [Britain] would have secured credit because it would borrow from itself and would pay to itself. It could happen that it would undertake something beyond the forces natural to it and would assert against its enemies an immense fictional wealth that the trust and the nature of its government would make real. In order to preserve its liberty, it would borrow from

From cosmic drama to cosmic irony

Gerald Postema argues that Hume is 'pivotal in the development of British legal theory'.[71] A similar case can be made for Hume's importance for British constitutional thought. Hobbes and the republican theorists examined in previous chapters still belong as much to the pre-modern world as the modern. There remains something alien about their writing, for all its undoubted brilliance and subsequent influence (the republicans on the United States Constitution especially;[72] Hobbes everywhere). Hume was a theorist of modern commercial society. He set out to explain the dynamics of social order in a new world distinguished by its complexity. How do we maintain social and political institutions, he asked, when things are too complicated for any one person or institution to command or even to understand? How can laws exist without a legislator? Hume's answers resonated through the eighteenth-century debate and were a notable influence on James Madison[73] and Edmund Burke,[74] whose political writings are examined in the next chapter. As such, his work provides one of the main intellectual sources for understanding the development of the British constitution in perhaps its most formative stage.[75]

Hume's theory took shape not only against the background of the financial and constitutional revolution but also against the creation of the new British state. Hume can be read as a North Briton 'committed to a restatement of English culture in such terms that it would become British and that Scotsmen would make their own way in it'.[76] His analysis of English

its subjects, and its subjects, who would see that its credit would be lost if it were conquered, would have a further motive to make efforts to defend its liberty.'

[71] Gerald J. Postema, *Bentham and the Common Law Tradition* (Oxford: Oxford University Press, 1986) 81. See also Knud Haakonssen, *The Science of a Legislator: The Natural Jurisprudence of David Hume and Adam Smith* (Cambridge: Cambridge University Press, 1981), 21.

[72] See, e.g., Pocock, *Machiavellian Moment*.

[73] See, e.g., Paul A. Rahe, *Republics Ancient and Modern: Classical Republicanism and the American Revolution* (Chapel Hill: University of North Carolina Press, 1992), 568–588.

[74] Phillipson, 'Politics and Politeness', 243: Hume's 'sceptical language of manners ... would be used by Burke to analyze the causes of the French Revolution, the catastrophe which brought about the destruction of the early modern state.'

[75] Martin Loughlin, *Public Law and Political Theory* (Oxford: Oxford University Press, 1992).

[76] J. G. A. Pocock, 'Hume and the American Revolution: The Dying Thoughts of a North Briton' in Pocock, *Virtue, Commerce, and History*, 128. See also John Robertson, 'The Scottish Enlightenment at the Limits of the Civic Tradition' in Istvan Hont and Michael Ignatieff (eds.), *Wealth and Virtue: The Shaping of Political Economy in the Scottish Enlightenment* (Cambridge: Cambridge University Press, 1983).

constitutional politics and history is that of a generally sympathetic, always intrigued, partial outsider, a position for which Hume's sceptical, urbane style is particularly well suited. The importance attached in his writing to sympathy, opinion and moderation fits the refashioned political culture of the early eighteenth century.[77] And, like other writers of the period, he is always in conversation with seventeenth-century predecessors, above all with Hobbes,[78] but also republicans (especially Harrington[79]) and ancient constitutionalists. Hume disagreed with their theories, but elements of each find their way into his own, albeit often subsumed or sublimated within a very different political vision. Virtue is replaced by interest.[80] Cosmic drama transmutes into cosmic irony.[81] Gothic nostalgia is exorcised by the 'enlightened spirit of the age'.[82] And Hobbes's constructivist absolutism rejected for a philosophy of evolution and moderation.[83]

Since our inquiry is juridical rather than philosophical, less attention will be paid to Hume's account of knowledge,[84] human nature (reason and the passions)[85] or his moral theory (including his distinctive account of justice)[86] than his constitutional theory. Before turning to his writings on commerce and jealousy of trade, especially germane to reason of state

77 Phillipson, 'Propriety, Property and Prudence', 304.

78 Hume, *History of England, vol. 6*, ch. LXII, 153: 'Hobbes's politics are fitted only to promote tyranny, and his ethics to encourage licentiousness. Though an enemy to religion, he partakes nothing of the spirit of scepticism; but is as positive and dogmatical as if human reason, and his reason in particular, could attain a thorough conviction in these subjects.'

79 Hume, 'Idea of a Perfect Commonwealth' in *Essays*, 514: 'All plans of government, which suppose great reformation in the manners of mankind, are plainly imaginary. Of this nature, are the *Republic* of PLATO, and the *Utopia* of Sir THOMAS MORE. The OCEANA is the only valuable model of a commonwealth, that has yet been offered to the public.' The essay contains a sketch of his own ideal state, which is indebted to Harrington. See also Hume, *History of England, vol. 6*, 153: 'Harrington's Oceana was well adapted to that age, when the plans of imaginary republics were daily subjects of debate and conversation ... The idea, however, of a perfect and immortal commonwealth will always be found as chimerical as that of a perfect and immortal man.'

80 Pocock, 'Virtues, Rights, and Manners', 48–50; Hampsher-Monk, 'From Virtue to Politeness'.

81 John Vladimir Price, *The Ironic Hume* (Austin: University of Texas Press, 1965), 102.

82 Hume, 'Of the Original Contract' in *Essays*, 477.

83 Hume, 'That Politics May Be Reduced to a Science' in *Essays*, 31: 'I would only persuade men not to contend, as if they were fighting *pro aris & focis* [for our altars and our hearths], and change a good constitution into a bad one, by the violence of their factions.'

84 David Hume, *A Treatise of Human Nature* (Harmondsworth: Penguin, ed. Ernest C. Mossner, 1985), Book I; David Hume, *An Enquiry Concerning Human Understanding* (Cambridge: Cambridge University Press, ed. Stephen Buckle, 2007).

85 Hume, *Treatise*, Book II. 86 Hume, *Treatise*, Book III.

matters, his writings on constitutions generally and on the British constitution in particular will be examined. As a political philosopher, Hume 'set himself to correct the excesses of vulgar Whiggism', particularly 'with respect to the contrast between the "free" government of Britain and the absolute monarchies of the continent'.[87] He distanced himself from that element within contemporary political culture that assumed a black-and-white conception of liberty in which 'English liberty' was set against 'French despotism'.[88] By contrast, Hume's perspective was that of a citizen of the republic of letters,[89] taking a European view of English politics and history.[90] His theory makes far more room for the contextual, the imperfect, even the happenstance, in politics.[91] It is a nuanced approach in which things tend to be measured by degrees rather than absolutes. All governments are a blend of authority and liberty.[92] Freedom exists on a continuum and, as such, is traded off against other values (survival, stability, peace, prosperity, etc.). This is very much the logic of the constitutionalism of the 'second best'.[93]

This perspective opened up the possibility of a comparative science of constitutions, a method that brought him into conversation with continental writers such as Montesquieu. It also meant that Hume could position himself as an advocate of moderation,[94] as someone above national and party prejudice.[95] His strong support for modern commercial society[96] – of trade, liberty and learning[97] – was matched by his

[87] Duncan Forbes, *Hume's Philosophical Politics* (Cambridge: Cambridge University Press, 1975), 153.

[88] Forbes, *Hume's Philosophical Politics*, 142–143. See also Pocock, 'Varieties of Whiggism'.

[89] John Robertson, *The Case for the Enlightenment: Scotland and Naples 1680–1760* (Cambridge: Cambridge University Press, 2005), 39–44.

[90] Forbes, *Hume's Philosophical Politics*, 140. See also Pocock, 'Hume and the American Revolution', 125–127.

[91] J. G. A. Pocock, 'David Hume: The *Essays* as Contemporary History' in Pocock, *Barbarism and Religion, Vol. 2: Narratives of Civil Government* (Cambridge: Cambridge University Press, 1999), 186.

[92] Hume, 'Of the Origin of Government' in *Essays*, 40.

[93] Adrian Vermeule, 'Hume's Second-Best Constitutionalism' (2003) 70 *University of Chicago Law Journal* 421.

[94] Hume, 'That Politics May Be Reduced to a Science', 27.

[95] Forbes, *Hume's Philosophical Politics*, 136.

[96] Hume, 'Of Interest' in *Essays*, 301: 'Without commerce, the state must consist chiefly of landed gentry, whose prodigality and expence make a continual demand for borrowing; and of peasants, who have no sums to supply that demand.' See also 'Of Money' in *Essays*, 293.

[97] Pocock, 'Hume and the American Revolution', 129.

hatred of superstition and enthusiasm, whether religious or political.[98] It also led Hume into a historical mode of inquiry. The urge to explain what was distinctive and distinctively 'modern' about European politics led Hume to trawl back through the past, not only, and most obviously, in his six-volume *History of England* but also in his political *Essays* and even his philosophy. (Nicholas Phillipson calls Hume 'the most historically minded of philosophers.'[99]) This historical perspective lends itself not only to an appreciation of the importance of contingency and change in human affairs[100] – and the related belief that 'the world is still too young to fix many general truths in politics'[101] – but also an awareness of the difficulty of controlling human affairs through legislation.

> Did one generation of men go off the state at once, and another succeed, as in the case with silk-worms and butterflies, the new race, if they had sense enough to choose their government, which surely is never the case with men, might voluntarily, and by general consent, establish their own form of civil polity, without any regard to the laws or precedents, which prevailed among their ancestors. But as human society is in perpetual flux, one man every hour going out of the world, another coming into it, it is necessary, in order to preserve stability in government, that the new brood should conform themselves to the established constitution, and nearly follow the path which their fathers, treading in the footsteps of theirs, had marked out to them.[102]

Note '*nearly* follow the path' of their fathers. Hume clearly accepts the inevitability and in some cases desirability of change.[103] But the overriding message is one of continuity in social and political life. The direct target of the essay from which this passage derives is the Hobbesian and Lockean model of the social contract that gives birth to the constitution

[98] Hume, 'Of Parties in General' and 'Of Enthusiasm and Superstition' in *Essays*. See also Hume, *Dialogues Concerning Natural Religion* (Cambridge: Cambridge University Press, ed. Dorothy Coleman, 2007).

[99] Phillipson, *David Hume*, 4. See also J. G. A. Pocock, 'The History of Great Britain: Hume's Modern History' in Pocock, *Barbarism and Religion, Vol. 2.*

[100] Hume, 'Of Civil Liberty', 89: 'Such mighty revolutions have happened in human affairs, and so many events have arisen contrary to the expectation of the ancients, that they are sufficient to beget the suspicion of still further changes.'

[101] 'Of Civil Liberty', 87.

[102] Hume, 'Of the Original Contract' in *Essays*, 466–467.

[103] The quoted passage continues: 'Some innovations must necessarily have place in every human institution, and it is happy where the enlightened genius of the age give these a direction to the side of reason, liberty, and justice.'

and explains authority and allegiance. People do not in fact choose their form of government – or at least almost never in the sense that the social contract model assumes.[104] Instead of an abstract and rationalist theory of the state, Hume provides a genetic story about how societies get to government, in which institutions are built on top of existing institutions.[105] It is a theory that accounts for social development. Law and government are cultural artefacts: 'Though a republic should be barbarous, it necessarily, by an infallible operation, gives rise to LAW, even before mankind have made any considerable advances in the other sciences. From law arises security: From security curiosity: And from curiosity knowledge.' The essay 'Of the Rise and Progress of the Arts and Sciences' is characteristic in the way it includes constitutional form, governing institutions, social and economic development, even social psychology, in its analytical framework. The argument that stems from it connects law to government structures and material conditions. Without laws, Hume argues, there can be no social progress. Laws necessarily arise in republics.[106] They can arise in monarchies too, but only through imitation.[107] Those who succeed in republics are likely to be seen as useful; in monarchies it is those who can make themselves agreeable. Sciences suit the temper of the former, the polite arts the latter. But national stories are complicated by international relations, as interactions between polities can be crucial: 'nothing is more favourable to the rise of politeness and learning, than a number of neighbouring and independent states, connected together by commerce and policy'.[108] This science of politics produces a more general political message: to govern a society through general laws 'is a work of so great difficulty, that no human genius, however comprehensive, is able, by the mere dint of reason and reflection, to effect it'. It is only the united 'judgments of many', a science of prudence, which is capable of doing so: 'Experience must guide their labour: Time must bring it to perfection' through a process of 'trials and experiments'.[109]

[104] Hume, 'Of the Original Contract', 472: 'Let not the establishment of the Revolution deceive us, or make us so much in love with a philosophical origin to government, as to imagine all others monstrous and irregular.'
[105] Postema, *Bentham and the Common Law Tradition*, 84.
[106] 'Of the Rise of Arts and Sciences', 118.
[107] 'Of the Rise of Arts and Sciences', 125.
[108] 'Of the Rise of Arts and Sciences', 118. (Hume's italics removed.)
[109] 'Of the Rise of Arts and Sciences', 124.

Law and politics of opinion

Government, in Hume's view, is not grounded on consent but on opinion: 'as FORCE is always on the side of the governed, the governors have nothing to support them but opinion. It is therefore, on opinion only that government is founded'.[110] Man is naturally social, but political society is an artificial form[111] whose purpose is to administer justice. States begin as little better than collections of robber bands. 'Camps are the true mothers of cities'.[112] Working in something like state-of-nature mode, Hume hypothesizes that things begin when a strong man takes over a social group during a war.[113] His long rule over the people, combined with their innate 'love of dominion', makes them accustomed to submitting to his authority and they come, in time, to perceive the benefits of peaceful coexistence. Stability of the governing structure only comes about, however, once the regime has a regular income to support it, after which point submission is no longer a matter of choice for most of the community but is 'rigorously exacted by the authority of the supreme magistrate'.[114] This pretty brutal, 'realist' account of the origins of government is meant to support the claim that it is habit that grounds our allegiance to governing structures: 'Habit soon consolidates what other principles of human nature had imperfectly founded; and men, once accustomed to obedience, never think of departing from that path, in which they and their ancestors have constantly trod, and to which they are confined by so many urgent and visible motives.'[115]

Government derives its authority by convention and the populace acquiesces in that rule by its own convention.[116] The passage of time is critical. Effective government rests on a process that combines the right proportions of memory and amnesia, of remembering the benefits brought by the regime and forgetting the moments of force, whether

110 Hume, 'Of the First Principles of Government' in *Essays*, 32.

111 Artificial because it is not natural for men 'to look farther than their nearest friends and acquaintances. 'Tis no less certain, that 'tis impossible for men to consult their interest in so effectual a manner, as by universal and inflexible observance of the rules of justice, by which alone they can preserve society': *Treatise*, Book III, 586.

112 *Treatise*, Book III, 592.

113 Compare *Treatise*, Book III, 591: 'I assert the rudiments of government to arise from quarrels, not among men of the same society, but among those of different societies.'

114 Hume, 'Of the Origin of Government', 39–40.

115 Hume, 'Of the Origin of Government', 39.

116 Russell Hardin, *David Hume: Moral and Political Theorist* (Oxford: Oxford University Press, 2007), 81.

arising from conquest or revolution, which brought it to power in the first place.[117] While this origins story may be bleak, its effects are anything but. European states have developed into complex juridical structures, a 'vast apparatus of our government' whose ultimate aim is to administer justice.[118] It makes little difference, Hume thought, whether the state is (more) monarchical or (more) republican.[119] Other writers of the Scottish Enlightenment considered these differences more significant. Adam Ferguson, for one, while also a believer in constitutional monarchy, tried to articulate a more republican vision aimed at stopping the ominous dialectic that he saw operating in commercial modernity between wealth, prosperity and culture on the one hand and apathy and decline on the other.[120] But it was Hume's view that, through a process of emulation and cross-fertilization, states have converged on a similar model of government under law. It is successful since the rule of law, once it has taken root, is a 'hardy plant' as 'being profitable to every mortal' it is an achievement unlikely to be forgotten.[121] Conventions help to preserve the benefits resulting from this process of trial and error and help stabilize the polity. This is perhaps most true in the case of 'fundamental laws'[122] that guard against those seventeenth-century spectres of revolution and civil war on the one hand and arbitrary power on the other.[123]

This account of constitutional conventions is consistent with Hume's emphasis on the importance of accident in history and his more general

[117] Phillipson, 'Politics and Politeness', 243: 'the natural disposition of human beings to *forget* how they acquired their ideas of interest, their proneness to fantasy, their extraordinary vulnerability to priestcraft, constituted both the greatest strength and weakness of human nature. This was the great theme of the *History of England*'.

[118] 'Of the Origin of Government', 37. And in so doing change the conditions in which men operate by ensuring that there are at least some (the governors) whose immediate interest is to do justice. See also *Treatise*, 588: 'as 'tis impossible to change or correct any thing material in our nature, the utmost we can do is to change our circumstances and situation, and render the observance of the laws of justice our nearest interest, and their violation our most remote. But this being impracticable with respect of all mankind, it can only take place with respect to a few, whom we thus immediately interest in the execution of justice.'

[119] See, e.g., 'Of Civil Liberty', 94–95.

[120] Adam Ferguson, 'Of the Separation of Departments, Professions and Tasks Resulting from the Progress of Arts in Society' in Ferguson, *Collected Essays* (Kyoto: Rinsen Book, ed. Yasuo Amoh, 1996), 142. See also Lisa Hill, 'Adam Ferguson and the Paradox of Progress and Decline' (1997) 18 *History of Political Thought* 677.

[121] Hume, 'Rise and Progress of Arts and Sciences' in *Essays*, 125.

[122] *Treatise*, 612.

[123] Andrew Sabl, *Hume's Politics: Coordination and Crisis in the History of England* (Princeton: Princeton University Press, 2012), 33.

account of the way that constitutional meaning can be said to unfold over time. Conventions, he argued, often arise by accident and solidify as they come to be seen as useful, becoming essential to political coordination, the *sine qua non* of constitutional politics.[124] Hume saw conventions relating to hereditary monarchy and Magna Carta as performing essential structuring roles of this sort within the British constitution, alongside additions such as *habeas corpus* and the Bill of Rights. Note that despite the central role it gives to history, the theory is not just another version of ancient constitutionalism. Hume was critical of those who saw it as their goal to reinstate the good old law. Let those who call for a return to the feudal constitution sign themselves over to a local baron, he said, 'and by submitting to slavery under him, acquire some protection to themselves; together with the power of exercising rapine and oppression over their inferior slaves and villains. This was the condition of the commons among their remote ancestors.'[125] The absence of nostalgia is striking and refreshing. The barons were a pack of criminals[126] and feudalism another name for warlordism. Just as for Harrington the Gothic constitution was nothing but a 'wrestling match' between king and nobles,[127] Hume saw it as 'an inconsistent fabric, whose jarring and discordant parts must soon destroy each other'.[128] Hume goes further and contests the plausibility of the very idea of an ancient *constitution*. Looking back, there was only 'an unlimited prerogative power in the king, and unlimited power of resistance in the feudal nobility, and an unlimited reverence for law which there was no means of enforcing but by violence'.[129]

The attack on ancient constitutionalism is part of a strategy to demystify authority. What we value in old things is the use they have in the present. But the project goes beyond a refusal to be enslaved by the past. Hume's constitution is one equipped for the needs of the times. Countering the civic republican critique of luxury and modernity advanced by Rousseau and Ferguson, he argued that warrior states like Sparta were both undesirable and obsolete, whereas the ages of refinement 'brought by modern

[124] David Miller, *Philosophy and Ideology in Hume's Political Thought* (Oxford: Oxford University Press, 1981), 160: 'Unlike most of his contemporaries, who regarded the British form of government as obviously the best, and as far superior to French "tyranny", Hume regarded it as a lucky and somewhat precarious historical accident. It was a system to be treasured while it existed.'

[125] Hume, 'Of the Coalition of Parties' in *Essays*, 497–498.

[126] See, e.g., Hume, *The History of England, vol. 2* (Indianapolis: Liberty Press, 1983), 331.

[127] See the discussion in Chapter 3.

[128] David Hume, *The History of England, vol. 5* (Indianapolis: Liberty Press, 1983), 59.

[129] Pocock, 'Hume's Modern History', 204.

commerce were 'both the happiest and the most virtuous'.[130] Government in a modern commercial society needs to be dynamic. It also must be capable of disciplining the passions and, as such, acting as a civilizing agent. We can see this at work, he says, if we look at what has happened over time on the margins of the constitution. The feudal 'constitution' was marked by the absolute or non-negotiable quality of its fundamental positions and provided no basis for reconciling them. The consequence was a frequent resort to extra-legal violence. The modern constitution reflects a more stable balance between competing claims of authority (monarchy) and liberty (Magna Carta and the Bill of Rights). It also has the capacity to prevent abuses that arise from a surfeit of liberty on the one hand and an excess of authority on the other, before either can become serious. Modern constitutions, which contain at their heart a balance or division of governmental powers, thus reduce the need for both prerogative and rebellion. Constitutions also change the character of power, from the 'barefaced' but weak powers of the feudal prince,[131] to the institutionalized and limited but massive power of the modern imperial state. The modern state offers its rulers power unimaginable to the feudal overlord or Renaissance prince. But the congealed force of the conventions that sustain them means that the modern prince, dependent on opinion, has to work within those constraints, acting in accordance with conventions rather than flouting them.

Hume approached prerogative power with the same equanimity and sense of historical sweep with which he studied just about everything else in the social and political world. He defined the field narrowly, as a limited set of defined executive powers – 'prerogatives' – in the manner of Hale, rather than a catch-all and extra-legal category of 'prerogative', in the manner of Locke. He did acknowledge, however, a more expansive notion of necessity in the emergency context, remarking that 'in every government, necessity, when real, supersedes all laws, and levels all limitations'.[132] In principle, though, even when defined narrowly, prerogative powers were suspect. Not only because they affect the rights of subjects,[133]

[130] Roy Porter, *Enlightenment: Britain and the Creation of the Modern World* (London: Allen Lane, 2000), 247–248.

[131] *Macbeth*, Act III, scene 1: 'though I could/ With barefaced power sweep him from my sight / And bid my will avouch it'.

[132] Hume, *History of England, vol. 5*, 329.

[133] Hume, *History of England, vol. 5*, 126: 'an eternal jealousy must be preserved against the sovereign, and no discretionary powers must ever be entrusted to him, by which the property or personal liberty of any subject can be affected'.

but also because they make claim to do the sorts of things now regarded as the province of legislation. As such, prerogatives are 'not discretionary powers so much as powers to rule by fiat'.[134] In practice, though, modern trends in government and society had both made prerogative less significant as a legal category and also made its exercise more regular. The political rudeness and institutional crudeness of ancient societies meant that they had a need for wide-ranging discretionary powers held in the person of the ruler. The normative and bureaucratic complexity of modern government structures, in which the idea of the rule of law has been institutionalized, depersonalize prerogative decision-making and tend to regularize and limit its use.

There are some parallels here with Blackstone's account of the British constitution, which is more familiar to lawyers, although these should not be overdrawn. Both wrote for the intelligent lay reader and for the legislator,[135] aiming to give a defence of the constitutional status quo. (Although neither found it a simple task to justify the Glorious Revolution.[136]) Both distrusted political enthusiasm, including those who made excessive claims for liberty, such as the populist radical John Wilkes.[137] Both opposed state-of-nature arguments on intellectual and political grounds and sought to refashion natural law into something more historical than metaphysical:[138] a society's laws could be called 'natural' if they were a

[134] Clement Fatovic, *Outside the Law: Emergency and Executive Power* (Baltimore: Johns Hopkins University Press, 2009), 114.

[135] Blackstone said that his work should furnish guidance to 'such as are, or may hereafter become, legislators': *Commentaries* IV, 11. Wilfred Prest, *William Blackstone: Law and Letters in Eighteenth Century England* (Oxford: Oxford University Press, 2008), 115: 'In short, the aim [of the *Commentaries*] was to present a broadly humane, liberal, and "scientific" overview, far removed from the arid, inchoate technicalities, the "mystic, dark, discordant lore" of traditional common law learning.' See also David Lieberman, *The Province of Legislation Determined: Legal Theory in Eighteenth-Century Britain*, chapter 2.

[136] Michael Lobban, 'Blackstone and the Science of Law' (1987) 30 *Historical Journal* 311, 327.

[137] Blackstone criticized 'over-zealous republicans' for formulating a sweeping doctrine of resistance. The doctrine was 'productive of anarchy, and (in consequence) equally fatal to civil liberty as tyranny itself' (*Commentaries* I, 244). As an MP, Blackstone said in a debate that Wilkes was guilty of 'an impious libel, with intent to blaspheme the Almighty God': Prest, *William Blackstone*, 237. Edmund Burke, by contrast, supported Wilkes on principled grounds: see 'Thoughts on the Cause of the Present Discontents' in Burke, *Pre-Revolutionary Writings* (Cambridge: Cambridge University Press, ed. Ian Harris, 1993), 163–166.

[138] Peter N. Miller, *Defining the Common Good: Empire, Religion and Philosophy in Eighteenth-Century Britain* (Cambridge: Cambridge University Press, 1994), 137.

good fit with that society.[139] However, while both shared the view that the British constitution owed its strength to the balance it had struck over time between authority and liberty,[140] their overall vision was quite different. Hume analysed political structures and institutions in terms of their appropriateness for modern commercial society. Blackstone articulated a version of ancient constitutionalism that carried more than a trace of nostalgia for the Gothic constitution, positions we have already seen Hume deride.

Blackstone's account of the balance struck in relation to prerogative power is particularly illuminating. In essence, his position here echoed the constitutional royalists of the previous century – and, through them, the idea of a Gothic balance. Blackstone claims that while the royal prerogative is not legally speaking entirely off-limits, in that its exercise is constrained by the ancient constitution and is to be used for the public good,[141] it amounts to a despotic power that operates in a space beyond the reach of normal law: 'in the exertion of lawful prerogative, the king is and ought to be absolute; that is, so far absolute, that there is no legal authority that can either delay or resist him.'[142] Edmund Burke, by contrast, writing in exactly the same period, said that prerogative was 'dead and rotten'. The Crown's authority now rested, he argued, on what we would call soft power but which he called 'Influence': 'an influence, which operated without noise and without violence, an influence which is converted the very antagonist, into the instrument, of power, which contained in itself a perpetual principle of growth and renovation'.[143] It was not for nothing, then, that Blackstone's political opponents called him 'a prerogative lawyer'.[144] Juxtaposed with this expansionary account of prerogative is an equally inflated conception of Parliament as absolute, despotic, even omnipotent.[145] The best way of trying to make sense of these apparently irreconcilable positions is to posit a division of labour between Crown and Parliament in which the former controls 'this nation's intercourse with foreign nations' and the latter 'it's own domestic government and

139 Willman, 'Blackstone and the "Theoretical Perfection" of English Law', 50; Lieberman, *Province of Legislation Determined*, 45.

140 *Commentaries* I, 155.

141 *Commentaries* I, 244.

142 *Commentaries* I, 243.

143 'Present Discontents', 123.

144 Prest, *William Blackstone*, 246. Some later commentators were no more generous. Harold Laski said that Blackstone's statements on the British Crown 'seem rather the occasion for irony than for serious political speculation': 'The Responsibility of the State in England' (1919) 32 *Harvard Law Review* 447, 447.

145 *Commentaries* I, 160.

civil polity'.[146] But this can at best be a very partial resolution, becoming increasingly less tenable with the interpenetration of the foreign and domestic, a feature of modern commercial society that we examine in detail in the next chapter.

In this unsuccessful attempt at reconciling an expansive royal prerogative and a sovereign Parliament, Blackstone unwittingly reveals the unsuitability of his Gothic and seventeenth-century sources. Claims of absolute jurisdiction cannot easily be reconciled with competing claims of absolute jurisdiction without resorting to conflict. His failure to make sense of prerogative demonstrates the accuracy of Hume's diagnosis of the structural weaknesses of Gothic governing structures and the importance of his insight into the impossibility of a modern style of 'civilized' constitutionalism when *any* institution makes too great or open a claim to supremacy. The constitution functions because it has grown up, becoming a system that emphasizes moderation and rejects as adolescent extreme claims about authority and liberty. While ideals surrounding liberty, such as the social contract or fundamental law, might initially sound particularly appealing, it is the hard won – and in the end rather fortuitous – success of the complex whole that counts.[147]

Commerce as an 'affair of state'

Hume recognized the benefits of government, both in its 'crude' form (peace) but also and more particularly in its more developed 'civilized' form. European states, whatever their precise governmental structure, seemed to be moving in the direction of greater freedom, stability and prosperity. 'I must observe, that all kinds of government, free and absolute, seem to have undergone, in modern times, a great change for the better'.[148] The general historical trend was away from superstition[149] and from the princely or baronial politics of ego and aggression towards the 'enlarged and benevolent sentiments' that had begun to characterize the Enlightenment state.[150] But this benign and rather optimistic picture had

[146] *Commentaries* I, 245. See Armitage, *Foundations of Modern International Thought*, 140–141.

[147] See also Vermeule, 'Hume's Second-Best Constitutionalism'.

[148] 'Of Civil Liberty', 93.

[149] Hume, 'Whether the British Government Inclines more to Absolute Monarchy, or to a Republic' in *Essays*, 51: 'Most people, in this island, have divested themselves of all superstitious reverence for names and authority'.

[150] Hume, 'Of the Jealousy of Trade' in *Essays*, 331. See also Montesquieu, *Spirit of the Laws*, 389: 'Since that time princes have had to govern themselves more wisely than they

a darker side. Hume was always aware of the fragility of constitutions, and of the precariousness of the gains of the recent past. This sensitivity did not arise simply out of historical and comparative study, but is also internal to his constitutional theory. A government that lives by opinion, after all, also dies by opinion. Conventions do not belong to the past but are things that have to be constantly lived, restated and reinvented in current political practice. Instead of a single 'ancient' constitution, England might more properly be said to have had several successive constitutions – from the 'settlement of our present plan of liberty' back to a more ancient constitution resting on a balance of forces between kings and nobles and again to a still more ancient constitution.[151] Not that Hume assumes that conventions are necessarily good, although there does seem to be an implicit belief that over time the good – or at least the useful – will win out. Just as 'good' conventions help stabilize and legitimate government, 'bad' conventions can undermine and ultimately destroy a constitution.[152]

Hume is attuned to the potential sites of instability and dysfunction within the British constitution. The balance between republicanism and monarchism on which he thinks the benefits of that constitution depend 'is really', he insists, 'so extremely delicate and uncertain'.[153] It was thus a constitution precariously poised upon a balance 'between monarchical torpidity and a "popular" military tyranny'.[154] He asks, in this mode, whether the British government is more likely to collapse into an absolute monarchy or a full-blown republic. His answer is that the worst outcome would probably be a republic. While he sympathizes with the republican ideal,[155] in reality a republic would open the way to the tyranny of faction, oppression and civil war, whereas absolute monarchy 'is the easiest

themselves would have thought, for it turned out that great acts of authority were so clumsy that experience itself has made known that only goodness of government brings prosperity.'

151 Hume, *History of England, vol. 4*, 345–347. See Eugene F. Miller, 'Hume on Liberty in the Successive English Constitutions' in Nicholas Capaldi and Donald W. Livingstone (eds.), *Liberty in Hume's History of England* (Boston: Kluwer Academic, 1990).

152 Miller, *Defining the Common Good*, 127.

153 Hume, 'Of the Parties of Great Britain' in *Essays*, 64.

154 M. M. Goldsmith, 'Liberty, Virtue, and the Rule of Law' in David Wootton (ed.), *Republicanism, Liberty, and Commercial Society, 1649–1776* (Stanford: Stanford University Press, 1994), 219.

155 He wrote in one of his letters 'I am an American in my Principles' and argued that a virtuous republic is in theory the ideal form of government: see Pocock, 'Hume and the American Revolution', 129–131. David Armitage argues that Hume 'remained firmly within the confines of the republican tradition': 'Empire and Liberty: A Republican Dilemma' in van Gelderen and Skinner, *Republicanism: A Shared European Heritage, Vol. II*, 44.

death, the true Euthanasia of the BRITISH constitution.'[156] Underpinning the essay is the sense that the constitution must 'incline one way or the other, and must end sooner or later in an easy death or a violent one.'[157] The unique balance achieved (or stumbled on) by the post-1689 constitution is constantly under threat from a potentially omnipotent House of Commons. Only the patronage – that is, informal, even corrupt – power that the Crown manages to exercise in Parliament currently prevents fragmentation.[158]

A deeper and more structural critique of the modern state appears in the important essay 'Of Public Credit'. The portrayal of Hume so far has revealed a man more than at home in the context of the eighteenth-century state, welcoming in particular the new world of commerce and refinement, together with the different form of government it entailed. Modern commercial ('refined') societies were better than pre-modern agrarian ('simple') ones.[159] Commerce not only pulls against political absolutism, as developments in France appeared to show.[160] It also militates against extremism of all kinds, including republican ideals of austerity and virtue.[161] Nonetheless, Hume was alive to dangers inherent to the relationship between commerce and politics. He observed that commerce had become for the first time an 'affair of state'.[162] Modern warfare created financial demands on a totally new scale and compelled even reluctant states to concern themselves with trade as a source of income. The international marketplace became crowded with states competing for every seemingly lucrative market. Writing during the unfolding commercial and colonial war between Britain and France, Hume was fiercely critical of such 'jealousy of trade' politics.[163] He feared that commerce had stopped being the gentle (and inadvertent) civilizer of nations, helping to transform 'the warlike worlds of universal monarchy, wars of religion, feudal disorder and the wars of ancient virtue' into 'a European republic of trading states',[164] and was instead fostering 'rivalries as intense as – and perhaps even more uncertain in their outcome than – any earlier forms of

156 'Whether the British Government Inclines More to Absolute Monarchy, or to a Republic', 53.

157 Pocock, 'Hume and the American Revolution', 133.

158 Hume, 'Of the Independency of Parliament' in *Essays*, 45. See also 'Of the First Principles of Government', 35–36.

159 'Of Money', 293. 160 'Of Civil Liberty', 92. 161 'Of Interest'.

162 'Of Civil Liberty', 88. 163 'Of the Jealousy of Trade'.

164 Pocock, 'The Problems of Hanoverian History' in *Barbarism and Religion, Vol. 2*, 169. See also Albert O. Hirschman, *The Passions and the Interests: Political Arguments for Capitalism Before Its Triumph* (Princeton: Princeton University Press, 2013), Part I.

conflict.'[165] As such, the new politics of trade presented a challenge to the Enlightenment project, a central tenet of which was that commerce and the development of civil society was the guarantee against the return of universal monarchy and religious war.[166]

What Hume was taking issue with was the new reason of state politics that had grown up in the context of commercial empire. He wrote at 'the high-water mark of reason of state economics. The policy of national aggrandizement based on transmarine colonies, commercial expansion and naval support had, seemingly, been vindicated and confirmed.'[167] Under huge military and commercial pressure from Louis XIV and Colbert's France, English political discourse had adopted a *raison d'état* idiom that was closer in spirit to Machiavelli's *Prince*.[168] Hume saw that this development was not just a matter of foreign relations, something that happened 'out there', but a constitutional question which had profound implications for domestic politics. The new security politics shifted debate to the domain of political economy, but Hume's target was extensive territorial empire, not trade.[169] Empire was not only stupid economics[170] but also put pressure on the 'home' constitution, breeding both faction and fanaticism.[171] Hume worried about the jealous and warlike streak within the British psyche, which had the capacity to undermine the European balance of power,[172] and argued, against the direction of the tide, for the adoption of free trade practices with other European nations, even France, on the basis that it would lead to the flourishing of them all.[173]

But Hume's overriding concern was the funding of war by means of a national debt. This was a defining feature of the modern state, as we have seen, but Hume saw it as the road to despotism. He decried the 'strange

[165] Istvan Hont, *Jealousy of Trade: International Competition and the Nation-State in Historical Perspective* (Cambridge, MA: Harvard University Press, 2005), 187. See also Montesquieu, *Spirit of the Laws*, 389; Benjamin Constant, 'The Character of Modern Nations in Relation to War' in *Political Writings* (Cambridge: Cambridge University Press, trans. and ed. Bianca Fontana, 1988), 53: 'War then becomes before commerce. The former is all savage impulse, the latter civilized calculation.'

[166] Pocock, 'European History and the Global Ocean', 231–232. See also Sankar Muthu, *Enlightenment against Empire* (Princeton: Princeton University Press, 2003).

[167] Miller, *Defining the Common* Good, 170.

[168] Hont, *Jealousy of Trade*, 17, 57–58.

[169] Armitage, *Ideological Origins of the British Empire*, 188–194.

[170] 'Of Interest', 305.

[171] Pocock, 'Hume and the American Revolution', 137–138.

[172] Hume, 'Of the Balance of Power' in *Essays*, 339.

[173] 'Of the Jealousy of Trade'.

supineness, from long custom' that had overtaken public debate on the topic. The 'real danger lay in the intimate entanglement of public debt with the vagaries of international politics. The national debt was inextricably connected to the wars and imperial ambitions which would cause its destruction.'[174] Modern states were sleepwalking into an 'empire of passion'. The competition for commercial and colonial aggrandizement driven by envy and vainglory would produce societies that could only be governed by imaginary hopes and fears.[175] The phenomenon was the economic equivalent of religious superstition, and presented an existential problem: 'either the nation must destroy public credit, or public credit will destroy the nation.' Hume runs at least two lines of argument. The first relates more generally to the 'liquid' quality of commercial modernity,[176] the second more specifically to public debt. He argues, first, that the quicksilver quality of the new financial markets fuelled by government debt undermined the stability of conventional (and national) structures of authority.[177] With convention undermined, 'the several ranks of men, which form a kind of independent magistracy in a state' are lost. What remains is a ruling class of stockjobbers 'owning nothing except the debts of the public and yet owning everything, since the value of every object would now be the extent of its indebtedness.'[178] With civil society gone, we are left with a nightmare vision of the untrammelled sovereign state: 'No expedient remains for preventing or suppressing insurrections, but mercenary armies: No expedient at all remains for resisting tyranny: Elections are swayed by bribery and corruption alone: And the middle power between king and people being totally removed, a grievous despotism must infallibly prevail.' Hume takes issue with a fundamental feature of commercial society, that it does not contain any ultimate check on the forces making for its corruption.

The second line of argument tells the story of public debt as it unfolds across generations. The present generation decides to mortgage the public revenues, trusting 'that posterity will pay off the incumbrances contracted by their ancestors'. The next generation, following 'so good an example of their wise fathers', do the same. The generation after that

[174] Istvan Hont, 'The Rhapsody of Public Debt: David Hume and Voluntary State Bankruptcy' in Phillipson and Skinner, *Political Discourse in Early Modern Britain*, 329.

[175] Pocock, 'Hume and the American Revolution', 139.

[176] Zygmunt Bauman, *Liquid Modernity* (Cambridge: Polity, 2000).

[177] Hont, 'Rhapsody of Public Debt', 340: 'The speed with which financial markets operated terrified Hume.'

[178] Pocock, *Machiavellian Moment*, 496–497.

follows suit more 'from necessity than choice'. The temptation for individual politicians is hard to resist and so 'will almost infallibly be abused', as the expedient 'enables him to make a great figure during his administration, without overburdening the people with taxes'. At some point, though, the house of cards must fall.[179] The government will default on the debt, probably when faced with an emergency threatening the nation. National bankruptcy, the 'natural death' of public credit, will 'bury thousands in its ruins'. Alternatively, later generations saddled with debt will fail to act when new European powers emerge 'till, at last, they themselves and their creditors lie both at the mercy of the conqueror. And this may properly enough be denominated the violent death of our public credit.'[180]

The unbalanced constitution?

The previous chapters focused on the way in which seventeenth-century authors were working out the new idea of the state as a juridical system of rule, a central aspect of which at the formal level concerned the royal prerogative and at the conceptual level the idea of reason of state. The debate over reason of state in that earlier period highlighted the unstable relationship in accepted theories of public law between personal and official conceptions of power and authority. In the ensuing period, that new idea of the state began to take shape. The state-building process after 1688 had at its heart the political and financial requirements of modern war. Constitutionally speaking, it had the effect of cementing 'an attributive structure that clearly identified the law's source, strictly separated the power of the state from the standing of singular persons, and conclusively consolidated the positive legislative operations of the state'.[181] This progression may well have been more obvious in Britain than elsewhere. The Glorious Revolution meant that monarchs did not rule 'primarily because of who they were. Nor because of who their ancestors had

[179] Compare Blackstone, *Commentaries* I, 316–318: 'We may boast of large fortunes, and quantities of money in the funds. But where does this money exist? It exists only in name, in paper, in public faith, in parliamentary security: and that is undoubtedly sufficient for the creditors of the public to rely on.' He continues: but 'it weakens the internal strength of a state, by anticipating those resources which should be reserved to defend it in case of necessity.'

[180] Hume, 'Of Public Credit' in *Essays*, 350, 352, 358, 360, 363, 365. Montesquieu argued that the existence of a high public debt could only be disadvantageous to a state: see *Spirit of the Laws*, 418–419. But compare *Spirit of the Laws*, 327.

[181] Thornhill, *Sociology of Constitutions*, 146.

been. Parliament had brought them to the throne, and Protestantism kept them there. They were essentially serviceable kings.'[182] In terms of Philip Bobbitt's model of state transformation discussed in the previous chapter, eighteenth-century Britain had managed the move from late medieval to modern. Seventeenth-century politics was defined by the conflict that surrounded the collapse of the old Tudor regime and its idea of princely *ragione di stato*.[183] A central feature of that conflict was a disagreement over how to modernize. Ought we to follow the route of the French, and adopt the idea of the absolute monarch's *raison d'état*, or that of the Dutch republic and adopt the idea of *Staats raison* grounded in the formal principles of the juridical (territorial) state?[184] Post-1688 politics showed a decisive move in favour of the latter.

The reconstitution of the prerogative is part of a general move from an early-modern world of transcendence and sovereignty to a self-consciously modern world of constitutions and 'balance'. The revived and modernized natural jurisprudence typical of the period[185] rested on the idea that the 'study of the variations of social behavior throughout space and time would reveal the underlying principles of human nature on which the diversities of conduct were based and from which *lois* took their *esprit*'.[186] As classically formulated by Montesquieu, who exerted considerable influence on British constitutional writers from Hume onwards,[187] the focus of constitutional analysis moved from *les principes de sa constitution* to *moeurs* and *manières* in their relation to laws.[188] Living in an age more comfortable with compromise and somewhat less legalistic, the writers of the period were more prepared to trade off the liberty protecting value of law for other values, such as security. As Hume argued, the maxim *fiat justitia et ruat caelum* 'by

[182] Colley, *Britons*, 47.

[183] Harold J. Berman, *Law and Revolution, Vol. II: The Impact of the Protestant Reformations on the Western Legal Tradition* (Cambridge, MA: Harvard University Press, 2003), 211: under Henry VII and Henry VIII, the king 'ceased to draw his retinue and his support chiefly from the clerical and feudal nobility, his vassals and tenants. Instead, like the German princes, he developed an inner circle of councilors, appointed by him primarily on the basis of their loyalty and their merit rather than on the basis of their lineage … Thus the earlier system of government by the royal household, which had functioned for centuries, was transformed into a rudimentary cabinet system operating through various departments of state.'

[184] Berman, *Law and Revolution*, 224.

[185] See Haakonssen, *Science of a Legislator*.

[186] Pocock, 'Virtue, Rights, and Manners', 49.

[187] See, e.g., Roger B. Oake, 'Montesquieu and Hume' (1941) 2 Modern Language Quarterly 25.

[188] Pocock, *Machiavellian Moment*, 488.

sacrificing the end to the means, shews a preposterous idea of the subordination of duties'. Common sense had taught that 'as government binds us to obedience only on account of its tendency to public utility, that duty must always, in extraordinary cases, when public ruin would evidently attend obedience, yield to the supreme obligaton. *Salus populi suprema Lex*, the safety of the people is the supreme law.'[189] But for the most part, questions did not need to be posed in such stark terms. The increasingly decent nature of European states, made moderate by the civilizing effects of commerce and the decline in superstition, led commentators to predict that reason of state – or at least its worst manifestations – might become a thing of the past. 'One has begun to be cured of Machiavellianism, and one will continue to be cured of it', Montesquieu wrote. 'There must be more moderation in councils. What were formerly called *coups d'état* would at present, apart from their horror, be only imprudences.'[190]

The post-1688 constitution depersonalized reason of state ('prerogative'). It also internalized the concept, at least to some extent.[191] As such, it was subject to the same institutional pressures that inclined towards moderation as were other sources of political power. We have already moved a long way from the 'cunning of princes' and *raison d'etat* politics as a kind of game of chess played among sovereigns. The pre-modern image of prerogative as a power necessarily clothed in secrecy and vested in the ruler and his trusted advisers who claimed to know what was good for their subjects and presumed to manipulate them accordingly was put under intense pressure in a political culture increasingly defined by open and free (and well-tempered) public debate.[192] The discovery of trade did not lead to a second English republic. It did, though, 'provide fertile ground for an insight central to the republican conception of "the empire of laws": that the welfare and survival of the nation rested on complex networks of social, political and economic cooperation. Necessities could not be resolved in secret; they required public discussion and public justification. It was this, ironically, that cemented the connection between power and representation, reason of state and the rule of law.'[193]

189 Hume, 'Of Passive Obedience' in *Essays*, 489.

190 Montesquieu, *Spirit of the Laws*, 389.

191 Braddick argues that this development occurred earlier: 'Reason of state had, by the restoration, ceased to be disreputable and had become instead a normal measure of policy': *State Formation in Early Modern England*, 279.

192 Robertson, *Case for the Enlightenment*, 37.

193 Alan Houston, 'Republicanism, The Politics of Necessity, and the Rule of Law' in Alan Houston and Steve Pincus (eds.), *A Nation Transformed: England after the Restoration* (Cambridge: Cambridge University Press, 2001), 270–271.

Reason of state, then, was not dead. It had mutated in line with the mutations in the structure of constitutional politics and changed as the object of statecraft changed.[194] Britain had become the paradigmatic modern state: 'commercial, calculating, and unperturbed by long-term cultural or religious concerns'.[195] The prerogative was all but dead and rotten, as Burke was able to claim in the 1760s, folded within normal structures of constitutional rule centred on parliamentary government. In a sense, this was a victory for Hobbesian or republican notions of the normalized or occluded prerogative over Locke's clearer articulation of an exceptional and free-floating prerogative operating outside and contrary to the law. Developments internal to Britain seemed to confirm the impression of the increasing normalization of politics under modern conditions. But the very importance and prominence of the normal in domestic politics led to heightened concerns about the exceptional elements of foreign affairs. In principle, you might imagine a world in which commerce is an almost unmitigated benefit. In practice, though, that does not seem to be how things are developing. The operation of jealousy of trade politics and commercial reason of state, over which governments had substantial unilateral control, had led to increasingly fevered and multipolar competition over land and resources.[196] As the Seven Years' War had shown, now almost everywhere on the globe was a potential flashpoint. 'Glory, overseas empire, and long-distance trade pushed reason of state far away from its narrow origins in patriotic self-defence in times of grave necessity. The boundaries of self-preservation became exceedingly elastic, potentially even global.'[197] Trade and the attendant concerns of intercontinental warfare and large-scale public debt financing were the new imperatives. The spread of reason of state politics into international commerce threatened to bring down the constitution by saddling the public with huge debts that could never be repaid, the eventual scenario one of bankruptcy or subjugation. This chapter looked at the development through the eyes of its most clear-sighted early British critic, David Hume. He observed that with war and commerce bound together, not only did the merchant become the sovereign but also the sovereign needed in part to become

[194] Steve Pincus, 'From Holy Cause to Economic Interest: The Study of Population and the Invention of the State' in Houston and Pincus, *A Nation Transformed*, 272.

[195] Anthony Pagden, *Lords of All the World: Ideologies of Empire in Spain, Britain and France c.1500–c.1800* (New Haven: Yale University Press, 1995), 129.

[196] Roberston, *Case for the Enlightenment*, 371: 'Commerce was not an alternative means to achieve empire ... it was an alternative to empire *tout court*.'

[197] Hont, *Jealousy of Trade*, 17.

the merchant. The alliance between governments and commercial elites was a structural feature of the new commercial empire. The Crown still enjoyed very considerable discretionary authority over many, if not all, of Britain's colonial possessions and dependencies. 'This freedom of action in the New World contrasted sharply with the limitations on royal power at home.'[198] The ongoing relationship between Crown and the merchant elites gave the distinct impression of cronyism and of elites acting in their own private interest rather than in the true interest of the state ('public' reason of state). The normalization of these arrangements was a particularly troubling prospect threatening to undermine the gains that resulted from the constitutionalization of reason of state within the domestic sphere. 'Extensive conquests when pursued, must be the ruin of every free government', Hume warned at the end of his essay on the ideal commonwealth, and every good state ought to have a fundamental law against conquest.

[198] J. H. Elliott, *The Old World and the New 1492–1650* (Cambridge: Cambridge University Press, 1970), 82.

5

Reason of state in the first age of global imperialism

The modern state was born, it has been said, out of the unstated alliance between *Leviathan* and *Oceana*.[1] It was the combination of Hobbes's theory of the state as a distinct and juridical union of a people and the advent of commercial society that created that modern representative republic, our current state form, in the eighteenth century.[2] The development of the idea of the state as an artificial legal body alongside and in combination with the notion of the expansionary possibilities of that body accentuated the importance of the 'join' between the inner and outer membranes or faces of the state. The way the state looked outwards – its external politics – helped to determine its internal characteristics – its internal politics and constitution. We saw in the previous chapter how writers on commercial society realized the impact that modern trade politics and war might have on the recently stabilized constitutional and political life of the nation. Reason of state, they came to realize, is not just an inescapable dimension of politics but also provides a crucial nodal point between the state's increasingly dynamic external actions – now taking place for the first time on a global stage – and the norms and conventions that shape the state's internal constitution.

This chapter picks up the story at the moment of 'imperial crisis'[3] that accompanied the end of the Seven Years' War in 1763. That war for

[1] J. G. A. Pocock, *The Machiavellian Moment: Florentine Political Thought and the Atlantic Republican Tradition* (Princeton: Princeton University Press, 2nd ed., 2003), 474–475. Although a less Anglo-centric focus would include the seminal work of Jean Bodin, especially his *Six Livres de la République* (1576), in identifying a conception of the state as an apparatus of power distinct from both the ruler and the ruled. See Quentin Skinner, *The Foundations of Modern Political Thought, Vol. II* (Cambridge: Cambridge University Press, 1978), 355.

[2] Istvan Hont, *Jealousy of Trade: International Competition and the Nation-State in Comparative Perspective* (Cambridge, MA: Harvard University Press, 2005), 21.

[3] J. G. A. Pocock, 'Political Thought in the English-Speaking Atlantic, 1760–1790: (i) The Imperial Crisis' in J. G. A. Pocock (ed.), *Varieties of British Political Thought, 1500–1800* (Cambridge: Cambridge University Press, 1993).

empire,[4] fought on an unprecedented scale, helped define and vindicate the nation, both against Spain and France and against 'native' others.[5] The aftermath of war saw Britain trying to come to terms with being the leading power in the 'first age of global imperialism'.[6] The ensuing period witnessed two revolutions (1776 and 1789) that in different ways shocked the body politic and led to soul-searching about what Britain, its empire and its entire structure of rule, exactly stood for.[7] As subjects watched 'the mesmerizing spectacle of Britain's global expansion',[8] India remained a focal point of political debate. The East India Company's extensive territorial gains on the Indian sub-continent during this period induced the most pronounced and significant confrontation to date with non-European cultures.[9] Going against the existing ideology of the British empire as Protestant, maritime, commercial and free,[10] these gains necessitated new ways of thinking. 'Acquired through conquest rather than established by trade and settlement, the new British empire was territorial, not maritime; it embraced large populations that were neither white nor Anglo-Saxon nor Protestant.'[11] The precise relationship between the state and a private company that exercised

[4] In south-eastern India the English and the French became allies of contestants for the succession of the Nawab of Arcot and the Nizam of Hyderabad. War ebbed and flowed across southern India between 1746 and 1761, at which point the territories of the English-backed Nawab of Arcot became a client state of the East India Company.

[5] Kathleen Wilson, *The Sense of the People: Politics, Culture and Imperialism in England, 1715–1785* (Cambridge: Cambridge University Press, 1998), 202.

[6] C. A. Bayly, 'The First Age of Global Imperialism, c.1760–1830' (1998) 26 *Journal of Imperial and Commonwealth History* 28.

[7] David Armitage, *Foundations of Modern International Thought* (Cambridge: Cambridge Univeristy Press, 2013), 148: 'the American War entailed the dismemberment, rather than the augmentation, of the British Empire and a fundamental reassessment of the authority of the British state'.

[8] Wilson, *Sense of the People*, 24.

[9] See, e.g., P. J. Marshall and Glyndwr Williams, *The Great Map of Mankind: British Perceptions of the World in the Age of Enlightenment* (London: Dent, 1982), chapter 3, esp. 74–78; Anthony Pagden, *European Encounters with the New World* (New Haven: Yale University Press, 1993), esp. chapter 5.

[10] David Armitage, *The Ideological Origins of the British Empire* (Cambridge: Cambridge University Press, 2000), 8. See also John Locke, *Two Treatises of Government* (Cambridge: Cambridge University Press, ed. Peter Laslett, 1967), 403: 'Conquest is as far from setting up any government, as demolishing an House is from building a new one in the place. Indeed it often makes way for a new Frame of a Common-wealth, by destroying the former; but without the Consent of the people, can never erect a new one.'

[11] Lynn Festa, *Sentimental Figures of Empire in Eighteenth-Century Britain and France* (Baltimore: Johns Hopkins University Press, 2006), 48–49.

quasi-sovereign functions and the responsibilities owed by that company to its subjects were defining issues of the period.[12]

This chapter explores the debate about reason of state in the commerce-driven 'military authoritarian empire'[13] in India. It does so through an examination of Adam Smith's political economy, read as a disquisition on reason of state, and the writings and speeches of Edmund Burke. For both, the Indian state under British rule represented a peculiar and obnoxious version of a structure predicated on commercial reason of state, as opposed to legitimate constitutional rule, to the extent that it operated as a state of exception which called into question not only British presence in India but also the justice of the British state itself. We consider first, though, the legal questions surrounding the rise of the East India Company.

Chartered imperialism

The East India Company obtained a Charter from Queen Elizabeth in 1600 giving it exclusive rights to trade with the East Indies.[14] It followed the model of established companies trading in Virginia, Hudson Bay, West Africa, and the Levant[15] and formed part of a pattern according to which England's overseas activities – war, trade, settlement – were undertaken through an administrative repertoire of delegation and government by licence.[16] The Company soon became by far the largest of the English chartered trading companies.[17] Its success naturally

12 Bernard S. Cohn, *Colonialism and Its Forms of Knowledge: The British in India* (Princeton: Princeton University Press, 1996), 58.

13 P. J. Marshall, 'Empire and British Identity: The Maritime Dimension' in David Cannadine (ed.), *Empire, the Sea and Global History* (London: Palgrave Macmillian, 2007), 54.

14 Samuel Williston, 'History of the Law of Business Corporations before 1800, I' (1888) 2 *Harvard Law Review* 105, 109. On the process of incorporation see W. S. Holdsworth, 'English Corporation Law in the 16th and 17th Centuries' (1922) 31 *Yale Law Journal* 382.

15 P. J. Marshall, 'The British in Asia to 1700' in Nicholas Canny (ed.,) *The Oxford History of the British Empire, Vol. 1: The Origins of Empire* (Oxford: Oxford University Press, 1988), 264. Far more than its Dutch counterpart the *Vereenigde Oost-Indische Compagnie*, the East India Company, like other joint-stock corporations, had guild-like characteristics. The regulations of the company applied to the personal as well as the commercial conduct of the members: Jelle C. Riemersma, 'Oceanic Expansion: Government Influence on Company Organization in Holland and England (1550–1650)' (1950) 31 *Journal of Economic History* 31.

16 Michael J. Braddick, 'The English Government, War, Trade, and Settlement, 1625–1688' in Canny, *Origins of Empire*, 286.

17 Ron Harris, 'The English East India Company and the History of Company Law' in Ella Gepken-Jager, Gerard van Solinge and Levinus Timmerman (eds.), *VOC 1602–2002:400 Years of Company Law* (Amsterdam: Kluwer, 2005).

encouraged other merchants to try to break into its exclusive monopoly.[18] The Company's close relationship with the Stuarts[19] proved almost fatal during the Commonwealth[20] and then again after the Glorious Revolution. Parliamentary opposition during the 1690s led to the creation of a rival company – the New East India Company.[21] But the Old Company staggered on, becoming the New Company's biggest shareholder and stymieing its operations. The two companies merged, under an arrangement brokered by the government, a process that took most of the first decade of the eighteenth century to complete.[22]

A late seventeenth-century case highlights the legal issues surrounding the Company. In 1683, proceedings were brought against a rival merchant for outfitting a ship with the intention of making a voyage to the East Indies. Considered as a constitutional matter in the Court of King's Bench, *East India Company v Sandys* raised fundamental questions about monopolies and prerogative on the one hand and the politics of empire on the other. Argument was joined on three main points. The first related to free trade, and invoked the right to liberty and property. Drawing on 'free seas' principles the Company itself had once used

[18] The overseas prerogative (and thus the East India Company's charter) was unaffected by the Statute of Monopolies of 1623. See Rederic A. Johnson, 'The Commerce Power, Monopoly and Contracts' (1956–1957) 30 *Temple Law Quarterly* 270, 274. The Crown sometimes granted other merchants concessions that infringed on the Company's monopoly. For instance, the Courten Association received a valuable grant from Charles I in 1635 that gave them the right to establish trade at Goa, China, Japan, Malabar, and other parts of the East Indies. The Association established a colony in Madagascar which, fortunately perhaps for the East India Company, was a total failure. See Alison Games, *The Web of Empire: English Cosmopolitans in an Age of Expansion 1560–1660* (Oxford: Oxford University Press, 2008), chapter 6.

[19] Arnold A. Sherman, 'Pressure from Leadenhall: The East India Company Lobby, 1660–1678' (1976) 50 *Business History Review* 329, 331: the Company 'did more than most to focus commercial anger, and to shape a belligerently anti-Dutch commercial and foreign policy'.

[20] Robert Brenner, *Merchants and Revolution: Commercial Change, Political Conflict and London's Overseas Traders, 1550–1653* (Cambridge: Cambridge University Press, 1993), chapter 1.

[21] Henry Horwitz, 'The East India Trade, The Politicians, and the Constitution: 1689–1702' (1978) 17 *Journal of British Studies* 1; K. N. Chaudhuri and Jonathan I. Israel, 'The English and Dutch East India Companies and the Glorious Revolution of 1688–9' in Jonathan I. Israel (ed.), *The Anglo-Dutch Moment: Essays on the Glorious Revolution and its World Impact* (Cambridge: Cambridge University Press, 1991), 436–437.

[22] Philip Lawson, *The East India Company: A History 1600-1857* (London: Routledge, 1993), 51–57; Julian Hoppit, *A Land of Liberty? England 1689–1727* (Oxford: Oxford University Press, 2000), 273–276.

against the Portuguese and Dutch,[23] but which had been disputed by the Crown at the time of *Ship Money* with the help of the polymath philosopher John Selden,[24] Sandys argued that 'the King cannot take away goods that a man has got by his trade, much less can he take away his whole trade'. The Company's response was that only a managed trade worked when distances were so great and the dangers so real, and only a monopoly organization could offer effective management. Second, the Company argued that East Indies trade was bound up with diplomacy and considerations of state policy. The king had a special interest in regulating commerce with the infidel inhabitants of the East Indies. Only a Christian prince could authorize interaction with infidels, such engagement being unnatural for a Christian subject. Sandys's lawyers sidestepped that claim with the suggestion that 'religion too often has been made a cloak and veil for other ends and purposes'. Third, the Company argued that foreign trade and international relations had always been under the exclusive purview of the monarch. Sandys's lawyers accepted that '[t]he prerogative is great', but suggested that 'it has this general and just limitation, that nothing is to be done thereby that is mischievous or injurious to the subject'. The cumulative effect of these arguments, the Company maintained, was to put the investigation of its trade into a different legal bracket, one where the common law ought to be applied only in light of 'such other Laws also as be common to other Nations as well as ours ... namely the General Law of Nations, the Law-Merchant, the Imperial or Civil Law'.[25]

The court sided with the Company and affirmed an expansive view of the king's overseas prerogative. That they did so was unsurprising. The lead judge, Jeffreys LCJ, had already established himself as Rottweiler to the king.[26] Only a few years separate it from *Godden v Hales* (1686),[27]

[23] Armitage, *Ideological Origins of the British Empire*, 111–112.

[24] John Selden's *Mare Clausum* (1636) was completely rewritten at the request of Charles I's government. See Chapter 2.

[25] The position is consistent with Sir Matthew Hale's *Prerogatives of the King*, written in the 1650s, where the king's absolute royal prerogative over newfound lands and the limited agency of the common law is asserted.

[26] J. P. Kenyon, *The Stuart Constitution: Documents and Commentary* (Cambridge: Cambridge University Press, 1966), 422: 'Jeffreys at his worst was worse than any English judge before or since.' On his ineptitude as a politician see G. W. Keeton, *Lord Chancellor Jeffreys and the Stuart Cause* (London: Macdonald & Co., 1965), 332–334, 338.

[27] Kenyon, *The Stuart Constitution*, 438–439. '[T]he laws of the England are the King's laws', Herbert CJ opined, and 'that it is an inseparable prerogative in the King, to dispense with penal laws upon necessity and urgent occasions' and that 'the King is sole judge in that

often thought of as the high-water mark of the prerogative in English law, which held that the king had a power to dispense with the laws. The judges viewed *Sandys* largely from the Crown's perspective.[28] The king had the 'undoubted prerogative' to grant exclusive trading charters, they said, a power that his courts would protect. The Company could not be classed as an illicit monopoly because it was not a private body in the normal sense. It acted for the public good, largely because it was performing at the king's behest tasks that the king would himself accomplish directly through his own agents if he could. On its face, the judgment seems to confirm the late Stuart plan for the assertion of monarchical dominance over the seas,[29] with the Company as one of the king's arms of enforcement. As such, it was true to the structure of delegated administrative authority that characterized the early years of overseas expansion.[30] But the reality of devolved imperial power, at least in the East Indies context, proved to be rather different. The royal grants the Company had received since 1600 contained attributes of sovereignty, such as the right to wage war and negotiate peace, to levy taxes, and to make laws for any territory that it controlled.[31] The vast distances involved in the Indies trade made it impossible for the state to exercise meaningful control over the Company's activities. Little surprise, then, that the Company took the *Sandys* decision as a green light to transform itself from 'a parcel of mere trading merchants or peddlers' into a 'formidable martial government in India'.[32] It turned out that Sandys's lawyers were not too far wide of the mark when they suggested that deciding for the Company would make

necessity'. See also the *Seven Bishops' Case* (1688) 12 State Trials 183. Compare *Thomas v Sorrell* (1674) Vaughan 330.

[28] Jeffreys CJ declared the case to be 'of so great concern and consequence as perhaps there was none other ever so great (I am sure none greater) in Westminster Hall wherein the prerogative of the King was more concerned on the one hand, and the liberty and property of the subject on the other'.

[29] Armitage, *Ideological Origins of the British Empire*, 123.

[30] Ken MacMillan, *Sovereignty and Possession in the English New World* (Cambridge: Cambridge University Press, 2009), 6: 'the English crown had a legal sovereign, prerogative, and imperial obligation to authorize, supervise, protect, and proclaim its overseas holdings, particularly when faced with challenges from other European colonizing monarchs'.

[31] Philip J. Stern, *The Company-State: Corporate Sovereignty and the Early Modern Foundations of the British Empire in India* (Oxford and New York: Oxford University Press, 2011), 23.

[32] Sir Josiah Child, dominant governor of the Company in the late seventeenth century, in a letter to Fort St George, the Company's outpost in Madras. Quoted in Steve Pincus, *1688 – The First Modern Revolution* (New Haven: Yale University Press, 2009), 378.

it unaccountable, 'independent from the government' and thus 'a sort of republic for the management of trade'.[33]

The regime change that occurred in 1688 did not favour the Company.[34] Another monopoly case brought by the Royal African Company immediately after the Glorious Revolution ended with the court ruling in favour of the private traders. In *Nightingale v Bridges*, Holt – recently appointed Chief Justice by William III – took the opportunity to extend common law protection to property rights formerly infringed by Crown grants of monopoly by requiring parliamentary sanction before any monopolistic grants could be legally enforced. The decision, it has been said, 'destroyed prerogative control of the economy'.[35] While that conclusion is almost certainly too stark, the case does seem to be in line with the general post-1688 trend. The House of Commons, on the back of a long public campaign against the Company and its Jacobite leanings, took umbrage with the king's decision to renew the East India Company's charter and passed an uncompromising resolution in January 1694 stating that 'all subjects of *England* have equal right to trade to the *East-Indies*, unless prohibited by Act of Parliament'. Coinciding with a probe into the Company's affairs, the resolution signalled Parliament's intention to replace the Crown as the dominant force in overseas and colonial affairs.[36] Thomas Sandys, sensing a change in political weather, then successfully sued two Company directors for preventing his ship from sailing to the East Indies back in 1683. Reversing the earlier ruling, Holt CJ said that 'royalty should not interfere because there was a remedy in the courts'. It was, he continued, 'a disparagement to the Christian Religion to think they [English merchants] should rather be converted by them', observing that this 'argument is only

[33] See also Sherman, 'Pressure from Leadenhall', 347: 'By the time James II became King in 1685, the Company had virtually sovereign powers east of the Cape of Good Hope, and enormous rights over the lives and properties of Englishmen.'

[34] The Revolution coincided with a disastrous military operation against Mughal forces in India: Chaudhuri and Israel, 'The English and Dutch East India Companies and the Glorious Revolution of 1688–9', 435–436.

[35] W. Stump, 'An Economic Consequence of 1688' (1974) 6 *Albion* 26, 28.

[36] This did not happen, at least not for quite some time. On the intricate nature of developments in this sphere see, e.g., Jack P. Greene, *Peripheries and Center: Constitutional Development in the Extended Polities of the British Empire and the United States, 1607–1788* (Athens, GA: University of Georgia Press, 1986) chapters 3 and 4. Greene writes (on p. 55) that in 'relations between the colonies and the home government before the mid-1760s, Parliament's authority over the colonies was an infinitely less important issue than that of the crown'.

a pretence anyway, for the restraint is only as to infidels within the limits of the East India Company'.[37]

Despite these legal and political setbacks, the Company nevertheless found itself perfectly positioned in the new era of statecraft defined through commercial competition.[38] It acted as one of the great money engines of state – the others being the Bank of England and the South Sea Company, the latter was incorporated in 1711 out of old government loans[39] – cementing a position at the heart of the metropolitan world of high finance because of the demands imposed upon the state by recurrent warfare.[40] It provided a nodal point connecting the City of London, the state and the nascent empire in a network of relationships based on mutual indebtedness.[41] The Company also supplied trading and diplomatic services that the state could not realize through its own agency. Philip Stern argues that the term 'Company-State' best characterizes the organization since it 'did what early modern governments did: erect and administer law; collect taxes; provide protection; inflict punishment; perform stateliness; regulate economic, religious, and civic life; conduct diplomacy and wage war; make claims to jurisdiction over land and sea; cultivate authority over and obedience from those people subject to its command'.[42] The activities of the Company were not in any real sense supervised by the government. Parliament was only sporadically interested in Indian matters before the 1750s, and politicians for the most part tended to accept that the Company offered the best way to secure profit and revenue from India.[43] Besides, as such an important part of Britain's

[37] *Sands v Sir Josiah Child, Franklin and Leach*, 3; Levinz, 352. See Sidney T. Miller, 'The Case of the Monopolies: Some of Its Results and Suggestions' (1907) 6 *Michigan Law Review* 1, 10–11.

[38] In the East Indies, too, the new Anglo-Dutch alliance meant that the English were now free to strengthen their trading position largely unhindered by the previously belligerent Dutch East India Company. The English Company also benefited from its non-involvement in the Franco-Dutch War in India 1689–1698 which, while immediately successful for the Dutch, ended up weakening the position of both participants. Chaudhuri and Israel, 'The East India Company and the Glorious Revolution of 1688–9'.

[39] Bruce G. Carruthers, *City of Capital: Politics and Markets in the English Financial Revolution* (Princeton: Princeton University Press, 1999), 78.

[40] H. V. Bowen, *The Business of Empire: The East India Company and Imperial Britain, 1756–1833* (Cambridge: Cambridge University Press, 2006), 30.

[41] L. S. Sutherland, 'The East India Company in Eighteenth-Century Politics' (1947) 17 *Economic History Review* 15, 19.

[42] Stern, *Company-State*, 3–6.

[43] H. W. Bowen, *Revenue and Reform: The Indian Problem in British Politics 1757–1773* (Cambridge: Cambridge University Press, 1991), 21: 'there was never any real prospect of any concessions being made to the free trade lobby: far too much was at stake'.

imperium, the Company could not be allowed to go to the wall.[44] It was simply too big to fail. Nor despite its best efforts were activities on the ground controlled by the Company's Directorate in London. The average time for an East Indiaman to make the round-trip to India was sixteen months.[45] Territorial expansion in India, whether by war and treaty, was almost always the result of the opportunism of Company servants.[46] 'The brutal truth of the matter was that Company policy failed to keep pace with events. The approach of the Company's Directors in London became irrelevant, in most cases, to the behaviour of its servants in India.'[47]

The second half of the eighteenth century saw the Company make spectacular gains. During this period, 'the nature, direction, and purpose of British activity in India underwent a dramatic and lasting transformation'.[48] There were two particularly important developments: the defeat of the Nawab of Bengal at the Battle of Plassey 1756 (not, in truth, much of a battle) which delivered Bengal into British hands and the acceptance of the Bengal *diwani* (right to collect revenues) from the Mughal Emperor Shah Alam II. The latter development in particular drew the Company into the detailed daily administration of Indian life.[49] These moves were largely driven by the need to obtain more revenues as a means of defraying escalating military expenses.[50] As such, they need to be placed 'in the broader context of the financial revolution, the expansionist forces it generated, and the problems these forces experienced on distant frontiers,

[44] Bowen, *Business of Empire*, 31.

[45] K. N. Chaudhuri, *The Trading World of Asia and the East India Company, 1660–1760* (Cambridge: Cambridge University Press, 1978), 74. Burke spoke eloquently of the importance of the tyranny of distance for the imperial constitution in his great speech 'Conciliation with America' in Burke, *Pre-Revolutionary Writings* (Cambridge: Cambridge University Press, ed. Ian Harris, 1993), 226: 'Three thousand miles of ocean lie between you and them. No contrivance can prevent the effect of this distance, in weakening Government. Seas roll, and months pass, between the order and the execution; and the want of a speedy explanation of a single point is enough to defeat an whole system.'

[46] Supidta Sen, 'Liberal Economy and Illiberal Trade: The Political Economy of "Responsible Government" in Early British India' in Kathleen Wilson (ed.), *A New Imperial History: Culture, Identity and Modernity in Britain and the Empire, 1660–1840* (Cambridge: Cambridge University Press, 2004).

[47] Lawson, *East India Company*, 107.

[48] Bowen, *Revenue and Reform*, 5.

[49] P. J. Marshall, *Bengal: The British Bridgehead. East India, 1740–1828* (Cambridge: Cambridge University Press, 1988); C. A. Bayly, *Indian Society and the Making of the British Empire* (Cambridge: Cambridge University Press, 1988).

[50] Anthony Webster, *The Twilight of the East India Company: The Evolution of Anglo-Asian Commerce and Politics 1790–1860* (Woodbridge: Boydell Press, 2009), 22.

where credit lines were fully stretched and where junctions made with representatives of indigenous financial and fiscal systems were a necessary precondition of commercial success'.[51]

'Strange absurdity': Smith on global trade and the East India Company

The euphoria surrounding the enormous gains in India soon turned sour. The stockmarket bubble that began with the news of the grant of the *diwani* burst at the end of the 1760s as the government passed a Dividend Act in 1767 forcing the Company to make a substantial annual payment and limiting the dividend to 10 per cent, and news of renewed warfare in south India reached London. The Company also failed to meet its monetary goals from the *diwani*. All this, plus the Bengal famine and a boycott of its once prosperous tea trade with the American colonies, combined to put the Company in a dire financial position.[52] A spectacular fall in the price of its stock led the Company to turn to the government for help. In response, the government passed the Regulating Act of 1773 which, as well as changing the voting structure for directors, curtailed the Company's freedom to manage its affairs in India. It introduced a five-man Council, with a new post of Governor-General of India at its head and a Supreme Court in Bengal with jurisdiction over all British operations in the sub-continent.[53] The Act represented a new form of partnership between the state and the Company, a partnership in which the state would increasingly have the upper hand.[54] Empire in India had become a matter of official state interest.

This was the context in which Adam Smith wrote his masterpiece, *An Inquiry into the Nature and Causes of the Wealth of Nations*. The East India Company features extensively in its pages. Smith described the work as a 'very violent attack' on the political principles of 'the whole commercial system of Great Britain' and the specious economic arguments harnessed to support it.[55] His frame of reference incorporated moral philosophy,

[51] P. J. Cain and A. G. Hopkins, *British Imperialism: Innovation and Expansion 1688–1914* (London: Longman, 1993), 94.

[52] Bowen, *Revenue and Reform*, 76–77 and chapter 8.

[53] For analysis of the workings of that court, see Lauren Benton, *Law and Colonial Cultures: Legal Regimes in World History: 1400–1900* (Cambridge: Cambridge University Press, 2002), 137–152.

[54] Bowen, *Revenue and Reform*, 131.

[55] Letter of Smith to Andreas Holt, 26 October 1780, *The Correspondence of Adam Smith* (Oxford: Oxford University Press, eds. E. C. Mossner and I. S. Ross, 1987), 251.

political economy and 'what might be called natural jurisprudence, or a theory of the general principles which ought to run through and be the foundation of the laws of all nations'.[56] The inquiry focused on the existence of a complex global system of power and trading relationships. 'The discovery of America, and that of the passage to the East Indies by the Cape of Good Hope, are the two greatest and most important events recorded in the history of mankind.'[57] Whereas Hume thought the discovery of America had initiated a new 'modern history',[58] Smith if anything saw the latter event as the more significant. It opened up a bigger market for commerce and exposed Europeans to more developed and sophisticated civilizations than in the Americas.[59]

Two aspects of Smith's moral theory require attention here,[60] since they set the philosophical platform from which Smith himself and later Burke mounted their attack on the East India Company and the reason of state politics it exemplified. First, the idea of the socially embedded self. In *The Theory of Moral Sentiments*, Smith's account of our moral faculties begins with a description of our immersion in society. Conscience emerges as sympathetic experience that insinuates itself into the human soul,[61]

[56] Adam Smith, *The Theory of Moral Sentiments* (Indianapolis: Liberty Fund, eds. D. D. Raphael and A. L. Macfie, 1982), VII.iv.37. Smith planned to write a book on jurisprudence as a sequel to *The Theory of Moral Sentiments*, but he never published what he wrote and destroyed his manuscript shortly before his death. Two sets of students' notes from his lectures on jurisprudence at the University of Glasgow survive.

[57] Adam Smith, *An Inquiry into the Nature and Causes of the Wealth of Nations* (Indianapolis: Liberty Fund, eds. R. H. Campbell and A. S. Skinner, 1981) IV.vii.c.80. Smith here paraphrases Raynal, whose *History of the Two Indies* (1770, English translation 1776) begins 'No event has been so interesting to mankind in general, and to the inhabitants of Europe in particular, as the discovery of the new world, and the passage to India by the Cape of Good Hope.' See J. H. Elliott, *The Old World and the New, 1492–1650* (Cambridge: Cambridge University Press, 1970), 1, 54–55.

[58] On the impact of the discovery of America on sixteenth-century European thought see Elliott, *The Old World and the New 1492–1650*.

[59] Smith, *Wealth of Nations*, IV.i.33.

[60] Smith positioned himself between 'whining and melancholy moralists' like Pascal who saw man as 'something separated and detached', and Stoic universalists who thought of man 'as a citizen of the world, a member of the vast commonwealth of nature'. *Theory of Moral Sentiments*, III.3.9–11. See also Nicholas Phillipson, 'Adam Smith as Civic Moralist' in Istvan Hont and Michael Ignatieff (eds.), *Wealth and Virtue: The Shaping of Political Economy in the Scottish Enlightenment* (Cambridge: Cambridge University Press, 1983).

[61] Smith's theory of rhetoric also approaches the subject as an aspect of the principles of sociability and suggests that the human personality is best understood in developmental terms as the story of how individuals learned to live sociably. See Adam Smith, *Lectures on Rhetoric and Belles Lettres* (Indianapolis: Liberty Fund, ed. J. C. Bryce, 1985),

hardens over time and ultimately becomes the inner tribunal that guides individual judgement and action.[62] The social contexts we inhabit provide us with 'a looking-glass by which we can, in some measure, with the eyes of other people, scrutinize the propriety of our own conduct.' In relation to my conduct I become in effect two persons.[63] The first, 'the spectator, whose sentiments with regard to my own conduct I endeavour to enter into'. The second, 'the agent, the person whom I properly call myself, and whose conduct, under the character of a spectator, I was endeavouring to form some opinion'.[64] The development of conscience, that 'demigod within the breast',[65] is a process through which the 'eyes of other people' become embedded in the individual soul. The social practice of sympathy is driven inside us and we become capable of self-judgement.[66] Though never completely successful, it is the ongoing search for a third standpoint of impartiality that makes social life possible.[67] Moral culture, understood as a practice of sympathy, is passed from each generation to the next, generating a 'thick' or 'sticky' account of social institutions.[68] Local context is always vital. 'It is never a matter of goodness or badness, justice or injustice, *per se*; but of goodness or badness, etc., against the background of a number of other values.'[69]

A second aspect requiring attention is the importance of contingency and unintended consequences, a defining feature of Smith's thought.[70] He was clear that, while an ideal theory of justice – and an attendant politics of natural liberty – might be identified, politics did not correspond to

Lectures 11, 23 and 'Considerations Concerning the First Formation of Languages, &c. &c', 223–224.

62 Smith, *Theory of Moral Sentiments*, III.I.2–3.

63 Dror Wahrman reads this account literally, tying it to the 'polymorphous identity play – and interplay, and double play, and counter-play' that characterized eighteenth-century notions of identity: *The Making of the Modern Self: Identity and Culture in Eighteenth-Century England* (New Haven: Yale University Press, 2006), 186–189.

64 Smith, *Theory of Moral Sentiments*, III.I.5–6.

65 Smith, *Theory of Moral Sentiments*, III.2.32.

66 Fonna Forman-Barzilai, *Adam Smith and the Circles of Sympathy: Cosmopolitianism and Moral Theory* (Cambridge: Cambridge University Press, 2010), 86.

67 Knud Haakonssen, *The Science of a Legislator: The Natural Jurisprudence of David Hume and Adam Smith* (Cambridge: Cambridge University Press, 1981), 58.

68 Christopher J. Berry, 'Sociality and Socialisation' in Alexander Broadie (ed.), *The Cambridge Companion to the Scottish Enlightenment* (Cambridge: Cambridge University Press, 2003), 243–257.

69 Haakonssen, *Science of a Legislator*, 62.

70 David Lieberman, 'Adam Smith on Justice, Rights, and Law' in Knud Haakonssen (ed.), *The Cambridge Companion to Adam Smith* (Cambridge: Cambridge University Press, 2006), 233.

natural law models in any straightforward way. Far from being close to the ideal, in fact, 'the natural course of things' has been 'in many respects, entirely inverted' in Europe and has resulted in an 'unnatural and retrograde order'.[71] In ways reminiscent of Harrington's critique of the Gothic constitution,[72] Smith's vision of medieval Europe is one of bleak and almost unremitting insecurity. The great landlords who ruled the roost were simply strongmen whose time and energy were spent either defending their territories or trying to extend them.[73] Only a few towns and cities managed to wrench themselves free from the domination of these landlords or 'petty princes'.[74] It was only in those cities, then, where people had sufficient liberty and security to consider improving themselves. They did so by producing things that were deeply attractive to the great lords, who would pay enormous sums for the latest gadget or pretty trinket. In this way, or so the story goes, 'for the gratification of the most childish, the meanest and the most sordid of all vanities, they gradually bartered their whole power and authority'.[75] Smith's stylized history aims to show how the freedom of the moderns, imperfect though it is, grew out of a process that was one part the workings out of natural laws and one part chance. Cities managed, often with a large dollop of luck, to free themselves from the control of petty princes. They then stumbled on a form of civic republicanism. This development led to another, as 'merchants and artificers', now free to act in their own interest, expanded and exploited a market in baubles for lords and ladies. The universal truth that the masters of mankind act according to the vile maxim 'All for ourselves, and nothing for other people' did the rest, working overtime to transform existing power structures.[76] Neither party intended to bring about a revolution, but that was exactly what was produced by 'the folly of the one, and the industry of the other'.[77]

While these two central elements in Smith's thought – the socialized individual and the idea of unintended consequences – are primarily

[71] See, e.g., Smith, *Wealth of Nations*, III.i.8–9.

[72] See the discussion in Chapter 3.

[73] Smith, *Wealth of Nations*, III.ii.7.

[74] Smith, *Wealth of Nations*, III.ii.3, III.iii.10–12 and III.iv.7.

[75] Smith, *Wealth of Nations*, III.iv.10.

[76] The distrust of the landed nobility was a consistent feature of Smith's thought. See, e.g., his *Lectures on Jurisprudence* (Indianapolis, IN: Liberty Press, ed. Ronald L. Meek, D. D. Raphael and P. G. Stein, 1982), 264: 'the nobility are the greatest opposers and oppressors of liberty that we can imagine. They hurt the liberty of the people even more than an absolute monarch.'

[77] Smith, *Wealth of Nations*, III.iv.17.

descriptive or analytical,[78] they combine to produce a normative position. The theory entails a principle of civility and restraint in politics, both in relation to one another and between subjects and the state. After all, the idea of the impartial spectator that lies at the core of Smith's moral theory is a recipe for taming passions and partiality and for reconciling the individual with her community.[79] The state, understood as a kind of super-community, should naturally be the object of our affection, as the prosperity and safety of all that we hold dear depends on its safety and prosperity.[80] This love of country drives two further principles: first, 'a certain respect and reverence' for the established constitution; second, a desire to make 'our fellow-citizens as safe, respectable, and happy as we can'.[81] Respect and reverence for the constitution involves accepting the supremacy of the state over the various orders, classes and communities within it. Additionally, it means accepting that seemingly unjust constitutional arrangements may not be unjustifiable. Since a successful constitution tends to preserve the existing balance between various social forces, it will at least sometimes operate so as to prevent change. But that may well be exactly what is required to ensure 'the stability and permanence of the whole system'.[82] Law and justice are here seen as a *system*. Smith believed that mankind's love of system was a sentiment that underpinned our desire to understand and improve the world.[83] The security offered by established governance structures was essential if individuals were to be able to seek the conveniences as well as the necessities of life. And it makes magistrates and rulers more inclined to regularize the systems on which continued security and progress depended.[84]

By extension, and though he was critical of many existing laws and arrangements, Smith was hostile to proponents of radical change – those 'projectors' and 'political mechanics' who thought that ideal principles

[78] Smith, *Theory of Moral Sentiments*, II.i.5.10.

[79] Smith, *Theory of Moral Sentiments*, III.3.4: 'It is reason, principle, conscience, the inhabitant of the breast, the man within, the great judge and arbiter of our conduct. It is he who, whenever we are about to act so as to affect the happiness of others, calls to us, with a voice capable of astonishing the most presumptuous of our passions, that we are but one of the multitude, in no respect better than any other in it. ... It is from him only that we learn the real littleness of ourselves, and of whatever relates to ourselves, and the natural misrepresentations of self-love can be corrected only by the eye of the impartial spectator.'

[80] Smith, *Theory of Moral Sentiments*, VI.ii.2.2.

[81] Smith, *Theory of Moral Sentiments*, VI.ii.2.11.

[82] Smith, *Theory of Moral Sentiments*, VI.ii.2.9–10.

[83] Phillipson, *Adam Smith*, 113.

[84] Smith, *Lectures on Jurisprudence*, 337–338.

could simply be legislated into existence to replace existing but imperfect legal arrangements. In the last additions he made to the 1790 edition of the *Theory of Moral Sentiments*, his 'parting shot from the republic of letters',[85] Smith took aim at the 'spirit of system' that animated so many contemporaries.[86] The man of system, 'enamoured with the supposed beauty of his own ideal plan of government', is dangerous because he wants to make his own judgement the supreme standard of right and wrong:

> He seems to imagine that he can arrange the different members of a great society with as much ease as the hand arranges the different pieces upon a chess-board. He does not consider that the pieces upon the chess-board have no other principle of motion besides that which the hand impresses on them; but that, in the great chess-board of human society, every single piece has a principle of motion of its own, altogether different from that which the legislature might chuse to impress upon it. If those two principles coincide and act in the same direction, the game of human society will go on easily and harmoniously, and is very likely to be happy and successful. If they are opposite or different, the game will go on miserably, and the society must be at all times in the highest degree of disorder.[87]

This view of politics derives from the idea that constitutions and laws are part of a community of sentiments. Like other Scottish Enlightenment thinkers, Smith saw that law and morals exist in a reflexive relationship which gave the modern or 'great' society the characteristic of a complex whole. For all his fears about the corrosive effect of capitalism on civic virtue and public spirit, Adam Ferguson, for instance, was equally clear that it was neither possible nor desirable to turn the clock back and resuscitate the 'perfect virtue' of the ancient republics. Political autonomy was archaic, appropriate for small, rude, homogenous and militaristic societies.[88] Differentiation and complexity were, by contrast, defining features of modern societies. Just as savage societies, it was possible for a man to say in a single word 'I have killed a bear', Smith argued, so too were they ones in which a man could be simultaneously a warrior, producer, statesman and judge. 'The "decomposition" of speech, the codification of

[85] Istvan Hont, 'Adam Smith and the Political Economy of the "Unnatural and Retrograde" Order' in Hont, *Jealousy of Trade*, 360.

[86] Smith, *Theory of Moral Sentiments*, VI.ii.2.15.

[87] Smith, *Theory of Moral Sentiments*, VI.ii.2.17.

[88] Adam Ferguson, *An Essay on the History of Civil Society* (Cambridge: Cambridge University Press, ed. Fania Oz-Salzberger, 1995), 72. See also Andreas Kalyvas and Ira Katznelson, *Liberal Beginnings: Making a Republic for the Moderns* (Cambridge: Cambridge University Press, 2008), 58–65.

a body of laws and the division of labour are all the determining features of a civil society. They make for difference, as well as for discord.'[89]

The 'savage patriotism' of ancient societies had gone, replaced by a more tolerant and inclusive society more comfortable with the idea of compromise and less likely to engage in bloody conflicts and annihilation.[90] Existing laws reflect, albeit imperfectly,[91] the society in which they operate, not least because each had matured alongside the other. The legal system helps to refine the people's sense of justice, particularly as modern judges and administrators tend to regularize and systematize their decision-making. By contrast, plans for radical reform offer unmoored and deeply unstable systems of government.[92] A newly minted order would lack for stability. At a stroke, the operating conditions in which both government and citizens could work to improve society would be removed. And the next new man (or faction) with the next new grand plan would be emboldened to plan his attack. The lesson of history, for Smith, was not to be found in 'superimposing the natural [ideal] order on the actual one, but rather in discovering how natural progress asserts itself in an imperfect but nonetheless forceful way, through the complex development of unintended consequences'.[93]

Smith's *Lectures on Jurisprudence*, given early in his career, were divided into two parts, the first on justice and the second on what he called police.[94] According to his star pupil John Millar, 'police' referred to 'those political regulations which are founded, not upon the principle of *justice*, but that of *expediency*, and which are calculated to increase the riches, the power, and the prosperity of a State'.[95] The category included political institutions relating to finance, commerce, foreign affairs and war. Smith saw the two sources of principles, justice and expediency, as related and insisted that justice was intimately connected with 'the proper means of introducing plenty and abundance into the country, that is, the

[89] Pagden, *European Encounters with the New World*, 150. See Smith, 'Considerations Concerning the First Formation of Languages'; *Wealth of Nations*, V.i.a.1–20.

[90] Kalyvas and Katznelson, *Liberal Beginnings*, 35.

[91] Particularly in his *Lectures on Jurisprudence*, Smith was critical of outdated law and customs, often those designed to service a feudal civilization that failed to meet the needs of modern commercial society.

[92] On the fragility of social life, see Smith, *Theory of Moral Sentiments*, II.ii.3.4.

[93] Hont, 'Adam Smith and the "Unnatural and Retrograde" Order', 375.

[94] Smith, *Lectures on Jurisprudence*, Part II.

[95] J. G. A. Pocock, 'Smith's Glasgow Lectures: Narrative and Philosophical History' in Pocock, *Barbarism and Religion, Vol. 2: Narratives of Civil Government* (Cambridge: Cambridge University Press, 1999), 320.

cheapness of goods of all sorts'.[96] Smith went on to explore these topics, which lay, as it were, on the far side of justice, systematically in the *Wealth of Nations*. Indeed, much of the book can be read as an analysis of reason of state in modern commercial society. Smith, in effect, divides the category into two. Reason of state is 'good' (or justifiable) when it can be accommodated within his theory of justice (natural jurisprudence) – in other words, when it is conducive to the security and well-being of individual subjects. It is 'bad' (or unjustifiable) when done for the private or self-interested reasons of rulers or powerful social groups, like merchants or soldier-adventurers.

Smith was ambiguous about commercial society. He believed that a free market economy, supplemented by appropriate institutions, was modern society's best hope for general well-being. And he shared the belief common to Enlightened thinkers that the advent of commercial society 'was the guarantee that neither ancient empire, medieval empire and papacy, nor early modern universal monarchy and religious warfare, would return to plague them'.[97] But he also saw that commercial life rested on a self-deception about our needs and happiness,[98] and joined Adam Ferguson in arguing that it tended to corrupt our moral sentiments and sap our public spiritedness.[99] Smith saw the potential benefits of international trade. Commerce should in principle unite distant parts of the world and, through stimulating one another's industry, should have a positive impact on both Europeans and non-Europeans.[100] Commerce not only marks an advanced state of civilization, it also '*creates* it by drawing the world together in the reciprocal exchanges that polish manners'.[101] In practice, though, the discovery of the East had proved 'ruinous and destructive' to native societies because of the 'savage injustice of the Europeans'[102] and their use of 'exclusive' trading companies for long-distance trade. He agreed with Raynal and Diderot that it was

96 Smith, *Lectures on Jurisprudence*, 333.

97 J. G. A. Pocock, 'European History and the Global Ocean' Pocock, *Barbarism and Religion, Vol. 4: Barbarians, Savages and Empires* (Cambridge: Cambridge University Press, 2005), 231. On the aspiration for universal monarchy in the history of the Spanish empire, see Anthony Pagden, *Lords of All the World: Ideologies of Empire in Spain, Britain and France c.1500-c.1800* (New Haven: Yale University Press, 1995), chapter 2.

98 See, e.g., Smith, *Theory of Moral Sentiments*, I.iii.3.7: 'There are hypocrites of wealth and greatness, as well as of religion and virtue.'

99 Ferguson, An Essay on the History of Civil Society, 223–232.

100 Smith, *Wealth of Nations*, IV.vii.c.80; IV.i.32–33.

101 Festa, *Sentimental Figures of Empire*, 58.

102 Smith, *Wealth of Nations*, IV.i.32.

a tragedy that the Europeans who broke into the world's oceans were themselves 'still half barbarous and had scarcely begun to be enlightened by *le doux commerce*'.[103] Monopoly trade brings an advantage to a small group – in this case, the big metropolitan merchants – at everyone else's expense.[104] British citizens have paid not just for the extraordinary profits that the East India Company has made on the back of its monopoly trade, but also for 'all the extraordinary waste which the fraud and abuse, inseparable from the management of the affairs of so great a company, must necessarily have occasioned'.[105]

The costs are not just monetary. The state has become so reliant on leviathan trading companies that it now resembles a body disfigured by a massive tumour. The body thus 'artificially swelled beyond its natural dimensions' is 'very likely to bring on the most dangerous disorders'. Given the tight nexus between merchant and state, reversing the process will be difficult 'without occasioning, for a time at least, still greater disorders'.[106] The 'spirit of monopoly' that Smith identifies extends beyond this, leading to the protection of domestic markets and 'beggar thy neighbour' trade policies which run counter to the interests of the state.[107] Worse still, India is in the process of moving to government by monopoly merchant, a 'perfectly destructive' system of rule. Company servants, 'plunderers of India', can operate in their own interest in the absence of competition or control by external authorities. A company of merchants acting as sovereign is a 'strange absurdity'. Trade being the merchant's principal business, it will always 'regard the character of the sovereign as but an appendix to that of the merchant'. Its instinct is to keep out all competitors. Government will be made subservient to the interest of monopoly. The interest of the Company will be to oppress and exploit the subject population – a predicament accentuated by the distance separating the Company's territories from its home base.[108] 'It is a very singular

[103] J. G. A. Pocock, 'The Antiquity of Asia: Priests, Legislators and the Tragedy of History' in Pocock, *Barbarism and Religion, Vol. 4*, 265. See Guillaume-Thomas Raynal, *Histoire philosophique et politique des établissements et du commerce des Européens dans les deux Indes* (Amsterdam, 1770). For analysis see Festa, *Sentimental Figures of Empire*, chapter 5.

[104] Smith, *Wealth of Nations*, IV.vii.c.62; IV.vii.v.47.

[105] Smith, *Wealth of Nations*, IV.vii.c.91.

[106] Smith, *Wealth of Nations*, IV.vii.c.43–44.

[107] Smith, *Wealth of Nations*, IV.iii.c.9–17.

[108] Smith, *Wealth of Nations*, IV.vii.b.4. See also Peter N. Miller, *Defining the Common Good: Empire Religion and Philosophy in Eighteenth-Century Britain* (Cambridge: Cambridge University Press, 1994), 184: 'Adam Smith ... recognized that

government in which every member of the administration wishes to get out of the country, and consequently to have done with the government, as soon as he can, and to whose interest, the day after he has left it and carried his whole fortune with him, it is perfectly indifferent "though" the whole county was swallowed by an earthquake.'[109]

The *Wealth of Nations* supplied a systemic criticism of the commercial reason of state politics of the first age of global imperialism. It was an immanent critique since it arose out of the values that lay at the heart of the ideology of the British state and its growing empire – summarized by David Armitage as Protestant, commercial, maritime and free. Smith did not seek to supplant existing values with some universalistic theory – an updated version of Stoicism,[110] for instance. Nor did he advocate disengaging from the modern world in the way he thought Rousseau was doing. And he rejected Lockean legalism as a way of modelling law and the constitution. Accepting that commerce on a global scale is the characteristic feature of the modern world, Smith saw virtue in doing business abroad, but only if it was divorced from monopoly double-dealing, colony and conquest. He was critical of the abuse of that other, more ancient dimension of reason of state, militarism and war, on grounds of both cost and justice. The only acceptable basis for waging war was on the basis of necessity, which he understood as being in this case anyway 'a part of justice'.[111] This two-pronged approach to global commercialism – honest trade and no offensive war – was Smith's solution to the rat race that threatened throughout much of the eighteenth century to spill out of control. National self-interest, when enlightened, might emulate cosmopolitan goodwill on a global scale and provide an alternative path towards cooperation and peace.

The proposed remedy was aimed at the internal dynamics of the British state as much as its external relations. Militarism and the extension of territory and power through conquest and exploitation, trade through monopolies, and government dependence on big trading companies,[112] these

distance was the overwhelming characteristic of British colonization and one which made it unique in world history.'

109 Smith, *Wealth of Nations*, IV.vii.v.101–106.

110 Adam Smith, *The Theory of Moral Sentiments* (Indianapolis, IN: Liberty Press, ed. A. MacFie and D. D. Raphael, 1982).

111 Smith, *Lectures on Jurisprudence*, 547. Smith is clear, though, that the idea of just war is particularly problematic in the East Indies context because of the disparity of force that exists between European and non-European combatants: *Wealth of Nations*, IV.vii.v.626.

112 Smith, *Wealth of Nations*, V.iii.35. See Sankar Muthu, 'Adam Smith's Critique of International Trading Companies: Theorizing "Globalization" in the Age of Enlightenment' (2008) 36 *Political Theory* 185.

were central features of the British fiscal-military state. Smith developed 'a critique of city-state civilization as driven to conquest, and as unable to sustain itself within the empires created by conquest'.[113] His point was that Britain was becoming in its actions, if not consistently in its ideology, a commonwealth for expansion.[114] It would soon, he warned, have a constitution to match – more ordered, more tightly regulated, more monopolistic, less free. Smith's analysis of the new political economy was unrivalled in its ability to knit together war, tax, trade and constitution, and provided a perceptive critique of the 'flawed metabolism' of East India Company rule.[115]

Burke and the dual constitution

The period in which Smith wrote the *Wealth of Nations* is familiar to lawyers as a time in which the relationship between liberty and the common law took its modern shape. The 1760s saw an upsurge in political radicalism, centred on the London radical John Wilkes and the new style of mass politics he helped to create.[116] In an echo of Harrington's redeployment of the term in which the people became the 'prerogative tribe' holding powers of legislation and judicature,[117] and of the close relationship in Locke's thought between the king's prerogative and the people's right of rebellion,[118] Wilkes accepted that the Crown had prerogative powers to be exercised with wisdom and judgement but asserted that 'the people too have their prerogative'.[119] The courts were dragged into the conflict between Wilkes and the Establishment on a number of occasions, led on the government side by Lord Chief Justice Mansfield.[120] In the most famous of

113 Pocock, 'Smith's Glasgow Lectures', 328.

114 Smith took aim at the people at home, scarcely touched even financially by foreign wars, 'reading in the newspapers the exploits of their own fleets and armies' and treating war as an 'amusement': *Wealth of Nations*, V.iii.37.

115 Nick Robins, *The Corporation That Changed the World: How the East India Company Shaped the Modern Multinational* (London: Pluto, 2nd ed., 2012), 121.

116 H. T. Dickinson, *Liberty and Property: Political Ideology in Eighteenth-Century Britain* (London: Methuen, 1977), 210–215.

117 James Harrington, *The Commonwealth of Oceana* (Cambridge University Press, ed. J. G. A. Pocock, 1992), 147, 166. See the discussion in Chapter 3.

118 Locke, *Two Treatises of Government*, Ch. XIV. See the discussion in Chapter 2.

119 Quoted in Arthur H. Cash, *John Wilkes* (New Haven: Yale University Press, 2006), 107.

120 David Bromwich, *The Intellectual Life of Edmund Burke: From the Sublime and Beautiful to American Independence* (Cambridge, MA: Harvard University Press, 2014), 132. Interestingly in the present context, the government also tried to buy Wilkes off with the offer to be made a director of the East India Company (also the governorship of Canada).

these cases, *Entick v Carrigton*, the court decided that the use of a general warrant which did not mention Wilkes by name to search for incriminating evidence was unlawful. 'If the king himself has no power to declare when the law ought to be violated for reason of state,' Lord Camden LCJ opined in response to an argument of state necessity, 'I am sure we his judges have no such prerogative.'[121] The same period also saw important developments in the legal fabric of the British empire. Lord Mansfield's decision on the status of slavery in England in *Somerset's Case* had implications for England and the colonies.[122] It also showed a path to a new judicial conception of freedom in which basic legal freedoms were available to all subjects irrespective of birth, race, religion or free status.[123]

Two years later, Lord Mansfield gave a classic 'restatement' of colonial law in *Campbell v Hall*.[124] There could be no difference in legal status, he ruled, within a colonial jurisdiction between native-born Britons and local subjects. Clear limits were placed on the king's prerogative to make law for a conquered territory. The case represents an attempt to update the legal 'map' of British imperial jurisdictions that had not changed substantially since Coke's judgment in *Calvin's Case*.[125] It signalled a shift away from the medieval understanding of sovereignty, given another lease of life in Coke's judgment.[126] The older conception, recrafted by Coke, saw allegiance (subjecthood) as a legal bond between sovereign and subject understood in personal terms. On this model, law itself was understood as being centrally about jurisdiction – that is, about who had the right to determine right and wrong and what were the boundaries of that power. The model that was beginning to emerge was grounded in a more

[121] (1765) 19 Howell's State Trials 1029. See also the House of Commons Resolution on General Warrants, 1766.

[122] *R v Knowles, ex parte Somerset* (1772) Lofft 1, 98 ER 499, 20 ST 1.

[123] George Van Cleve, 'Somerset's Case and Its Antecedents in Imperial Perspective' (2006) 24 *Law and History Review* 601, 606. If this was a 'new English idea of freedom', it was one that drew heavily on non-native sources, especially '[t]he Roman code, the law of nations, and the opinion of foreign civilians': Armitage, *Foundations of Modern International Thought*, 148.

[124] (1774) 98 Eng. Rep. 1045.

[125] (1608) 7 Co Rep 1a. The case was discussed in Chapter 2. Blackstone still used a framework of analysis derived essentially from *Calvin's Case* in his discussion of the legal status of the American colonies: *Commentaries*, I.4.104–105. See also William Searle Holdsworth, *A History of English Law, Vol. 9* (London: Methuen, 1926), 76–87.

[126] Daniel J. Hulsebosch, 'The Ancient Constitution and the Expanding Empire: Sir Edward Coke's British Jurisprudence' (2003) 21 *Law and History Review* 439, 461; P. G. McHugh, *Aboriginal Societies and the Common Law: A History of Sovereignty, Status, and Self-Determination* (Oxford: Oxford University Press, 2004), chapter 2.

substantive conception of allegiance (citizenship) which contained principles of liberty and authority, and where law was increasingly seen as jurisprudence – that is, a rational system of rules that bound government and private parties.[127]

In a parallel development at about the same time, the courts removed some of the uncertainty surrounding the legal position of colonial governors.[128] *Mostyn v Fabrigas* established that a governor was not the king's substitute but the king's servant and, as such, could be sued in English courts if he inflicted damage upon one of his subjects by breaking the law or by exceeding the powers with which he was invested.[129] On the basis of this new principle, two Armenian merchants, former business partners of disgruntled ex–East India Company servant Williams Bolts, sued Governor of Bengal Harry Verelst for abusing his ascendancy over nominally independent local rulers to procure their arrest for private motives.[130] The suits for wrongful imprisonment were successful and resulted in significant damages. The case went twice to the (judicial) House of Lords, whose handling of the case indicated that British courts of justice should accept responsibility for the expanding empire and enable those subject to British power abroad to appeal to British courts and laws.[131]

During the same period, Parliament made moves in the direction of a more sophisticated system of colonial regulation, an activity no doubt influenced by the increasingly troubled situation in the American colonies. Outside the North American arena, where lasting developments included the Quebec Act 1774, Parliament passed a significant statute (the India Act 1784) which sought to impose greater controls on Company rule in India. More dramatically, Parliament was also the venue for the impeachment of Warren Hastings, who as Governor of Bengal was effectively head of government in India from 1773 to 1785. The fact that the impeachment happened at all was due to the indefatigable efforts of opposition politician Edmund Burke. A seminal figure of the age, the

[127] Daniel J. Hulsebosch, *Constituting Empire: New York and the Transformation of Constitutionalism in the Atlantic World, 1664–1830* (Durham, NC: University of North Carolina Press, 2005).

[128] *Witham v Dutton* (1688) 3 Mod. 160, on appeal as *Dutton v Howell* (1694) Showers' 'Parliamentary Cases', 24.

[129] (1774) Cowper, 161.

[130] *Gregore Cojamaul v Harry Verelst*, 21 June 1774 English Reports, Vol. II House of Lords, 280.

[131] Willem G. J. Kuiters, *The British in Bengal 1756–1773: A Society in Transition seen through the Biography of a Rebel: William Bolts (1739–1808)* (Paris: Les Indes Savantes, 2002), chapter 16.

'conscience of his country' in the 1770s and 1780s,[132] Burke was obsessed with India. His involvement with Indian affairs spans almost the whole of his public life and his writings on India constitute a majority of his published works.[133] In that body of work, Burke 'theorized empire as a political form more deeply than anyone else of his time'.[134] 'There is no more difficult subject for the understanding of men', he told Parliament as early as 1766, 'than to govern a large Empire upon a plan of Liberty.'[135] Burke and Smith were friends, participated in the same intellectual society in the 1770s and 1780s ('the Club').[136] Burke was influenced by Smith's work and more generally by Scottish Enlightenment thought.[137] The connections between them should not be overstated. Burke cherished the ancient constitution in a way that Smith certainly did not,[138] and their position on empire differed in certain respects.[139] Nonetheless, they shared a historical approach to understanding society and morality, a not uncritical fascination with the power dynamics of modern commercial society, a conception of law as intimately connected to the life of a particular society, an attachment to the local and the concrete as opposed to the abstract and universal, and a marked preference for measured progressivism over radical reform.[140]

Burke's main works on India include some important speeches in Parliament,[141] several Committee reports[142] and, above all, his central

[132] Bromwich, *Intellectual Life of Edmund Burke*, 265.

[133] Uday Singh Mehta, *Liberalism and Empire: A Study in Nineteenth-Century British Liberal Thought* (Chicago: University of Chicago Press, 1999), 166.

[134] Jennifer Pitts, 'Burke and the Ends of Empire' in David Dwan and Christopher J. Insole (eds.), *The Cambridge Companion to Edmund Burke* (Cambridge: Cambridge University Press, 2012), 145.

[135] 'Speech on Declaratory Resolution', 3 February 1766.

[136] Forman-Barzilai, *Circles of Sympathy*, 133.

[137] And, like those Scottish theorists, Burke was also influenced by Montesquieu: Richard Bourke, 'Edmund Burke and the Politics of Conquest' (2007) 4 *Modern Intellectual History* 403.

[138] J. G. A. Pocock, 'Burke and the Ancient Constitution – A Problem in the History of Ideas' (1960) 3 *Historical Journal* 125.

[139] Iain Hampsher-Monk, 'Edmund Burke and Empire' in Duncan Kelly (ed.), *Lineages of Empire: The Historical Roots of British Imperial Thought* (Oxford: Oxford University Press, 2009), 128–136.

[140] On Burke's parliamentary record, see F. P. Lock, *Edmund Burke: Vol. II: 1784–1797* (Oxford: Oxford University Press, 2006), 21–22.

[141] Edmund Burke, 'Speech on Fox's India Bill' (1 December 1783) in David P. Fidler and Jennifer M. Welsh (eds.), *Empire and Community: Edmund Burke's Writings and Speeches on International Relations* (Boulder, CO: Westview Press, 1999).

[142] 'Ninth Report of the Select Committee of the House of Commons on the Affairs of India' (25 June 1783) and the 'Eleventh Report of the Select Committee of the House of Commons on the Affairs of India' (18 November 1783), for both of which Burke was

role in the Hastings impeachment. Burke's crusade against Hastings, 'one of the consuming passions of his life',[143] culminated in a seven-year trial before the House of Lords that resulted in Hastings's acquittal. The impeachment amounted to the revival of an ancient process which even Burke had earlier thought 'in danger of being lost, even the idea of it'[144] and was huge political theatre – 'the greatest spectacle of late-eighteenth-century Britain'.[145] It was entirely apt that the playwright and MP Richard Brinsley Sheridan, Burke's fellow Irishman, was its star performer.[146] It was clear to Burke, as to many others, that the proceedings against Hastings went far beyond the attempt to hold a powerful individual to account for his actions. He believed that he was putting the empire on trial before the entire nation. 'Indeed, the reputation of British justice, all that was good and sacred about the ancient constitution, was on trial as well. To convict Warren Hastings was to uphold the foundations of British sovereignty.'[147] As such, it was entirely appropriate to hold a great 'Inquest of the Nation',[148] in the name of the Commons of Great Britain in Parliament assembled, on the question Burke regarded as the most complicated of his age, namely, the fragile relationship between *imperium* and *libertas*.

Burke's case against Hastings centred on an attack on 'geographical morality' – the idea that the ordinary rules do not apply to power exercised outside the jurisdiction. This had long been his approach to Indian matters. In his *Speech on Fox's India Bill* (1783) Burke tried to make India comprehensible to British moral sensibilities by comparing the patchwork quilt of sovereignties and loyalties in India with the German empire.[149] In another speech, on the *Nabob of Arcot's Debts*, he argued that 'Fraud, injustice, oppression, peculation engendered in India, are crimes of the same blood, family, and cast, with those that are born and bred in

the chief author: Edmund Burke, *The Writings and Speeches of Edmund Burke: Vol. VIII* (New York: Cosimo Classics, 2008).

143 Lock, *Edmund Burke*, 62.

144 Edmund Burke, 'Thoughts on the Cause of the Present Discontents' in *Pre-Revolutionary Writings*, 162.

145 Nicholas B. Dirks, *The Scandal of Empire: India and the Creation of Imperial Britain* (Cambridge, MA: Harvard University Press, 2006), 85.

146 Lock, *Edmund Burke*, 188–190.

147 Dirks, *Scandal of Empire*, 106–107. Edmund Burke, 'Speech on Opening of Impeachment' (15 February 1788) in Fidler and Welsh, *Empire and Community*, 204.

148 'Speech on Opening of Impeachment', 203.

149 'Speech on Fox's India Bill', 176.

England.'[150] This rhetorical strategy is consistent with the view that sympathy plays a central role in moral judgement, a feature of his early essay on aesthetics[151] and something he shared with Scottish Enlightenment thinkers. Its aim was to bring India within the reach of a universal moral and legal code, to put it firmly on what he called 'the Great Map of Mankind'.[152] His specific target was the claim that British agents in India could govern arbitrarily. Burke was adamant that the Company ought to 'govern upon British principles', understood to comprise 'that spirit of equity, the spirit of justice, that spirit of safety, [and] that spirit of lenity'. No claim to arbitrary power could ever be legitimate, whatever the source. 'Was there ever heard, or could it be conceived, that a man would dare to mention the practices of all the villains, all the mad usurpers, all the thieves and robbers in Asia, that he should gather them all up, and form the whole map of abuses into one code, and call it the duty of a British Governor?'[153]

Claims like these, and the practices they are meant to justify, are bad for Indians but they are also bad for us. They carry the potential to cannibalize the British constitution. They disrespect particular systems of law – Indian, British, natural, divine – and the idea of law itself.[154] Through this pollution of 'the spirit of all laws', they 'endanger the nature of our constitution itself'.[155] The unnaturalness of British rule in India is exemplified by its social and institutional characteristics. Not only does Company rule amount to a perversion of government because it confuses commercial and sovereign functions – 'a State in disguise of a Merchant'.[156] It is also unnatural because it allows untutored boys to rule an ancient community. Using exactly the sort of framework for moral development articulated by Scottish Enlightenment writers, and perhaps above all Smith, Burke argued that the Company provided in India a kind of unsentimental education for British youth. 'Young men

150 Edmund Burke, 'Speech on the Nabob of Arcot's Debts' in Burke, *Writings and Speeches, Vol. 5* (Oxford: Oxford University Press, ed. P. J. Marshall, 1981), 488.

151 Edmund Burke, *Philosophical Enquiry into the Origin of Our Ideas of the Sublime and the Beautiful* (1757) (Oxford: Oxford University Press, 1990), I.XI-XIV.

152 Letter to William Robertson (9 June 1777) in Edmund Burke, *Correspondence* (Cambridge: Cambridge University Press, 1958) vol. iii., 351, quoted in Lock, *Edmund Burke*, 163.

153 'Speech on Opening of Impeachment', 223.

154 Peter J. Stanlis, *Edmund Burke and the Natural Law* (New Brunswick, NJ: Transaction Publishers, 2003), 240.

155 'Speech on Opening of Impeachment', 204.

156 'Speech on Opening of Impeachment', 211.

(boys almost) govern there; without society and without sympathy with the natives.' Note the way in which 'sympathy', or rather its absence, is deployed here to reveal the essential 'adolescence of the colonizing mind'[157] central to which is a juvenile disrespect for local laws and customs. Government should be an important and onerous responsibility. Instead it has become a game subject to 'the desperate boldness of a few obscure young men'.[158] Having come into 'a power of which they saw neither the purposes nor the limits, tossed about, subverted, and tore to pieces, as if it were in the gambols of a boyish unluckiness and malice, the most established rights, and the most ancient and most revered institutions, of ages and nations'.[159] Animated by avarice, the slippage from (mature) man to (untutored) boy to (wild) animal is complete. The new rulers of India, Burke opined, are like 'birds of prey and passage, with appetites continually renewing for a food that is continually wanting'.[160]

Burke here provides a parable of misrule that applies to Britain and her growing empire but speaks more broadly of the danger posed by structures of authority divorced from custom and precedent, a worry that we have seen that Smith shared. It brings into relief fundamental aspects of his philosophy of government. In a speech in 1769 on the Wilkes crisis, Burke said that his ideas of liberty were tempered by the knowledge that 'Peace is the great end in *all* Governments; Liberty is an End only in the Best.' He was, he said, 'an hater of violence and *innovation*'. The innovation that he most feared in the turbulent years of the Wilkes crisis of the late 1760s was the establishment of a 'regular martial police', the 'blending the Army into the civil Government', as a first instrument rather than a last resort of government.[161] Such a move – the application of maxims of reason of state into the body politic – quickly fractures the community of sentiment which makes the constitution of liberty possible. 'Nations are not primarily ruled by laws; less by violence.'[162] A government that innovates – and uses force to defend its innovations – relies increasingly on law

[157] Sara Suleri, *The Rhetoric of English India* (Chicago: University of Chicago Press, 1992), 32.

[158] 'Speech on Fox's India Bill', 180.

[159] Compare Edmund Burke, *Reflections on the Revolution in France* (New Haven, CT: Yale University Press, ed. Frank M. Turner, 2003), 75: 'Their attachment to their country itself is only so far as it agrees with some of their fleeting projects; it begins and ends with that scheme of polity which falls in with their momentary opinion.'

[160] 'Speech on Fox's India Bill', 180.

[161] 'Speech of March 8, 1769', quoted in Bromwich, *Intellectual Life of Edmund Burke*, 142–143.

[162] 'Present Discontents', 117.

and legal rights and prerogatives. The juridification of civil life helps to harden the opposition between government and a people fearing oppression. Underlying this sentiment is a consistent vision of government 'as a bond of trust rather than a system of abstract rights, an affair of sentiment and of interest rather than a rationalized system of juridical relations'.[163] The natural end of a system built on abstract rights and deracinated laws is a collapse into 'lofty despotism'.[164] 'Do not dream', he enjoined fellow MPs in his *Speech on Conciliation with America*, 'that your letters of office, and your instructions, and your suspending clauses, are the things that hold together the great contexture of this mysterious whole [the empire]. These things do not make your government. Dead instruments, passive tools as they are, it is the spirit of English communion that gives all their life and efficacy to them.'[165]

It was just such an innovation that Burke opposes in the government of India. What most worries Burke is what happens when the Company boys come back home from India schooled in 'avarice, rapacity, pride, cruelty, ferocity, malignity of temper, haughtiness, insolence'[166] as rich and influential men.[167] The sins of the children will be visited on their fathers as 'they are transformed from slippery youth to perilous independence' and corrupt British moral sentiments. Their 'prey is lodged in England'. Accustomed to buying and selling political power, to breaking treaties and agreements whenever it suits them, to exploiting populations through arbitrary power, these men will destroy British power structures from within. England and English liberty stood in the same perilous

[163] Richard Bourke, 'Liberty, Authority, and Trust in Burke's Idea of Empire' (2000) 61 *Journal of the History of Ideas* 453, 462.

[164] 'Speech on Fox's India Bill', 182. This worry was by no means unique to Burke. Lord Chatham, speaking in the House of Lords in 1770, declared that 'The riches of Asia have been poured in upon us, and have brought with them not only Asiatic luxury, but, I fear, Asiatic principles of government.' Quoted in Bowen, *Business of Empire*, 16.

[165] 'Conciliation with America', 265.

[166] 'Speech on the Opening of Impeachment', 206.

[167] Mehta, *Liberalism and Empire*, 170–171. See also William Fullarton, *A View of English Interests in India* (1787), 270: 'let it never be forgotten that in the present state of national depravity, wherever a latitude of power is lodged, whether in civil or military hands, the eye of justice must be more piercing, and her sword more severely pointed against delinquency, before you can hope to restrain the repetition of abuse'. Quoted in James Epstein, *The Scandal of Colonial Rule: Power and Subversion in the British Atlantic During the Age of Revolution* (Cambridge: Cambridge University Press, 2012), 72. Fullarton went on to pursue impeachment proceedings against Sir Elijah Impey, chief of the Supreme Court of Bengal from 1774 to 1781, articulating in so doing a concept of colonial authority subject to humanitarian restraint and strict review.

relationship to empire as did Rome and Roman liberty: 'The downfall of the greatest empire this world ever saw, has been, on all hands agreed upon to have originated in the mal-administration of its provinces.'[168] The process is already well underway. As he said in his *Speech on the Nabob of Arcot Debts*:

> all England, Scotland, and Ireland had for years been witness to the immense sums laid out by the servants of the Company in stocks of all denominations, in the purchase of lands, in the buying and building of houses, in the securing quiet seats in Parliament or in the tumultuous riot of contested elections, in wandering throughout the whole range of those variegated modes of inventive prodigality.

In his engagement with the law and morals of empire, Burke fashioned an account of a dual constitution, or rather a series of dual constitutions. The East India Company is a constitutional entity of sorts. In principle, it is public, rule-bound, transparent and reasonably, if imperfectly, accountable. In practice, it acts as a commonwealth of thieves operating 'an oppressive, irregular, capricious, unsteady, rapacious, and peculating despotism'.[169] The nature of that enterprise, when understood as the administrative agent of the British state, gives rise to a second dualism: between the British constitution as understood by those, including Burke, who see it as a near-ideal guarantor of 'a manly, moral, regulated liberty'[170] – he spoke elsewhere of Britain having a monopoly on freedom[171] – and that constitution in reality once its offshore additions, most notably in India, are included. Whereas Smith reached for a biological metaphor when describing this state of affairs, calling it a 'massive tumor' on the body politic, Burke characteristically deploys a juridical vocabulary and describes the operation of a state of exception. In India, normal moral and legal rules do not apply. Decision-making is arbitrary and policy made on the basis of the rulers' own immediate interest. 'Crimes so convenient, crimes so politic, crimes so necessary, crimes so alleviating of distress, can never be wanting to those who use no process, and who produce no proofs.'[172] This creates a topsy-turvy world that violates one of

[168] Burke, 'Motion for the Papers' in Edmund Burke, *Works and Speeches, Vol. 6: India: The Launching of the Hastings Impeachment, 1786–1788*, 63, quoted in Hampsher-Monk, 'Edmund Burke and Empire', 134.

[169] 'Speech on Fox's India Bill', 194.

[170] *Reflections*, 7. See also 209.

[171] 'Conciliation with America', 265.

[172] 'Speech on Fox's India Bill', 188.

the first principles of the commonwealth: that no government 'should act as if they were the entire masters'.[173] There is a humanitarian dimension to this analysis. But establishment and acceptance of the state of exception in India represents, Burke argues, a threat to the constitution. The danger comes from the fact that powerful people become accustomed to acting in this way, not least because it provides massive rewards for the rulers (the new class of 'nabobs'). This being so, the state of exception threatens to become the norm. The blowback effect from colonial rule – which is the reverse, and darker, narrative of moral sentiments – creates what is for Burke the final and most serious dualism: between the British constitution as it is supposed to be, and the British constitution as it may be in the process of becoming. A constitution dominated by commercial reason of state thinking, arbitrary and lawless, adolescent in its disavowal of precedent, extractive and oppression, run for the benefit of rulers, abusive of the right of war and peace:[174] in a word, unfree.

Burke developed his account of reason of state and constitutional exceptionalism primarily in the context of India and imperial rule.[175] But the relationship he perceived between shock, force and the regression of sentiments emerges even more strongly in his later writings on revolutionary France. The framework he applied there was essentially the one that he had worked out on the basis of his theory of the sublime and had applied to the question of empire. In the Indian context, he observed that imperial engagements, even if driven by commercial interest, are likely without proper management to become exploitative and violent. The need to use sustained force in turn drives the inclination to favour monopolist companies, the effect of which is to deepen and perpetuate exploitative relationships. 'Any *état police*', as Pocock observes in respect of similar observations made by French thinkers, 'necessarily corrupts its subjects if these do not retain and develop the free activity, commercial and civil, of the independent proprietor'.[176] And just as we adjust ourselves to the habit of peaceful civil engagement, so we adapt ourselves to violent conditions to the extent that we may at last be equipped to deal with nothing else. 'Unlike later theorists of the sublime – Walter Benjamin, for example, in

[173] *Reflections*, 81.

[174] 'Speech on Fox's India Bill', 179; 'Speech on Opening of Impeachment', 211: 'where powers of peace and war are given, it wants but time and circumstance to make this supersede every other'.

[175] Pitts, 'Burke and the Ends of Empire', 153: 'Burke's political thought was undoubtedly shaped by his sense of the distinctively imperial space in which he acted.'

[176] Pocock, 'The Antiquity of Asia', 267.

his writings on modernism and the city – Burke did not suppose that any tolerable life could be made from the human induration to daily shocks', David Bromwich argues in a recent study. From Burke's point of view, he continues, 'to say that "all men hate war" or that "all men hate anarchy" is false. It is equally false to say that we love those things. We are fascinated by them; and what fascinates us may draw us in.'[177]

Reflections on the Revolution in France, written while proceedings against Hastings were ongoing, can be read as an attack on the state of exception instigated by the French Revolution and the mortal threat it poses the British constitution. Indeed, Burke makes the connection himself in a telling passage:

> It is impossible not to observe, that, in the spirit of this geometrical distribution, and arithmetical arrangement, these pretended citizens treat France exactly like a country of conquest. Acting as conquerors, they have imitated the policy of the harshest of that harsh race. The policy of such barbarous victors, who contemn a subdued people, and insult their feelings, has ever been, as much as in them lay, to destroy all vestiges of the ancient country, in religion, in polity, in laws, and in manners; to confound all territorial limits; to produce to general poverty; to put up their properties to auction; to crush their princes, nobles, and pontiffs; to lay low everything which had lifted its head above the level, or which could serve to combine or rally, in their distress, the disbanded people, under the standard of old opinion.[178]

The *Reflections* draws on much the same imagery developed in the attacks on Company rule in India. The new rulers in France are 'juvenile'.[179] Government has become a game – the 'great object in [their] policies is to metamorphose France from a great kingdom into one great play-table'.[180] Combined with familiar warnings about the dangers inherent in 'new, experimental government' and the wholesale rejection of the past comes a sweeping critique of power unlimited by law. 'In such a state of unbounded power for undefined and undefinable purposes, the evil of a moral and almost physical inaptitude of the man to the function must be the greatest we can conceive to happen in the management of human affairs.'[181] The stark power claimed by the new rulers is dehumanizing. It strips people down to their bare existence. From this perspective, 'a king is but a man, a queen is but a woman; a woman is but an animal, and an animal not of the highest order'.[182] We become little better 'than the flies of a summer'.[183] Burke

[177] Bromwich, *Intellectual Life of Edmund Burke*, 236–237.
[178] *Reflections*, 155. [179] *Reflections*, 55. [180] *Reflections*, 164.
[181] *Reflections*, 39. [182] *Reflections*, 66. [183] *Reflections*, 81.

here uses the same declension from 'rounded' or socialized man to 'natural' man to animal as when criticizing Company rule in India. But here the argument draws on the contrast between the natural and established order that subsists under the British constitution, where government works with the grain of the customs of the people, and the perverse and unnatural order being established in France.[184] The revolutionaries spawned a 'monster of a constitution'[185] structured around the power of war and peace: 'this military democracy, which … must be the true constitution of the state'.[186] That is to say, contemporary France is not so much a constitutional order as a state of exception, and as such has no more legitimacy than the abusive government of a newly conquered territory:

> I can never consider this Assembly as anything else than a voluntary association of men, who have availed themselves of circumstances to seize the power of the state. They have not the sanction and authority of the character under which they first met. They have assumed another of a very different nature; and have completely altered and inverted all the relations in which they originally stood.[187]

Burke developed this analysis in his *Letters on a Regicide Peace*, written between 1795 and 1797, in which he urged the British government to wage an aggressive war aimed at the annihilation of the new regime and the restoration of the *ancien régime*. The analysis of the situation in France remains essentially unchanged. What is different is the existentialism with which it is now freighted. 'They made a schism with the whole universe.'[188] Burke provides a sharper characterization of the state of exception that he thinks exists in France, and of the clear and present danger posed to Britain and British liberty as a result. In addition, the *Letters* cast the problem as a Europe-wide problem, threatening the collapse of civilized government across the entire continent. The revolution, Burke argues, ought to be seen more like a proselytizing religion than a political revolt.[189] A 'hideous phantom', which despises 'all common maxims and all common means',[190] it is a phenomenon entirely new to European politics. The revolutionaries present a radical conception of politics based on original principles of state and government. They are

184 *Reflections*, 9. 185 *Reflections*, 166.
186 *Reflections*, 180. 187 *Reflections*, 139.
188 Edmund Burke, *Letters of a Regicide Peace* (Indianapolis: Liberty Press, 1999), 134.
189 Iain Hampsher-Monk, 'Burke's Counter-Revolutionary Writings' in Dwan and Insole, *Cambridge Companion to Edmund Burke*, 215.
190 *Letters*, 65.

intent on spreading those new politics and overturning established governments. Revolutionary ideology already has a foothold in countries outside France: 'It has, by it's essence, a faction of opinion, and of interest, and of enthusiasm, in every country.'[191]

All this makes the conflict with France categorically different from normal intra-European wars. 'We are at war with a system, which, by it's essence, is inimical to all other Governments, and which makes peace or war, as peace and war may best contribute to their subversion.'[192] We see here a repetition of one of the central charges Burke made against Company rule of India – the systematic use of the power to make peace and war for self-interested ends and in furtherance of a plan to dominate others. A defining feature of commercial reason of state in the imperial sphere now threatens to dominate European politics. At base, Burke now argues, Europe is basically a commonwealth on account of its shared religion, laws and manners.[193] 'Old' European constitutions are similar in that none has been 'formed upon a regular plan or with any unity of design' and, as such, they are not 'directed to any *peculiar* end'.[194] The 'total departure of the Jacobin Republick' from these shared legal and moral ideals and customs, and her use of 'studied violence' to do so, amounts to a 'violent breach of the community of Europe'.[195] This accusation has a pronounced juridical dimension. It is primarily through the violent rejection of the *ius publicum europeaum*, the jurisprudence that contained the elements and principles of the law of nations, 'the great ligament of mankind', that opens France up for differential treatment. 'With a fixed design, they have outlawed themselves, and, to their power, outlawed all other nations.'[196]

Indeed, Burke presses the case that the republican leaders of France should not be understood as a new government running a transformed state so much as a criminal enterprise that has seized power through robbery and murder. France, he says, 'is under the sway of a sect'.[197] Its governing apparatus has been hijacked by terrorists. We therefore 'encounter France, not as a State, but as a Faction'[198] – a 'pretended Republick' not the

[191] *Letters*, 76. [192] *Letters*, 169.

[193] *Letters*, 133. America is counted among the 'European Powers' for these purposes: 231.

[194] *Letters*, 180. [195] *Letters*, 134.

[196] *Letters*, 124. Iain Hampsher-Monk, 'Edmund Burke's Changing Justification for Intervention' (2005) 48 *Historical Journal* 65, 95 notes that Burke's point is both that the revolutionaries have rejected the laws but also the methods of engagement, including the very language of diplomacy itself, that customarily attached themselves to those laws.

[197] *Letters*, 123. [198] *Letters*, 154.

nation as a moral esssence.[199] At times, the analysis slips into the metaphysical (as well as the animal). Burke talks, for instance, of 'the evil spirit that possesses the body of France'. Exhibiting 'a false reptile prudence'[200] rather than any real wisdom, this 'Republick of Regicide'[201] is a place of killing and destruction and death. Even when it comes to the laws, the republicans have replaced living law, with its imperfections and messiness, with crystal clear but stillborn prescriptions: 'No! the law is clear, but it is a dead letter. Dead and putrid, it is insufficient to save the State, but potent to infect and to kill.'[202]

Conclusion

The previous chapter offered a picture of a Britain that was beginning to grow into itself as a nation. Hume, turning to the past to help him specify the distinctive contours of the present, saw the society he inhabited as a vast improvement on the older versions out of which it had arisen. In part, this was due to the complexities of modern commercial society. Social pluralism, the seemingly boundless possibilities and energy of commerce, developed political institutions, an integrated system of laws – all these factors seemed conducive not only to peace and prosperity but also to reducing the scope for personal, and therefore arbitrary, rule. It was also due in part to the fact that the rule of law, that 'hardy plant', had taken root in British political institutions – and within the political imagination. One might almost see this development as a result of historical accident, and certainly fortune attended it, but for the fact that other European states seemed to be travelling in a similar direction. Power was becoming socialized and domesticated – and, as a result, made normal.

The main cloud on the horizon concerned the destabilizing potential of commercial reason of state and the jealousy of trade politics that attended it. Here, Hume was far from being his usual equanimous self. The riskiness of these policies, and the public debt required to sustain them, he insisted, would spell the ruin of the free state. This chapter has picked up where that last one finished. Here, we read Smith's *Wealth of Nations*, the culmination of a life's work on questions of morals and political economy, as an essay on reason of state. The book supplied a systemic criticism of the commercial reason of state politics that had so exercised Hume in his

[199] *Letters*, 139. [200] *Letters*, 68. [201] *Letters*, 66.

[202] *Letters*, 75. Compare Burke's remark elsewhere in the *Letters* that 'Manners are of more importance than laws': 126.

Essays and, through it, an immanent critique of British commercial and political practice in the first age of global imperialism. A vital dimension of that critique focused on the delegated nature of the power relations that structured the commercial empire in the East Indies. Here, Smith can be seen making a parallel move to the one we saw Hobbes and the republican theorists make, except that for them the move was to do with conditions on the home front, whereas for Smith it was primarily about extra-territorial activities. The seventeenth-century writers had called for a state-consolidating process capable of creating conditions in which a public interest could emerge and dominate various competing private interests. Smith's specific solution to the problem represented by the East India Company is a two-pronged approach of honest trade and no offensive war. But for that plan to have any chance of working the whole operation needs to be taken within state control. Only then is there a chance that 'good' (public-interested) reason of state will triumph over the 'bad' (private-interested) version that currently predominates.

Turning to Burke after encountering Hume and Smith, it is hard not to be struck by what Dror Wahrman calls 'the overdramatized effusions of the man who turned sentimental pathos into a political art form'.[203] But for all that, it is not an exaggeration to describe him as the preeminent early-modern theorist of reason of state.[204] While moving in the terrain mapped out by Hume and Smith, Burke was uniquely capable of recasting those arguments in juridical form. His success in managing to get the Hastings impeachment up and running shows that he could be politically effective and, perhaps more to the point, was able to tap into widespread sentiments and anxieties about the dangers of overseas empire. The impeachment itself has been criticized at the time and since for its unfocused and overly dramatic handling. But the drama may not have been entirely without point – and may well have had a role to play in the normalizing of reason of state politics within developing constitutional structures. Burke also had an exceptionally keen awareness of the interconnectedness of the internal and external facets or membranes of the state. He saw clearly how the 'internal' dimension of the constitution, the sphere of law and liberty, could be affected by what happens in the 'external' dimension, not least because he understood them as being really two parts of the same thing.

[203] Wahrman, *The Making of the Modern Self*, 222.

[204] David Armitage, 'Edmund Burke and Reason of State' (2000) 61 *Journal of the History of Ideas* 617, 633.

In a manner entirely consistent with the Scottish theorists and Montesquieu, for whom the constitution was akin to a living entity with a character or spirit developed over time through a process that paralleled the socialization of individuals, Burke was able to capture the *regression* of moral sentiments that threatened to tear apart the constitution of liberty. He developed a compelling account of the feedback loops and possibilities of contagion that activity in the external sphere might have on the other, being particularly alive to the cascading effect of reason of state thinking and practice. Good government cannot be legislated into existence. Just as good practice can flow through social and legal arteries and be sustained thereby, so can bad reason of state practices and mentalities warp the body politic by occupying precisely the same channels.[205] The rapacious behaviour of Company officials in India is not a matter of esoteric or purely humanitarian concern. It is a clear and present danger for the British constitution, understood as a particularly good instantiation of a constitution of liberty (or, in Hume's terms, a constitution that is fortunate in providing a good balance between authority and liberty). *Novis orbis victus vos vicit*, as the influential Tacitean thinker Justus Lipsius wrote in 1603 – the New World, conquered by you, has conquered you in its turn.[206]

In relation to India, reason of state provided the threat against which Burke marshalled a full array of Ciceronian arguments, including those derived from both national and natural legal sources. In the case of revolutionary France, reason of state thinking provided both the framework and the basis on which to make the case for all-out war. With the continent's most powerful country controlled by a bunch of ideologically motivated bandits, reason of state thinking threatened to become the new norm and the new basis for inter-state relations in Europe, just as it had long threatened to be in their commercial and imperial competition outside the European legal space. Given the predicament that Europe now

[205] Nowhere does the author of the *Origin of Our Ideas of the Sublime and the Beautiful* express this idea more eloquently than in 'Thoughts on the Cause of the Present Discontents', 153: 'When the people conceive that laws, and tribunals, and even popular assemblies, are perverted from the ends of their institution, they find in those names of degenerated establishments only new motives to discontent. Those bodies, which, when full of life and beauty, lay in their arms, and were their joy and comfort, when dead and putrid, become but the more loathsome from remembrance of former endearments. A sullen gloom, and furious disorder, prevail by fits: the nation loses its relish for peace and prosperity, as it did in that season of fullness which opened our troubles in the time of Charles the First.'

[206] Quoted in Elliott, *The Old World and the New*, 63.

found itself in, nothing else but the logic of the exception would do. The remedy Burke proposed – a war to bring about regime change – while in violation of accepted standards of the European legal order was necessary, he argued, precisely because that same legal order was threatened by the continued existence of the revolutionary regime. 'Fidelity was heading for extinction, and with its demise all known instruments of social negotiation and accommodation would collapse in the face of an unyielding competition of powers. On this scheme of things, revolutionary society is an altogether more brutal affair than the military societies of early European history.'[207]

With Burke in particular we see the age of reason slipping into the age of revolution and counter-revolution. His articulation of a theory of dual constitutionalism, pivoting around the tension between rule of law and reason of state, and played out on both the outer and inner faces of the state, was a juridically sophisticated and politically potent response to what he saw as the crises of his times. Somewhat ironically, the existential notes that we encounter in Burke's treatment of both the Indian and French cases provide more than a foretaste of the age that was dawning. Like many constitutional theories with a strong normative bent, Burke's account opened the possibility of both constitutional redemption and constitutional failure in which the gap between norm and exception is pronounced and carries an almost existential significance. If we fall into the trap of the British in India – or of revolutionary France – and pursue reason of state politics without reserve or restraint, oblivious to established precedents and practice, it will take over our polity, eradicate the moral sentiments that bind us together and keep us civil, and lead us into a season in hell.

[207] Bourke, 'Liberty, Authority, and Trust in Burke's Idea of Empire', 467.

6

Reason of state and the legislating empire

The previous chapter closed with Burke's angry panegyric to the old British constitution and the old legal pathways that he grouped under the banner of the *ius publicum europaeum*, both of which he thought were on the verge of transformative and possibly fatal change. As Burke predicted, the French Revolution did indeed change European politics and its legal order irrevocably. Britain found itself a major participant in the Napoleonic Wars, the 'first total war' according to one of its leading historians,[1] which gave birth to the idea of the 'nation in arms' and, through a process of military, political and cultural reconfiguration, a new constitutional model.[2] Although France was ultimately defeated, Philip Bobbitt observes, 'the constitutional result of the epochal war waged from 1792 to 1815 was not to restore the *ancien régimes* of the territorial states' but to instigate the era of the 'state nation', a state that 'mobilizes a nation – a national, ethnocultural group – to act on behalf of the state'.[3]

The century that separated the Congress of Vienna in 1815 and the outbreak of the First World War was one of fundamental change for Britain on numerous fronts, not least in basic conceptions of law, politics and society and also in the character of imperial rule. This chapter isolates two central sites of juridical change that were integral to the creation of modern government structures. The first is *legislation*. The rise of legislation

[1] David A. Bell, *The First Total War: Napoleon's Europe and the Birth of Modern Warfare* (London: Bloomsbury, 2007).

[2] In reaction to defeat by Napoleon, for instance, Prussia instigated a 'revolution from above' – the abolition of rural serfdom and urban guilds, the opening up of the professions, an equalization of the tax burden and a measure of religious toleration – in order to modernize the state along French lines. Friedrich Meinecke applauded the reform on the basis that it changed the army 'from a mere tool in the hands of the commander-in-chief into a living institution': *The Age of German Liberalism, 1795–1815* (Berkeley: University of California Press, ed. Peter Paret, 1977), 93, quoted in Bell, *The First Total War*, 253.

[3] Philip Bobbitt, *The Shield of Achilles: War, Peace, and the Course of History* (New York: Alfred A. Knopf, 2002), 538, 146. The 'nation state' is a later phenomenon, Bobbitt argues, which creates a state in order to benefit the nation it governs.

as the predominant lawmaking form is a familiar feature of legal histories of the period.[4] As important were the conceptual and attitudinal changes that accompanied it. What we might call the normalization of legislation corresponds to a different way of thinking about law and lawmaking.[5] The sovereign legislator, seen as an active agent representing the will of the nation, could and should recast the legal relationships among subjects where it was in the interests of the community to do so.[6] Legislation, Dicey wrote in *Law & Public Opinion in England during the Nineteenth Century*, his last major work, 'is a science based on the characteristics of human nature, and the art of lawmaking, if it is to be successful, must be the application of legislative principles'. It was Bentham, he continued, 'the prophet' of 'scientific legislation', who forced the idea that law is in fact made, rather than grown, upon the attention of a generation of Englishmen.[7]

The second phenomenon is the growth of *bureaucracy*. Bureaucracies, in one form or another, have existed as long as governments. But its modern Weberian form – hierarchical, structured through norms of expertise, independence and professionalism themselves connected to a rational-legal conception of authority – was largely a nineteenth-century invention.[8] It is true that administrative structures of this sort had existed before. Eighteenth-century England knew at least one. The Excise Office developed an extremely cohesive and efficient 'modern' bureaucratic form,[9] and had special legal powers in order to perform its work, much to the consternation of common lawyers like Blackstone.[10] Again, it was not

[4] Stuart Anderson, 'Parliament' in William Cornish, Stuart Anderson, Raymond Cocks, Michael Lobban, Patrick Polden and Keith Smith (eds.), *The Oxford History of the Laws of England: Volume XI, 1820–1914: English Legal System* (Oxford: Oxford University Press, 2010).

[5] Gerald J. Postema, *Bentham and the Common Law Tradition* (Oxford: Oxford University Press, 1986).

[6] Compare Burke's classical account of Parliamentary lawmaking in 'Thoughts on the Cause of the Present Discontents' in Burke, *Pre-Revolutionary Writings* (Cambridge: Cambridge University Press, ed. Ian Harris, 1993), 169: 'We do not *make* laws. No; we do not contend for this power. We only *declare* law; and, as we are a tribunal both competent and supreme, what we declare to be law becomes law, although it should not have been so before.'

[7] A. V. Dicey, *Lectures on the Relation between Law and Public Opinion in England during the Nineteenth Century* (Indianapolis: Liberty Fund, ed. Richard VandeWetering, 2008), 98.

[8] See, e.g., Oliver MacDonagh, *Early Victorian Government, 1830–1870* (London: Weidenfeld and Nicolson, 1977).

[9] See the discussion in Chapter 4.

[10] William Blackstone, *Commentaries on the Laws of England* (Chicago: University of Chicago Press, ed. Stanley N. Katz, 1979), vol. I: 308.

only the very substantial increase in the size of bureaucratic governance that counted, but also the way in which that increase changed ideas about government and the relationship between state and citizen. One vital dimension of the issue was the unprecedented rise of mass social and political movements and the vast scale of the administrative enterprise that these movements helped precipitate.[11] The unrelenting examination of the relationship between self and group was a defining feature of the new politics, connecting back to the roots of much of this new politics in the nonconformist and Evangelical religious revival earlier in the century.[12] Just as we can read Weber – or, for that matter, Kafka – as rethinking what it means to be human given the realities of the modern state, so we can understand Dicey as attempting to reconcile the common law tradition with the new legislative state, and J. S. Mill as reworking the Anglo-British tradition of liberalism to accommodate new forms of participatory democracy and political action.

But how do the modern phenomena of legislation and bureaucracy, and the habits of mind that pertain to them, relate to reason of state? The connection between them is not obvious. The waters are muddied still further by the development during the same period of a modern and professional body of 'international law' (the term was coined by Jeremy Bentham towards the end of the previous century).[13] Thinking about the external properties of the state – the traditional domain of reason of state thinking – became, towards the tail end of the nineteenth century, increasingly the preserve of international lawyers and international relations theorists.[14] This chapter continues the focus on India which, as one of the most visible manifestations of British control and dominion, continued to play a sustained and extensive role in nineteenth-century British political debate.[15] 'Almost without exception, all the important British political

[11] One interesting aspect of this shift is the 're-evaluation of the Puritan Revolution [that] first took place between the age of the French Revolution and the days of Peterloo', as a result of which the Puritan Revolutionaries, and Oliver Cromwell in particular, became the most important source of inspiration for popular radical movements: see Eugenio F. Biagini, *Liberty, Retrenchment and Reform: Popular Liberalism in the Age of Gladstone, 1860–1880* (Cambridge: Cambridge University Press, 1992), 41–46.

[12] See, e.g., Melvin Richter, *The Politics of Conscience: T.H. Green and His Age* (London: Weidenfeld and Nicolson, 1964), chapter 1.

[13] Jeremy Bentham, *An Introduction to the Principles of Morals and Legislation* (1780/1789) (Oxford: Oxford University Press, eds. J. H. Burns and H. L. A. Hart, 1996), 6, 296.

[14] Martti Koskenniemi, *The Gentle Civilizer of Nations: The Rise and Fall of International Law 1870–1960* (Cambridge: Cambridge University Press, 2001).

[15] Sandra den Otter, '"A Legislating Empire": Victorian Political Theorists, Codes of Law, and Empire' in Duncan Bell (ed.), *Victorian Visions of Global Empire* (Cambridge: Cambridge University Press, 2007), 88.

theorists from the late eighteenth century into the twentieth century dealt in an extensive and focused manner with India.'[16] Analysis in this chapter concentrates on just a handful of these figures. It considers the colonial writings of Bentham and James Mill, before situating J. S. Mill's argument for technocratic imperialism in India against his wider political theory. Both Mills worked for most of their adult lives in the East India Company. It then examines Walter Bagehot's constitutional writings against this background, observing his application to the domestic arena of some of the arguments and language that underpinned British imperialism, particularly the distinction between civilized and uncivilized. The chapter concludes with an analysis of the Victorian debates on martial law and the work of W. F. Finlason and A. V. Dicey in particular. That debate ended inconclusively, and neither events surrounding the Jamaica uprising in the late 1860s nor the *fin-de-siècle* Boer War produced much clarity. In practice, martial law (or martial law-like) powers were increasingly legislated by imperial and colonial parliaments as officials sought increasing reassurance from positive law sources. This gradual process led to the old common law/prerogative framework for martial law being displaced by a statutory and bureaucratic one.

James Mill and the science of imperial legislation

In his classic work *The English Utilitarians and India*, Eric Stokes relates an incident that occurred in 1827 at a farewell dinner for Lord William Bentinck, who had been appointed Governor-General of India. Bentinck apparently turned to James Mill and said, 'I am going to British India, but I shall not be Governor-General. It is you that will be Governor-General.'[17] The anecdote illustrates, for Stokes, utilitarianism's influence on imperial theory and practice, in India perhaps above all. (Although Bentham's influence elsewhere could hardly be called negligible. The Central American reformer José del Valle called him the 'legislator of the world'.[18]) James Mill was Bentham's foremost philosophical disciple,[19]

[16] Uday Singh Mehta, *Liberalism and Empire: A Study of Nineteenth-Century British Liberal Thought* (Chicago: University of Chicago Press, 1999), 64.

[17] Eric Stokes, *The English Utilitarians and India* (Oxford: Oxford University Press, 1959), 51.

[18] José del Valle to Jeremy Bentham, 21 May 1826, quoted in David Armitage, *Foundations of Modern International Thought* (Cambridge: Cambridge University Press, 2013), 173.

[19] Although the influence may not have been entirely one-way: see J. R. Dinwiddy, 'Bentham's Transition to Political Radicalism' (1975) 35 *Journal of the History of Ideas* 683, 685–686.

although their relationship became increasingly strained. Mill's *Essay on Government* (1817) was the manifesto of the philosophic radicals, read as an attempt to prepare the middle classes for the leadership of a reformed British politics.[20] His *History of British India* (1818) has been described as transforming utilitarianism into a militant faith,[21] and was probably the most influential book on India written in the first half of the century – 'the book that became a grammar of Indian civilization' for British officials.[22] Publication secured him a job as a leading official in the East India Company, a position he retained until shortly before his death in 1836. By the time the elder Mill joined the Company, it had lost its trading monopoly, and the important aspects of its governance of India were detailed in an Act of Parliament.

The position of Mill's master, Jeremy Bentham, on colonial and imperial matters has been the subject of much debate.[23] No one can deny the universal range of his concerns or his global vision and ambition. But questions remain about the consistency of his stance on specific matters of imperial law and politics. Some statements reveal a pro-imperialist sensibility that occasionally borders on the jingoistic. There are echoes of Harrington, for instance, in this passage from *Defence of a Maximum* (1801):

> colonies, though still a drain, are notwithstanding, and even because they are a drain, a relief. The retribution for the past experience is a scene from *Paradise Lost* – a prospect such as the angel shewed to Adam: men spreading in distant climes, through distant ages, from the best stock, the earth covered with British population, rich with British wealth, tranquil with British security, the fruit of British law.[24]

This expansionary perspective may even have grown stronger towards the end of his life. In 1831, under the influence of Edward Gibbon Wakefield's free trade imperialism,[25] he put forward a scheme for colonizing South

[20] Javed Majeed, 'James Mill's *The History of British India*: The Question of Utilitarianism and Empire' in Bart Schultz and Georgios Varouxakis (eds.), *Utilitarianism and Empire* (Lanham, MR: Lexington, 2005), 98.

[21] Duncan Forbes, 'James Mill and India' (1951–52) *Cambridge Journal* 5, 31.

[22] Balachandra Rajan, *Under Western Eyes: India from Milton to Macaulay* (Durham, NC: Duke University Press, 1999), 96.

[23] Donald Winch, 'Bentham on Colonies and Empire' (1997) 9 *Utilitas* 147, 154.

[24] *Jeremy Bentham's Economic Writings* (London: Allen & Unwin, ed. W. Stark, 1952–4), vol. III: 355–357.

[25] Bernard Simmel, *The Rise of Free Trade Imperialism: Classical Political Economy, the Empire of Free Trade and Imperialism 1750–1850* (Cambridge: Cambridge University Press, 1970).

Australia.[26] More typically, though, Bentham was sceptical of empire, largely on the grounds Adam Smith had articulated.[27] Colonies were unnecessary, wasteful and prone to corruption.[28] The colonial enterprise led to war, which increased both taxation and executive power, which in turn led to more war.[29] 'Reform the world by example, you act generously and wisely; reform the world by force, you might as well reform the moon, and the design is fit only for lunatics' seems more often than not to have been his mantra.[30] Admittedly, this position tended to be expressed in works addressed to other nations: to France in the early 1790s ('Emancipate Your Colonies')[31] and to Spain in the early 1820s ('Rid Yourselves of Ultramaria').[32]

India as always remained a limit case. It is true that Bentham once said that he aspired to play the role of 'the dead legislative' for India, with James Mill as her 'living executive'. But perhaps this was said tongue in cheek. Bentham showed considerable sensitivity to local customs and conditions when considering the prospect of law reform in Bengal.[33] He was privately critical of Mill's *History of British India*, which he said made him melancholy. He nonetheless shared many of the views typical of contemporary liberals, views that the Mills were to develop in their particular ways. Emancipation, however admirable a goal in principle, was inappropriate

[26] Schofield, *Utility and Democracy*, 219.

[27] Jennifer Pitts, *A Turn to Empire? The Rise of Imperial Liberalism in Britain and France* (Princeton: Princeton University Press, 2005), chapter 4.

[28] Lea Campos Boralevi, *Bentham and the Oppressed* (Berlin: Walter de Gruyper, 1984), 121–134.

[29] Stephen Conway, 'Bentham on Peace and War' (1989) 1 *Utilitas* 82, 90.

[30] Jeremy Bentham, *The Works of Jeremy Bentham* (Edinburgh: W. Tait, ed. John Bowring, 1843), vol. IV: 416.

[31] 'Short Views of Economy' (1789), 'Jeremy Bentham to the National Convention of France' (1792, republished in 1830 as *Emancipate Your Colonies! Addressed to the National Convention of France*) in Jeremy Bentham, *Rights, Representation, and Reform* (Oxford: Oxford University Press, eds. Philip Schofield, C. Pease-Watkin and C. Blamires, 2002).

[32] 'Emancipation Spanish', 'Summary of Emancipate Your Colonies' and 'Rid Yourselves of Ultramaria', written between April 1820 and April 1822 in Jeremy Bentham, *Colonies, Commerce, and Constitutional Law* (Oxford: Oxford University Press, ed. Philip Schofield, 1995).

[33] From Bentham's point of view, local customs and prejudices were relevant to the science of legislation: 'Essay on the Influence of Time and Place in Matters of Legislation' in *The Works of Jeremy Bentham* (Edinburgh: W. Tait, ed. John Bowring, 1838), vol. I: 180: legislators had to 'be possessed fully of the facts, to be informed of the local situation, the climate, the bodily constitution, the manners, the legal customs, the religion of those with whom they have to deal'.

in India's case. Its inhabitants appeared incapable of giving themselves the security that only a stable framework of property could bring.[34] The Indians 'must have masters', he declared, and they ought to get the 'least bad ones'. Native governments would undoubtedly be more oppressive. Since European stewardship was deemed necessary, who better to do the job than the East India Company? 'I question whether you will find any less bad than our English company.'[35]

There is less uncertainty surrounding Bentham's status as 'archetypal legal codifier and legislative *machiniste*'[36] – although his campaign to reform and codify international law is less well known.[37] He argued that British laws, still largely based on common law, were incapable of ordering a modern state. The reverence for things past that Blackstone and Burke exemplified he dismissed as the 'relentless tyranny of the dead'.[38] Obscurity in the laws meant lack of clarity about legal rights and obligations and alienated subjects from the law. It also made it easier for conservative forces (the 'sinister interest') to manipulate the system to their own advantage. As commercial society made people more individualistic, so they were less likely to obey a rule simply on account of its antiquity ('ancestor-worship'); they needed to be convinced of its present utility. The complexity of modern life meant that a 'centralized, systematic, and fully public structure of law' had become necessary.[39] Current governance structures, with the common law at the centre, were so corrupted by the 'pestilential breath of fiction'[40] that only radical reform would do. As well as root and branch institutional reform, we need also to change the way we think about law and legality. Law should be seen as something made rather than inherited, justified by reference to the open

[34] Schofield, *Utility and Democracy*, 218.

[35] Jeremy Bentham, 'Emancipate Your Colonies! Addressed to the National Convention of France, Anno. 1793' in *Works of Jeremy Bentham*, IV, 415, 417. See also Bentham, 'Institute of Political Economy' (1804) in *Economic Writings of Jeremy Bentham* (London: Allen & Unwin, ed. W. Stark, 1952–4), vol. III: 356: it is an advantage to the people of the Orient 'to be regulated by minds such as those of Hastings's, Teignmouths, Cornwallises, Wellesleys ... rather than those of the Tippoo's, the Wan Lan Yun's ... or those of the disciples and associates of Thomas Payne [*sic*]'.

[36] Stefan Collini, Donald Winch and John Burrow, *That Noble Science of Politics: A Study in Nineteenth-Century Intellectual History* (Cambridge: Cambridge University Press, 1983), 93.

[37] Armitage, *Foundations of Modern International Thought*, 180.

[38] Bentham, 'Parliamentary Reform' (1794) UC, 5.

[39] Postema, *Bentham and the Common Law Tradition*, 310.

[40] Majeed, 'James Mill's *The History of British India*', 98.

and inclusive process through which it is made (democracy) and its consequences for the public good (utility) rather than its antiquity.

In Britain, despite the prominence of Benthamite reformers,[41] the goal of radical legal reform was never close to being achieved. Things abroad were rather different.[42] Benthamite ideas were influential in Indian administration throughout the nineteenth century. 'Benthamites who felt they were too regularly thwarted in England by entrenched powers and the recalcitrant body of common law', Jennifer Pitts observes, 'reveled in the opportunity that they believed despotic power provided for the establishment of a complete legal code (what Bentham liked to call a *pannomion*) and a rational bureaucracy'.[43] James Mill played a crucial role in the transformation of the utilitarian tradition on questions of law and empire. Whereas Bentham's application of his own philosophy to colonial matters was unsystematic and often complicated, Mill's use of the same principles was more blunt. His interest in India grew out of a frustration with the conservatism of home-grown institutions. The *History* is critical of the East India Company's activities in India on familiar political economy grounds, but it is also utterly disparaging of Indians, condemning Hinduism as the product of the 'wild and ungoverned imagination ... of a rude and credulous people'.[44]

Even in the context of his own time Mill's views on Indian culture were extreme.[45] As Balachandra Rajan remarks, 'rude', 'ignorant', 'superstitious' and 'credulous' are 'epithets he uses of Hindu civilization so frequently that it is difficult to find occasions on which they are not employed'.[46] Applying a bastardized version of the Scottish conjectural

41 Dicey, *The Relation between Law and Public Opinion*, Lecture VI, especially 119–131; S. E. Finer, 'The Transmission of Benthamite Ideas 1820–50' in Gillian Sutherland (ed.), *Studies in the Growth of Nineteenth-Century Government* (London: Routledge, 1972).

42 Bentham applied the same principles of law and morals to the new penal colony of New South Wales, developing in his *A Plea for the Constitution* (1803) a critique that in addition to offering classic utilitarian arguments against the ability of a distant penal colony to serve as a deterrent to criminals in England also argued that the absence of a written law framing the new colony and an effective legislature made the new settlement unconstitutional. See Lauren Benton, *A Search for Sovereignty: Law and Geography in European Empires, 1400–1900* (Cambridge: Cambridge University Press, 2010), 191–197.

43 Jennifer Pitts, 'Jeremy Bentham: Legislator of the World?' in Schultz and Varouxakis, *Utilitarianism and Empire*, 57.

44 Mill, *History of British India*, I. 143.

45 Pitts, 'Jeremy Bentham: Legislator of the World?', 59.

46 Rajan, *Under Western Eyes*, 93.

historians' model of development from primitive to more complex stages of social organization,[47] Mill categorized societies as either barbarous or civilized and, in so doing, 'assimilated all "rude" peoples into a single category of moral and political inferiority'.[48] Indians' intellectual and moral capacities are dismissed as representing the 'rudest and weakest state of the human mind'.[49] India had not yet arrived at the stage of civilization that Europe had reached in the Middle Ages.[50] The gulf being so wide, British rule in India must continue 'for the sake of the natives' – for the British, 'India has never been anything but a burden'. 'Even the utmost abuse of European power, is better, we are persuaded, than the most temperate exercise of Oriental despotism.'[51]

So, despite being under no illusions about either the unenlightened nature of British government or in relation to the activities of the Company, Mill was still able to conclude that the British should establish despotic rule in India as part of a duty to improve the Indians.[52] No doubt one of the purposes in devaluing Indian culture 'beyond the possibility of reinstatement' was to justify precisely this conclusion.[53] But the exercise also served as a ground-clearing one aimed at conceptualizing India as a *tabula rasa*[54] on which the 'new moral arithmetic' of utility might freely be applied.[55] His target was the so-called Orientalists, whose leading figure was Sir William Jones, judge of the Supreme Court of Bengal and pioneer of Sanskrit studies and champion of India's civilizational richness. Jones began the compilation of a digest of Indian law in order to help reconstitute a Hindu polity – India's 'ancient constitution' – on the basis of a legal tradition predating the Mughal invasions which the British would define.[56] Mill saw this as a dangerously quixotic manifestation of Burkean conservatism. The idea behind the *History*, then, is to write a

[47] Knud Haakonssen, 'James Mill and Scottish Moral Philosophy' (1985) 33 *Political Studies* 628; Collini, Winch and Burrow, *That Noble Science of Politics*, 116–118.

[48] Mehta, *Liberalism and Empire*, 90; Pitts, *A Turn to Empire*, 130.

[49] Mill, *The History of British India*, I: 115.

[50] Mill, *History of British India*, I: 466–467.

[51] James Mill, 'Review of *Voyage aux Indes Orientales*', 371, quoted in Pitts, *A Turn to Empire*, 125.

[52] Javed Majeed, 'James Mill's *The History of British India*: A Reevaluation' in Martin I. Moir, Douglas M. Peers and Lynn Zastoupil (eds.), *J.S. Mill's Encounter with India* (Toronto: University of Toronto Press, 1999), 56.

[53] Rajan, *Under Western Eyes*, 94.

[54] Majeed, 'James Mill's *The History of British India*', 95.

[55] Francis Jeffrey, writing in the *Edinburgh Review* IV (1804), quoted in Postema, *Bentham and the Common Law Tradition*, 148.

[56] Majeed, 'James Mill's *The History of British India*: A Reevaluation', 53; Majeed, *Ungoverned Imaginings: James Mill's* The History of British India *and Orientalism* (Oxford: Oxford

history of India, the effect of which is to remove the need to take history seriously, to write a new text and not to amend an old one.[57] 'Mill was here initiating a new mode of argument that would demand that the ethics of colonial conquest should be judged not so much by the motivations but rather by its consequences.'[58]

Benthamite techniques were well suited to this end. Applied absent Bentham's own advice that in legislating for any country we must take into account the habits, feelings and prejudices of its inhabitants, and allow for their ideas of what constitutes happiness,[59] Mill's *History* embodies what Ernest Gellner called a world-levelling, unificatory epistemology.[60] Utility, freed from unnecessary constraints of locality and custom, can function as 'the ruler and decider of all things'.[61] From this perspective, the physical, cultural and imaginative distance between observer (and would-be legislator) and observed subject could be seen as an enabling rather than limiting condition. Distance freed the lawmaker from the biases and prejudices that might otherwise interrupt or distort the application of the felicific calculus.[62] It was this style of universalism rather than the principle of utility itself that alienated other liberals. In a stinging review of Mill's essay on government, Macaulay claimed that this approach expressed the 'contempt of ignorance', arguing that it was the product of 'ordinary men, with narrow understandings and little information … whose attainments just suffice to elevate them from the insignificance of dunces to the dignity of bores'.[63] Dicey, writing many decades later, made a similar charge. 'The weakness of the Benthamites as legislators has been, not their devotion to the principle of utility, but their feeling that laws which in the nineteenth century promoted the happiness

University Press, 1992), 40–46. Compare Mill in Moir, Peers and Zastoupil, J.S. Mill's Encounter with India, 155: 'with respect to the sciences it is worse than a waste of time to employ persons either to teach or to learn them in the state in which they are to be found in the Oriental books'.

57 Rajan, *Under Western Eyes*, 90.

58 Partha Chatterjee, *The Black Hole of Empire: History of a Global Practice of Power* (Princeton: Princeton University Press, 2012), 64.

59 Bentham, 'Essay on the Influence of Time and Place', I: 173; *Principles of Morals and Legislation*, 51–72.

60 Ernest Gellner, *Relativism and the Social Sciences* (Cambridge: Cambridge University Press, 1985), 76.

61 Postema, *Bentham and the Common Law Tradition*, 155.

62 Mill, *History of British India*, VI: 479. See also Majeed, 'James Mill's *The History of British India*: A Reevaluation', 56.

63 Thomas Babington Macaulay, 'Mill on Government' (March 1829) in James Mill, *Political Writings* (Cambridge: Cambridge University Press, ed. Terence Ball, 1992), 272.

of Englishmen must, with rare exceptions, promote at all times the happiness of the inhabitants of all countries.'[64]

Nonetheless, the same argument from distance was later to justify many other imperial habits, including the role of the sovereign Imperial Parliament, later given authoritative exposition by Dicey. As William Huskisson declared in Parliament in 1828, 'standing aloof, as we do, from the party feelings and local jealousies … our decision will be the more respected; first, as coming from a high and competent authority; and next, on account of our manifest impartiality'.[65] Rajan identifies the remoteness and austerity articulated by Mill, the most bureaucratic of political philosophers, as 'a commonplace of bureaucratic arrogance' which 'goes well with the hauteur of the British administration' in India.[66] But it also illustrates one prominent and influential attempt to apply a science of legislation, grounded in *a priori* methods and structured around a universalizable notion of utility, and the implications such a conception might have on the rule of law. The implications of this were felt most keenly in India where, as in the colonial empire more generally,

> the idea of a rule of law became fatally confused with that of a rule by law under which 'civil society', while perhaps directed by general legal principles, is denied any part itself in formulating those principles; while the state may make law for its subjects, it posits itself as above that law and as unaccountable to it. British-Indian law became less a tool of liberty than an instrument of despotism.[67]

J. S. Mill: the art and science of colonial governance

John Stuart Mill spent most of his adult life in the service of the East India Company.[68] Having entered the Company at 17 as an assistant to his

[64] Dicey, *Relation between Law and Opinion*, 101.

[65] 2 May 1828, *Parliamentary Debates (Commons)*, XIX, col. 302, quoted in Peter Burroughs, 'Imperial Institutions and the Government of Empire' in Andrew Porter (ed.), *The Oxford History of the British Empire: The Nineteenth Century* (Oxford: Oxford University Press, 1999), 178. Huskisson, a leading politician of his day, is best remembered now as the first reported railway casualty, run over by George Stephenson's *Rocket* in 1830.

[66] Rajan, *Under Western Eyes*, 96.

[67] D. A. Washbrook, 'India, 1818–1860: The Two Faces of Colonialism' in Porter, *Oxford History of the British Empire: The Nineteenth Century*, 407.

[68] Lynn Zastoupil, *John Stuart Mill and India* (Stanford: Stanford University Press, 1994); R. J. Moore, 'John Stuart Mill at East India House' (1983) 20 *Historical Studies* 497; Abram L. Harris, 'John Stuart Mill: Servant of the East India Company' (1964) 30 *Canadian Journal of Economics and Political Science* 185.

father, Mill was in charge of political department dispatches for most of his 35-year career.[69] This made him responsible for interaction with dozens of native princes who were officially recognized as 'independent' allies of the Company.[70] Mill went on to argue against Parliament's decision to extinguish the Company in the wake of the Indian Rebellion of 1857,[71] and at the onset of Crown rule turned down the offer of a seat on the new Council for India. The younger Mill's involvement with Indian affairs was at least as extensive as his father's. Far from being of peripheral interest to those involved in reforming governing structures, Indian government was influential within administrative discourse, providing the source of not just the name 'civil servant'[72] but also many of the practices of modern bureaucratic government. The Indian Civil Service was 'in many ways more efficient than the Home Civil Service'[73] and many notable reformers served within it, including Sir Charles Trevelyan. Mill found himself at Leadenhall Street at the cutting-edge of nineteenth-century administrative reform. It was this environment that produced what Amartya Sen and Bernard Williams call 'Government House utilitarianism', that is, 'an outlook favouring social arrangements under which a utilitarian élite controls a society in which the majority may not itself share those beliefs'.[74] It also raised in exceptionally clear form the perennial nineteenth-century question of democratic versus aristocratic government, public opinion versus expertise. India also acted as a key battleground in the wider intellectual war between utilitarian arguments of the rationalizing kind – and more generally of Western 'scientific' learning – and non-utilitarian, often anti-rationalistic, arguments about the benefits of a wider, more emotionally supportive 'culture'.[75]

J. S. Mill was the foremost British political thinker of the nineteenth century, attaining an authority that was 'positively papal'.[76] No attempt is

[69] Martin Moir, 'John Stuart Mill's Draft Dispatches to India and the Problem of Bureaucratic Authorship' in Moir, Peers and Zastoupil, *J.S. Mill's Encounter with India*.

[70] Lynn Zastoupil, 'J.S. Mill and India' (1988) 32 *Victorian Studies* 31, 33.

[71] Douglas M. Peers, 'Imperial Epitaph: John Stuart Mill's Defence of the East India Company' in Moir, Peers and Zastoupil, *J.S. Mill's Encounter with India*.

[72] Distinguishing those of the East India Company's servants in its civilian employment from those who served in its armed forces.

[73] Jennifer Hart, 'The Genesis of the Northcote-Trevelyan Report' in Sutherland, *Growth of Nineteenth-Century Government*, 72.

[74] Amartya Sen and Bernard Williams (eds.), *Utilitarianism and Beyond* (Cambridge: Cambridge University Press, 1982), Introduction, 16.

[75] Alan Ryan, 'Utilitarianism and Bureaucracy: The Views of J.S. Mill' in Sutherland, *Growth of Nineteenth-Century Government*, 39.

[76] Collini, Winch and Burrow, *That Noble Science of Politics*, 130.

made here to offer a comprehensive survey of his work. The focus instead falls on two main themes. First, his vision of a system of government that combined Greek ideals of freedom and self-government with a modern emphasis on good bureaucratic administration. Second, the distinction between civilized and uncivilized that he used to justify both the differential treatment of native subject peoples and as a way of specifying the limits of the sphere of liberty, representative government and the rule of law. These themes are important in their own right, but we also explore their connections with other writers on the British constitution, especially Walter Bagehot and A. V. Dicey.

Mill's neo-Grecian homage

Mill often saw himself positioned at the confluence of two great and apparently opposing streams of thought – and usually as being able to provide a philosophical synthesis of the two.[77] His general approach to reform was to introduce the scientific method into the study of human behaviour. But he did not intend the scientific approach to dictate governmental action. 'The "Scientist" does not make normative decisions, but his findings enable the "Artist" to avoid futile and foolish proposals.'[78] The reconciliation of science and art, *thesis* and *praxis*, Enlightenment rationalism and Romanticism, scientific laws and moral laws had deep personal resonance for Mill. Brought up in hothouse fashion to be a model utilitarian – he was taught Greek by his father when he was three – he had a 'mental crisis' as a young man.[79] He worked his way through it with the help of the Lake Poets, above all Wordsworth. His intellectual and psychological dissatisfaction with orthodox utilitarianism led to what he later described as the 'weaving anew' of his philosophical framework.[80] In two early essays on 'Bentham' (1838) and 'Coleridge' (1840), 'the two great seminal minds of England in their age',[81] Mill gives philosophical

[77] See, e.g., the beginning of *Considerations of Representative Government*, which begins by describing 'two conflicting theories' concerning political institutions.

[78] Frank M. Robson, *The Improvement of Mankind: The Social and Political Thought of John Stuart Mill* (Aylesbury: University of Toronto Press, 1968), 160.

[79] Richard Reeves, *John Stuart Mill: Victorian Firebrand* (London: Atlantic Books, 2007), chapter 3.

[80] Zastoupil, 'J.S. Mill and India', 49, which also makes a connection between this more general development and influences Mill encountered in his administrative work for the East India Company, both of which led him to a partial accommodation of Romanticism.

[81] 'Bentham' in *Collected Works of John Stuart Mill, Vol. X* (London: Routledge & Kegan Paul, ed. John M. Robson, 1963) 77.

voice to this psychological journey. He used these essays to criticize Bentham and 'the Bentham school' for failing to provide a moral message or uplifting theme, the absence of which amounted to a 'very serious evil'.[82] The Romantic conservatism of Coleridge, where mind was more than a reasoning faculty and in which value was attached to human desires, long-held beliefs and to stability and 'the feeling of allegiance, or loyalty', offered a corrective.[83] But the point of the two essays in combination is that neither author gives a complete picture. 'Coleridge is ignorant of experience lying outside tradition; Bentham, of that within tradition.'[84]

Mill's reshaping of the utilitarian position on method and morals had a political corollary. He focused on two vital sites of modern politics and government: bureaucracy and democracy. 'Mill's central contribution to democratic theory is his prescient attempt to develop the model of constitutional democracy "compatible with the development and increasing role of bureaucracy".'[85] The first site, the move from personal power to rational administration, Mill took to be the prime index of modernity.[86] John Austin, at one point Mill's tutor and who may have influenced his jurisprudential thinking,[87] wrote an extended essay on the subject of 'Centralization' in the *Edinburgh Review* (1847) in which the easy elision between the importance of the new-style 'administrative machine', colonial legal policy and modernity can be seen clearly. Janet McLean has called the essay the most sustained defence of nineteenth-century public administrative reform from a utilitarian perspective.[88] The purpose of the centralization, Austin argues, is to realize the new ideal of rational administration under the direction of the sovereign power: 'In a country whose government is centralized, the administrative system is highly

[82] CW X: 15–16. See also Frederick Rosen, 'The Method of Reform: J.S. Mill's Encounter with Bentham and Coleridge' in Nadia Urbinati and Alex Zakaras (eds.), *J.S. Mill's Political Thought: A Bicentennial Reassessment* (Cambridge: Cambridge University Press, 2007).

[83] CW X: 119–120, 132–136. On Coleridge's philosophical and political writings see Richard Holmes, *Coleridge: Darker Reflections* (London: HarperCollins, 1998).

[84] Robson, *The Improvement of Mankind*, 191–192.

[85] Nadia Urbinati, *Mill on Democracy: From the Athenian Polis to Representative Government* (Chicago: University of Chicago Press, 2002), 44.

[86] CW XVIII: 76.

[87] J. S. Mill, 'Austin on Jurisprudence', *Edinburgh Review*, 1863. See also Stefan Collini, *Public Moralists: Political Thought and Intellectual Life in Britain 1850–1930* (Oxford: Clarendon Press, 1991), 261–265; Wilfrid E. Rumble, *The Thought of John Austin* (London: Athlone Press, 1985), 39, 95, 215.

[88] Janet McLean, *Searching for the State in British Legal Thought: Competing Conceptions of the Public Sphere* (Cambridge: Cambridge University Press, 2012), 42.

regular. A high civilisation, therefore, is an imperative moral condition of centralization. In imperfectly civilized countries whose governments are apparently centralized, (as, for example, Russia,) the centralization is merely formal.' Further down the scale of civilization, Austin extols the bespoke administrative techniques developed in India, which have had 'wonderful success in attaching [Britain's] Hindoo subjects to her naturally invidious rule; and in tincturing an Asiatic people whose prejudices were all but indelible, with the morality and knowledge of Christian and civilised Europe'.[89]

Mill broadly shared the same understanding of modernity and bureaucracy. As civilizations progress, he argued, individuals become increasingly interdependent. Agreement and civility become the norm rather than the exception in modern societies, and there is a corresponding move in government from personal power to rational administration, a 'relative routinization of political ability and choice'.[90] The existing nature of the British constitution was a favourite target, especially the eighteenth-century idea of 'constitutional balance'. Even if the metaphor was allowed, Mill argued, equilibrium between the 'balancing forces' of the constitution meant logically that 'the machine must stand still'.[91] Bureaucratizing the administration of government was a 'natural' way for civilized societies to order themselves. Great talents are not needed for carrying on the government of a well-ordered society. Mill supported the development of a professional class of civil servants. He shared the belief that underlay the Northcote-Trevelyan reforms in expertise and independent opinion, the faith in the man who can press his view without fear or hope for his own position.[92] In defending that position, he presented something like a watered-down version of Coleridge's advocacy of a 'clerisy', a class of enlightened leaders in moral and intellectual matters, not least on the basis that it might serve as a correction to the levelling and despotic tendencies of representative government.

At the same time, Mill was clear about the limits of bureaucratic governance, however enlightened. Although a Francophile, Mill wrote disparagingly about 'bureaucracy-ridden nations of the continent'.[93] Bureaucracy easily becomes pedantocracy, stifling independent thinking and judgement, and gradually sapping a state of its vital energy. 'The disease which

[89] 'Centralization', *Edinburgh Review*, 1 Jan. 1847, 233–234.

[90] Duncan Kelly, *The Propriety of Liberty: Persons, Passions and Judgement in Modern Political Thought* (Princeton: Princeton University Press, 2011), 211.

[91] J. S. Mill, 'Parliamentary Reform' (1), August 1824, quoted in Reeves, *John Stuart Mill*, 56.

[92] Ryan, 'Utilitarianism and Bureaucracy', 51–52.

[93] *Representative Government*, 268.

afflicts bureaucratic governments, and which they usually die of, is routine. They perish by the immutability of their maxims; and, still more, by the universal law that whatever becomes a routine loses its vital principle.'[94] The extent of Mill's concern on this point distinguishes him from Austin – and, for that matter, earlier utilitarian thinkers including his father – who tended to downplay the dangers inherent to bureaucratic government. To save it from these ills, rational bureaucracy needs to be set within a system of representative government, itself dependent on and part of a greater flow and free exchange of opinion. Indeed, Mill saw the development of active social and political movements as an index of a civilized society.

Representative government can cure introspection ('group-think') and stagnation within bureaucracies; bureaucracy can ameliorate democracy's tendency towards mediocrity and despotism via the tyranny of the majority.[95] Together, the combination holds out the possibility of stemming the tendency of modern societies to bring about too much by way of social cohesion[96] – the tyranny of conformity that was the primary target of *On Liberty*. The aim was to balance the utilitarian concern with good management with the ideal of the independent-minded, self-critical, engaged and public-spirited citizen. Stated in these terms, the Greek inflection of Mill's political thought is clear. 'The nineteenth-century was the century of both Greek revivalism and the slow transition to democracy.'[97] Confronting the aftermath of both Enlightenment and revolution, Europeans turned afresh to ancient Greek models in order to make sense of their disruptive political, social and intellectual experience.[98] Democratic Athens had in previous centuries generally been regarded as a byword for civic lawlessness, political disorder and the absence of personal security. We saw in Chapter 3 how Marchamont Nedham's advocacy of the Athenian model put him at odds even with other republicans. Now, under the spell of (Mill's friend) George Grote's magisterial *History of Greece* (1846–56),[99] Athens became the ancient equivalent of Victorian England's better self, a society that had mastered the art of self-government and where artistic excellence, rational thought and individual liberty had

94 *Representative Government*, 290.

95 *Representative Government*, 313.

96 Alan Ryan, 'Bureaucracy, Democracy, Liberty: Some Unanswered Questions in Mill's Politics' in Urbinati and Zakaras, *J.S. Mill's Political Thought*, 160–161.

97 Urbinati, *Mill on Democracy*, 33.

98 Frank M. Turner, *The Greek Heritage in Victorian Britain* (New Haven: Yale University Press, 1981), 1–2.

99 Mill reviewed the twelve volumes of Grote's *A History of Greece* between 1846 and 1853, the three volumes of *Plato and the Other Companions of Sokrates* (1865) in 1866 and *Aristotle* (1872) in 1873.

largely, if not always perfectly, flourished. Advancing the case on the political front, Mill argued that the moderns needed to choose Athens as their political model. 'Their task was not to thwart or stunt individual potential but to create a "secure" democracy that would preserve the two features of ancient *eleutheria*: political liberty as the right "common to every citizen rich and poor" to participate in "public discussion and public action", and moral liberty as "reciprocal indulgence of individual diversity".'[100]

Mill and the politics of civilization

But how does all this relate to colonial questions and the matter of reason of state? We have seen already how the idea of civilization is built into Mill's conception of bureaucracy and democracy. His neo-Athenian blend of democracy and bureaucracy applies only to modern nations: that is, to political communities that are sufficiently well developed to sustain them. Played out in the imperial domain, Mill supported the colonial reformers' advocacy of a Greek as opposed to Roman model, proposing settlement colonies that would replicate English institutions and society, but would have the character of self-contained societies, independent of the mother country.[101] Colonies were not just useful in that they provided opportunities for excess labour. They also provided an escape from the parochialism and class-ridden nature of British life and were, as such, 'spaces for innovation and forms of progressive self-fashioning ... allowing – demanding – experimentation in ways of living'.[102] Writing in support of Edward Gibbon Wakefield's plan to colonize South Australia, Mill said:

> Like the Grecian colonies, which flourished so rapidly and so wonderfully as soon to eclipse the mother cities, this settlement will be formed by transplanting an entire society, and not a mere fragment of one. English colonies have almost always remained in a half-savage state for many years from their establishment. This colony will be a civilized country from the very establishment.[103]

[100] Urbinati, *Mill on Democracy*, 37–38, quoting Grote, *History of Greece*, VI: 182–183 and Mill, *Complete Works*, II: 314–326. See also Jonathan Riley, 'Mill's Neo-Athenian Model of Liberal Democracy' in Urbinati and Zakaras, *J.S. Mill's Political Thought*.

[101] Pratap Bhanu Mehta, 'Liberalism, Nation, and Empire: The Case of J.S. Mill' in Sankar Muthu (ed.), *Empire and Modern Political Thought* (Cambridge: Cambridge University Press, 2012), 252; Georgios Varouxakis, *Liberty Abroad: J.S. Mill on International Relations* (Cambridge: Cambridge University Press, 2013), 125–140.

[102] Duncan Bell, 'John Stuart Mill on Colonies' (2009) 38 *Political Theory* 34, 46.

[103] J. S. Mill, 'Wakefield's *The New British Province of South Australia*', *Examiner*, 20 July 1834, *Complete Works*, XXIII: 742.

But this model is not suitable and perhaps even dangerous for civilizations that have yet to leave the age of heroes and warriors, still less for those at an even earlier stage of development. To understand why we must appreciate how central the idea of progress is within Mill's thought. The first object of government, he says in *Representative Government*, is progress rather than security or order.[104] Progress represents something more than efficiency gains ('scientific' progress). It is a rich concept that includes 'the qualities of mental activity, enterprise, and courage' and beyond them ideas of 'Originality, or Invention'.[105] Progress so conceived provides not only the centrepiece of a style of politics that sees the state ideally in dynamic (progressive) as opposed to static (conserving) terms but also a limit concept with which to separate the societies suited to this new model ('us') from those that aren't ('them'). Mill is clear that the new idea of freedom developed in writings such as *On Liberty* is suitable only for the 'stage of progress into which the more civilized portions of the species have now entered'.[106] This theory of freedom in turn delimits the scope of legitimate state action. What counts as unduly paternalistic action ('reason of state') in relation to the citizens in an advanced society like England might be entirely legitimate when applied to other societies in an earlier stage of development.

There is an intimate connection, then, between the core of Mill's political theory and his imperial views. All that needs to be added is an account of native peoples as inhabiting an earlier stage of development. This his father had already provided, at least in relation to British India. Mill accepted in all significant respects his father's assessment of Indians. The new democratic model simply cannot apply to a case like India:

> A rude people, though in some degree alive to the benefits of civilized society, may be unable to practise the forbearances which it [representative government] demands: their passions may be too violent, or their personal pride too exacting, to forgo private conflict, and leave the laws the avenging of their real or supposed wrongs. In such a case, a civilized government, to be really advantageous to them, will require to be in a considerable degree despotic[.][107]

The message is clear. Despotism is 'a legitimate mode of government in dealing with barbarians', provided that it aims at their improvement.[108] Neither liberty nor representative government is appropriate for societies

[104] *Representative Government*, 223.
[105] *Representative Government*, 220–221. [106] *On Liberty*, 5.
[107] *Representative Government*, 209. [108] *On Liberty*, 14–15.

that had not as yet come of age. Civilized states – and for all his criticism Mill was sure of Britain's superior standing even among developed nations, seeing in it a source of additional obligations in the international sphere[109] – had a right and perhaps also the duty to govern uncivilized states. Barbarian and savage societies are static. (Given his preference for dynamism, social 'stagnation' was unsurprisingly one of Mill's greatest fears.) They are incapable of discipline so have no hope of progressing up the ladder of civilization without the help of a more advanced nation. Undisciplined, they will follow their immediate whim or appetite and so cannot be depended upon to observe any rules or treaties concluded with civilized powers.[110] Barbarians can therefore have no rights as a nation, except a right to such treatment as may fit them for becoming one.[111] Faced with the destabilizing effect of uncivilized nations, civilized states in the end found themselves almost 'obliged to conquer them, or to assert so much authority over them, as to break their spirit, that they gradually sink into a state of dependence'.[112] In a disconcerting reversal of Burke's handling of the same motif,[113] the parent-child dynamics of the imperial relationship so understood are apparent – the analogy between barbarians and children 'emerges repeatedly in Mill's thought to justify imperial rule and a suspension of international norms'.[114] Within this model of 'parental despotism',[115] progressiveness, the cardinal human quality, it transpires, was also the monopoly of a select group of societies.

What did this mean in the case of India, where much of this argument was played out? For Mill the fundamental test of government is the extent to which it assists 'progress' among its subjects. For India, a 'great distance' still from being sufficiently civilized,[116] self-rule would not provide that. The salient question becomes: which external government works best for India? Britain, as 'the Power which, of all in existence, best understands

[109] Collini, *Public Moralists*, 134.

[110] J. S. Mill, 'A Few Words on Non-Intervention' in *Complete Works*, XXI: 118–120. See also J. S. Mill, 'Civilization' in *Complete Works*, XVIII: 120.

[111] Varouxakis, *Liberty Abroad*, 121–122; Jennifer Pitts, 'Boundaries of Victorian International Law' in Bell, *Victorian Visions of Global Empire*, 76–78.

[112] Mill, 'A Few Words on Non-Intervention', 118–119.

[113] See the discussion in Chapter 5.

[114] Pitts, *A Turn to Empire*, 143; Karuna Mantena, 'The Crisis of Liberal Imperialism' in Bell, *Victorian Visions of Global Empire*, 120.

[115] Gregory Claeys, *Mill and Paternalism* (Cambridge: Cambridge University Press, 2013), 99. See also Eileen P. Sullivan, 'J.S. Mill's Defense of the British Empire' (1983) 44 *Journal of the History of Ideas* 599.

[116] *Representative Government*, 447.

liberty',[117] is best placed to provide such government. To be 'really advantageous' to the Indians, British rule will have to be 'in a considerable degree despotic', since 'a vigorous despotism is in itself the best mode for training the people in what is specifically wanting to render them capable of a higher civilization', namely discipline to follow rules prescribed by a recognized governing authority.[118] Good native despots are very rare. But there is no reason why a more civilized people ought not be able to supply good government constantly[119] since they have developed the necessary techniques. The special conditions that pertain in the management of uncivilized peoples mean that, in their case, the purer the form that bureaucratic management takes the better. Enlightened bureaucratic despotism works best when free from the meddling of uninformed and self-interested public opinion based in the imperial home country.

Progress and civilization were structuring concepts within Mill's new theory of liberal democracy. The same concepts played a role in the developing public law of empire, although the precise contours of that role are much harder to track. Later in the chapter, we look at the debates over martial law in the colonies that occupied many of Mill's later years. But here we examine a series of cases that arose from an earlier period of conquest and subsequent restructuring of authority. Given his high-level position in the East India Company, Mill was intimately familiar with such jurisprudential and administrative details. The first case, *Nabob of the Carnatic (or Arcot) v East India Company* (1791), turned on a number of treaties that the Company had concluded with the Nabob (or Nawab) of the Carnatic, the ruler of an area of southern India over which the British had been competing with the French. By 1765, the Nawab had fallen under the Company's *de facto* control, which later became *de jure* with his formal resignation of sovereignty in 1801. The case before the English courts saw the Nawab chafing against the realities of this creeping extension of imperial control. His lawyers claimed that the Company had received more from the concession to collect revenue in the Carnatic than the treaties allowed. The Company replied that both parties to the case were 'sovereign independent powers' exercising the capacity to make peace or war with other princes. That power was outside the jurisdiction of the court, even in those cases where the prince had delegated that power (here to the Company) rather than exercise it personally. The Nawab countered

[117] *Representative Government*, 451.
[118] *Representative Government*, 208, 453.
[119] *Representative Government*, 454.

that the powers granted to the Company reflected its nature as 'a species of corporation created for the purposes of trade' and did not 'in any degree create them a sovereign, much less an independent state'. Even assuming that they had the power 'to rob any of the powers in India', that was no reason to prevent the court from forcing them to pay their debts. The court held that the Company could not claim the total exemption of a sovereign state. But the source of its power ('participation in the prerogative') entailed a right to enter into treaties on behalf of Britain. The treaties on the basis of which the Nawab brought suit were 'engagements of a political nature and matters of State'. As such, they were not amenable to the jurisdiction of the court.

Nabob of the Carnatic confirms that there was indeed a sovereign dimension to the East India Company's activities in India and that this dimension was as immune from the jurisdiction of ordinary law as any other sovereign act.[120] This ruling was later confirmed. In *Gibson v East India Company* (1839), Tindal CJ said the Company possessed a double nature encompassing, first, the (private) power to carry on trade as merchants and, second, the (sovereign) power to acquire, retain and govern territory, to raise and maintain armed forces by sea and land and to make peace or war. Acts done in pursuance of its sovereign authority bound only *in foro conscientiae* but not before a court of law.[121] On its face, these rulings treat the local ruler in the same manner as a European prince, on equal footing with the British Crown. But turning the question into one of public law in this way weakens the juridical situation in a way that systematically disfavours the Indian claimant. As such, the cases show much less of an adherence to principles of legal equality than the cases examined in the previous chapter in which two Armenian merchants successfully sued the Governor of Bengal (in 'private law') for false imprisonment. They sit uneasily too alongside the principle of imperial public law enunciated in *Campbell v Hall*, also discussed in the previous chapter, that in general the pre-cessional law of a territory remains in force under the new sovereign until altered by that sovereign.[122]

Two other cases from the same period illustrate the same juxtaposition of formal equality (in public law) and substantive inequality (in private law). *Elphinstone v Bedreechund* (1830) arose out of the declaration of

[120] (1839) 132 ER 1105 at 1110.

[121] See also *Cook v Sprigg* (1899) AC 572.

[122] See Peter Wesley-Smith, 'Act of State: Lord Diplock's Curious Inconsistency' (1986) 6 *Legal Studies* 325.

martial law by the Company in the wake of the victory of British forces over the Peishwa. The former treasurer of Peishwa was kept under house arrest some distance from where there was still actual fighting until he handed over a sum of money. Bedreechund, the treasurer's executor, subsequently claimed that the money ought to be returned. Company lawyers argued that military necessity must provide the legal framework. Any other approach 'would tend to unnerve the arms of the soldier, and to render quite fruitless the conquest he had obtained'. A conquering army commander has a choice: 'He may either deliver it up to the ravages of his soldiery, if he is cruelly disposed, or may place commissioners in it to preserve tranquility, till final arrangements are made respecting it … but this does not deprive the commander of his power, or free the country from military government.' The Privy Council, reversing a decision of the Supreme Court of Bombay, agreed. What took place was a hostile seizure made while war had not ceased and so could not be adjudicated on by any court. The case has an interesting footnote. The judge advised Bedreechund to petition the King in Council. The same judge sitting on that (political) body advised the king that the money should in fact be returned. It may be, then, that Bedreechund got the money back. But if so, it was paid out of royal grace and not through a claim of legal right. The case proper stood as a central authority for determining the legal status of parties subject to martial law and was relied upon as such in many subsequence decisions, including *Ex parte Marais* considered later in the chapter.[123]

Secretary of State in Council of India v Kamachee Boye Sahaba (1859) also involved a seizure of property. The British, by now entrenched practically everywhere in the subcontinent, assumed control of the Raj of Tanjore when the Rajah died without an obvious heir. A series of treaties concluded between the East India Company and successive Rajahs had already given the British very substantial powers but no *de jure* sovereign rights over the territory. Nonetheless the Company simply declared on the Rajah's death that the Raj had lapsed to the British government and seized the late Rajah's property. In court, the Rajah's widow claimed that some of that property was the personal property of the Rajah as opposed to public property of the Raj. The government argued that the taking of the property was an act of state, and so no court had jurisdiction to entertain the question. At first instance, the court accepted that the Company

[123] W. S. Holdsworth, 'Martial Law Historically Considered' (1902) 18 *Law Quarterly Review* 117, 129–130.

must be 'considered to have become the Sovereign power throughout the kingdom of Tanjore from the death of Rajah Sevajee' despite the lack of public pronouncement or legal title. But this power gave them no right to the personal property of the late Raj, which ought to be returned to his widow. That decision was overturned on appeal, where Lord Kingsdown held that if the court cannot inquire into an act because it is an act of state, it cannot inquire into any part of that act, and that the government – here acting through its delegate, the East India Company – must be understood as intending to act according to its own notions of what is just and reasonable, not those of the court.[124] 'The transactions of independent States between each other are governed by other laws than those which Municipal Courts administer: such Courts have neither the means of deciding what is right, nor the power of enforcing any decision which they may make.'[125]

These cases indicate that the shift into the register of public law – or perhaps of the *ius publicum europaeum* – did little to protect the rights or interests of indigenous rulers and subjects. On the contrary, the ascription to the East India Company of the Crown's sovereign rights and the equation of local Indian rulers with European princes had the effect of pushing the matter outside the jurisdiction of courts into another realm altogether harder to specify, that of politics, diplomacy, force and grace. Even an exception such as the *Bedreechund* case, where the plaintiff may actually have got some redress, proves the rule. For even there it is clear that compensation occurs not through the application of ordinary state laws but by dint of exceptional reasons of state. While on the surface respectful of Indian claimants, this jurisprudence amounts to a hollowing out of the common law, the assertion of a public law of state's interest stripping out much of its normal (private) law substance. This is the scenario about which Smith and Burke had nightmares. It is the world of force and the pact, inhabited by rapacious and all but uncontrollable Company agents ransacking India under the cover of a veneer of legality. Not that it is an entirely lawless world. Treaties can be made, which take legal form, and martial law may be said to supply the rudiments of legal order. Principles – derived from the law of nations or natural law or Roman Law – float around the margins. But this law in its operation is paper-thin.

[124] On the act of state doctrine see Amanda Perreau-Saussine, 'British Acts of State in English Courts' (2008) *British Yearbook of International Law* 176.

[125] (1859) 15 ER 9 at 28–29.

It provides almost no break on superior force or on the manipulation of legal forms in self-interested ways.

Mill and the late Victorian crisis of empire

The Indian Rebellion of 1857 had a seismic effect on British attitudes to empire. The uprising challenged the assumptions that Victorians held about the imperial mission – although, it must be said, rarely for the better. One might have expected the jurisprudence of empire to provide a focal point of debate, not least because of the brutality of the exercise of martial law in suppressing the uprising. Strangely, however, the legal debate on imperial authority had to wait until the aftermath of the Morant Bay (Jamaican) rebellion. The post-1857 debate concerned questions of imperial *authority*, not liberty, and concentrated on whether East India Company rule should be replaced with direct imperial rule. Mill argued unsuccessfully in favour of the former option.[126] While Mill had both privately and publicly expressed his dismay at the brutality used to suppress the Rebellion,[127] it did not alter his view that rule under the auspices of the reformed and the no longer commercial East India Company was the best possible form of government for India. Writing in 1858, Mill maintained that the Company represented 'a Government of which perpetual striving towards improvement is the vital principle'. Ideal despotic government must contain its own checks and balances, and this was already provided through the 'double government' of the Company and Parliament.[128] The Company also had long experience in working to ensure that the government of India was run by qualified individuals, a project that included the

126 Mill drafted a petition to Parliament on behalf of the Company that began: 'That your Petitioners, at their own expense, and by the agency of their own civil and military servants, originally acquired its magnificent empire in the East. That the foundations of this empire were laid by your Petitioners, at that time unaided nor controlled by Parliament, at the same period at which a succession of administrations under the control of Parliament were losing to the Crown of Great Britain another great empire on the opposite side of the Atlantic.' (Quoted in Reeves, *John Stuart Mill*, 258.)

127 Varouxakis, *Liberty Abroad*, 107; Claeys, *Mill and Paternalism*, 105. For an account of the Indian Rebellion see Saul David, *The Indian Mutiny* (Harmondsworth: Penguin, 2002). Unlike the situation in respect of the Morant Bay uprising, where Mill took a leading role in the campaign against Governor Eyre but was supported by a great many significant figures, in these criticisms of British activities in India 'Mill was much more of a lone voice in protesting against racial hatred. It should be borne in mind that the first major work by a British author in which the British share of the atrocities was acknowledged was not published until 1925.' Peers, 'Imperial Epitaph', 207.

128 Peers, 'Imperial Epitaph', 210.

establishment of the East India College at Haileybury in 1806. The 'cardinal principle of Indian administration', Mill wrote, was 'the personal qualities and capacities of the agents of government'.[129] This was Mill's answer to Burke's fear that British rule in India amounted to government by juvenile delinquents. True, British officials go out to India young. But working up the bureaucratic ladder ensures that they are educated in the effective and constrained use of power. They 'go through the necessary course of preparation in subordinate functions before they can arrive at the higher ones'.[130]

Although the Rebellion itself did not persuade Mill to change his view that despotism was best for India, British attitudes towards the Rebellion induced a despairing note when speaking of the future of British rule. 'It has been the destiny of the government of the East India Company', he wrote in the final paragraph of *Representative Government* (published in 1861) 'to suggest the true theory of the government of a semi-barbarous dependency by a civilized country, and after having done this, to perish'.[131] Duncan Bell refers to the 'melancholic colonialism' of Mill's later years. While still clinging on to the ideal of colonialism as transcending a reactionary past and opening up new vistas of human possibility, the earlier romance and optimism of that vision was replaced by 'an anxiety, even despondency, about the direction of (colonial) history'.[132] This change of heart was brought about by an increased awareness of the pathologies of colonialism, apparent not just in the high drama of the Indian and the Jamaican uprisings but also in the prevalence of settler violence against indigenous peoples in Australia and New Zealand in particular.[133]

There is not all that much separating the Mill of these later years and the more pessimistic strands of liberal imperial thought developed at the same time by James Fitzjames Stephen and Henry Maine. After a series of imperial setbacks, later Victorians showed less interest in 'improving' imperial subjects, putting more of a focus on the superiority of the English and the need for strict control over violent and irredeemably 'savage' peoples.[134] Maine's account of the singular nature of ancient society, based on

[129] *Representative Government*, 463.

[130] Parliamentary Papers 1852–3, XXX: 303, quoted in Ryan, 'Utilitarianism and Bureaucracy', 44.

[131] *Representative Government*, 466.

[132] Bell, 'John Stuart Mill on Colonies', 34.

[133] Katherine Smits, 'John Stuart Mill on the Antipodes: Settler Violence against Indigenous Peoples and the Legitimacy of Colonial Rule' (2008) 54 *Australian Journal of Politics and History* 1, noting the importance of the New Zealand land wars of the 1860s.

[134] Smits, 'John Stuart Mill and the Antipodes', 9.

a corporate notion of the family ('status') whereas in modern society the individual was the primary legal unit ('contract'), became foundational in comparative social theory and imperial ideology.[135] 'In highlighting the difference from the dynamics of modern society', Karuna Mantena argues, 'the newly "ethnologized" ancient world would be bracketed together with primitive, feudal-medieval, and Eastern social forms as traditional societies defined through a common opposition to the unique trajectory of industrializing societies in the West.'[136] What is missing from Maine's account is the idea of progress, unquestionably the driving force in Mill's social and political theory.[137] With it goes any real hope for improvement and the removal of the duty on civilized nations to educate and bring on the less civilized. We are left with a more rigid dichotomy of civilized and backward peoples understood as something like a perpetual condition. This leaves the world to spin indefinitely around a master/servant polarity with little chance of improvement or transformative redemption.

Fitzjames Stephen wondered slyly why Mill's analysis of civilized and backward civilizations should apply to societies and not to individuals within them. Why, indeed, should it not apply to Britain? The principles of discipline and coercion that Mill was prepared to apply in India were just as applicable to the equally ignorant British peasant or petty shopkeeper: 'it seems to me quite impossible to stop short of this principle if compulsion is the case of children and "backward" races is admitted to be justifiable; for, after all, maturity and civilization are matters of degree'.[138] In fact, Walter Bagehot had already made a similar move. *The English Constitution* can be read as the internal application of the principle of difference that Mill and others had developed in the imperial arena. The book begins, curiously enough, with a quote from Mill (' "On all great subjects", says Mr Mill, "much remains to be said", and of none is this more true than of the English Constitution.'[139]) Bagehot's central argument is

[135] Henry Sumner Maine, *Ancient Law: Its Connection with the Early History of Society, and Its Relation to Modern Ideas* (London: John Murray, 1861).

[136] Karuna Mantena, *Alibis of Empire: Henry Maine and the Ends of Liberal Imperialism* (Princeton: Princeton University Press, 2010), 73.

[137] Although Maine was later to argue that India and the West were on a continuum of development: see Henry Sumner Maine, *Village-Communities in the East and West: Six Lectures Delivered at Oxford* (London: John Murray, 1876).

[138] James Fitzjames Stephen, *Liberty, Equality, Fraternity* (1873) (Indianapolis: Liberty Fund, ed. Stuart D. Warner, 1993), 19.

[139] Walter Bagehot, *The English Constitution* (1867) (Cambridge: Cambridge University Press, ed. Paul Smith, 2001), 3.

familiar. Intent on pulling back the veil on the British constitution, he distinguished between its 'dignified' and 'efficient' parts. The former by historical accretion – what he elsewhere called the 'cake of custom'[140] – gave the government the necessary authority, reverence and force. The latter exercises the power so accrued. It was the elements of show, and above all the traditional and mysterious institution of monarchy,[141] that held people's allegiance. The basis of stability is national character: 'the mass of the English people yield a deference rather to something else than to their rulers. They defer to what we may call the *theatrical show* of society'.[142] This left the middle classes, that 'heavy sensible class', to get on with 'dull government'.[143] 'The middle classes – the ordinary majority of educated men – are in the present day the despotic power in England.'[144] They ruled through an institution (Parliament) that tapped this reservoir of popular power and exercised it through a body (the Cabinet) in which met the 'fusion' of legislative and executive powers.

In part an argument against the widening of the franchise, the very defined 'us' versus 'them' framework is striking, simultaneously flattering and frightening its middle-class readership.[145] One of the striking things about this analysis is the similarity between its treatment of the British proletariat and peasantry and Mill's justification for the rule of backward peoples by civilized nations. Indeed, Bagehot approaches the domestic situation by way of an analysis of the 'unequal development of the human race' before panning in on the 'narrow-minded, unintelligent, incurious' lower orders, represented by the servant figures of 'the housemaid and the footman'. The lower orders do not – like 'us' – act rationally. 'The ruder sort of men … will sacrifice all they hope for, all they have, *themselves*, for what is called an idea.' Uninterested in the 'plain, palpable ends of government', these people are drawn in to the '*theatrical* elements; those

[140] Walter Bagehot, *Physics and Politics* (1873) (Cambridge: Cambridge University Press, 2010), 27.

[141] *English Constitution*, 41: a monarch 'should not be brought too closely to real measurement … [The English royalty] is commonly hidden like a mystery, and sometimes paraded like a pageant, but in neither case is it contentious'.

[142] *English Constitution*, 30.

[143] Walter Bagehot, 'Dull Government' in *The Collected Works of Walter Bagehot* (London: ed. Norman St John Stevas, 1965–78), IV, 85: 'The English people have never yet forgotten what some nations have scarcely ever remembered – that politics are a kind of business … Steady labour and dull material – wrinkles on the forehead and figures on the tongue – these are the English admiration.'

[144] *English Constitution*, 30.

[145] M. J. C. Vile, *Constitutionalism and the Separation of Powers* (Indianapolis: Liberty Fund, 1998), 247.

which appeal to the senses, which claim to be embodiments of the greatest human ideas – which boast in some cases of far more than human origin'.[146] There is more than a trace here of both Mills' analysis of the Indians as a race apart – emotional, irrational, religious, resolutely unmodern, easily duped. The elision is even clearer in Bagehot's late book *Physics and Politics*, a work heavily influenced by Maine's ethnological jurisprudence.[147] The book seeks to explain changes within political culture given two fundamental parameters: the nature of post-revolutionary[148] politics (the advent of the 'age of discussion') and Darwinian natural science. Here, we see not just the division between the East and the West along the familiar poles of civilized/uncivilized (Mill) and modern/ancient (Maine),[149] but also the connection between savages, beasts and children: 'A savage tribe resembles a herd of gregarious beasts; where the leader goes they go too; they copy blindly his habits, and thus soon become that which he already is ... Children, in the same way, are born mimics.' And finally a connection between savages and ignorant people of all races: 'The persecuting tendency of all savages, and, indeed, of all ignorant people, is even more striking than their imitative tendency.'[150]

Physics and Politics is a more ambitious work than *The English Constitution*, drawing widely on contemporary science and philosophy to deal with its grand themes. This allowed Bagehot to gloss his earlier account of the role played by chance in constitutional development[151] with the new language of genetic mutation.[152] But as far as the substantive analysis of the constitution is concerned, the two works are of a piece. Bagehot is clear that the idea of the 'cake of custom' belongs to the pre-modern, uncivilized world, relating to the 'condition of the primitive man', a condition that describes both to Indian society in its entirety and the ordinary inhabitants of his native Somerset. Such people are to be

[146] *English Constitution*, 6–7.

[147] *Physics and Politics*, 12, where Bagehot refers to Maine as 'the greatest of our living jurists – the only one, perhaps, whose writings are in keeping with our best philosophy'.

[148] *Physics and Politics*, 29–30: 'What are called in European politics the principles of 1789, are therefore inconsistent with the early world; they are fitted only to the new world in which society has gone through its early task; when the inherited organisation is already confirmed and fixed.'

[149] *Physics and Politics*, 156: 'The greatest living contrast is between the old Eastern and customary civilisations and the new Western and changeable civilisations.'

[150] *Physics and Politics*, 100–102.

[151] *English Constitution*, 8: 'We have made, or rather stumbled on' a constitution which is both efficient and imposingly august.

[152] Collini, Winch and Burrow, *That Noble Science of Politics*, 173.

'drilled', subjected to the straightforwardly Hobbesian rules of the older world (the 'preliminary age'), to '*law* – rigid, definite, concise law'.[153] Elite Europeans, on the contrary, have left the 'age of status' and have entered a new age of free government, discussion and choice, one of whose beneficial effects is its civilizing effects – that 'it counteracts the excessive inherited impulses of humanity'.[154] The stark difference between the two forms of rule is clear in the very different treatment ancient Greece, especially Athens, receives at different phases. Seen from the perspective of the primitive constitution, Athens is the great 'free failure' of the ancient world, beaten by the 'drilling aristocracies' of Sparta and Rome.[155] Seen through modern eyes, Athens becomes both the fountainhead and the greatest exemplar of the free state.[156] The difficulty for us, Bagehot claims, lies precisely in the fact that we inhabit a political community where some people are barely civilized, and so not fit for the politics of the new age, while others are as advanced as any who have ever lived. 'The Greek legislator had not to combine in his polity men like the labourers of Somerset, and men like Mr. Grote. He had not to deal with a community in which primitive barbarism lay as a recognized basis to acquired civilization. *We have*.'[157] Bagehot's answer was the scheme of 'double government'[158] that was meant to appeal in different ways to both civilized and barely civilized, modern and Gothic, social groups.

Martial law: a 'demented economy of principles'

Mill's defence of special provisions for India, distinct from the liberal regime that he prescribed for developed states, amounts to carving out a general exception aimed at kick-starting that country out of stagnation. As Duncan Kelly observes, this temporarily paternalist government applies 'something like emergency powers to recast unenlightened states'.[159] The ideal balance of skilled bureaucracy and representative government, the latter capable of tapping into the moral resources of public opinion, gives way to a despotism of enlightened and remote officials. Arguments based on the exception are not restricted to the management of internal affairs

[153] *Physics and Politics*, 18, 21, 27.
[154] *Physics and Politics*, 158, 195.
[155] *Physics and Politics*, 28.
[156] *Physics and Politics*, 158.
[157] *English Constitution*, 35.
[158] *English Constitution*, 180.
[159] *The Propriety of Liberty*, 211.

of less civilized states. In his writings on international law, Mill argues that rules governing intervention amongst states do not apply to barbarians. Nor need treaties concluded with uncivilized peoples be respected, since 'barbarians will not reciprocate. They cannot be depended on for observing any rules. Their minds are not capable of so great an effort, nor their will sufficiently under the influence of distant motives.'[160]

Beyond these general exceptions, one of Mill's more particular targets was martial law. Although it had not been a feature of domestic practice since the Gordon Riots of 1780, even in Ireland,[161] martial law had been used as an 'instrument of imperial statecraft' throughout the nineteenth century.[162] The issue became the subject of intense debate in the aftermath of the uprising in Morant Bay, Jamaica in 1865, becoming *the* polarizing topic of the Victorian debate on law, prerogative and empire. Mill had been quietly critical of the excesses that accompanied the suppression of the Indian Rebellion, as we have seen. But he threw himself into the Jamaica affair, zealous in advancing the case against those responsible for putting down the uprising with what he regarded as excessive force,[163] especially Governor Edward Eyre.[164] Mill was the most prominent member of the Jamaica Committee, set up with the purpose of bringing Eyre to trial, becoming its chairman in July 1866. The Committee was supported, in one way or other, by many leading Victorian liberals, including Walter Bagehot, James Fitzjames Stephen and the young Albert Venn Dicey.[165] These men were ashamed at the mistreatment of Jamaican blacks during

[160] Mill, 'A Few Words on Intervention'.

[161] In Ireland, martial law was declared in 1798 and 1803, but not again until the Easter Rising of 1916. A series of Coercion Acts were passed, however, starting with Gladstone's Protection of Person and Property Act 1881 which allowed, for instance, for imprisonment without trial.

[162] Including in Barbados 1805, 1816; Ceylon 1817, 1848; Demerara 1823; Jamaica 1831–2; Cape Colony 1835, 1846, 1850–1; Canada 1837–8; Cephalonia 1849; India (in some form or other) 1857–8; St Vincent 1862: R. W. Kostal, *A Jurisprudence of Power: Victorian Empire and the Rule of Law* (Oxford: Oxford University Press, 2005), 201.

[163] The disturbances lasted just a week, but Eyre kept martial law in force for two months, during which time his troops burnt a thousand houses, executed 439 Jamaicans and flogged at least 600 more.

[164] Discussing the business in Parliament for 1865–6, Mill said: 'There is no part of it all, not even the Reform Bill, more important than the duty of dealing justly with the abominations committed in Jamaica.' (Letter to William Fraser Rae, *Complete Works*, XVI: 1126.)

[165] In addition to other Victorian luminaries including John Bright, Charles Darwin, Thomas Huxley, Charles Lyell and Herbert Spencer. Eyre received considerable support from many other leading men of letters, including Thomas Carlyle, John Ruskin, Charles Dickens, Alfred Tennyson and Charles Kingsley, who saw Eyre as heroic saviour

the suppression, but their main concern was for the ramifications of the episode for Britain's domestic politics, specifically its constitutional foundations. Mill thought that the conduct and defence of the deployment of martial law in Jamaica supplied evidence that the governing classes were resiling from 'the transcendent principle of British political culture: the supremacy of law and the constitution over men, and most especially over men of state'.[166] Good government, at home and abroad, was worth fighting for. Eyre's actions were the antithesis of good colonial policy, indicative as they were of 'an arbitrary colonialism that exploits the colonized for the benefit of the colonizer'.[167] The question at stake, then, was nothing less than whether 'British dependencies, eventually even perhaps Great Britain itself, were to be under the government of law, or of military license'.[168]

The Jamaica affair petered out indecisively. Attempts to bring a private criminal prosecution against Eyre failed.[169] So too did a case against the military commander and the president of the court martial, despite Lord Chief Justice Cockburn's lengthy charge to the grand jury in which he argued that the Jamaica statute authorizing the use of martial law did not of itself justify the use of arbitrary power.[170] A civil action, funded by members of the Committee, also ended in defeat for those who wanted the Governor brought to book.[171] Outside the courtroom, Eyre lost his job and was mildly censured by Parliament. Mill's involvement in the campaign probably cost him his seat in Parliament. Even the debate over

of order and empire. J. Joseph Miller, 'Chairing the Jamaica Committee: J. S. Mill and the Limits of Colonial Authority' in Schultz and Varouxakis, *Utilitarianism and Empire*, 157, 160; Kostal, *Jurisprudence of Power*, 472, 456; Collini, *Public Moralists*, 145–146.

166 Kostal, *Jurisprudence of Power*, 148–149. Although, in truth, Mill was never shy in his criticism of the British constitution. The existing constitution, he wrote, was 'at best a shattered fragment of the feudal system', where 'religious intolerance' and the 'domination of a despotic aristocracy' were so powerful that he found it 'astonishing that mankind should ever have emancipated themselves' from their clutches. (Kelly, *The Propriety of Liberty*, 176).

167 Miller, 'Chairing the Jamaica Committee', 155.

168 J. S. Mill, *Autobiography*, I, 281, quoted in Miller, 'Chairing the Jamaica Committee', 159.

169 Kostal, *Jurisprudence of Power*, 296–315, 373–403. Lord Blackburn's charge to the grand jury in one of those cases, *Regina v Eyre*, is discussed in Charles Fairman, 'The Law of Martial Rule and the National Emergency' (1942) 55 *Harvard Law Review* 1253, 1262–1263.

170 *Regina v Nelson and Brand* (1867). Frederick Cockburn (ed.), *Charge of the Lord Chief Justice of England to the Grand Jury at the Central Criminal Court, in the Case of* The Queen Against Nelson and Brand (London: William Ridgway, 1867).

171 *Phillips v Eyre* (1869) L.R. 4 225 (QB); *Phillips v Eyre* (1870) L.R. 6 (QB) 1 (Ex. Ch.).

the law and politics of martial law generated much more heat than light. 'Partly because of the violence of the dispute it engendered, the Eyre case tended if anything to *obscure* the issue of martial law.'[172]

The period did, however, produce two significant and opposing contributions to the theory of martial law. The first, by William Finlason, chief legal writer for *The Times*, was written at the height of the Jamaica affair with the intention of influencing its outcome. The second, written by Dicey in 1885, was a later response to the post–Morant Bay debate in general and Finlason's conception of martial law in particular. Finlason's *A Treatise on Martial Law*,[173] described as 'the most comprehensive discussion of martial law that had ever been written in English',[174] offered something like a legal manual for the discipline of imperial subjects through terror. Signalling a move towards a model of empire based on race and *realpolitik*, Finlason conceived martial law as an essential element to protect the civilized in remote outposts within Britain's sprawling empire where they were vastly outnumbered by semi-savage peoples. Largely obsolete in the British mainland, martial law 'had been revived by the military, demographic, and racial exigencies of the expanding empire'.[175] To perform this task, colonial governors and military commanders needed at their disposal almost unlimited discretionary power with which to deter the always potentially unruly native populations. Terror was thus of its very essence.[176] 'To be anything, it [martial law] must be *absolute*.'[177]

Finlason defined martial law as the 'right or prerogative of the Crown' in time of rebellion to restore peace, declare war and 'exercise its severities'.[178] Such a right or power entitles the Crown to 'absolute and discretionary military power'.[179] In the imperial sphere, this 'tremendous power' vests in the colonial governor.[180] Finlason was contemptuous of Lord Cockburn's attempt in his Grand Jury Charge to normalize martial law by trying to bind it to common law notions of legality. In reality,

172 Charles Townshend, 'Martial Law: Legal and Administrative Problems of Civil Emergency in Britain and the Empire, 1800–1940' (1982) 25 *Historical Journal* 167, 173.

173 W. F. Finlason, *A Treatise on Martial Law as Allowed by the Law of England in Time of Rebellion* (London: Stevens & Sons, 1866). See also Finlason, *Commentaries on Martial Law* (London: Stevens & Sons, 1867).

174 Kostal, *Jurisprudence of Power*, 229.

175 Kostal, *Jurisprudence of Power*, 231.

176 Finlason, *Treatise on Martial Law*, xxxii.

177 Finlason, *Commentaries*, 33.

178 Finlason, *Commentaries*, 1.

179 Finlason, *Commentaries*, 10.

180 Finlason, *Commentaries*, 11.

martial law draws its authority from a very different source. It follows the 'principle of authority' rather than the ordinary principle of law and justice.[181] Like war, it seeks to impose order where there is none. It operates where the constitution has ceased to operate. Martial law thus tracks the logic of war rather than the logic of law. Normal modes of accountability do not apply: 'The question of legality can practically never be settled by judicial determination, seeing that, if men in authority have acted honestly in a great public emergency, no jury will be likely to find against them in any proceeding, civil or criminal, added to which, there is certain to be (as there is in the Jamaica case), a bill of indemnity.'[182]

Despite this vast inchoate reserve of power into which colonial governors and military commanders might tap with almost complete freedom, Finlason also made a case for the legalization of martial law. If colonial officials act under the authority of an Act of Parliament – including an Act of a colonial parliament – and under the orders from the highest civil and military authorities within the colony, they cannot be criminally liable for their actions, unless bad faith is shown.[183] He gives examples of legislation of this sort being passed in relation to Ireland, India[184] and Jamaica. His argument for greater use of martial law legislation rests on the same basis as his argument for a discretionary royal prerogative to combat rebellion, namely, to free up officials and soldiers in the field. But although they are both based on an assessment of operational need, the two legal techniques are very different. One relies on explicit advance authorization; the other does not.[185] As we soon see, while Finlason's argument concerning the prerogative basis of martial law was not adopted by either the courts or government,[186] his argument for *ex ante* statutory grants of discretionary powers to deal with uprisings and emergencies became something like

[181] Finlason, *Commentaries*, 18–19.

[182] Finlason, *Commentaries*, 25, 26, 30.

[183] Finlason, *Commentaries*, 30.

[184] These took the form of regulations drawn up by the East India Company, then of course the governing authority, and not strictly speaking the imperial or colonial legislature. See Finlason, *Commentaries*, 33. Despite these regulations, and the contemporaneous State Offences Act, the Heinous Offences Act and the Mutiny and Desertion Act 1857, and further legislation providing for collective punishment and confiscation, the legal status of at least some of the actions taken in response to the Sepoy Rebellion remained unclear: A. W. Brian Simpson, *Human Rights and the End of Empire: Britain and the Genesis of the European Convention* (Oxford: Oxford University Press, 2001), 77.

[185] Simpson, *Human Rights and the End of Empire*, 75.

[186] William Harrison Moore, *Act of State in English Law* (New York: E. P. Dutton, 1906), 48–49.

the operating framework, in as much as there was one, for crisis management within the British state and empire.

This development reflects the administrative state's tendency to move from discretion to rules – or, rather, its use of rules (and especially statute) to grant discretionary powers to officials. Dicey, writing more than a decade after the Jamaica crisis, was better placed than Finlason to make sense of these trends. Dicey moved in the same circle as the leaders of the Jamaica Committee – Fitzjames Stephen was a cousin – and was an admirer of Mill.[187] It is not surprising, then, to see him take up the topic of martial law in the *Law and the Constitution* (1885), nor to see him develop a position that aimed at subjecting martial law to the control of the ordinary law. At all points, Dicey's account of martial law could hardly have been more different from Finlason's treatment. Whereas for Finlason martial law was an element of the Crown's sovereign right to put down rebellious subjects, part of the prerogative of war and peace, for Dicey it is just another name for the common law right and duty to suppress breaches of the peace. No doubt in practice the right is generally invoked by the Crown and its agents, but in principle it is one held by all legal subjects. 'Every subject, whether a civilian or soldier, whether what is called a "servant of the government" (such for example as a policeman) or a person in no way connected with the administration, not only has the right, but is, as a matter of legal duty, bound to assist in putting down breaches of the peace.'[188] Officials and ordinary citizens thus occupy the same position in law. They are bound to put down breaches of the peace, authorized to employ as much force as is necessary for the purpose, but no more. And they are liable to be called to account for their actions before a court for the use of excessive or unnecessary force, or indeed for their non-performance of their duty to do what they can to keep order.[189]

Dicey's intent is to normalize and domesticate martial law to the greatest possible extent and to leave no scope for Finlason's idea of an extraordinary reservoir of sovereign terror. The extra-legal route, Dicey argues, is the equivalent of the French idea of the 'state of siege', during which the government operates by military force and 'constitutional guarantees

[187] 'At Oxford we swallowed Mill, rather undigested', Dicey later recalled. 'He was our chief intellectual food until 1860.' Quoted in Collini, *Public Moralists*, 326.

[188] A. V. Dicey, *The Law of the Constitution* (Oxford: Oxford University Press, ed. J. W. F. Allison, 2013), 161. See also excerpt from the 6th edition, Dicey, *Law of the Constitution*, 353.

[189] Dicey refers to the case of *Rex v Pinney* 5 C&P 254 which considered the duty of the Mayor of Bristol in reference to the Reform Riots of 1831.

are suspended'. Thinking in all likelihood of the recent suppression of the Paris Commune and *la semaine sanglante*, Dicey wrote: 'We shall hardly go wrong if we assume that during this suspension of ordinary law any man whatever is liable to arrest, imprisonment, or execution at the will of a military tribunal consisting of a few officers who are excited by the passions natural to civil war.'[190] Dicey's specific target is Finlason, although his name is not mentioned. Finlason argued repeatedly that martial law involves the 'suspension of all law' and confers 'an absolute discretion for the doing of anything which possibly could be deemed necessary or expedient'.[191] It is 'a state of things in which there is no *law* at all, but the will of the Commanding officer'.[192] Dicey uses here the same technique of aversive comparative analysis that he deploys elsewhere in the *Law of the Constitution*, most notably in his dismissal of administrative law – or *droit administratif* as he insists on calling it – as something alien to English constitutional and legal sensibilities.[193] The reader is faced with the same sort of stylized choice in respect of martial law. Either, with Dicey, a native English law that is straightforward, limited and egalitarian. Or, with Finlason, what amounts to a French import, foreign both in its provenance and in the licence it allows for despotic force.[194]

In reality, though, the Victorians and Edwardians went for neither option entirely. It is probably true that on the narrow issue of whether martial law was a prerogative or a common law power the Diceyans had the better of the battle. There was a general acceptance of Dicey's position that martial law was in principle subject to common law oversight – although few believed post-Eyre that this would have much practical bite.[195] In the Boer War (1899–1902), discussions on martial law took

[190] *Law of the Constitution*, 163.

[191] *Treatise*, 107.

[192] *Treatise*, vii.

[193] *Law of the Constitution*, 1st ed., 101–119; 3rd ed., 235–249. See also J. W. F. Allison, *The English Historical Constitution* (Cambridge: Cambridge University Press, 2007), 166, 177–178.

[194] Cockburn LCJ had adopted a similar strategy in *R v Nelson and Brand*, where he called the prerogative theory of martial law 'repugnant to the genius of our people, to the spirit of our laws and institutions, to all which we have been accustomed to revere and hold sacred': *Charge of the Lord Chief Justice of England*, 23.

[195] The most spectacular failure of the Diceyan model was the treatment of Brigadier-General Rex Dyer who ordered his troops to open fire on a crowd of 20,000 that had gathered in Amritsar, India. Around 380 were killed and more than 1,000 wounded; 180 people were sentenced to death and 264 to transportation for life at subsequent *in camera* trials. Dyer was never prosecuted, his only 'punishment' was to be invalided out of the army.

place both in Parliament and the courts (chiefly those of the colonies concerned). While the cases were not consistent,[196] in general the courts reconciled conflict between the ordinary law and martial law regulations by allowing the latter to prevail, subject to their being satisfied of the need to enforce the military jurisdiction.[197] The well-known Privy Council decision in *Ex parte Marais* short-circuited arguments of principle by declaring that, as a state of war was shown to exist, the maxim *inter arma silent leges* applied: 'The fact that for some purposes some tribunals have been allowed to pursue their ordinary course in a district where martial law has been proclaimed, is not conclusive that war is not raging.'[198] The judgment applied the ruling of *Elphinstone v Bedreechund*, discussed earlier, for the first time to British subjects.

If this period marks the end of prerogative-based martial law,[199] it was largely not the common law's doing, as *Ex parte Marais* illustrates. What had happened was that the legal terrain on which martial law operated had shifted, largely outside the terms set by Dicey.[200] First in the Jamaica affair and then in relation to the Boer War, the common law had not been able to provide sufficiently clear standards by which the exercise of martial law might be structured.[201] It is possible to see this omission as part

See David Dyzenhaus, 'The Puzzle of Martial Law' (2009) 59 *University of Toronto Law Journal* 1, 31; Simpson, *Human Rights and the End of Empire*, 64–66.

196 Compare, for instance, *Fourie's Case* (1900) Buchanan xvii. 166, with *R v De Preez* (1900) Buchanan xvii. 53.

197 G. G. Phillimore, 'What Is a State of War in Law?' (1902) 4 *Journal of the Society of Comparative Legislation* 128,131.

198 *Ex parte D.F. Marais* [1902] AC 109. The Privy Council decided that the fact that ordinary courts were open in a country parts of which were in a 'state of war' did not of itself bar the trial of civilians by military tribunals. This ruling might be seen as a qualification to the stricter position outlined by Cockburn and Dicey in the previous century. Dyzenhaus, 'The Puzzle of Martial Law', 31; Townshend, 'Martial Law', 182.

199 Phillimore, 'What Is a State of War in Law?', 133: 'At the present day, however, it is hardly likely to be contended that the prerogative rights of the Crown include the proclamation and enforcement of martial law by military courts'. Compare Lord Halsbury's more sardonic dictum in *Tilonko v Attorney-General of Natal* (1907) AC 93: 'If there is a war, there is a right to repel force by force, but it is found convenient and decorous, from time to time, to authorize what are called "courts" to administer punishments, and to restrain, by acts of repression, the violence that is committed in time of war.'

200 See, e.g., the remark in the discussion of martial law in the 6th edition of the *Law of the Constitution* that Acts of Indemnity 'have been invariably, or almost invariably, passed after the determination of a period of civil war or disturbance, e.g., after the Rebellions of 1715 and 1745' (359–360).

201 *Ex parte Marais* led to a series of articles in the *Law Quarterly Review*: see, e.g., Holdsworth, 'Martial Law Historically Considered'; Cyril Dodd, 'The Case of Marais' (1902) 18 LQR 145; Frederick Pollock, 'What Is Martial Law?' (1902) 18 LQR 155. The 6th

of a wider tactic of avoidance of the more awkward questions of colonial rule.[202] Historians have identified such a 'strategy of self-deception' as a common feature of imperial discourse. Cheryl Welch detects patterns of evasion – irony, containment, comparison, avoidance – in Alexis de Tocqueville's refusal in his pro-imperialist writings to confront violations of the *jus in bello* in imposing French authority in North Africa. These avoidance techniques enable the imperialist to avoid confronting the moral consequences of political choices and 'illustrate recurring responses to a particularly modern moral anxiety about violating internalized liberal norms'.[203]

The fudging of martial law might be typical of the false consciousness of nineteenth-century imperialism, adding to the disquiet that at least some contemporaries felt when confronted with the dissonance between colonial practice and the moral and legal standards that they took to be defining of the character of the nation. But the lack of legal clarity was also a practical problem for government and colonial officials. Mill's claim that after the Jamaica affair colonial governors 'though they might escape the actual sentence of a criminal tribunal, they were not safe against being put to some trouble and expense in order to avoid it' might have been self-serving, but was not untrue.[204] The passage of martial law statutes – which even when Finlason was writing his *Treatise* was already a gathering trend – picked up pace after the Jamaica crisis. Ad hoc legislation, ordinances and official instructions to provide authorization for exceptional use of force became an increasingly common feature of colonial lawmaking, issued by colonial authorities looking for legal clarity and wanting to avoid Eyre's fate.[205] The process was not much different from how the administrative state developed in other areas. The growth of nineteenth-century bureaucracies typically followed a similar pattern. A social problem was identified and subjected at first to piecemeal and targeted legislation, accompanied by a new body of officials charged with

edition of Dicey's *Law of the Constitution* (1902) contains a more extensive treatment of martial law and includes a critical treatment of the case: 352–366, esp. 359.

202 Townshend, 'Martial Law', 194.

203 Cheryl B. Welch, 'Colonial Violence and the Rhetoric of Evasion: Tocqueville on Algeria' (2003) 31 *Political Theory* 235, 247.

204 *Autobiography*, 219, quoted in Dyzenhaus, 'The Puzzle of Martial Law', 30.

205 In the wake of the Eyre affair, for instance, a circular sent by the Colonial Office to all colonial governors outlining the British government's understanding of the legal situation. The circular is quoted at some length in G. G. Phillimore, 'Martial Law in Rebellion' (1900) 2 *Journal of the Society of Comparative Legislation* 45, 61.

carrying the statute into effect. The activities of the officials tended to have a centralizing effect, which in turn generated calls for more general legislation. Once passed, this legislation often failed to deliver the desired knockout blow, leading to a pattern of rolling, dynamic regulation led by now expert and experienced officials acting under the shadow of a developed regulatory regime.[206]

The same pattern of legalization and bureaucratization occurred with martial law. The best specific example again comes from the Boer War.[207] Martial law was 'proclaimed' in an area covering the whole of Natal and much of Cape Colony by the end of 1899. The insecurity felt by officials because of the fuzzy legal position is plain. The Attorney General to the Colony, Richard Solomon, taking his cue from official documents dating back to the Eyre crisis, doubted the legality of the proclamation and remarked: 'I am exceedingly anxious that nothing should be done by Military Authorities, under the cloak of such a proclamation, which will provoke an application to the Supreme Court, whereby such a proclamation might be declared null and void.'[208] Such concerns about 'legal risk' led to regulations being issued that specified the powers of the military tribunals. The commander-in-chief sent a circular to magistrates identifying and elaborating on the new provisions. As the conflict deepened, new legislation was passed and model regulations prepared to replace local ad hoc measures. A Martial Law Board – as Townshend notes 'a wonderfully incongruous title' – was created to regulate administration under the various legal provisions produced during the war.[209] After the war was over, the problems encountered by civilian and military officials led to calls for the comprehensive legislation of martial law.[210] Nothing of the

[206] Oliver MacDonagh, 'The Nineteenth-Century Revolution in Government: A Reappraisal' (1958) 1 *Historical Journal* 52, 58–60.

[207] Another example is the gradual extension of temporary emergency provisions statutes in Ireland during roughly the same period: Protection of Life and Property (Ireland) Act (1871); An Act for the Better Protection of Person and Property in Ireland (1881); Prevention of Crime (Ireland) Act (1883). This Irish legislation 'introduced in embryo the idea of a code of emergency powers', although it did not involve delegating legislative power to the executive: Simpson, *Human Rights and the End of Empire*, 79–80.

[208] Report by the Attorney-General, Cape Colony, 25 November 1899, quoted in Townshend, 'Martial Law', 176.

[209] Townshend, 'Martial Law', 176–182.

[210] Phillimore, 'What Is a State of War in Law?', 134: 'It has been suggested that in view of the constitutional and legal difficulties and doubts surrounding the adoption and administration of martial law, legislation should be passed to deal clearly and comprehensively with the whole subject; and our recent experiences in the South African War seem to show that this is no less necessary now.'

sort was forthcoming. But the development of a model of statutory martial law in the Boer War and elsewhere culminated in the Defence of the Realm Acts (DORA). Passed by Parliament at the start of the First World War, DORA granted unprecedentedly wide-ranging powers to the executive to make and modify laws without further reference to Parliament.[211] They also allowed for the treatment of both foreign and British subjects 'in like manner as if such persons were subject to military law and had in active service committed an offence' under the Army Act. The courts construed the Regulations that came through the DORA structure liberally in the government's interest according to the maxim *salus populi suprema lex*.[212] In the words of the Lord Chief Justice in the leading case *R v Halliday, ex parte Zadig*, 'by reason of the emergency arising out of the war and the necessity of providing for the national safety without delay Parliament thought that the making of the necessary provisions for that purpose might be entrusted to His Majesty in Council'.[213] (Note the repetition of necessity/necessary in that sentence, and the need to inject majesty into the equation.) The Great War had brought martial law home, in its new and comprehensive legislative form, instigating the rule of enlightened executive government cut loose from the restraining force of both representative government and common law. Many DORA provisions found their way onto the statute book after 1918. Other provisions formed the basis of the restrictive general legislation of the 1930s, such as the Incitement to Disaffection Act 1934 and the Public Order Act 1936: 'what began life as emergency powers to deal with the defence of the realm gradually became part of the general law and as such of the peace-time powers of the public authorities for dealing with dissent and opposition'.[214]

Conclusion

Martial law is a paradigmatic area in which arguments pertaining to reason of state have found expression in British legal history. Studying the topic against a background that interweaves legislation and bureaucracy

[211] For analysis and criticism see Harold M. Bowman, 'Martial Law and the English Constitution' (1916) 15 *Michigan Law Review* 93.

[212] *Michaels v Block* [1918] 34 TLR 438.

[213] (1916) 1 KB 738, at 741. See also *R v Halliday* [1917] AC 260 (House of Lords); *Ex parte Norman* (1916) 114 LT 232.

[214] K. D. Ewing and C. A. Gearty, *The Struggle for Civil Liberties: Political Freedom and the Rule of Law in Britain, 1914–1945* (Oxford: Oxford University Press, 2000), 93.

on one hand, with imperialism and constitutional development on the other, is particularly valuable. Far from being divorced from the legislating and bureaucratizing trends that elsewhere characterize the developing nineteenth-century state, martial law in fact is almost as good an example of these phenomena as any, even mirroring the characteristically piecemeal way that it developed. In the case of martial law, these modernizing developments left the common law scrambling. Bentham's charge that the common law was methodologically unsuited to providing the clear comprehensive direction required by modern men and the modern state had more obvious purchase at the close of the century than when he had made it at its beginning. The common law showed itself incapable of policing martial law effectively. Actors in the field – the Colonial Office, governors, officials, commanders – were left to find their own solutions, albeit ones that drew in a variety of ways on their understanding of common law principles, usually in the resources that were becoming increasingly familiar to them: statute, regulations and soft law. The result of these developments was the practical displacement of the old paradigm of 'prerogative versus common law'. It was obvious, if not at the close of the Boer War (*Marais*), then certainly by the First World War (*Zadig*), that the common law had lost any claim it might have to a central role in the articulation of the constitutional discourse on reason of state. The old common law pathways were effectively bypassed by legislative and official practice, and the common law found itself in a responsive and ancillary role, filling in the gaps within the grand or not so grand designs of others.

DORA signals the arrival of the modern administrative state. From that point on, it becomes far harder to see the government apparatus as being surrounded by and working within the principles of the common law constitution. In an age of statutes the common law must increasingly work within the interstices of government. Dicey came to realize as much when late in life he modified his earlier implacable opposition to the whole idea of *droit administratif* and called instead for a common law of judicial review.[215] What we need, he now recognized, was not no administrative law at all but rather a style of administrative law which was channelled through the ordinary courts and which drew on the old common law's reserve of principles. He might have made a similar corrective move in relation to martial law – after all, he returned to the topic with renewed vigour after the Boer War cases. But the opportunity was

[215] A. V. Dicey, 'The Development of Administrative Law in England' (1915) 31 *Law Quarterly Review* 148.

passed up. The common law would remain pure, in this domain at least, but barely relevant.

The formalization and bureaucratization of martial law, which had its apotheosis in DORA, parallels an argument made by both James and J. S. Mill about the need for exceptional bureaucratic rule for India. Perhaps a stronger claim might be made. It is not simply that the colonial context provided a space in which new ideas and new arrangements might be tried out, a kind of laboratory of government and administration.[216] It was also that, as Burke predicted, these ideas and arrangements were always likely to come back in one form or another, spilling into metropolitan legal and constitutional structures. The link is particularly clear in relation to martial law or emergency powers. Martial law was in practice for a long time all but reserved for the colonial 'other'. Indeed, mid-Victorian debate was conducted almost entirely on this assumption. A vague and largely informal power to instigate martial law was gradually replaced in the colonial arena with first ad hoc and then increasingly more general and 'standing' legislation, complete with its own administrative structure. It was in this new statutory form that martial law (sweeping executive emergency powers) came home, as the conflict between the imperial powers outside the European continent found a new and particularly deadly expression on European soil. Writing in 1900, G. G. Phillimore observed that it was true that the Crown in the colonies has the powers it enjoys in Britain. '*Vice versa*, whatever power in this respect the Crown has in the Colonies, except by colonial enactment, it also has in the United Kingdom.'[217] Martial law offers a good example, then, of the permeable nature of the dichotomies British authors and officials tended to operate within – between the inside and the outside, the British and the imperial, the civilized and the barbarian.

The study of martial law also shows how forces inside government worked towards juridifying what had historically been an area from which law had been largely absent – *inter arma silent leges* – or at least at its thinnest. This development reflects J. S. Mill's theory of civilizational development and the state. Modern man requires a different structure of rule, one that fits his more individualist temperament. Social development will be accompanied by an increase in the use of formal, positive law

216 Compare Bell, 'John Stuart Mill on Colonies', 46: 'He saw the colonies, I would argue, as laboratories of character development, as vast case studies of his proposed science of ethology.'

217 Phillimore, 'Martial Law in Rebellion', 52.

as a mode of regulation and by the creation of bureaucracies charged with the expert application of that law. 'As respects such new laws, and as much new agency as is needed to ensure their observance, the function of the State naturally does widen the advance of civilization.'[218] The lack of legal clarity in the relationship between state and subject was as problematic for Mill as it had been for Bentham. Even worse were remnants of ancient discretionary authority operating in the gaps and silences between the laws. Hence his stance on martial law. Even in an emergency, power should be determined so far as possible by law. This was also Dicey's position, although he wrote in the simultaneously ancient and modern idiom of the common law. What Mill did not clearly foresee was how the trend towards democracy, statute and bureaucracy might operate to install exceptional modes of governing *within* the legal framework and the operating structures of the modern state. By the turn of the century, as the Victorian and Edwardian experience with martial and emergency laws showed, these progressive developments had themselves produced two substantial constitutional problems. It had become clear, first, that legislation through a more active Parliament and applied through more effective bureaucracies, while essential for progressive change, also carried a threat to liberty. And, second, it was becoming apparent that the common law did not have the institutional and constitutional capacity to provide an adequate check in the event of an unruly government.

[218] Mill, *Complete Works*, XIX: 602, quoted in Claeys, *Mill and Paternalism*, 69.

7

War, law and the modern state

The constitutionalizing project charted in this book involved the normalization of politics via the subjection of sites of arbitrary power, especially those associated with reason of state, to ordinary law and parliamentary politics. By the twentieth century this project had run into difficulty, having become in a sense a victim of its own success. Previously, the assumption shared by many writers – including those, like Burke and Bentham, who otherwise disagreed on most things – was that greater legal coherence and rationality led to more effective government and a more willing populace, thereby increasing the stability and potency of the state. The same belief supported the codification project that accompanied the birth of the 'state-nation' in the Age of Revolution, exemplified by the establishment of the Code Napoléon in 1804.[1]

Events showed that this assumption did not necessarily hold. As the nineteenth century progressed, Benthamite notions of law as the command of a sovereign lawmaker displaced the older, Burkean idea of parliament as a law-*declarer* bound by conventional restraints and principles of natural law. The law was made subject to the state, but then the state was itself made subject to the nation.[2] These developments, in as much as they were consciously motivated, were animated by the goal of strengthening the state.[3] And indeed by the First World War the state *had* become more potent than ever before. But the apparent triumph of the state was a prelude to disaster. Looking back from the rubble left by the Second

1 Maurice Amos, 'The Code Napoléon and the Modern World' (1928) 10 *Journal of Comparative Legislation and International Law* 222, 223: with the promulgation of the Civil Code, the 'law of the whole country was unified, laicized, democratized and simplified'.

2 Phillip Bobbitt, *The Shield of Achilles: War, Peace, and the Course of History* (New York: Alfred A. Knopf, 2002), chapter 8. See also Hannah Arendt, *The Origins of Totalitarianism* (Chicago: University of Chicago Press, 1985), 275: 'the nation had conquered the state'.

3 See, e.g, the analysis in the previous chapter of John Austin on centralization and Walter Bagehot on the English constitution.

World War, 'the entire era resembled (in the words of Charles de Gaulle) a "second", but more devastating, "Thirty Years War", a time in which any fleeting moments of hope or optimism had at best been an expression of naivety'.[4] Not only did Europe see death and destruction on an unprecedented, 'mechanized' scale. It also saw decades of political turbulence, of revolution and counter-revolution – it was an age of political experiment geared towards 'making peoples and remaking souls'.[5]

The apotheosis of the state in the early twentieth century also marked the high point of empire. The period saw the European states complete their march across the globe.[6] Competition among European states for the reflected glory that came from imperial possession reached almost obscene heights with the 'Scramble for Africa' from the 1880s. For Britain, India still seemed vital. 'As long as we rule India', the Viceroy of India Lord Curzon remarked at the dawn of the century, 'we are the greatest power in the world. If we lose it we shall drop straightaway to a 3rd rate power.'[7] The First World War was both a war of nation-states and a war of global empires. 'When Britain declared war on Germany and its allies in August 1914, it did so in the name of the empire. In making this declaration, Britain expected that all parts of the empire … were perforce at war' and did not seek agreement from any part of the empire, even the self-governing dominions.[8]

While the experience of fighting together as an imperial force sometimes led to a greater sense of imperial connectedness,[9] the seeds of the move 'from empire to nation'[10] were sown during and immediately after the Great War. True, the British empire reached its greatest geographical extent after the war. 'But within a year of the Armistice the British Empire came to resemble not so much a vista of power as a landscape of

[4] Robert Gerwarth, 'Introduction' in Robert Gerwarth (ed.), *Twisted Paths: Europe 1914–1945* (Oxford: Oxford University Press, 2007), 1.

[5] Jan-Werner Müller, *Contesting Democracy: Political Ideas in Twentieth-Century Europe* (New Haven: Yale University Press, 2011), 49.

[6] Duncan Bell, 'Introduction' in Duncan Bell (ed.), *Victorian Visions of Global Empire: Empire and International Relations in Nineteenth-Century Political Thought* (Cambridge: Cambridge University Press, 2007), 3.

[7] Quoted in Brendan Simms, *Europe: The Struggle for Supremacy, 1453 to the Present* (London: Allen Lane, 2013), 271.

[8] Stephen Garton, 'The Dominions, Ireland, and India' in Robert Gerwarth and Erez Manela (eds.), *Empires at War 1911–1923* (Oxford: Oxford University Press, 2014), 154–155.

[9] Garton, 'The Dominions, Ireland, and India', 171–172.

[10] Samuel Moyn, *The Last Utopia: Human Rights in History* (Cambridge, Mass.: Harvard University Press, 2010), 117.

rebellion on which the sun never set',[11] a crisis that embraced the West Indies, Ireland, Egypt, Palestine, South Africa, Hong Kong and India. The year 1919, during which the Treaty of Versailles was signed, also saw the massacre at Amritsar. Woodrow Wilson's promotion of the concept of self-determination at Versailles crystallized incipient nationalist aspirations.[12] Later in the century, the principle took root and widened to include non-Europeans.[13] Within forty years, the British empire 'had become a commonwealth – a constitutional simulacrum shorn of might and meaningful majesty'.[14] War was again a catalyst, the Second World War having shown clearly that colonial control depended ultimately on force and that British national interests would trump those of its Imperial subjects.[15]

The mechanized slaughter of 1914–18 and the killing fields of 1939–45, as well as what happened during the intervening years, put paid to an easy presumption that modernity lent itself internationally to peace and domestically to constitutional normalization.[16] Earlier generations had assumed that Europe was the cradle of civilization and that alegal barbarism was a matter for the extra-European wilds. It was the vocation among civilized nations to legislate, Hegel wrote, an aspect of the infinite urge of our times to systematize. Barbarians, though, 'are governed by drives, customs, and feelings, but they have no consciousness of these' just as the 'sun and the planets also have their laws, but they are unaware of them'.[17] By 1945, barbarism had conquered the *ius publicum*

[11] Adam Tooze, *The Deluge: The Great War and the Remaking of Global Order* (London: Allen Lane, 2014), 374.

[12] Margaret MacMillan, *Peacemakers: Six Months that Changed the World – The Paris Peace Conference of 1919 and Its Attempt to End War* (London: John Murray, 2003), 19–20; Antony Anghie, *Imperialism, Sovereignty and the Making of International Law* (Cambridge: Cambridge University Press, 2004), 139; Gerry Simpson, *Great Powers and Outlaw States: Unequal Sovereigns in the International Legal Order* (Cambridge: Cambridge University Press, 2004), 158–159.

[13] Mazower, *Governing the World*, 250–272.

[14] Garton, 'The Dominions, Ireland, and India', 172.

[15] Keith Jeffery, 'The Second World War' in Judith M. Brown and Wm. Roger Louis (eds.), *The Oxford History of the British Empire: The Twentieth Century* (Oxford: Oxford University Press, 1999), 326–327. See also Wm. Roger Louis, *Imperialism at Bay, 1941–45: The United States and the Decolonization of the British Empire* (Oxford: Oxford University Press, 1977), 101–103.

[16] Paul Kennedy, *The Parliament of Man: The Past, Present, and Future of the United Nations* (Toronto: HarperCollins, 2006), chapter 1.

[17] G. W. F. Hegel, *Elements of the Philosophy of Right* (Cambridge: Cambridge University Press, ed. Allen W. Wood, 1991), 243 at para. 211.

Europeaum. The preceding years had seen violence subjected to the 'urge to systematize' in a way that would have been beyond the wildest imaginations of Hegel's 'barbarians'.[18] Indeed it was not only barbarism that had come home to European soil but the full techniques of imperial rule. In the Second World War, the might of the state was mobilized for the first time to conquer and exploit other Europeans.[19] Those who fell under German rule after 1939 were made slaves of the Reich or destroyed. Much of post-war Europe became, in the words of one of the century's great writers, 'the necropolis of a foreign, mysterious people, torn from its civil existence and its history, thrown back to the evolutionary stage of nomadic gatherers'.[20]

The mystery of lawlessness

A pervasive, if relatively undramatic, feature of the juristic and political thought of the first half of the twentieth century was a preoccupation with the rise of the administrative state. The topic provided a focus for humanistic concerns about the automatizing of political and social life that the arrival of the 'Machine Age' seemed to augur. For those interested in the juridical dimensions of the state, a central worry was the displacing or the warping effect of the modern state on law and legality. The post-1918 state was a 'positive state', as Harold Laski called it, which 'through the agency of government, has directly undertaken the control of national life'.[21] Society became an object that the state might manage and transform with a view towards perfecting it. An Enlightenment belief in the self-improvement of man had become a 'high modernist' belief in the perfectibility of social order: 'It was possible to conceive of an artificial, engineered society designed, not by custom and historical accident, but according to conscious, rational, scientific criteria. Every nook and

[18] Anghie, *Imperialism, Sovereignty and the Making of International Law*, 138: the War 'had not merely devastated Europe, but also severely weakened its claims to moral superiority – and, indeed, to be civilized'.

[19] Tony Judt, *Postwar: A History of Europe since 1945* (London: Pimlico, 2007), 14: 'For Europeans this was a new experience. Overseas, in the colonies, European states had habitually indentured or enslaved indigenous populations for their own benefit.' See also Mark Mazower, *Dark Continent: Europe's Twentieth Century* (London: Penguin, 1999).

[20] W. G. Sebald, *On the Natural History of Destruction* (London: Penguin, trans. Anthea Bell, 2004), 36.

[21] Harold Laski, *The Foundations of Soveriegnty* (New York: Harcourt, Brace & Co., 1921), 30, 33–34.

cranny of the social order might be improved upon.'[22] Law within the state so conceived was understood principally as a social technique, subordinate to politics, whose purpose was primarily functional: to provide a framework for the effective realization of the social goals specified by legislation through an often fragmented and complex administrative sphere.[23]

This development had profound consequences. The increased demands on the state, in part a response to the sacrifices made by ordinary citizens during the First World War, disrupted existing patterns of government.[24] The inter-war years saw a transformation of the function of parliaments. Parliaments across Europe increasingly resorted to broad delegations of power to executive or administrative bodies.[25] On the back of their control over a purportedly technocratic administrative apparatus, executives increasingly claimed normative authority in their own right.[26] As Max Weber was among the first to observe, the evolution of the West had produced a bureaucratic state, an industrial capitalist economy characterized by means/end rationality and a formally rationalized legal system.[27] Within such a state, the *Rechtsstaat* ideal was threatened as demands for redistributive justice induced a move away from general statutes to more specific measures and decrees aimed at particular situations or groups of citizens. Offering only an emotionally and spiritually unsatisfactory 'mastery' through 'calculation', the 'mass state' and its 'rule by officials' had the potential to produce, Weber argued, 'the greatest form of

[22] James C. Scott, *Seeing Like a State: How Certain Schemes to Improve the Human Condition Have Failed* (New Haven: Yale University Press, 1998), 92.

[23] Martin Loughlin, 'Modernism in British Public Law, 1919–1979' [2014] *Public Law* 56, 58–66.

[24] The situation tended to be more pronounced in those states which had been restructured in the aftermath of the war or following the Treaty of Versailles. On Germany see, e.g., Arthur Jacobson and Bernhard Schlink (eds.), *Weimar: A Jurisprudence of Crisis* (Berkeley: University of California Press, 2002) and on the inter-war European situation more generally the essays in Gerwarth, *Twisted Paths: Europe 1914–1945*.

[25] A development not just feared by those on the right: see, e.g., Harold J. Laski, *Liberty in the Modern State* (Harmondsworth: Penguin, 1937), 73: 'There has accreted today about the departments of State a type of discretionary power which seems to me full of danger unless it is exercised under proper safeguards.'

[26] Peter L. Lindseth, 'The Paradox of Parliamentary Sovereignty: Delegation, Democracy, and Dictatorship in Germany and France, 1920s–1950s' (2004) 113 *Yale Law Journal* 1341, 1344; Edward L. Rubin, 'Law and Legislation in the Administrative State' (1989) 89 *Columbia Law Review* 369.

[27] Dana Villa, 'The Legacy of Max Weber in Weimar Political and Social Theory' in Peter E. Gordon and John P. McCormick (eds.), *Weimar Thought: A Contested Legacy* (Princeton: Princeton University Press, 2013), 75–76.

collective enslavement the world had ever known', the 'steel-hard casing' of universal rationalization and bureaucratization.[28]

This chapter examines the response of Carl Schmitt, Friedrich Hayek and Michael Oakeshott to these developments, exploring what each has to say about the modern idea of reason of state. While all are seminal figures in twentieth-century political and constitutional thought, only two fit at all neatly within the British tradition. Oakeshott taught at Cambridge and in 1948 succeeded Laski as Professor of Political Science at the London School of Economics. Hayek, though Austrian by birth and training, came to the LSE in 1931 and saw himself as leading a revival of British Enlightenment political thought. Schmitt, on the contrary, was German, an authoritarian and sometime Nazi jurist. There are, though, strong reasons for including him here. First, and most obvious, he was a giant of twentieth-century constitutional thought who made particularly significant contributions to thinking on reason of state and the 'exception'. His reputation in the area is such that to leave him out of the discussion here would create a problematic lacuna. Second, his ideas about reason of state were influential even on liberal and conservative thinkers like Hayek and Oakeshott, who would sometimes adopt parts of his analysis even while denying his normative conclusions. In more recent times, his influence has increased, especially among scholars on the Left.[29] Third, his thought may be said to reflect Burke's idea of the regression of sentiments, discussed in an earlier chapter. Burke argued that just as we adjust ourselves to the habit of peaceful civil engagement, we become inured to violence so that in the end we are equipped to deal with nothing else. Germany in the period of the twentieth-century's Thirty Years' War saw dynamics of this sort. Schmitt needs to be read contextually, I argue here, as a reactionary modernist incapable of finding a stable route away from the shock and violence of the First World War.

While the phenomena of modern reason of state politics and the rise of the administrative state might seem unconnected, they are in fact anything but. On the contrary, as Weber observed, 'the relationship of the state to violence is particularly close at the present time'.[30] Understanding

[28] John P. McCormick, *Carl Schmitt's Critique of Liberalism: Against Politics as Technology* (Cambridge: Cambridge University Press, 1997), 39; Müller, *Contesting Democracy*, 28.

[29] See, e.g., Giorgio Agamben, *Homo Sacer: Sovereign Power and Bare Life* (Stanford: Stanford University Press, trans. Daniel Heller-Roazen, 1998); Agamben, *State of Exception* (Chicago: University of Chicago Press, trans. Kevin Attell, 2005).

[30] Max Weber, 'Politics as a Vocation' in Weber, *The Vocation Lectures* (Indianapolis: Hackett Publishing, ed. David Owen and Tracy B. Strong, 2004), 33.

the inter-war state was very much a matter of getting to grips with the sharp end of state action of the type long associated with the category of reason of state: war, crisis, diplomacy. The twentieth century saw plenty of action on all these fronts. The earlier part of the century in particular made manifest the new 'massification' of both war and politics. Preparing for and waging mechanized and global warfare now necessitated a vast state apparatus.[31] The heightened coordinating functions accrued by the state during wartime were substantially carried over into its constitutional structure during the peace.[32]

Schmitt, struggling to make sense of the juridical challenge presented by these years of turmoil and change, characteristically resorted to theology. Drawing on one of the most enigmatic of apocalyptic texts, St Paul's second letter to the Thessalonians, Schmitt turned repeatedly to the phrase the 'mystery of lawlessness', as if that – and the need to find an earthly Restrainer (*katechon*) while we awaited the Redeemer on Judgment Day – was the defining problematic of the age.[33] While they would have rejected the apocalyptic language, the basic sentiment was one that Hayek and Oakeshott shared.[34] They too were alarmed at the prospect of the masses, manipulated by a demagogue or elite interest, unleashing the vast destructive capacity of the modern state and viewed 'with horror the swallowing up of other values in the all-consuming interests of the society which is considered to be identical with the

[31] In Britain, these and related concerns led to a mini crisis over the administrative state. The repeated use of skeleton legislation to pass social laws, which effectively transferred regulatory power from Parliament to the executive, Lord Chief Justice Hewart and others argued, created a regime of 'departmental despotism' that spread 'administrative lawlessness' and destroyed self-government: G. Hewart, *The New Despotism* (London: Ernest Benn, 1929). See Janet McLean, *Searching for the State in British Legal Thought: Competing Conceptions of the Public Sphere* (Cambridge: Cambridge University Press, 2012), 172–174.

[32] Poggi, *The State*, 112. In the United Kingdom, government spending accounted for 8.9 per cent of gross domestic product in 1890 but 20.2 per cent by 1920. See also Chris Thornhill, *A Sociology of Constitutions: Constitutions and State Legitimacy in Historical-Sociological Perspective* (Cambridge: Cambridge University Press, 2011), 275. The same pattern emerged after the Second World War. See Ross McKibbin, 'Great Britain' in Gerwarth, *Twisted Paths*, 56.

[33] 2 Thessalonians 2: 'The mystery of lawlessness doth already work; only there is one that restraineth now, until he be taken out of the way; and then shall be revealed the lawless one, whom the Lord Jesus will slay with the breath of his mouth, and bring to nought with the manifestation of his coming.'

[34] Perry Anderson, 'The Intransigent Right: Michael Oakeshott, Leo Strauss, Carl Schmitt, Friedrich von Hayek' in Anderson, *Spectrum: From Right to Left in the World of Ideas* (London: Verso, 2005), 26–27.

state'.[35] They searched for someone, some institution, some conceptual scheme that might contain the risks of unbridled democracy, 'seen and feared through the prisms of their theories of law, as the abyss of its absence: *to misterion tes anomias*, the mystery of lawlessness'.[36] The problem had a political specification: Europe groping for a new form of governance and a new legal order, internal and external – a *novus ordo seclorum* to replace the one that had died in the trenches in 1914–1918. It also had a conceptual specification: rescuing the normative in law out of the modern idea of law as technique, as that which the machine of state wills.

'Now the machine runs itself': Schmitt *v* the law

Schmitt saw himself as the 'cleric of postneutralization Europe',[37] his self-appointed task being to make contemporaries aware of the dangers of technicity inherent to the twentieth-century 'total state'.[38] His message to a post-war generation full of complaints 'about a soulless age of technology in which the soul is helpless and unconscious' is that their romantic pessimism 'has been carried to an end'.[39] In his early book *Political Romanticism* (1919), the target was a certain style of nineteenth-century romanticism that Schmitt thought now dominated politics. Those who accepted the liberal, bureaucratic and technocratic status quo were charged with 'effeminate passivity', an 'inability to decide' and 'subjective occasionalism'. People of this sort lived not real lives but 'a kind of lyrical paraphrase of existence'.[40] As such, they were incapable of engaging in

[35] Ernst Fraenkel, *The Dual State: A Contribution to the Theory of Dictatorship* (New York: Oxford University Press, trans. E. A. Shills, 1941), 60.3.

[36] Anderson, 'The Intransigent Right', 26.

[37] McCormick, *Carl Schmitt's Critique of Liberalism*, 103.

[38] Carl Schmitt, *The Concept of the Political* (Chicago: University of Chicago Press, trans. George Schwab, 1996) ('CP'), 23. See also Carl Schmitt, *Dictatorship* (Cambridge: Polity, trans. Michael Hoelzl and Graham Ward, 2014), 9: 'This orientation towards dictatorship – an orientation consisting of the three elements of rationalism, technicality and the executive – is at the origins of the modern state.'

[39] Carl Schmitt, 'The Age of Neutralizations and Depoliticizations' (1929) trans. Matthias Konzett and John P. McCormick (1993) 96 *Telos* 130, 140.

[40] Carl Schmitt, *Political Romanticism* (Cambridge: MIT Press, trans. Guy Oakes, 1991) ('PR'), 128, 117, 140, 159. Ellen Kennedy describes the 'romanticism vs. politicism dilemma' as 'the major question for his [Schmitt's] generation': '*Hostis* Not *Inimicus*: Toward a Theory of the Public in the Work of Carl Schmitt' in David Dyzenhaus (ed.), *Law as Politics: Carl Schmitt's Critique of Liberalism* (Durham, NC: Duke University Press, 1998), 93.

politics other than as a spectacle for gossip and idle criticism.[41] Schmitt offers instead the image of the 'romantic politician', pointing (quite bizarrely) to Don Quixote as a model. He was a man, we are told, with 'the enthusiasm for a real knight of his rank', who 'was capable of seeing the difference between right and wrong and of making a decision in favour of what seemed right to him'. The battles he fought may have been fantastically absurd. But at least they were real battles in which he exposed himself to personal dangers.[42]

In little of this was Schmitt original. He was one of a group of reactionary modernists that included Oswald Spengler, Ernst Jünger, Martin Heidegger and Werner Sombart.[43] This 'masculine cult of action and will' saw decision as good, deliberation ('endless talk') bad. Its associates were existentialists who used the same 'jargon of authenticity' and espoused what Goebbels was to call 'steellike romanticism'. Positivism, liberalism, Marxism and Parliament they hated as inimical to life. They wanted for the future not more of the same *Entseelung* (desouling) but a renewal of the soul in a modern setting.[44] Walter Benjamin captured some of the spirit of this movement when he wrote in his essay 'The Work of Art in the Age of Mechanical Representation' that 'fascism sees its salvation in giving [the] masses not their rights but instead a chance to express themselves'.[45]

Schmitt pushed the rightist critique of Weimar more deeply into the field of jurisprudence than anyone else and became the most important conservative critic of liberal constitutional theory. His route to what he called 'the political' – that is, authentic politics that is substantive rather than procedural, decisionistic not deliberative, existential as opposed to just muddling through – was through the 'exception'. Whereas liberals

41 PR, 159: 'following political events with marginal glosses, catch phrases, viewpoints, emphases and antitheses, but always without making its own decision and assuming its own responsibility and risk. Political activity is not possible in this way. But criticism is.'

42 PR, 147–148.

43 See also F. A. Hayek, *The Road to Serfdom* (Chicago: University of Chicago Press, ed. Bruce Caldwell, 2007), 189 n. 27, where Schmitt is listed alongside Sombart, Spengler, Jünger, Arthur Moeller van den Bruck, Othmar Spann and Hans Freyer as the 'intellectual leaders of the generation which has produced nazism'.

44 Jeffrey Herf, *Reactionary Modernism: Technology, Culture, and Politics in Weimar and the Third Reich* (Cambridge: Cambridge University Press, 1984), 23, 27. See also Eric D. Weitz, *Weimar Germany: Promise and Tragedy* (Princeton: Princeton University Press, 2007), 332–341, discussing the broader social and political context, and shared language, of the 'conservative revolution', naming Schmitt as one of its leading intellectual figures.

45 Walter Benjamin, 'The Work of Art in the Age of Mechanical Representation' in Benjamin, *Illuminations* (London: Pimlico, ed. Hannah Arendt, 1999).

were scared of the exception and so shied away from it,[46] the philosopher of concrete life 'must not withdraw from the exception and the extreme case, but must be interested in it to the highest degree'.[47] Reason of state, seen traditionally as a central problem for constitutional politics, becomes the route to solving the apathy and stagnation of the West.[48] Concentrating on the steely edges of *raison d'état* is a prerequisite, Schmitt maintains, for identifying the dynamic flow of power through state institutions,[49] the source of state power in notions of community and identity,[50] the true relationship between politics and public law, and the connection between the internal and external faces of the state. It is in relation to the exception and not the rule, he says, that we must look to uncover the secrets of constitutional theory: 'In the exception the power of real life breaks through the crust of a mechanism that has become torpid by repetition.'[51]

Schmitt observes that 'the exception' refers to a general concept in constitutional theory and not merely a construct applied in situations of emergency.[52] The exception is internally related to the norm, not just its dirty little secret. Although a 'limit case', it is part of a constitutional order rather than somehow outside or in a straightforward sense opposed to it. 'Although he [the sovereign] stands outside the normally valid legal system, he nevertheless belongs to it, for it is he who must decide whether the constitution needs to be suspended in its entirety.'[53] Schmitt argues that his analysis of the exception enables him to get closer to sovereignty

[46] Carl Schmitt, *Political Theology: Four Chapters on the Concept of Sovereignty* (Chicago: University of Chicago Press, trans. George Schwab, 1985) ('PT'), 13–15. Oakeshott also thought that liberalism, because of its obsession with the threat of the reappearance of absolute monarchy, was blind to other threats and 'lacked appropriate doctrinal weapons for combating what has turned out to be the real danger': *The Social and Political Doctrines of Contemporary Europe* (London: Basic Books, 1940), 4.

[47] PT, 15.

[48] See also Carl Schmitt, *The Crisis of Parliamentary Democracy* (Cambridge, MA: MIT Press, trans. Ellen Kennedy, 1985) ('CPD'), 37–38, suggesting that *Arcana rei publicae* 'belong to every kind of politics', not just absolutism.

[49] Schmitt's most extensive analysis of reason of state and the development of constitutional theory is to be found in the first chapter of *Dictatorship*, where he connects the growth of the concept with the spread of the technical conception of the state, derived from a reading of Machiavelli's *Il Principe* and refracted through the state theory of Hobbes and Bodin.

[50] Carl Schmitt, *Constitutional Theory* (Durham, NC: Duke University Press, trans. Jeffrey Seitzer, 2008) ('CT'), 61: 'Constitution = the principle of the dynamic emergence of political unity, of a process of constantly renewed formation and emergence of this unity from a fundamental or ultimately effective power and energy ... Political unity must form itself daily out of various opposing interests, opinions, and aspirations.'

[51] PT, 15. [52] PT, 5. [53] PT, 7.

than liberal and neo-Kantian jurists like Hans Kelsen, who obfuscate or 'radically suppress' the idea.[54] Close attention to the prerogative zone also enables Schmitt to make connections between the state and the people. The contrast is again with Kelsen and those for whom the state was an entirely normative – that is, in this context, formal – structure. Schmitt, by contrast, insists that 'the state is a specific entity of people'.[55]

The exception is vital because it connects with the creation, renewal and sustenance of an individual political community. It is necessarily, Schmitt thinks, the world unstructured by prior norms and so marked by the absence of constrained legalistic thinking. 'What characterizes an exception is principally unlimited authority, which means the suspension of the existing order ... The decision frees itself from all normative ties and becomes in the true sense absolute.'[56] This is the realm of decision, of might rather than right, and so the space where a real choice can be made about the goals as ambitions of the nation. The exception allows the nation to determine its *raison d'être*. Literally so, since Schmitt sees the political properly so-called to be a matter of the survival and flourishing of this particular community, a condition understood existentially[57] as being defined according to its fundamental enmities, that is, its readiness to fight against those it constructs as its enemies.[58] 'Political democracy, therefore, cannot rest on the inability to distinguish among persons, but rather only on the quality of belonging to a *particular people*. This quality of belonging to a people can be defined by very different elements (ideas of common race, belief, common destiny, and tradition).'[59]

[54] PT, 21. Also CT, 187: 'A logically consistent and complete Rechtsstaat aspires to suppress the political concept of law, in order to set a "sovereignty of the law" in the place of a concrete existing sovereignty. In other words, it aspires, in fact, to not answer the question of sovereignty and to leave open the question of which political will makes the appropriate norm into a positively valid command. ... [T]his must lead to concealments and fictions, with every instance of conflict posing anew the problem of sovereignty.'

[55] CP, 19. [56] PT, 12.

[57] McCormick, linking Schmitt to Nietzsche, calls the former the 'infamous, early-twentieth-century political existentialist' and the latter 'the renowned, late-nineteenth-century philosophical existentialist': *Carl Schmitt's Critique of Liberalism*, 85.

[58] CT, 76: 'The constitution does not establish itself. It is, rather, given to a concrete political unity. ... Every existing political unity has its value and its "right to existence" not in the rightness or usefulness of norms, but rather in its existence. Considered juristically, what exists as *political* power has value because it exists. Consequently, its "right to self-preservation" is the prerequisite of all further discussions; it attempts, above all, to maintain itself in its existence, "*in suo esse perseverare*" (Spinoza); it protects "its *existence*, its *integrity*, its *security*, and its *constitution*", which are all existential values.'

[59] CT, 258.

Alternative models of the modern state (liberal, parliamentary, positivist) attempt a 'formalist-functionalist hollowing out' of the state; pluralism is a recipe for chaos and anarchy.[60] Their effect is to remove from the state all sense of substantive value, and with it any sense of community and meaning. As David Dyzenhaus observes, Schmitt feared that Hobbes's description of Leviathan as a great machine might supplant all other meanings that animated the state. 'The product of [this] rationalist impulse was the destruction of the state's soul which rendered the state insubstantial and thus open to enemy capture.'[61] This is not only a problem at the socio-psychological level, in that it produces effete political romantics helpless against the modern state machine. It also removes the bedrock of values with which a system of law sustains itself. Legality is thus deprived 'of its persuasive power' and rendered incapable of distinguishing between justice and injustice.[62]

Prioritizing the exception in this way enables Schmitt to specify a hierarchy in which law is subordinate to the political – politics, that is, in its 'authentic' sense as normatively unconstrained decision. One reading of this position emphasizes the relatively conventional nature of Schmitt's theory, maintaining that Schmitt is claiming no more than what many political theorists before him would have thought obvious, namely, the lexical priority of order over justice and the truth of the maxim *auctoritas non veritas facit legem*. Andreas Kalyvas sees Schmitt's aim as being to combine 'Hobbes's absolutist concept of sovereignty and Emmanuel Sieyès's notion of *le pouvoir constitutant*, that is, the power of a political subject to create a new constitution'. Schmitt's concern throughout his Weimar works, Kalyvas maintains, was to theorize a two-level constitution not all that different from Bruce Ackerman's theory of dualist democracy,[63] capable of protecting 'the general will of the popular sovereign from the particular wills of ephemeral majorities'.[64]

60 CP, chapter 4.

61 David Dyzenhaus, '"Now the Machine Runs Itself": Carl Schmitt on Hobbes and Kelsen' (1994) 16 *Cardozo Law Review* 1, 8.

62 Carl Schmitt, *Legality and Legitimacy* (Durham, NC: Duke University Press, trans. Jeffrey Seitzer, 2004) ('LL'), 29.

63 Bruce Ackerman, *We the People: Foundations* (Cambridge, MA: Harvard University Press, 1991).

64 Andreas Kalyvas, *Democracy and the Politics of the Extraordinary: Max Weber, Carl Schmitt, and Hannah Arendt* (Cambridge: Cambridge University Press, 2008), 88. See also Adrian Vermeule, 'Our Schmittian Administrative Law' (2009) 122 *Harvard Law Review* 1095.

This revisionist reading has the virtue of making us pause before making too quick a move from extraordinary to ordinary when interpreting Schmitt's theory. It is true that Schmitt's writings offer a theory of constitutional change and dynamism. As such, they can be seen as an attempt to inject life into a situation that their author feared was becoming torpid. In that sense, Schmitt's theory may be seen as a characteristic response to a familiar early twentieth-century predicament. But the attempt to normalize Schmitt fails to convince. The reading does not do justice to the tone and conceptual vocabulary Schmitt deployed. His choice of language is that of a reactionary modernist of the Weimar period, inclined to embrace the existential and extraordinary at the expense of the normal and quotidian.[65] Even the closest thing Schmitt wrote to a standard legal treatise, his *Constitutional Theory* (1928), is largely taken up with considerations of constituent power and the prioritization of the 'positive' concept of the constitution, 'the constitution as the complete decision over the type and form of the political unity', over the constitution in the normative sense, referred to dismissively as the 'bourgeois *Rechtsstaat*'. The book does show considerable sophistication in its handling of deep-lying historical trends, for instance in analyzing the liberal constitutionalist paradigm. But its real interest lies in emphasizing and prioritizing the idea of systematic constitutional change. This is at odds with standard theoretical and doctrinal treatments, although its unorthodox position arguably makes sense in an era of radical instability, revolution and counter-revolution.

The role the extraordinary plays in Schmitt's theory is far more extensive than an account of a process in which epoch-making constitutional moments end up shaping public law for a generation and more.[66] One of the most consistent themes within Schmitt's work, an essential part of his critique of liberal legalism and positivism, was his insistence on the penetration of the ordinary by the extraordinary. Existential moments 'bleed into the quotidian', as Nomi Claire Lazar puts it, 'in part because every quotidian moment is potentially existential'.[67] Schmitt envisages a

[65] Michael Stolleis, *A History of Public Law in Germany 1914–1945* (Oxford: Oxford University Press, trans. Thomas Dunlap, 2004), 79: Schmitt invoked the 'dissolution of the order-generating state in ever-new apocalyptic images as the end of statehood as such, as a ship adrift without a rudder, as the slaughtering and devouring of Leviathan by egotistical particularistic powers, as blindness toward the existentially necessary distinction between friend and foe'.

[66] CT, 77: 'Prior to the establishment of any norm, there is a fundamental *political decision by the bearer of constitution-making power.*' (Schmitt's italics.)

[67] Nomi Claire Lazar, *States of Emergency in Liberal Democracies* (Cambridge: Cambridge University Press, 2009), 41.

situation in which normal juridical relations are always and everywhere subject to and structured by the political (i.e., the substantive decision on the basis of friend/foe). 'The political decision, which essentially means the constitution, cannot have a reciprocal effect on its subject and eliminate its political existence. This political will remains alongside and above the constitution.'[68] Anything less pervasive would lack the redemptive quality Schmitt seeks in the political and would amount to an acceptance of the status quo. As John McCormick observes, Schmitt consistently presents the normal liberal political order as being 'so utterly corrupted by science and technology that it is actually *redeemed* by the exception and the sovereign dictatorial action for which it calls'.[69] The exception is jurisgenerative and life-affirming, while an excess of normativity leads to civic death. It is only by virtue of this primacy of the prerogative, not just during exceptional moments but at all times, that the 'power of real life' can constantly break through 'the crust of the mechanism'.

The exception also enables Schmitt to connect the internal constitution of the state with its external manifestation. The friend/enemy distinction, the definition of the political, is the attribute of a sovereign power that is itself determined in the exceptional moment. The pre-eminent act of sovereign power is the decision that fixes the nature and frontier of any community.[70] Internally it defines community and constitution, stipulating who counts as 'friend' and on what basis. Externally it is enmity-constructing and pregnant with the possibility of conflict. 'War is neither the aim nor the purpose nor even the very content of politics. But as an ever present possibility it is the leading presupposition which determines in a characteristic way human action and thinking and thereby creates a specifically political behavior.'[71] We have already met a precursor of this position in the figure of the romantic politician Don Quixote, who made a decision on what was right and wrong and lived by it, as exemplified by his preparedness to do battle, even where to do so was seen by others as absurd. His later writings on war and international law are equally illuminating, not least in that they reveal a different dimension of the destabilizing force of Schmitt's commitment to decisionist politics. Here, we see the state almost bursting at the

[68] CT, 125–126.

[69] John P. McCormick, 'The Dilemmas of Dictatorship: Carl Schmitt and Constitutional Emergency Powers' in Dyzenhaus, *Law as Politics*, 225.

[70] On the way Schmitt connects this primary move of boundary-fixing to the normative (*nomos*), see his *The Nomos of the Earth in the International Law of the Jus Publicum Europeaum* (New York: Telos Press, 2003).

[71] CP, 34.

seams. In 'The *Großräum* Order of International Law' (1939–1941), Schmitt seems prepared to subordinate the state to the political decision, whereas before it was the decision that gave the state its shape and animating purpose.[72] He argues in this essay for a new order of international law to reflect new political realities, chief among which was the expanding *Großdeutsche Reich*. 'Today we think planetarily and in *Großräume* [large spaces].' The new international law should be 'grounded in concrete *Großräume*' and not the 'universalistic-humanitarian world law' that currently dominates. Within this order, states are obsolete. They are to be replaced by *Reichs* as the central legal subject, *Reichs* being 'the leading and bearing powers whose political ideas radiate into a certain *Großräum* and which fundamentally exclude the interventions of spatially alien powers into this *Großräum*'. The immediate political message is clear. The new *Deutsches Reich*, spreading its control across increasing parts of the European continent, 'has the holy honour of defending a non-universalistic, *völkisch* order of life with respect for the nation'.

> Today, however, a powerful German *Reich* has arisen. From what was only weak and impotent, there has emerged a strong centre of Europe that is impossible to attack and ready to prove its great political idea, that respect of every nation as a reality of life determined through species and origin, blood and soil, with its radiation into the Middle and European space, and to reject the interference of spatially alien and un-*völkisch* powers.[73]

Schmitt was only one of a number of German lawyers to press this geopolitical case.[74] What is noteworthy, though, is Schmitt's preparedness to sacrifice the state on the altar of the political. The decision is now the property of the nation (*Volk*) rather than the state, and may have expansionary properties – certainly where the nation is strong and

[72] It is at least arguable, though, that in his slightly earlier work *The Leviathan in the State Theory of Thomas Hobbes: Meaning and Failure of a Political Symbol* (Chicago: University of Chicago Press, trans. George Schwab and Erna Hilfstein, 2008), Schmitt is making the case against the 'quantitative total state' that Germany had become under the Nazis and reiterated his argument in favour of the 'qualitative total state' comprising a strong authoritarian state and an unrestricted economy. See also his 1932 address 'A Strong State and Sound Economics' before the *Langnam Verein* (literally the 'Long Name Association' or northwestern industries) in Renato Cristi, *Carl Schmitt and Authoritarian Liberalism* (Cardiff: University of Wales Press, 1998).

[73] Carl Schmitt, 'The *Großräum* Order of International Law with a Ban on the Intervention for Spatially Foreign Powers: A Contribution to the Concept of *Reich* in International Law' in Schmitt, *Writings on War* (Cambridge: Polity, trans. Timothy Nunan, 2011), 96, 101, 102, 111.

[74] Franz Neumann, *Behemoth: The Structure and Practice of National Socialism, 1933–1944* (Chicago: Ivan R. Dee, 2009), 150–171.

decisive enough for its political idea to radiate and take on continental proportions. We see here a reasonably comfortable alliance between Schmitt's prerogative-dominated state theory and Nazi race imperialism. (Incidentally, the anti-semitism in 'The *Großräum* Order' is as apparent as it is odious.[75]) In Schmitt's hands, Franz Neumann observed, 'the exception becomes the rule. There is no one international law but as many as there are empires, that is, large spaces. The *großdeutsche Reich* is the creator of its own international law in its own space.'[76]

Schmitt's relentless exploration of the prerogative zone brings insight into the dynamic energy that underpins constitutions, orients them and flows through and outside them. It is nonetheless problematic, not least because in paying insufficient attention to the normal juridical sphere Schmitt's theory is radically unstable. Schmitt's obvious and increasing relish throughout the Weimar period for the use of quasi-dictatorial powers to enable an authoritarian president to bypass the liberal/parliamentary framework of checks and balances is indicative, for in this context practice and theory come together. The idea of a continuing or floating sovereignty that pervasively inhabits normal constitutional and legal structures combines with a streamlined model of supposedly authentic political activity – of myth-encrusted political life, existentially freighted decision, popular acclamation, immediate enactment. The state, Schmitt writes, 'intervenes everywhere. At times it does so as a *deus ex machina*, to decide according to positive statute a controversy that the independent act of juristic perception failed to bring to a generally plausible solution; at other times it does so as the graceful and merciful lord who proves by pardons and amnesties his supremacy over his own laws.'[77] This is a theory of the sovereign as Old Testament God. Its dynamism is capable of undermining a framework of 'settled, stable law'. The theory folds the realm of law into the world of the exception, the artificial reason of law into the political reason of state.

Schmitt's antinomian position glories in the image of the statesman-sovereign cut free from the baggage of parliamentary democracy and constitutional laws and acts authentically in what he takes to be the interest of state. This transition is sketched with mesmerizing skill in a chapter in *Legality and Legitimacy* on the President's decree powers under

[75] 'The *Großräum* Order', 108 ('the Jew Laski'), 121–122 ('The relation of a nation to a soil arranged through its own work of colonization and culture and to the concrete forms of power that arise from this arrangement is incomprehensible to the spirit of the Jew.')

[76] Neumann, *Behemoth*, 158. [77] PT, 38.

Article 48 of the Weimar Constitution. It starts solidly enough, with the text itself and an account of the settled practice that even refers to two court cases. Soon, though, these conventional legal trappings disappear, submerged by Schmitt's *modus operandi* of 'categorical elision and rhetorical manipulation'.[78] The 'simple truth of legal scholarship becomes evident through all the normative fictions and obscurities', we are told, and it is 'that norms are valid only for normal situations, and the presupposed normalcy of the situation is a positive-legal component of its "validity".' And who gets to decide whether normality exists? 'By his own discretion, the extraordinary lawmaker determines the presupposition of his extraordinary powers (danger for public security and order) and the content of "necessary" measures.' It is thus 'evident' that the President is superior to the Reichstag, 'that is, to the ordinary, national legislature in regard to the scope and content of its recognized legislative power'.

This position is reached despite it being the opposite of the constitutional text on which the analysis supposedly rests. We are left with something that looks very much like bare power – as straightforward, untrammelled and de-institutionalized as possible.

> The practice that was only a groundless theory in parliament becomes self-evident in the dictator, and the legislative power becomes the weapon useful for completing his mission. Instead of issuing a general decree, therefore, the dictator can issue an individual order, even immediately and directly… In this way, he renders practically meaningless the entire system of legal protections that was built up with great artistry to counter the orders of the executive ... But for the extraordinary law-maker of Article 48, the distinction between statute and statutory application, legislative and executive, is neither legally nor factually an obstacle. The extraordinary lawmaker combines both in his person.[79]

[78] McCormick, 'The Weimar Crisis of Law', 67. See also Stolleis, *A History of Public Law in Germany*, 173, referring to Schmitt's 'conceptual playfulness, combined with fundamental and intentional obfuscation'.

[79] LL, 67, 69, 70–71. Schmitt's earlier article 'The Dictatorship of the President of the Reich according to Article 48 of the Weimar Constitution', developed from a keynote address given in 1924 to the conference of German Constitutional Jurists and which appeared as an appendix to the second edition of *Die Diktatur* in 1928, is somewhat more nuanced, less obviously an endorsement of sovereign dictatorship, for instance, in its discussion of the difference between true 'laws' and executive (emergency) 'measures'. But the thrust of the piece is identical to that pursued more decisively in later works such as *Legality and Legitimacy*, arguing for the maximum possible reach, and the minimum possible interference, with the President's use of Article 48 emergency powers: see *Dictatorship*, 183, 185, 208 and 225: 'The truth is that in 1919, in view of the incredibly difficult situation, the National Assembly was concerned first to give as far-reaching authorisations as possible

In passages such as this one, it is almost impossible to identify when Schmitt is talking about normal constitutional operations and when he is talking about emergency ones.[80] As Gopal Balakrishnan notes, echoing Fraenkel's contemporaneous analysis of Schmitt's role in fashioning the Nazi prerogative state,[81] 'the distinction between the normal and the exceptional had become so thoroughly effaced that the question of what the normal procedures were could no longer be answered except politically.'[82] To an extent, such a move is perfectly understandable for a jurist trying to make sense of the inter-war crisis years. The exception has unquestionably become a much more common feature of political life. Older conceptions of law are threatened by social and political developments and by other ideas of what (modern) law really is. There is a concern, which Schmitt shared, about the deadness of modern life, at one extreme, and a Leftist revolutionary culture that seems the most obvious alternative, at the other. Redemption from the former is sought in authentic political life. Protection from the latter is sought in the unity of the nation at the level of political will – the state as a 'specific entity of people' – and a lack of squeamishness about protecting that unity from internal and external enemies. One of the problems, though, with Schmitt's vision is that it saves law – or what Schmitt liked to call the 'persuasive power' of the juridical – almost at the expense of law itself. For in his scheme, it is not law or legality that acts as a binding agent. That role is taken by the popularly acclaimed decider, who represents the unity of the people. The subordination of norm to exception and the juridical to the political deprives law of its autonomous capacity, its characteristic of

[to the President]; and it left the fulfillment of the constitutional requirements to a later, "detailed" regulation, which was not forthcoming.'

80 John P. McCormick, 'From Constitutional Technique to Caesarist Ploy: Carl Schmitt on Dictatorship, Liberalism, and Emergency Powers' in Peter Baehr and Melvin Richter (eds.), *Dictatorship in History and Theory: Bonapartism, Caesarism, and Totalitarianism* (Cambridge: Cambridge University Press, 2004), 208.

81 Fraenkel refers to Schmitt's *Über die drei Arten des rechtswissenschaftlichen Denkens* ('On the Three Types of Juristic Thought') of 1933 as the 'most influential juridical study of recent years': *Dual State*, 142. See also *Dual State*, 25: 'Schmitt's theory has been adopted by the *Gestapo*.' There are more references to Schmitt in the index of the book than to any other figure. See also Neumann, *Behemoth*, 43, 49 where Schmitt is referred to as 'the ideologist of this sham' and 'the most intelligent and reliable of all National Socialist constitutional lawyers'.

82 Gopal Balakrishnan, *The Enemy: An Intellectual Portrait of Carl Schmitt* (London: Verso, 2002), 158. See also Ellen Kennedy, *Constitutional Failure: Carl Schmitt in Weimar* (Durham, NC: Duke University Press, 2004), 85: Schmitt's claim that sovereignty *is* order 'introduces an apparently unlimited space of legal indeterminacy in which sovereignty is that very aspect of law that is not determined. Schmitt seems to remove all law'.

providing a settled framework of rights and duties capable of operating coherently and at arms-length from the ministrations of those in power. Contrary to his intentions, then, Schmitt's theory threatens to make law instrumental to the needs of the political unit as perceived by the decider. This, as it turned out, was precisely the fate of law within the Nazi dual state, where prerogative, understood as the will of the decider, was always and everywhere capable of trumping law. Just as troubling, Schmitt's theory also reduces law and constitutional politics to a game, played without much rhyme or reason. The essential qualities of law and politics are made mysterious, myths designed simultaneously to shroud and prop up the authority of an imagined central decider. We are left with a 'huge cloak-and-dagger drama',[83] as Schmitt called it, to be marvelled at by a largely uncomprehending people, in whose name, we should remember, the whole thing is said to take place.

Hayek: dethroning politics

Hayek's constitutional theory was not just written against the background of the twentieth-century crisis of law and the administrative state, but also and more specifically against Schmitt's solution to that problem, which he saw as offering the pathological elements of a legal system as the cure of its present ills.[84] Schmitt's theory of concrete order formation, he wrote, provided 'the instrument of arrangement or organization by which the individual is made to serve concrete purposes. This is the inevitable outcome of an intellectual development in which the self-ordering forces of society and the role of law in an ordering mechanism are no longer understood.'[85] Arguing against precisely such a formulation, Hayek's theory is a self-conscious attempt to reinvigorate older strands of liberal thought, particularly the British tradition made explicit by the Scottish moral philosophers 'led by David Hume, Adam Smith, and Adam Ferguson, seconded by their English contemporaries Josiah Tucker, Edmund Burke, and William Paley', all of whom drew on a tradition rooted in the jurisprudence of the common law in which the key figure is Matthew Hale.[86] By contrast, Schmitt's decisionist theory, which

[83] PT, 38.

[84] Friedrich A. Hayek, *Law, Legislation and Liberty: A New Statement of the Liberal Principles of Justice and Political Economy* (London: Routledge, 1982), *Vol. I: Rules and Order*, 71 ('*Rules and Order*').

[85] *Rules and Order*, 71.

[86] F. A. Hayek, *The Constitution of Liberty* (London: Routledge, 2010), 50; *Rules and Order*, 22. As a number of commentators have noted, the evolutionary liberal dimensions of

sought to narrow decision-making and to de-institutionalize political decision, was a particularly egregious case of synoptic delusion, the 'fiction that all relevant facts are known to some one mind, and that it is possible to construct from this knowledge of the particulars a desirable social order'.[87] The idea that an authoritarian leader might present the truest form of representative government Hayek would have dismissed as spectacular nonsense. Schmitt was 'in the grip of a picture', the relevant picture being the theological one within which one credulously accepts the 'argument from design'.[88]

Hayek's work sits squarely within a broader liberal tradition, a characteristic of which is its 'distrust of determinate, personal authority, authority whose power was visible and traceable to a specific person, such as a pope or monarch'.[89] One way of reading his constitutional analysis is as a systematic attempt to do away with reason of state altogether, to fade even the idea of a moment of decision into a system of laws understood as non-purposive social rules that have evolved over time. The image of common law development as the epitome of law understood as *nomos* (the law of liberty) is crucial to this enterprise. Historically, the common law provided the anchor of the eighteenth-century liberty that Britain enjoyed and the rest of Europe admired.[90] The common law demonstrates the process by which 'rules that have never been deliberately invented but have grown through a gradual process of trial and error in which the experience of successive generations has helped to make them what they are'.[91] The common law shows how an order of laws can develop largely in the absence of design, with very little commanding intelligence[92] or substantive purpose beyond peaceful coexistence.[93]

This account of the common law as a model for the free society corresponds to a sceptical account of human intelligence. There is no other

Hayek's theory often sit uneasily next to its more Kantian liberal elements. See Chandran Kukathas, *Hayek and Modern Liberalism* (Oxford: Oxford University Press, 1989), 17.

87 *Rules and Order*, 14.

88 Edna Ullmann-Margalit, 'The Invisible Hand and the Cunning of Reason' (1997) 64 *Social Research* 181, 183.

89 Sheldon Wolin, *Politics and Vision: Continuity and Innovation in Western Political Thought* (Princeton: Princeton University Press, 2006), 311.

90 *Rules and Order*, 85.

91 *Constitution of Liberty*, 138.

92 *Constitution of Liberty*, 140: 'Much of the opposition to a system of freedom under general laws arises from the inability to conceive of an effective co-ordination of human activities without deliberate organization by a commanding intelligence.'

93 *Rules and Order*, 112: 'to conceive as a goal an abstract order, the particular manifestation of which no one could predict, and which was determined by properties no one could precisely define'.

theme that Hayek emphasizes more 'than the need for human reason to recognize the limitations of human reason'.[94] Man's 'unavoidable ignorance' is for Hayek a 'fundamental fact'.[95] Indeed, it becomes all the more so as people and the societies that they inhabit become more complex. 'The more civilized we become, the more relatively ignorant must each individual be of the facts on which the working of his civilization depends.'[96] Counter-intuitively, then, the seemingly archaic common law is perfectly adapted to modern conditions. Seen as a collective intelligence device, a vast system of trial and error on matters of law and coordination, it is a near perfect way, so Hayek argues, of aggregating experience and of transmitting the accumulated stock of knowledge through time. Admittedly, Hayek's use of the term 'common law' is imprecise. His conception of *nomos* conflates two distinctive types of law: customary law and common law. While at one point in the long history of English common law there would not have been all that much that separated the two, certainly by the nineteenth-century common law courts applied 'both procedural and substantive rules of law consistently with the rules announced in prior judicial decisions' and aimed to develop and maintain 'a consistent and coherent body of rules'.[97] It is arguably customary law, rather than common law as it developed into the modern era, that better reflects Hayek's idea of spontaneous order. Still, we might modify the claim and suggest that (modern) common law nonetheless offers a model different from and preferable to legislation, one that is interstitial, evolutionary, both backward- and forward-looking, and in which authority is depersonalized and dispersed.[98]

In fact, Hayek presses his objection to rationalist accounts further, arguing that reason is significantly shaped by culture. Intelligence and the

94 Ullmann-Margalit, 'The Invisible Hand and the Cunning of Reason', 185.

95 *Constitution of Liberty*, 21.

96 *Constitution of Liberty*, 25. Also, *Rules and Order*, 14.

97 John Hasnas, 'Hayek, the Common Law, and Fluid Drive' (2005) 1 *New York Journal of Law and Liberty* 79, 94.

98 T. R. S. Allan makes precisely this argument, drawing on Hayek in order to do so, in *Law, Liberty and Justice* (Oxford: Oxford University Press, 1994). For a defence of the position from a law and economics perspective see George L. Priest, 'The Common Law Process and the Selection of Efficient Rules' (1977) 6 *Journal of Legal Studies* 65. Others are sceptical of claims for the superiority of common law, given the pace of social change: see Giacomo A. M. Ponzetto and Patricio A. Fernandez, 'Case Law vs. Statute Law: An Evolutionary Comparison' 2008 37 *Journal of Legal Studies* 379; Adam J. Hirsch, 'Evolutionary Theories of Common Law Efficiency: Reasons for (Cognitive) Skepticism' (2005) 32 *Florida State University Law Review* 425; Adrian Vermeule, *Law and the Limits of Reason* (New York: Oxford University Press, 2009), 109–112.

pathways reason takes in the human mind are themselves products of the social order in which they have evolved. 'Man is as much a rule-following animal as a purpose-seeking one', he argues, and 'his thinking and acting are governed by rules which have by a process of selection been evolved in the society in which he lives.'[99] Society is in essence a 'social order of actions' that arises from a system of rules.[100] What identifies a society – and differentiates it from other societies – is the particular set of rules that it has developed (actually the rules that have developed as that society has developed) and the way that it relates to and identifies with those rules.[101] To describe this process, Hayek uses an analogy to evolutionary theories in biology. Rules are to orders of action as genes are to organisms. In essence, 'in Hayek's account rules play a role analogous to genes in biological evolution; whereas individual organisms are constituted by following the instructions of genes, a Great Society is constituted by following the instructions of rules.'[102] Complex societies in particular are apt to be self-maintaining. It might be possible synoptically to control a warrior band or village community. Aspiring to do the same thing in a social order as complex as the modern state is quite a different proposition,[103] especially if you want that society to be even remotely free. Complex societies are characterized by constant novelty, so that all the relevant data could never be given to single mind. Their operating principle is the natural selection of traditions.[104] Social evolution

[99] *Rules and Order*, 11. Also 17: 'mind is an adaptation to the natural surroundings in which man lives and … has developed in constant interaction with the institutions which determine the structure of society.'

[100] F. A. Hayek, 'Notes on the Evolution of Systems of Rules of Conduct: The Interplay between Rules of Individual Conduct and the Social Order of Actions' in Hayek, *Studies in Philosophy, Politics, and Economics* (Chicago: University of Chicago Press, 1967). See also Douglas Glen Whitman, 'Hayek contra Pangloss on Evolutionary Systems' (1998) 9 *Constitutional Political Economy* 45.

[101] Hayek, 'Notes on the Evolution of Systems of Rules of Conduct', 68; see also *Fatal Conceit*, 6.

[102] Gerald F. Gaus, 'Hayek on the Evolution of Society and Mind' in Edward Feser (ed.), *The Cambridge Companion to Hayek* (Cambridge: Cambridge University Press, 2006), 238, 243. Note, however, that Hayek argued that the idea of evolution is older in the humanities and social sciences than in the natural sciences and suggests that Darwin, who was reading Adam Smith when formulating his own theory, 'got the basic ideas of evolution from economics'. F. A. Hayek, *The Fatal Conceit: The Errors of Socialism* (Chicago: University of Chicago Press, ed. W. W. Bartley III, 1988), 24.

[103] Hayek, *Fatal Conceit*, 113.

[104] John Gray, *Hayek on Liberty* (London: Routledge, 3rd ed., 1998), 55. See *Rules and Order*, 18; *Fatal Conceit*, 43: an evolutionary account of customs must show the 'distinct advantages by those groups that kept to such customs, thereby enabling them to expand more

specifies a mechanism of selection according to which certain social traits are selected in a competitive environment over others. As Hayek sees it, 'evolutionary accounts provide the real alternative to design theories, and they articulate precisely the "explanations of principle" that are appropriate to complexity.'[105]

Reason of state, seen from this perspective, is twice damned. First, conceived as the reflection of the reason of the individual or relative small group of individuals who happen to be at the helm of state at a given time, it is necessarily limited, certainly when set against the accumulated knowledge gains of generations embodied in the evolved law (*nomos*). It is even more limited than the law of legislation (*thesis*), which is at least refracted through a series of institutions (that is., more and larger groups) before becoming law.[106] Institutionally speaking, reason of state represents an attenuated structure of decision-making and is as such even more subject to Hayek's observations about the limits of individual human intelligence. Secondly, reason of state often presents itself as operating, in a certain sense, outside time. The moment of decision interrupts the normal flow of social intercourse and development.[107] The sort of intelligence that this kind of action presupposes is antithetical to Hayek: 'Any attempt to use reason to control or direct the social process threatens not only to impede the development of our powers of reason but also to bring the growth of knowledge to a halt.'[108] The exception, understood as a kind of caesura in constitutional time, was for Schmitt the nation's potential saviour, perhaps even a reflection of the voice of God. For Hayek, the same phenomenon, not all that dissimilarly understood,[109] threatens the evolution of the spontaneous order of freedom and is, as such, necessarily problematic.

So much for the 'reason' part of reason of state. What Hayek says about the 'state' side of the equation is also important. His interpretation of the constitutional maxim *salus populi suprema lex esto* is particularly

rapidly than others and ultimately to supersede (or absorb) those not possessing similar customs'.

105 Gaus, 'Hayek on the Evolution of Society and Mind', 237. See also Gerald F. Gaus, *The Order of Public Reason: A Theory of Freedom and Morality in a Diverse and Bounded World* (Cambridge: Cambridge University Press, 2011), 415–424.

106 Hayek, *Rules and Order*, chapter 6, esp. 129–131.

107 See Vermeule, *Law and the Limits of Reason*, 33–36, which points to the necessarily diachronic aspect of Hayek's evolutionary theory.

108 Kukathas, *Hayek and Modern Liberalism*, 61.

109 Hayek says of Schmitt: 'It has been contended with some plausibility that whoever has the power to proclaim an emergency and on this ground to suspend any part of the constitution is the true sovereign' (*Rules and Order*, 125).

illuminating. The principle is historically linked to reason of state, providing a justification for agents of government to act on their own initiative outside and sometimes even against the requirements of the ordinary law. This is exactly the sort of action that Hayek wants to foreclose. 'Correctly understood', Hayek argues, *salus populi* 'means that the end of the law ought to be the welfare of the people, that the general rules should be so designed as to serve it, but *not* that any conception of a particular social end should provide a justification for breaking those general rules.'[110] This passage is a reminder that the relevant unit of his theory is the group – or, rather, the order of actions of a group.[111] A group is defined not by the will of a group of living agents (a people) but through shared identity with a system of non-positive laws (a public). 'This means that our units are systems of cooperation – arising out of a system of rules – and for Hayek this means that the rules actually regulated people's actions.'[112] This entails that there is nothing either special or mysterious about the state – it is just the form that a system of cooperation under rules tends to take in modern politics. Certainly, there is no cause to reify or personify the state, nor any justification for imbuing it with any special notion of agency. The rules that are contained within the state's legal order (or, perhaps better, the rules that as a system define the state) ought to serve the welfare of the people, and should do so where lawmaking operates as *nomos*. Breaking these rules is highly unlikely to benefit the public, as opposed to a powerful group within it.

This conception of state and law is remarkable in how far it goes to deny agency on the part of the state or its officials. Hayek's model constitution is designed to enclose the decision-making capacity of individual agents within dense institutional structures whose purpose is to remove agency from government as far as possible.[113] We are entitled to ask whether this position is plausible, especially in the conditions of modernity that Hayek acknowledged. In normal conditions, the ideal of legal development that Hayek presents, modelled on the common law understood as a species of customary law and resting on an organic selection between competing traditions, seems too slow to accommodate the pace of change that occurs in modern societies.[114] In this environment, as Vermeule notes, statutes

[110] *Constitution of Liberty*, 139.

[111] Hayek, 'Notes on the Evolution of Systems of Rules of Conduct', 72.

[112] Gaus, 'Hayek on the Evolution of Society and Mind', 241.

[113] Hayek, *Law, Legislation and Liberty, Vol. III: The Political Order of a Free People*, chapter 17.

[114] As Richard Bellamy points out, the pluralism of contemporary societies also challenges the possibility of the well-ordered, co-operative society based upon the sort of

(and other types of directive legislation) 'can innovate more rapidly and completely than the common law, when there is an abrupt change of circumstances'.[115] In respect of exceptional conditions, Hayek's escape from reason of state is not complete. In his more engaged political writings, Hayek was not afraid to use reason of state type arguments to justify, for instance, a proposal for 'real political and economic union with France' at the outset of the Second World War.[116] In his theoretical work, reason of state emerges briefly from the shadows in a short passage in his discussion of the model constitution in *Law, Legislation and Liberty.* Hayek here recognizes that the basic principles of a free society may have to be temporarily suspended when the long-run preservation of that order is itself threatened:

> Though normally the individuals need be concerned only with their own concrete aims, and in pursuing them will best serve the common welfare, there may temporarily arise circumstances when the preservation of the overall order becomes the overruling common purpose, and when in consequence the spontaneous order, on a local or national scale, must for a time be converted into an organization.[117]

This way of conceptualizing emergency action is unconvincing, not least because there are few resources within Hayek's theory that might account for it. He presents the shift in the register of the state – from common law to reason of state – as a natural thing, like 'a wounded animal in flight from mortal danger'. Hayek is elsewhere very critical of the application of animistic vocabulary and imagery to describe large societies like the state. Such extended orders are formed into a concordant structure through observance to similar rules of conduct and do not correspond to a model of intimate fellowship. It is misleading, he says in *The Fatal Conceit*, to treat the state 'animistically, or to personify it by ascribing to it a will, an intention, or a design'.[118] But here, for an instant, he moves into the territory of the Schmittian exception, adopting Schmitt's conceptual scheme, even parroting his rhetoric. But Schmitt had extensively, even

shared universal principles that Hayek defends: '"Dethroning Politics": Liberalism, Constitutionalism and Democracy in the Thought of F. A. Hayek' (1994) 24 *British Journal of Political Science* 419, 434.

[115] Adrian Vermuele, *Law and the Limits of Reason* (New York: Oxford University Press, 2008), 109.

[116] F. A. Hayek, 'War Aims', letter to *The Spectator*, 17 November 1939, in Bruce Caldwell (ed.), *The Collected Works of F.A. Hayek – Socialism and War: Essays, Documents, Reviews* (Indianapolis: Liberty Fund, 1997), 162.

[117] LL, 124. [118] *Fatal Conceit*, 113.

excessively, laid the groundwork for this in his theory of the exception and its prime importance to juridical order, the necessity of sovereign authority to the legal system, and an account of substantive popular unity and representation which focuses on exceptional moments. Hayek has done the opposite. He has tried to eradicate even the conditions that make the Schmittian exception possible. In Hayek's vision, there is no sovereign. There is little by way of individual or small-group political agency. There is only an attenuated notion of the state.[119] This makes his theory of emergency powers feel like a drop-in. As such, it has a similar conceptual logic to Schmitt's exception, but the opposite normative logic. The exception in Hayek has the same *deus ex machina* structure as in Schmitt, but here the descending gods are figured as would-be tyrants rather than welcomed as redeemers.

Hayek's is a second characteristic response to twentieth-century conditions, one that steers a very different path from Schmitt's embrace of the idea of reason of state as a rejuvenating and purifying force. On this second account, reason of state becomes an illegitimate exotic, aberrant and dangerous, to be distinguished sharply from normal juridical conditions and pushed to the margins as much as possible. But Hayek does not tell us why reason of state should present itself differently from all other aspects of political life. If the pattern of development within a complex order of action proceeds in the way Hayek imagines, then reason of state too must be subject to evolutionary development, and must develop a particular and complex institutional, conceptual and rule-bound shape over time. We choose between competing traditions of reason of state politics just as surely as we select from competing traditions of ordinary rule.

Oakeshott's dual state

In exploring Michael Oakeshott's contribution to the idea of reason of state, I proceed by way of an exploration of two somewhat different layers

[119] Hayek faces parallel difficulties in relation to that important area in which reason of state operates: international relations. As he wrote in *The Road to Serfdom*, if 'the resources of different nations are treated as exclusive properties of … nations as wholes, if international economic relations, instead of being relations between individuals, become increasingly relations between whole nations organized as trading bodies, they inevitably become the source of friction and envy between nations' (224). The only legitimate options this leaves is a universal state, with no restrictions on movement, or alternatively national states with no redistribution. Neither option is plausible in the world as it exists today. See Harold James, *The Roman Predicament: How the Rules of International Order Create the Politics of Empire* (Princeton: Princeton University Press, 2006), 37–38.

within his work. The first, most clearly visible in his more polemical writings, connects reason of state thinking straightforwardly to the errors of Rationalism. The second, based on a reading of *On Human Conduct*, reluctantly accepts the inclusion of reason of state politics within the state understood as a complex and conflicted whole.

At first sight, reason of state seems to fit neatly within Oakeshott's scheme as one of the errors of Rationalism. He is deeply antagonistic to the Schmittian (or indeed Lockean[120]) exception, regarding it as belonging to a political imagination that is both revolutionary and perfectionist. As such, it adopts a view of politics which takes wartime or other moments of national crisis as the norm and attempts to use them as a model for times of peace.[121] This model mistakenly views politics and statecraft as a science of 'technique'. Machiavelli, writing a crib on politics for the new prince, inadvertently invented a species of political thought (Machiavellianism, *raison d'état*, Rationalism) whose founding tenet was the 'sovereignty of technique' epitomized by the belief that 'government was nothing more than "public administration" and could be learned from a book'.[122]

Oakeshott finds this perspective, which he calls the 'politics of the book', both specious and dangerous. To think of politics as a purposive endeavour is to conceive the state as an instrument of its rulers. It thus reflects the 'unpurged relic of "lordship"'[123] within the modern state. To apply this model in practice endangers the continuity of otherwise stable political traditions and the moral practices out of which they arise. It also has massive destructive potential. Providing a kind of genealogy of the practice of reason of state in the last chapter of *On Human Conduct*, Oakeshott links the disposition to consider the state as an enterprise (or purposive) association[124] with the history of colonialism and commercial

[120] 'Rationalism in Politics', 30–34, where the Second Treatise of Civil Government is described as 'as valuable a political crib' as there has ever been, responsible in part for the Rationalistic errors of the early history of the United States of America.

[121] Steven B. Smith, 'Practical Life and the Critique of Rationalism' in Efraim Podoksik (ed.), *The Cambridge Companion to Oakeshott* (Cambridge: Cambridge University Press, 2012), 138.

[122] Michael Oakeshott, 'Rationalism in Politics' in Oakeshott, *Rationalism in Politics and Other Essays* (Indianapolis: Liberty Fund, 1991), 29–30.

[123] Michael Oakeshott, *On Human Conduct* (Oxford: Oxford University Press, 1975), 268.

[124] *On Human Conduct*, 315: 'An enterprise association is composed of persons related in terms of a specified common purpose or interest and who recognize one another in terms of their common engagement to pursue or to promote it. Each associate knows himself as the servant of the purpose being pursued … This mode of association is, then, substantive; it is association in co-operative "doing".'

empire. 'What is important for us is that the notionally uninhabited lands of the New World were understood to belong, by right of conquest or occupation, to the rulers of the states whence the settlers came. They were extensions of a royal domain.'[125] The activities of expansionary colonialism, in the first instance typically undertaken by private enterprises backed by rulers of states, such as the East India Company, ended up fostering the sense that government was a matter of both lawmaking and man-management:

> They were enterprises, promoted directly or indirectly by the rulers of states, in which government and management were indistinguishable engagements. And the consequence of this colonial experience was to familiarize modern Europe with states which were, in some significant respects, enterprises and with governments which were managers of enterprises.[126]

The argument, here channelling Adam Smith and Edmund Burke, is that jealousy of trade and competition for colonial possessions – the imperatives of enterprise association played out *in foro externo* – led inevitably to war. Not only did the perspective of politics as technique lend itself to risk-tasking behaviour among rulers and ruling groups, who tied the destiny of the state to their own self-interest, it also produced complex feedback effects that tended to embed the same associational model *in foro interno*. 'War is the enemy of civil association; belligerence is alien to civil association.' In war, the subject of the law gives ground to the agent performing tasks prescribed by the state. The word 'public', Oakeshott adds, 'loses its meaning as considerations of civility to be subscribed to by *cives* in pursuing their chosen satisfactions and comes to stand for the now compelling corporate purpose of the association'.[127] Preparing for war and repairing the ravages of war became the normal condition of the European state. The instantiation of the managerialist and purposive political culture in peacetime as well as times of war produced a near-despotism that required 'not only a "poor" who neither had nor could have any incentive to resist the intrusive management of their lives, but a whole people who had been, in this sense, pauperized, that is, persons deprived of their status as "subjects" obligated to subscribe to conditions of civility and transformed into the servants of a compulsory corporate enterprise'.[128] The corruption of civil association naturally also had an institutional dimension: Parliaments became 'markets where

[125] *On Human Conduct*, 271.
[126] *On Human Conduct*, 272.
[127] *On Human Conduct*, 273.
[128] *On Human Conduct*, 305.

private interests clamour for awards from patron governments' and laws are degraded into 'instruments of managerial policy'.[129]

This first-blush reading of Oakeshott, in which reason of state is simply a core aspect of an impoverished conception of civil life – *universitas* or enterprise association – is consistent with many aspects of his writings. And it is true that, in full polemical mode, Oakeshott's emphasis on the traditional character of human conduct can reach an extraordinary pitch. He comes close to doubting even the possibility of exceptional moments of political crisis and transformation for instance, when dismissing the French and Russian Revolutions as themselves tradition-bound.[130] His Manichean rendering of European history and politics can also sometimes border on the maniacal. In the essay 'The Masses in Representative Democracy', Oakeshott splits the history of Europe from the twelfth century to the twentieth into two. The good part – which began with the emergence of human individuality in Renaissance Italy – produced the new image of human nature distinguished by its multiplicity and endless self-transformative power and generated a governing structure combining sovereign power, representative legislatures and the rule of law, in which individuality could flourish. The bad part spawned the counterpart to the individual, the mass man or individual *manqué*, scared of modern life and resentful of the individual, banding together out of cowardice and seeking a leader to relieve them of the burden of freedom and impose their misery on the whole population.[131]

It is hard to take this just-so story, iced with patrician disdain, entirely at face value. Were we to do so, it would represent an even more radical attempt than Hayek's to eradicate reason of state, and as sweeping an attack on modern parliamentarism as Schmitt's.[132] To insist on the triumph of *societas* (civil association) over the idea of the state understood as *universitas* (enterprise association) is not so much a window into reason of state and like political concepts as a flat denial that it should exist at all. Such an outcome is distinctly odd coming from a philosopher for whom the deep historical currents of European political life were so important.

[129] *On Human Conduct*, 312.

[130] Michael Oakeshott, 'Political Education' in *Rationalism in Politics*, 59, fn 6: 'The Russian Revolution … was a modification of *Russian* circumstances. And the French Revolution was far more closely connected with the *ancien regime* than with Locke or America.'

[131] Oakeshott, 'The Masses in Representative Democracy' in *Rationalism in Politics*.

[132] Compare Oakeshott's 'The Masses in Representative Democracy', 377–380 and *Social and Political Doctrines of Contemporary Europe*, xvi–xvii and *On Human Conduct*, 312 with Schmitt, *Crisis of Parliamentary Democracy*, 6–8, 48–50.

These traditions of thought are all that we have, he insisted, 'each of them is an expression of something in our civilization, in some cases of what were better forgotten, in others of what to our loss we have failed to remember, and in all of what we cannot merely ignore. And we cannot merely regret them without regretting our civilization – a fruitless, if heroic, act.'[133] It is true that Oakeshott sometimes seems to offer a pure and austere constitutional theory which leaves no room for collective purpose and state action, other than the operation of a structure of general laws that specify conditions of conduct. His essay on the Rule of Law, for instance, attributes 'a *persona* to the occupant or occupants of this office which reflects the engagement of enacting authentic rules: a *persona* without interests of its own and not representative of the interests of others. That is, a *persona* which is the counterpart of the *persona* of those related in terms of the rule of law.'[134] The theory, when generalized, threatens to produce an account of political life that is shapeless, stripped of meaning. As Perry Anderson observes, 'For if their association was void of purpose, why should individual agents ever accept a public authority at all? In Oakeshott's construction, government without goal yields what looks very much like an *état gratuit*. His famous image of politics – a vessel endlessly ploughing the sea, without port or destination – is all too apt. For why then should any passengers want to board the ship in the first place?'[135]

A second reading of Oakeshott is available, which is to be preferred not just because the first reading is so problematic but also on the ground Oakeshott himself provided in his early book *Experience and Its Modes*, namely, that a unified interpretation is to be preferred since 'pluralism or dualism are not, as we are frequently invited to believe, the final achievement in experience with regard to some ideas'.[136] The reading builds on the fuller rendition of the history of the European state in *On Human Conduct*, the filigree of liberty within which now being connected to the *civitas peregrina* – 'an association, not of pilgrims travelling to a common destination, but of adventurers each responding as best he can to the ordeal of consciousness in a world composed of others of his kind'.[137] This account retains the same set of binary distinctions, enterprise and civil

[133] *Social and Political Doctrines of Contemporary Europe*, xii.

[134] Michael Oakeshott, 'The Rule of Law', in Oakeshott, *On History and Other Essays* (Indianapolis: Liberty Fund, 1999), 150. See also *On Human Conduct*, 128–129.

[135] Anderson, 'The Intransigent Right', 19.

[136] Michael Oakeshott, *Experience and Its Modes* (Cambridge: Cambridge University Press, 1933), 33.

[137] *On Human Conduct*, 243.

association, *societas* and *universitas*, and the same astringent attitude to weakness.[138] The state understood as *universitas* models itself, on one of its versions, as 'an association of invalids, all victims of the same disease and incorporated in seeking relief from their common ailment: and the office of government is remedial engagement. Rulers are *therapeutae*, the directors of a sanatorium from which no patient may discharge himself by a choice of his own.'[139] Even so, Oakeshott is here prepared to recognize, albeit grudgingly, that both practices of association – *societas* and *universitas* – are inescapably part of the character of the state structures we inhabit. We see this first in the analysis of state action initially at the margins, particularly in emergencies. In such situations, the 'invasion of "public" by "private", of ruling by lordship, may indeed be recognized (somewhat equivocally) as a contingent situation which may emerge in the history of a civil association, and not as a direct denial of the civil condition, when the common concern that the prescriptions of *lex* shall be acknowledged is circumstantially transformed into a substantive purpose'. So, in cases where the civil association is threatened, or in lesser emergencies to which judicial remedies are unable to restore the situation, 'the common concern may become a common purpose and rulers may become managers of its pursuit'.[140]

But given the way the European state has developed, the margins are not just marginal. Oakeshott says that the use of the word 'state' to identify the emergent associations of early-modern Europe was a 'masterpiece of neutrality' in that it could encompass both models of association.[141] There is no plausible way of eradicating the aspects of enterprise association from the modern state, not least because they are intertwined not just within our cultural and institutional practice but even in our conceptual thinking. Indeed, it is hard to imagine what a state so reconstructed might look like. A world of pure *lex* seems more like a theoretical postulate, a kind of philosophical glass bead game, than a remotely viable constitutional idea. In his essay on the topic, Oakeshott calls power the third condition of association in terms of the rule of law. Rather embarrassed by the idea, he devotes just one sentence to the matter.[142] Under what conditions is that power to be retained, but for some sense of allegiance to

[138] See, e.g., *On Human Conduct*, 276: 'The relatively weak are apt to seek safety in the protection of the relatively more powerful and are usually gratified if they can find an adequate and not over-exacting patron'.

[139] *On Human Conduct*, 308.

[140] *On Human Conduct*, 146.

[141] *On Human Conduct*, 233.

[142] 'The Rule of Law', 160–161.

the political community understood in some sense or other as purposive community? Even the adjective 'European' – as in 'the character of the European state', the title of the final chapter in *On Human Conduct* – connotes some state of belonging, or of community – that is not purely or even primarily formal or juristic.

Even if crafting such a hollow state were plausible, it is hard to see it as desirable. Internally, what would glue it together? Externally, it is hard to imagine it surviving long in a world where other states are just not made this way. These points are given added weight by Oakeshott's renunciation of Rationalist reform projects. The type of reason Oakeshott sees as appropriate in relation to the state – practical knowledge as opposed to technical or scientific knowledge, *mētis* rather than *techne* – is contextual and particular. While this perspective acknowledges that something can be said about state, revolution or constitution in general, this will only take us so far in understanding *this* state, *this* revolution, *this* constitution. As James C. Scott observes, such local knowledge is by its nature '*partisan* knowledge as opposed to generic knowledge', the holder of such knowledge typically having 'a passionate interest in a particular outcome'. In as much as Oakeshott can be read as extolling local knowledge while seeking to give various localities (states) the identical core based on generic knowledge (*lex*), he not only stands accused of muddled contradiction but also of advocating a state theory doomed to fail. 'A mechanical application of generic rules that ignores these particularities is an invitation to practical failure, social disillusionment, or most likely both.'[143] Besides, if all that passed for government within a state was the maintenance of an abstract framework of rules granting entitlements and imposing obligations, then it really wouldn't be all that hard to teach and understand it by means of a treatise or crib.

The only way Oakeshott can escape this trap is to accept that state and government contain both dispositions, towards *societas* and towards *universitas*, neither of which is able to predominate. He reaches just such a conclusion in the closing pages of *On Human Conduct*. 'It may be true that, hidden in human character, there are two powerful and contrary dispositions, neither strong enough to defeat or to put flight the other.'[144] In this way, Oakeshott manages to reconcile the historian and the political philosopher within him. The manner in which we got here makes it inconceivable that the state will suddenly become a pure civil association;

[143] *Seeing Like a State*, 318. [144] *On Human Conduct*, 323.

even assuming such an option were possible. We are inheritors of a deeply imperfect, confused and fractured political condition, at the base of which lies a never-ending conflict between the liberty-supporting framework of *societas* and the community-supporting idea of *universitas*. Given the state we find ourselves in, some sense of community-giving purpose seems to be essential to the political condition, and even to the maintenance of the liberty-protecting dimensions of the state. But that does not mean that we need to accept them as equals. On the contrary, whereas it is right to cherish and protect those strands within our associational life that relate to *civitas peregrina*,[145] our stance towards manifestations of *universitas*, including reason of state, ought to be nearly the opposite, regarding it as something like a necessary evil and particularly open to abuse. Reason of state is part of a tradition with deep cultural and institutional roots and which connects to a larger conception of the state as a purposive entity. The pathways of *lex* and reason of state are ineluctably bound up together in the history of the state. As reason of state flows through the same channels as the rule of law, it has the capacity to warp those channels from the inside as well as from the outside. Repeated recourse to reason of state leads to an infantilized subject. Man is the subject of the rule of law state; mass man the subject of the security state, the individual *manqué* who demands security like a comfort blanket.[146]

Oakeshott's final position thus reflects a third characteristic twentieth-century reaction to modern reason of state politics. This can be seen as either a pragmatic response to the existence of pathways of political and legal thought and action that have a very deep heritage. Or it works in a tragic register: the way we have developed makes it impossible now to recast political life in a way that would allow us to be truly free. This response in its pragmatic mode is arguably the most common reaction to the crisis years of the first half of the century. One might link it with the rise of Christian democracy in Europe after 1945, a point

[145] See, e.g., *On Human Conduct*, 241–242: the idea of individuality 'although, later, it was almost buried under a mountain of rubbish, confused with trivial liberations, romanticized, mistaken for the exercise of "subjective will", confounded with a "sacred inner light" and with a banal individualism, and finally corrupted in being confused with "sentience" (a capacity for feeling pleasure and pain) or with so-called "libidinal instinct", it has remained the strongest strand in the moral convictions of the inhabitants of modern Europe.' The passage refers to Pico della Mirandola, Rabelais, Luther, Cervantes and Pascal.

[146] *On Human Conduct*, 275.

developed in the next chapter.[147] But at least as Oakeshott presents it, it is deficient on a number of fronts. It threatens to leave law and legality in its twentieth-century limbo, perched uncomfortably between conflicting accounts – law as normative order versus law as managerial technique. And while the theory provides at least the outlines of a discernible normative position, it is one that we are told is unrealizable. Although this is not part of Oakeshott's immediate theoretical objectives, it leaves us short of answers to some of the most pressing questions concerning reason of state. When ought you to trade off the demands of *societas* (rule of law) for the needs of *universitas* (reason of state)? Who makes that choice and under what institutional conditions?

Conclusion

The writers considered in this chapter present three contrasting accounts of reason of state and of the role that it plays within Modern constitutional politics. For Schmitt, reason of state is connected with what is for him the central idea of the exception, tied to a substantive politics of belonging and thus to the basic political question of who counts as our friend and who the enemy. Reason of state offers a source of redemption and escape from the humdrum realities of the creeping bureaucratic state. Hayek, by contrast, sees reason of state as the antithesis of the common law *Rechtsstaat*,[148] a constitution of liberty fashioned out of the crooked timber of *nomos*, the evolutionary body of law tied closely to the lived experience of the people and which contains the virtues of the many-minds principle in juridical form. His response to the threat presented by reason of state is to try to eradicate it, both normatively and as a matter of institutional design, a move especially evident in his model constitution. This attempt is problematic in several respects, not least because it allows reason of state to re-emerge as part of an animistic (non-cognitive, de-institutionalized) account of emergency politics. Oakeshott shares Hayek's distrust of reason of state, even deepening some of the criticisms. But he recognizes that the practice of reason of state lies at the heart of one of two conceptions of politics that vie for prominence within the modern European state. Built into the institutional structures and pathways of government, reason of

[147] Müller, *Contesting Democracy*; Stathis N. Kalyvas, *The Rise of Christian Democracy in Europe* (Ithaca: Cornell University Press, 1996); Wolfram Kaiser, *Christian Democracy and the Origins of the European Union* (Cambridge: Cambridge University Press, 2011).

[148] Gray, *Hayek on Liberty*, 69.

state may be impossible to eradicate but we may be able to check its more dangerous excesses.

The differences between the three writers, stated in this way, are marked. Each may be said to reflect a characteristic response to the crisis-ridden decades of the first half of the twentieth century. But it is important to acknowledge what the three writers share. In each, there is a palpable yearning for wholeness, to become one again after the fracturing and dehumanizing experiences of what Eric Hobsbawm called the 'age of catastrophe'.[149] The juridical dimension is of paramount importance to all three, notably in the need to make sense of the 'ordinary' and 'extraordinary' at a time when the difference between the two categories had become increasingly blurred. Here again, though, the precise strategies diverge, and in revealing ways. Schmitt seeks to infuse the ordinary with the extraordinary. Hayek looks to make the extraordinary properly extraordinary, so as to ring-fence and reinforce the ordinary. Oakeshott regards the categories as at least partially redundant – both the ordinary and extraordinary have, in a sense, become ordinary now, through long use and interbreeding. But, while Oakeshott comes closer than the others to recognizing the developmental lines of reason of state, noting its evolutionary and institutional aspects, he fails to develop a reflexive account of the relationship between the ordinary and extraordinary within constitutions in which normality is always the outcome of a process of normalization.[150]

[149] Eric Hobsbawm, *The Age of Extremes: The Short Twentieth Century, 1914–1991* (London: Michael Joseph, 1994), Part 1.

[150] For an argument of this sort see Hans Lindahl, 'Law as Concrete Order: Schmitt and the Problem of Collective Freedom' in David Dyzenhaus and Thomas Poole (eds.), *Law, Liberty and State: Schmitt, Hayek and Oakeshott on the Rule of Law* (Cambridge: Cambridge University Press, 2015).

8

Rights, risk and reason of state

The concept of reason of state has come into focus once again, and not necessarily for the best of reasons.[1] But the response of those liberal theorists who acknowledge it is often to deny its salience as a constitutional concept. Wojciech Sadurski has defended this strategy of avoidance. The concept of reason of state is either otiose, he says, in that it can be subsumed within the more familiar and less tarnished framework of public reason as modeled by John Rawls. Or it is pernicious: understood as applying to the security and survival of the state and 'based on the insight that, "if the political order is assumed to be an essential condition of free moral existence, the survival of this order becomes crucial" ',[2] reason of state fails to provide a useful working concept since it is not 'something that people of diverse viewpoints and ideologies may agree on'.[3]

There is something initially attractive about Sadurski's call to exclude reason of state from the constitutional lexicon. If right, it would deprive government of a historically important, and potentially morally suspect, category of pre-emptive reasons capable of overriding normal calculations about what it ought to do or refrain from doing. Claims grounded in security and necessity would then take their place alongside a host of other arguments that inhabit the realm of public reason, and secrecy – always closely allied to reason of state and the antithesis of public reason[4] – might become a thing of the past. Before we are seduced

[1] See, e.g., Conor Gearty, *Liberty and Security* (Cambridge: Polity Press, 2013); Duncan Kelly, 'Reconfiguring Reason of State In Response to Political Crisis' in David Dyzenhaus and Thomas Poole (eds.), *Law, Liberty and State: Schmitt, Hayek and Oakeshott on the Rule of Law* (Cambridge: Cambridge University Press, 2015).

[2] Wojciech Sadurski, 'Reason of State and Public Reason' (2014) 27 *Ratio Juris* 21, 26, quoting Carl J. Friedrich, *Constitutional Reason of State* (Providence: Brown University Press, 1957), 6.

[3] Sadurski, 'Reason of State and Public Reason', 27.

[4] Remo Bodei, 'From Secrecy to Transparency: Reason of State and Democracy' (2011) 37 *Philosophy and Social Criticism* 889.

into accepting this position, we should note that it adopts essentially the same strategy that we saw Hayek deploying in the previous chapter, although now presented in the language of analytical jurisprudence. But Hayek did not manage to drive reason of state off the field. Rather, in situations of emergency he imagined that the state would somehow suddenly turn itself into a managerial association charged with the task of saving the political community. The theory's inadequacy at this point exposed a more general weakness, namely, an inability to make sense of political agency. If this is true of Hayek, then we might wonder whether recent attempts by liberals to eradicate reason of state are similarly flawed. Do they even aim at providing, in Sadurski's phrase, a working conceptual map of constitutional politics, or are they more concerned with keeping liberal theory pure? If there is something to this charge, then it might also prove to be the case that the search for purity means neglecting the external dimension of the constitution that, as we have seen throughout the book, was such a vital feature of older styles of liberal thought.

The chapter explores these intuitions in the context of contemporary constitutional politics. As in previous chapters, it does so by setting the juridical changes that relate to reason of state within a broader historical and political frame. The constitutional politics that developed out of the post-Second World War reordering centred on the need to prevent the re-emergence of the prerogative state and the imposition of legal limits on potentially arbitrary authority more generally. In that sense, the post-1945 constitution has seen a reversion to the trend towards the juridification of reason of state. This move in the direction of liberal constitutionalism, although it channels and to an extent transforms reason of state, does not eliminate it and may not even reduce its frequency. The instantiation in the same period of risk as an important principle of government has resulted in a scenario that is particularly prone to conflicts between human rights and reason of state. As a result, the courts are called upon more often to pronounce on reason of state questions. The chapter then surveys a number of recent case studies drawn from areas that resonate with the material covered so far in this book – empire, trade, diplomacy and emergency. The final section develops the proposition that reason of state has a special role to play in mediating between two competing models of what the *salus populi* principle entails, the first of which emphasizes the state's normative structure and democratic and juridical fundamentals, the second the duty to provide security for its citizens.

Constitutional politics in an age of anxiety

The foundations of the constitutional politics of the present era were laid after the Second World War. The period of reconstruction was essentially reactive, partaking 'more of the spirit of restoration than it did of revolution (and the fundamental role of Catholics in the postwar promotion of talk of human rights extended this spirit)'.[5] The end of the First World War had seen broadly similar legal and institutional aspirations, of course, and these gave rise in particular to the League of Nations and a host of international treaties in the 1920s and 1930s. Unfortunately, these developments did not take root, not least because of the decision of America and Russia not to join the League.[6] While many, including Hayek,[7] had thought that socialism would probably emerge victorious after 1945, in fact it was the Christian democratic parties which became the strongest political force, especially in Continental Western Europe.[8] (In Britain, dominated by the post-war Keynesian consensus, the closest equivalent was the 'One Nation' Toryism of Harold Macmillan and Rab Butler.) This was the Age of Anxiety, in Auden's phrase,[9] in which a Europe divided by the Iron Curtain lived under the shadow of the Bomb. And it developed a constitutional politics to match.[10] The priority was to foster states that were the opposite of 'the hypertrophied, pagan, racially based and aggressive nation-state' of national socialist Germany and its lesser fascist and

[5] Samuel Moyn, *Human Rights and the Uses of History* (London: Verso, 2014), 12.

[6] Paul Kennedy, *The Parliament of Man: The Past, Present, and Future of the United Nations* (Toronto: HarperCollins, 2005), 12–24.

[7] F. A. Hayek, *The Road to Serfdom* (1944) (Chicago: Chicago University Press, ed. Bruce Caldwell, 2007).

[8] Wolfram Kaiser, *Christian Democracy and the Origins of the European Union* (Cambridge: Cambridge University Press, 2007), 164. See also Stathis N. Kalyvas, *The Rise of Christian Democracy in Europe* (Ithaca: Cornell University Press, 1996), 2: 'Christian Democracy is rightly considered the most successful western European political movement since 1945' (citing *The Economist*, Mar. 1990), whose 'importance cannot be overstated'.

[9] In his introduction to the poem, Alan Jacobs points out that Auden worked for the Morale Division of the US Strategic Bombing Survey right at the end of the war, and was posted to Germany as part of the effort to understand the psychological impact of the Allied bombing campaigns. It was here that he came 'to understand more clearly the extent of the Nazi's devastation of German Jewry: *The Age of Anxiety* is among the first poems in English, perhaps the very first, to register the fact of the Nazi's genocidal murder of millions of Jews'. W. H. Auden, *The Age of Anxiety: A Baroque Eclogue* [1947] (Princeton: Princeton University Press, 2011), xiii.

[10] Tony Judt, *Postwar: A History of Europe since 1945* (London: Vintage, 2010), 155, 242.

clerical-dictatorial relatives.[11] In practice this meant the triumph of a new chastened Weberian politics, 'not charismatic, but firmly centred on the executive and pragmatic leaders; not geared towards generating meaning, but based on more than economic success (namely, moral foundations, such as natural law); not animated by a comprehensive liberal vision, but attempting to integrate citizens through shared values rooted in the rejection of the fascist past and the Communist threat from the East in the present'.[12]

The campaign against the 'hypertrophied and aggressive nation-state' highlights the way in which the post-1945 state sought to transcend itself externally and limit its powers internally. In Western Europe, the dull but worthy style of politics, technocracy with a human face, was transposed onto the European level – Alcide De Gasperi, Konrad Adenauer and Robert Schuman, the founders of the European Community, were all Christian Democrats.[13] Fearing nationalism, these leaders advocated subsidiarity and a Europe united in its 'Christian-humanist' heritage.[14] The supranational character of the European Community became more pronounced from the 1960s, and its constitutional character became from the 1990s a main theme in the analysis of the EC's transformation.[15] The old nation state operated also within a transformed international order. The erection and subsequent development of the UN Charter system can be seen retrospectively as 'the construction of an autonomous, global, increasingly integrated legal order of constitutional quality claiming supremacy that has profoundly modified state sovereignty'.[16] Its defining

[11] Peter Pulzer, 'Nationalism and Internationalism in European Christian Democracy' in Michael Gehler and Wolfram Kaiser (eds.), *Christian Democracy in Europe since 1945* (London: Routledge, 2004), 21.

[12] Jan-Werner Müller, *Contesting Democracy: Political Ideas in Twentieth-Century Europe* (New Haven: Yale University Press, 2011), 129. See also Kaiser, *Christian Democracy and the Origins of the European Union*, 172: the style of government was the precise opposite of the flamboyant dictatorial style of Hitler and Mussolini in being 'a deliberately conservative, dull form of political representation and decision-making by indistinguishable "men in suits"'.

[13] Kaiser, *Christian Democracy and the Origins of the European Union*, 171.

[14] Müller, *Contesting Democracy*, 141.

[15] J. H. H. Weiler, *The Constitution of Europe* (Cambridge: Cambridge University Press, 1999), Chapter 6; Neil Walker, 'European Constitutionalism in the State Constitutional Tradition' (2006) 59 *Current Legal Problems* 51.

[16] Jean L. Cohen, 'Sovereignty in the Context of Globalization: A Constitutional Pluralist Perspective' in Samantha Besson and John Tasioulas (eds.), *The Philosophy of International Law* (Oxford: Oxford University Press, 2010), 269. For stronger versions of the constitutionalization thesis see Andreas L. Paulus, 'The International Legal System as a Constitution' in Jeffrey L. Dunoff and Joel P. Trachtman (eds.), *Ruling the World? Constitutionalism, International Law, and Global Governance* (Cambridge: Cambridge

feature was the articulation of the principle of collective security eliminating the *jus belli* exception for self-defence, 'an unprecedented attempt to legally regulate the use of force'.[17] The UN Charter mentions the *concept* of human rights,[18] but the idea received more detailed specification with the 1966 UN Covenants on Civil Political Rights and on Economic, Cultural and Social Rights, which created legal obligations. The Universal Declaration of Human Rights 1948 evolved from its original status as an aspirational statement to a body of norms many of whose provisions are now regarded as authoritative.[19] Over the ensuing decades, states have bound themselves not to torture or summarily execute citizens, not to convict them without due process of law, not to discriminate on the basis of race, religion or gender, and not to do various other things which are sources of despair (including commit genocide or enslave populations).[20] 'The advent of the international human rights machinery', Gerry Simpson writes, 'modified the view that a state's internal affairs were ... matters for the state alone and not subject to international supervision or surveillance. The domestic jurisdiction of states underwent shrinkage as the human rights regime became more and more intrusive.'[21]

These Declarations, Covenants and Conventions, the self-limiting actions of states at the international level, although submerged for a period by more urgent calls for self-determination and decolonization as well as Cold War *realpolitik*,[22] had a profound feedback effect on regional

University Press, 2009); Jan Klabbers, Anne Peters and Geir Ulfstein, *The Constitutionalization of International Law* (Oxford: Oxford University Press, 2011).

17 Cohen, 'Sovereignty in the Context of Globalization', 269. Although hopes 'of an end to the traditional politics of aggression, and the customary deterrence through competing alliance system, proved abortive', despite some successes: Jeremy Black, *A History of Diplomacy* (London: Reaktion Books, 2010), 212.

18 UN Charter, Arts 1(3), 13, 55–56, 68. See Tom J. Farer and Felice Gaer, 'The UN and Human Rights: At the End of the Beginning' in Andrew Roberts and Benedict Kingsbury (eds.), *United Nations, Divided World: The UN's Roles in International Relations* (Oxford: Oxford University Press, 2nd ed., 1993), 245.

19 Philip Alston and Ryan Goodman, *International Human Rights* (Oxford: Oxford University Press, 2012), 82.

20 Farer and Gaer, 'The UN and Human Rights', 244. Some of these matters, including slavery (1926 Slavery Convention), had been subject to international agreement before the UN era.

21 Gerry Simpson, *Great Powers and Outlaw States: Unequal Sovereigns in the International Legal Order* (Cambridge: Cambridge University Press, 2004), 299.

22 Samuel Moyn, *The Last Utopia: Human Rights in History* (Cambridge, MA: Harvard University Press, 2010), Chapters 2 and 3; Mazower, *Governing the World*, 317–322, tying the emergence of an international human rights movement with the normative transformation of American power from 1977.

and domestic constitutional orders.[23] This was especially true of Europe, where the European Convention of Human Rights (1950) developed an effective litigation structure as individual petitions became commonplace, a right granted to British citizens in 1966.[24] Compliance was so consistent that the judgements of the European Court of Human Rights became 'as effective as those of any domestic court'.[25] The increasing recourse to the ECHR and the shaming factor that accompanied judgements against the United Kingdom, combined with the increased salience of human rights as an index of good government, led to the incorporation of the ECHR into British law with the passing of the Human Rights Act 1998. Symbolically at least the Act 'marks the shift from a positivist, liberal democratic model to a rights-based conception of law as a set of architectonic principles which frames the political order'.[26] Not unreasonably, that transition was held out at the time as 'Bringing Rights Home',[27] not so much for the usual reason that is given – that we British drafted the ECHR in the first place[28] – as for more content-specific reasons. True, declarations of rights are unusual, if not unknown, within the British constitutional tradition.[29] But the structuring ideals of the European Convention are consonant with the tradition traced in this book. The cardinal idea of government through and under law (recall Hobbes); a rejection of personal or charismatic authority (Harrington); the principle of legal equality (Dicey); the idea that there are limits on what legitimate government

[23] Although it is worth noting that by 1939, most state constitutions contained declarations and guarantees of individual rights: A. W. Brian Simpson, *Human Rights and the End of Empire: Britain and the Genesis of the European Convention* (Oxford: Oxford University Press, 2001), 91.

[24] See, e.g., Helen Keller and Alec Stone Sweet, 'Assessing the Impact of the ECHR on National Legal Systems' in Keller and Stone Sweet (eds.), *Europe of Rights: The Impact of the ECHR on National Legal Systems* (Oxford: Oxford University Press, 2008).

[25] Lawrence Helfer and Anne-Marie Slaughter, 'Toward a Theory of Effective Supranational Adjudication' (1997) 107 *Yale Law Journal* 273, 283.

[26] Martin Loughlin, 'Rights, Democracy, and Law' in Tom Campbell, K. D. Ewing and Adam Tomkins (eds.), *Sceptical Essays on Human Rights* (Oxford: Oxford University Press, 2001), 55.

[27] 'Rights Brought Home: The Human Rights Bill', Home Office Policy Paper, 24 October 1997.

[28] Simpson, *Human Rights and the End of Empire*, chapters 7–8 and 12–14; Geoffrey Marston, 'The United Kingdom's Part in the Preparation of the European Convention on Human Rights 1950' (1993) 42 *International and Comparative Law Quarterly* 796.

[29] We have encountered two such declarations during the course of this book: the Petition of Right 1628 and the Bill of Rights 1689. On the consequences of declarations see Lynn Hunt, *Inventing Human Rights: A History* (New York: W. W. Norton & Co., 2007), chapter 4, which discusses the French Declaration of 1789.

may do (Burke);[30] the hostility to arbitrary power and the concomitant duty on public authorities to justify their actions (J. S. Mill); the belief in reason itself, and in the connection of reason to law (Smith); the idea that some things, like torture, are simply beyond law's pale (Locke);[31] perhaps even the Convention's open-ended or negotiable elements (Hume) that exasperate some commentators[32] – all these would be familiar to the writers whose thought has dominated the book. (The partial exception as ever is Hobbes, and even here it depends on whether you see him as an authoritarian or something of a proto-Whig.[33]) This relationship between old and new should not surprise us, bearing in mind that the ECHR was a plank of the conservative and anti-Communist (Western) European ideological armoury.[34] The post-war constitution was essentially a restoration and, as such, looked to the past for legitimacy and normative inspiration. But, as is so often the case, the act of restoration was also and profoundly a creative act, leading to the restructuring of our perspective on the past and the generation of a constitutionalism that was at the same time familiar enough and yet profoundly new. As Isaiah Berlin observed, it was precisely because the rules of natural law were flouted so spectacularly in the twentieth century that we have been forced to become conscious of them.[35]

[30] A point reinforced at the international level by the development of the concept of 'the responsibility to protect', 2005 World Summit Outcome, GA Res. 60/1, paras 138–139 (24 Oct. 2005). See Gareth Evans, 'The Responsibility to Protect: Rethinking Humanitarian Intervention' (2004) 98 *Proceedings of the Annual Meeting of the American Society of International Law* 78; Carsten Stahn, 'Responsibility to Protect: Political Rhetoric or Emerging Legal Norm?' (2007) 101 *American Journal of International Law* 99.

[31] Compare Jeremy Waldron's idea of the prohibition on torture being a 'legal archetype': 'Torture and Positive Law: Jurisprudence for the White House' (2005) 205 *Columbia Law Review* 1681.

[32] A theme effectively explored in Grégoire C. N. Webber, *The Negotiable Constitution: On the Limitation of Rights* (Cambridge: Cambridge University Press, 2009).

[33] On the latter interpretation see, e.g., Richard Tuck, *Philosophy and Government 1572–1651* (Cambridge: Cambridge University Press, 1993), 345; David Dyzenhaus, 'Hobbes on the Authority of Law' in David Dyzenhaus and Thomas Poole (eds.), *Hobbes and the Law* (Cambridge: Cambridge University Press, 2012); Larry May, *Limiting Leviathan: Hobbes on Law and International Affairs* (Oxford: Oxford University Press, 2013).

[34] For a more nuanced interpretation of the origins of the ECHR see Andrew Moravcsik, 'The Origins of Human Rights Regimes: Democratic Delegation in Postwar Europe' (2000) 54 *International Organization* 217, which argues that the primary proponents of reciprocally binding human rights obligations were the governments of newly established democracies rather than established democracies such as Britain.

[35] Isaiah Berlin, 'European Unity and Its Vicissitudes' in Isaiah Berlin, *The Crooked Timber of Humanity* (London: Chatto & Windus, 1991), 204.

What *is* at least relatively novel when set against the older British tradition, even though most of the writers in this book used the word 'rights' in a sense that went beyond the Benthamite sense of a legal right granted by positive law, is the rights foundationalism that the new declaratory rights regimes seem to entail. I agree with those who think the language of human rights can seem almost adolescent, presenting complex moral problems as though they were amenable to logical deduction from abstract universals.[36] But that in a sense is precisely their point. Rights provide a deliberately basic script or code for a world that had entirely lost its bearings[37] – and if Samuel Moyn is right, a world that has lost its faith in world-changing ideologies.[38] The choice to use 'human rights' rather than the more historically resonant 'natural rights' was part of this simplifying move in that it removed some of the problems associated with grounding rights in nature. The idea 'was to seek agreement on *norms* (rules), without seeking agreement on fundamental values and beliefs'.[39] Just as significantly, the concept of *human* rights also shatters the civilized/barbarian binary which, as we saw in Chapter 6, was such an entrenched feature of European thought.

A troubling feature of the inter-war period, we saw in the previous chapter, was its complexity. The growth of the administrative state served to alienate people from government, raising deep concerns about the possibility of a free and self-chosen life under modern conditions. From the juridical standpoint, it threatened to make the task of

[36] See classically Jeremy Bentham, 'Anarchical Fallacies' [1796] in Jeremy Waldron (ed.), *'Nonsense Upon Stilts': Bentham, Burke and Marx on the Rights of Man* (London: Methuen, 1987). For a recent contribution see, e.g., John Milbank, 'Against Human Rights: Liberty in the Western Tradition' in Costas Douzinas and Conor Gearty (eds.), *The Meaning of Rights: The Philosophy and Social Theory of Human Rights* (Cambridge: Cambridge University Press, 2014).

[37] Compare Michael Ingatieff, *Human Rights as Politics and Idolatry* (Princeton: Princeton University Press, 2001).

[38] Moyn, *The Last Utopia*. Jeremy Black connects the shift in global politics in the 1970s to the *Ostpolitik* of the new Social Democrat-Free Democrat coalition under Willy Brandt that came to power in 1969. The new government sought a more benign relationship with Eastern Europe. 'This strategy reached its height with détente and the Helsinki Accords, while in the final stages of the Cold War the Americans took the strategy over.' *A History of Diplomacy*, 224–225. Saskia Sassen agrees that there was a fundamental change in global politics in approximately the same period – although she would date it slightly later, 'beginning in the late 1970s and strengthening in the 1980s' and would connect it to globalization outside the state and the 'privatization, deregulation and marketization of public functions' within the state: *Territory, Authority, Rights: From Medieval to Global Assemblages* (Princeton: Princeton University Press, 2008), 17.

[39] Michael Freeman, *Human Rights* (Cambridge: Polity Press, 2002), 35.

subjecting government to law impossible.[40] We have since learned perhaps to live with an administrative state larger and even more complex than its inter-war predecessor. But rights help cut through that structure to an extent, providing a relatively straightforward moral-legal template with which to assess the legitimacy of any governmental action. As such, rights perform an increasingly significant role in the law of judicial review of administrative action whose growth has been a feature of modern constitutional politics.[41] At its most appealing, judicial review provides a means by which the individual can require a public authority to give reasons for an action against his or her right or interest before an independent body before which both parties, state and individual, appear as equals.[42]

The prominent role that courts play in the articulation and protection of rights, and in the constitutional politics of the modern state more generally, is perhaps another anomaly when set against the tradition of thought traced in this book, although here again we should recall the instances analyzed in this book when courts were called upon to decide whether a government intent on matters of state and empire had violated a subject's rights. We return to the court's role in contemporary constitutional politics later. What needs emphasis here is that the new constitutional order of which the concept of human rights forms a vital part carries a clear, if implicit, conception of the state, including its external character, and the role that reason of state plays within it. 'The normative foundations of the international legal order', Ruti Teitel writes in a work on the transformation of the relationship of law and violence since 1945, 'have shifted from an emphasis on state security – that is, security defined by borders, statehood,

[40] Laski, although an advocate of the administrative state, realized this early on. See Harold J. Laski, 'The Responsibility of the State in England' (1919) 32 *Harvard Law Review* 447, 462: 'The development of administrative law needs to be closely scrutinized in the interests of public liberty. If a government department may make regulations of any kind without any judicial tests of fairness or reasonableness being involved, it is clear that a fundamental safeguard upon English liberties has disappeared. If administrative action can escape the review of the courts, there is no reality in official responsibility; and cases like *Entick v Carrington* become, in such a contest, of merely antiquarian interest.'

[41] See, e.g., Martin Shapiro and Alec Stone Sweet, 'The Success of Judicial Review and Democracy' in Martin Shapiro and Alec Stone Sweet, *On Law, Politics and Judicialization* (Oxford: Oxford University Press, 2002). On British developments see Thomas Poole, 'The Reformation of English Administrative Law' (2009) 68 *Cambridge Law Journal* 142.

[42] Lon L. Fuller, 'The Forms and Limits of Adjudication' (1978) 92 *Harvard Law Review* 353.

territory, and so – to a focus on human security: the security of persons and peoples'.[43]

This post-1945 transformation amounts at the constitutional level to an affirmation of the principle that the state's primary aim is the material and psychological well-being of its people. This position requires the restatement of that ancient first principle of state legitimacy, *salus populi suprema lex esto*, along precisely those lines that we saw Hayek insist upon in the previous chapter. 'Correctly understood', Hayek wrote, the principle 'means that the end of the law ought to be the welfare of the people, that the general rules should be so designed as to serve it, but *not* that any conception of a particular social end should provide a justification for breaking those general rules'.[44] The principle so interpreted entails that the state be construed as existing in a posture of peace. The idea of war as a sovereign prerogative of states has been replaced by the rule that, in the absence of UN authorization, a state may go to war against another state only in individual or collective self-defence against aggression.[45] Britain ran up against this new reality of post-war global politics early on when it sought to embark on its late-imperial adventure in Suez in 1956.[46] The conduct of states in warfare has been subject to a comprehensive and sophisticated body of law.[47] Of more immediate relevance, cases such as *Al-Skeini* have revealed that human rights obligations may attach themselves in some circumstances to the wartime conduct of a state operating outside its jurisdiction.[48]

Relevant developments go beyond the context of war, vital though it has been in shaping constitutions,[49] and involve structural changes that

[43] Ruti G. Teitel, *Humanity's Law* (New York: Oxford University Press, 2011), 4.

[44] F. A. Hayek, *The Constitution of Liberty* (London: Routledge, 2010), 139.

[45] Ingrid Detter, *The Law of War* (Cambridge: Cambridge University Press, 2000), 157–158.

[46] Judt, *Postwar*, 294–298.

[47] There were steps in this direction before 1945, notably with the Hague Regulations of 1899 and 1907, but these tended to focus on restricting particular weaponry whereas the emphasis of the post-war Geneva Conventions of 1949 and the Protocols Additional to the Geneva Conventions of 1977 were more focused on protecting individuals in the context of war. See Sandesh Sivakumaran, 'International Humanitarian Law' in Daniel Moeckli, Sangeeta Shah and Sandesh Sivakumaran (eds.), *International Human Rights Law* (Oxford: Oxford University Press, 2nd ed., 2013).

[48] *Al-Skeini v United Kingdom* [2011] ECHR 1093; *Al-Jedda v United Kingdom* [2011] ECHR 1092. Note also the recent decision of the ECHR Grand Chamber *Hassan v UK* (16 Sep. 2014) Case app. no. 29750/09 whereby rules of international humanitarian law circumscribe what protections are afforded by human rights law.

[49] Philip Bobbitt, *Terror and Consent: The Wars of the Twenty-First Century* (New York: Knopf, 2002), 23: 'Warfare and constitutional order exist in a mutually

have taken place *within* state constitutional orders.[50] What is interesting is not so much the sheer amount of new international and transnational law and the way those bodies of law have been taken up within the legal orders of states but that the interpenetration of international law and national law forces us to rethink our understanding of the relationship between them. The classical distinction between the domestic and international spheres has become, Nico Krisch writes, 'increasingly blurred, with a multitude of formal and informal connections taking the place of what once were relatively clear rules and categories'.[51] Seeking to make sense of this 'global disorder of normative orders',[52] which now includes to an unprecedented degree more or less autonomous sites of *private* networked power and transnational 'privatized norm-making',[53] jurists have offered various maps of the new global legal pluriverse, including constitutional pluralism,[54] constitutional dualism[55] and global constitutionalism.[56]

There are two important points to make about the effect of this transformation of law and politics on reason of state. The first is that despite similarities in their basic orientation, the strategy in the new constitutional order is not the same as Hayek's vision of a reason-of-state-less (perhaps almost state-less[57]) world. There is an attempt to curb, to limit it, certainly. But the ambition is not to eradicate reason of state so much as

affecting relationship. Fundamental innovations in war bring about fundamental transformations in the constitutional order of states, while transformations in the constitutional order bring about fundamental changes in the conduct and aims of war.'

[50] Karen Knop, 'Here and There: International Law in Domestic Courts' (2000) 32 *New York University Journal of International Law and Politics* 501; Teitel, *Humanity's Law*, Chapter 3.

[51] Nico Krisch, *Beyond Constitutionalism: The Pluralist Structure of Postnational Law* (Oxford: Oxford University Press, 2010), 4.

[52] Neil Walker, 'Beyond Boundary Disputes and Basic Grids: Mapping the Global Disorder of Normative Orders' (2008) 6 *International Journal of Constitutional Law* 373.

[53] Anne-Marie Slaughter, *A New World Order: Government Networks and the Disaggregated State* (Princeton: Princeton University Press, 2004); Sassen, *Territory, Authority, Rights*, 265.

[54] Krisch, *Beyond Constitutionalism*; Günther Teubner, *Constitutional Fragments: Societal Constitutionalism and Globalization* (Oxford: Oxford University Press, 2014); Neil Walker, 'The Idea of Constitutional Pluralism' (2002) 65 *Modern Law Review* 317.

[55] Jean Cohen, *Globalization and Sovereignty: Rethinking Legality, Legitimacy, and Constitutionalism* (Cambridge: Cambridge University Press, 2012).

[56] Mattias Kumm, 'The Legitimacy of International Law: A Constitutionalist Framework of Analysis' (2004) 15 *European Journal of International Law* 907.

[57] Chandran Kukathas, 'Hayek's Theory of State' in Dyzenhaus and Poole, *Law, Liberty and State*.

to transform it, to ensure that it flows wherever possible through ordinary legal channels and made subject to scrutiny, often 'multi-layered'.[58] The post-war trend has thus been a strengthening and deepening of the pattern identified over the course of this book. If the inter-war period saw something of a reversion to the prerogative state, post-war developments have seen both a renewed commitment to constitutional politics and a more or less consistent attempt to extend that trend beyond the confines of the *ius publicum Europaeum*. There is still room for reason of state in the new order, a characteristic feature of which has been to attempt to make provision for it. We examine some examples shortly, but familiar instances include Article 15 ECHR, which allows a state to derogate in public emergencies from certain Convention rights. Britain has by no means been immune to this trend. The Civil Contingencies Act 2004, for instance, aspires to provide a comprehensive framework for emergency planning and response[59] and there even appears to be a convention developing within Britain that would require the Prime Minister to seek parliamentary approval before taking the country to war.[60]

The second point appears almost paradoxical in light of these developments. Despite the attempts to curb it, reason of state may actually become *more* common in the current constitutional climate and will almost certainly give rise to more frequent legal dispute. One reason for this is globalization. In an increasingly interconnected world, one state's interests are more likely to rub up against the interests of other state and non-state actors. Increased globalization makes it more likely that actors enter into denser legal and institutional relationships.[61] This increased demand for cross-border law in turn amplifies the call for transnational and international legal structures capable of dealing with the disputes that necessarily arise. The corollary of this rise in global law of various types is that what once might have been seen as a political, diplomatic or economic problem will now also present as a *legal* problem. A second

[58] See, e.g., Nicholas Bamforth and Peter Leyland (eds.), *Public Law in a Multi-Layered Constitution* (Oxford: Hart Publishing, 2003); Ingolf Pernice, 'Multilevel Constitutionalism and the Treaty of Amsterdam: European Constitution-Making Reconsidered?' (1999) 36 *Common Market Law Review* 703.

[59] Clive Walker and James Broderick, *The Civil Contingencies Act 2004: Risk, Resilience and the Law in the United Kingdom* (Oxford: Oxford University Press, 2006).

[60] James Strong, 'Why Parliament Now Decides on War: Tracing the Growth of the Parliamentary Prerogative through Syria, Lybia and Iraq' (2014) *British Journal of Politics and International Affairs* (published online 11 June 2014).

[61] Jeffrey L. Dunoff and Joel P. Trachtman, 'A Functional Approach to International Constitutionalization' in Dunoff and Trachtman, *Ruling the World?*, 5–6.

reason relates to the new structural importance of human rights, especially within domestic legal orders, one of the familiar features of which is the capacity to transform political disputes into (also) juridical ones.[62] In 'the rights-based conception', as Martin Loughlin writes, 'law provides the frame within which politics is conducted'.[63] Rights have an open-textured[64] *and* an imperial quality – as indeed they must if they are to achieve even some of the objectives expected of them. As we see in the next section when we turn to the cases, they have already shown their capacity to infiltrate what would have been considered until very recently the *sanctum sanctorum* of state action.[65]

This analysis seems particularly cogent when we recall that the central feature of the contemporary state is its duty to protect its citizens. This is not to say that the state in its earlier incarnations did not have this as a central goal – a glance at *Leviathan* would show otherwise. The point is that the contemporary state tends to abjure certain goals it might in earlier ages also have aspired towards – territorial expansion, imperial conquest, *gloire*. One index of this transformation is the rise to predominance of the related ideas of risk and security as hallmarks of contemporary governance. Some go so far as to argue that risk has become a dominant paradigm in thinking about state and society[66] and risk management the central organizing principle of government.[67] This development is not merely a contingent feature of supposedly cossetted modern society and its politics of fear as some commentators believe,[68] echoing

[62] See, e.g., J. A. G. Griffith, 'The Political Constitution' (1979) 42 *Modern Law Review* 1; Jeremy Waldron, *Law and Disagreement* (Oxford: Oxford University Press, 1999).

[63] Loughlin, 'Rights, Democracy, and Law', 56.

[64] This characteristic of rights is systematically explored in Kai Möller, *The Global Model of Constitutional Rights* (Oxford: Oxford University Press, 2012).

[65] See, e.g., *Lawless v Ireland* (1961) 1 EHRR 15. For a critical analysis of this development see Ran Hirschl, 'The Judicialization of Mega-Politics and the Rise of Political Courts' (2008) 11 *Annual Review of Political Science* 93.

[66] See, e.g., Ulrich Beck, *Risk Society: Towards a New Modernity* (London: Sage, 1992); Mary Douglas and Aaron Wildavsky, *Risk and Culture: An Essay on the Selection of Technical and Environmental Dangers* (Berkeley: University of California Press, 1982).

[67] See, e.g., Michael Power, *The Risk Management of Everything: Rethinking the Politics of Uncertainty* (London: Demos, 2004); Christopher Hood, Henry Rothstein and Robert Baldwin, *The Government of Risk: Understanding Risk Regulation Regimes* (Oxford: Oxford University Press, 2004); Anthony Giddens, 'Risk and Responsibility' (1999) 62 *Modern Law Review* 1; Cass Sunstein, *Laws of Fear: Beyond the Precautionary Principle* (Cambridge: Cambridge University Press, 2005).

[68] See Judith Shklar, 'The Liberalism of Fear' in Stanley Hoffmann (ed.), *Political Thought and Political Thinkers* (Chicago: University of Chicago Press, 1998); Frank Furedi, *Politics of Fear* (London: Continuum, 2005).

Oakeshott's arraignment of modern 'mass man' as the individual *manqué* who through craven fear demands security like a comfort blanket.[69] Rather, a structural connection exists between the post-war state, especially its foundation in rights and consent, and risk. As Phillip Bobbitt explains, since the contemporary state adds to the old duty of providing security from external and internal threat a new commitment to manage risks, as well as asserting that a pluralism grounded in human rights is what distinguishes it from other state forms, protecting civilians from risks of catastrophes that threaten such pluralism becomes an overriding aim.[70] Human rights themselves and the institutional structures designed to realize them in fact fit comfortably in this risk framework, at least at a high level of generality. Rights are risk management tools whose task is to guarantee the security of individuals, arguably the key normative objective of constitutional politics in the age of anxiety.[71] The historian and philosopher François Ewald's definition of risk applies equally to rights documents. They provide 'first and foremost a schema of rationality, a way of breaking down, rearranging, ordering certain elements of reality'[72] and serve to select certain risks, thereby representing or reflecting social and political choices about which hazards we foreground – a classic purpose of risk management techniques.[73]

At lower levels of generality, differences between rights and risk emerge, of course. Whereas human rights are juristic, risk management techniques more generally are bureaucratic and technical, even actuarial.[74] Whereas human rights shunt questions to the great institutions of state, to the legislature and even more the courts, risk management tends to be the preserve of the executive and expert administrators.[75] Some of

[69] Michael Oakeshott, *On Human Conduct* (Oxford: Oxford University Press, 1974), 275.

[70] Bobbitt, *Terror and Consent*, 215. See also Ian Loader and Neil Walker, *Civilizing Security* (Cambridge: Cambridge University Press, 2007); Peter Ramsay, *The Insecurity State: Vulnerable Autonomy and the Right to Security in the Criminal Law* (Oxford: Oxford University Press, 2012).

[71] Indeed, Adrian Vermeule goes further in this direction, arguing that constitutions should be seen as instruments of risk management: *The Constitution of Risk* (New York: Cambridge University Press, 2014).

[72] François Ewald, 'Insurance and Risk' in Graham Burchell, Colin Gordon and Peter Miller (eds.), *The Foucault Effect: Studies in Governmentality* (Chicago: University of Chicago Press, 1991), 199.

[73] Julia Black, 'The Emergence of Risk-Based Regulation' [2005] *Public Law* 512, 519.

[74] See, e.g., Elizabeth Fisher, 'The Rise of the Risk Commonwealth and the Challenge to Administrative Law' [2003] *Public Law* 455.

[75] Beck, *Risk Society*, 57: the government of risk evokes 'the possibility of objectively and obligatorily determining hazards in a specialized fashion and through expert authority'.

the conflicts between rights and risk at this lower level are explored later in the chapter. For now, it is important to note a less salutary aspect of the new politics of rights and risk, namely, a propensity to think in terms of catastrophe. Such thinking stems from two sources that represent different aspects of the inheritance of 1945. First, the post-war rights regime was designed above all to prevent the extraordinary acts of savagery and violence that characterized the first half of the century. As such, post-war rights nevertheless also project extreme fears, a negative image of utopia, into the future on the basis of isolated but undeniably real events – the Holocaust, the Gulag, the killing fields of the Second World War – the very striking nature of which tends to dominate the way in which subsequent disputes are framed. Second, as the post-war order became a more individualist society its social and psychological resources became harder to mobilize[76] – except where the political community can be said to face grave danger. This development has a juridical dimension. 'Averting and managing these [catastrophes] can include the *reorganization of power and authority*. Risk society is a *catastrophic* society. In it the exceptional condition threatens to become the norm.'[77] Rights are designed to dampen down expressions of the exception. But even if they achieve this they also tend to open up or exacerbate a norm/exception dynamic.

In the context of counter-terrorism where it is most visible, though not only there,[78] developments have led jurists to consider afresh the dynamics of norm and exception.[79] There tends to be some confusion among commentators, perhaps understandably so given the complex relationship between rights and exception in today's constitutional politics. On one side of this debate there are those like Judith Butler who see evidence

See Michel Foucault, 'Governmentality' in Burchell, Gordon and Miller, *The Foucault Effect*.

76 Recent social scientific analysis links this trend, as both cause and effect, to the decline of traditional political parties: see, e.g., Peter Mair, *Ruling the Void: The Hollowing of Western Democracy* (London: Verso, 2013).

77 Beck, *Risk Society*, 24. Italics in the original.

78 Another prominent recent example relates to the political and legal response to the global financial crisis: see, e.g., Günther Teubner, 'A Constitutional Moment? The Logics of Hitting the Bottom' in Paul Kjaer, Günther Teubner and Alberto Febbrajo (eds.), *The Financial Crisis in Constitutional Perspective: The Dark Side of Functional Differentiation* (2011).

79 See, e.g., Giorgio Agamben, *State of Exception* (Chicago: University of Chicago Press, trans. Kevin Attell, 2005); Oren Gross, 'The Normless and Exceptionless Exception: Carl Schmitt's Theory of Emergency Powers and the "Norm-Exception" Dichotomy' (2000) 21 *Cardozo Law Review* 1825; Nomi Claire Lazar, *States of Emergency in Liberal Democracy* (New York: Cambridge University Press, 2009).

of a 'resurgent prerogative'. They think post-9/11 developments represent the birth of a new type of sovereignty politics central to which is the reassertion of 'a lawless sovereign power over life and death … through animating and deploying the extra-legal dimension of governmentality'. Within this new paradigm, existing institutions including courts become conceived merely as instruments for use 'in the service of national security, the protection of principality and the continuing and augmented exercise of state sovereignty'.[80] On the other side, there are those like Jack Goldsmith who claim that in the contemporary world prerogative has become all but irrelevant. Older conceptions of prerogative, especially those predicated on the Lockean idea of executive action in open defiance of law or legal authority, are 'no longer part of a president's justificatory tool kit'. The real danger, Goldsmith suggests, lies in government secrecy, specifically in the phenomenon of 'executive auto-interpretation of executive authorities, and in particular *secret executive branch interpretation of law*'.[81]

Both interpretations are in a sense right, in that they identify important features common to a number of recent developments. Butler dramatizes the admittedly fairly familiar point about the rise in executive power and about the propensity of executives to use both crises and scare tactics in order to increase their power.[82] Incidentally, this last point is one that we have seen in this book a number of Enlightenment writers, including Hume and Bentham, make. Goldsmith picks out for juridical attention the growing domain of secrecy that seems to attend the new politics of terrorism, in particular the insidious connection between growing executive power and increased claims for *government privacy*,[83] while at the same time cutting down on the privacy rights of citizens. As such, they are worthwhile contributions. But they miss a larger truth. What we see in the terrorism context and elsewhere are not so much aberrant dynamics as normal practices in a hypertrophic state. When combined with our penchant for thinking in terms of risk and catastrophes, rights may make

[80] Judith Butler, *Precarious Life: The Power of Mourning and Violence* (London: Verso, 2006), 95.

[81] Jack Goldsmith, 'The Irrelevance of Prerogative Power, and the Evils of Secret Legal Interpretation' in Clement Fatovic and Benjamin A. Kleinerman (eds.), *Extra-Legal Power and Legitimacy: Perspectives on Prerogative* (New York: Oxford University Press, 2013), 215. Italics in the original.

[82] See, e.g., Eric A. Posner and Adrian Vermeule, *The Executive Unbound: After the Madisonian Republic* (New York: Oxford University Press, 2011).

[83] Sassen, *Territory, Authority, Rights*, 179.

'exceptional claims' more common. And given the prevalence of rights and risk in modern government, the exceptional is now as often as not folded up in, and all but indistinguishable from, the normal. The danger, then, is an updated version of Oakeshott's warning about the modern dual constitution. While it might be possible to divide the world cleanly along conceptual lines (although Oakeshott also worried that we were losing our ability to do this too) between the juridical or *societas* conception and the purposive or *universitas* conception, in practice it can be extremely hard to distinguish one from the other. There is not always a separate channel for reason of state, and in as much as there is, there is no obligation on reason of state to use it.

I should summarize the argument of the chapter so far. The post-war ambition might be summed up in terms of the phrase 'never again', as long as we bear in mind that this phrase carried a strong conservative charge. The restoration as so often has had radical effects. The project was to reorder a world in such a way as to put *homo abyssus occidentalis* (Auden again) back on the path of civilization, or at least ordinary decency. This meant decommissioning the aggressive, sovereign, national and imperial state. The colonial aspect was tackled by decolonization.[84] Its aggressive side was wrapped up in a new system of collective security based on the illegality of aggression and a strengthened law of war. And sovereignty was tackled by two interconnected developments: internationalism and human rights. Especially since the upswing in the politics and activism of rights in the late 1970s, human rights have been quite successful in transforming the conceptual structure of the modern constitution. That constitution aims to eliminate the prerogative, lessen the power of the executive vis-à-vis the legislature and judiciary and to drive certain things shown to have been deleterious to the safety and well-being of the people outside the sphere of legitimate authority. As such, it echoes the prescriptions of the vast majority of thinkers whose work has been discussed in this book, beginning with the seventeenth-century republicans.

But the modern constitution has only been partially successful in fulfilling its ambitions. Reason of state has not gone away. (Nor has charismatic leadership or war, although they operate on a very different scale now than before 1945.) Instead, it finds expression within a constitutional politics in which both rights (individualism) and risk (catastrophe) feature strongly. Introducing the concept of human rights was meant to simplify things morally and juridically – and in some ways it may have done

[84] On the British experience see Simpson, *Human Rights and the End of Empire*, Chapter 6.

so. But two properties of rights arguably increase the incidence of reason of state in courts, and complicates the way reason of state is handled. First, human rights are juridical tools designed at least in part for use by courts, but their principled and open-textured nature are attractive to litigants wanting to harness the protective capacity of the law for novel ends or in novel means.[85] Second, despite this open-ended fluidity, human rights retain a formally hard-edged property. A judicial decision about rights formally settles whether or not an action falls within the domain of legitimate authority. Counter-intuitively, the urge that underpins rights-based decision-making results in more emphasis being placed on the dynamics of norm and exception. Some modern liberals – I take Sadurski to be representative – seem animated by the desire to find a clear, substantive solution to reason of state. They want to be able to draw a line, good for all time between legitimate and illegitimate state action. The urge to do so is natural, even admirable. But the magic bullet they seek is not available. The remedy – rights – is in a sense now related to the disease – reason of state. An alternative, essayed in the final part of the chapter, rejects the static, once-and-for-all solution in favour of a more dynamic model that connects the deliberative properties of rights to the institutional structure of the modern state.

Reason of state in court

So far in this chapter we have been painting with a broad brush. This section aims to secure a finer-grained understanding of modern reason of state. As such, it presents a number of contemporary case studies that correspond to the main topics covered in the book – empire, trade, diplomacy and emergency.[86] All four cases come from Britain. While in certain respects specific to the British tradition of constitutional politics that has been the focus of the book, these cases have more general relevance or application, as we shall see.

[85] See, e.g., Möller, *The Global Model of Constitutional Rights*; Mattias Kumm, 'The Idea of Socratic Contestation and the Right to Justification: The Point of Rights-Based Proportionality Review' (2010) 4 *Law & Ethics of Human Rights* 142.

[86] War has also been a focus of some of the 'reason-of-state' cases – see, e.g., *Al-Skeini v Secretary of State for Defence* [2007] UKHL 26; *Al-Jedda v Secretary of State for Defence* [2007] UKHL 58. Both cases are good examples of the importance of the European Court of Human Rights in helping to determine the shape of the modern constitutional settlement between reason of state and the rule of law: *Al-Skeini v United Kingdom* (2011) 53 EHRR 18; *Al-Jedda v United Kingdom*, App. No. 27021/08, 7 July 2011.

Empire

We start with a relatively rare[87] and important case about Britain's imperial past and post-imperial present. *Bancoult (No. 2)*[88] concerned a challenge to the UK government's decision not to repatriate inhabitants of the Chagos Archipelago, a group of about sixty islands in the Indian Ocean ceded to Britain after Napoleon's defeat in 1814. The archipelago was turned into a separate territory (the British Indian Overseas Territory, or BIOT) in 1965 and depopulated in order to make room for a US military base on the archipelago's chief island, Diego Garcia. All this was achieved through the exercise of prerogative powers – first the BIOT Order 1965 and then the Immigration Ordinance 1971, which gave the newly established BIOT Commissioner the authority (in colonial boilerplate) to 'make laws for the peace, order and good government of the territory'.

There had been a number of previous cases relating to the expulsion of the Chagossians in British courts. In *Bancoult (No. 1)*, the 1971 Ordinance was held unlawful on the ground that a power to legislate for the 'peace, order and good government' of BIOT, while broad, did not include a power to exile a people from their homelands. The people of the islands, Laws LJ said, 'are to be governed: not removed'.[89] The government issued a statement that it would not challenge the ruling. A feasibility study reported that while resettlement was possible (although expensive) in the short term, global warming would make the archipelago uninhabitable in the longer term. The government decided, in light of the report, not to support resettlement. The US government also made known its concern

[87] Interestingly, there has recently been a rise in cases involving imperial questions, although many relate to the misdeeds of the colonial past. On the Mau Mau litigation see, e.g., Devika Hovell, 'The Gulf Between Tortious and Torturous: UK Responsibility for Mistreatment of the Mau Mau in Colonial Kenya' (2013) 11 *Journal of International Criminal Justice* 223, discussing *Ndiku Mutua and Others v The Foreign and Commonwealth Office* [2011] EWHC 1913 (QB). See also the Pitcairn Island cases, especially *Christian and Others v The Queen* [2006] UKPC 47 and *Christian v The Queen* [2004] UKPC 52. On those cases see Dawn Oliver (ed.), *Justice, Legality and the Rule of Law: Lessons from the Pitcairn Prosecutions* (Oxford: Oxford University Press, 2009); Sue Farran, 'The "Re-Colonising" of Pitcairn' (2007) 38 *Victoria University of Wellington Law Review* 435.

[88] *R (Bancoult) v Secretary of State for Foreign and Commonwealth Affairs* [2008] UKHL 61.

[89] *R (Bancoult) v Secretary of State for Foreign and Commonwealth Affairs* [2001] QB 1067, at [57], referring to s. 11(1) of the BIOT Order 1965, S.I. 1965/1920. See also *Chagos Islanders v. Attorney General* [2004] EWCA Civ 997, where the Court of Appeal held that this unlawful conduct did not give rise to liability in damages, affirming a settlement package agreed by the United Kingdom and Chagossian representatives in 1982.

that repopulating the Chagos Islands might compromise what it regarded as the unique security of Diego Garcia. New orders were passed in 2004 reinstating full immigration control.

The claimants in *Bancoult (No. 2)* challenged these new orders. A preliminary issue concerned the reviewability of prerogative *legislation*, as opposed to *exercises* of prerogative power that the court had decided some time ago were at least in principle reviewable.[90] The court unanimously accepted that judicial review applied to prerogative legislation too, despite being technically a type of primary legislation. This opened the way to reviewing the legality of this particular exercise of prerogative power. A majority of the court held the 2004 orders lawful, holding that the phrase 'peace, order and good government' relates to the governance of the entire Crown realm and not just to those residing in BIOT. The phrase has been treated historically 'as apt to confer plenary law-making authority'.[91] The case fell within a 'macro-political field' and as such raised a 'political, not judicial' question.[92] A 'rule of abstinence' should apply: however 'distasteful' the court might consider the provisions at issue, it should avoid interfering with 'what is essentially a political judgment'.[93] Two dissenting judges argued that there was no prerogative power to exile a population – 'the reciprocal duties of allegiance and protection ... cannot ordinarily be discharged by removing and excluding the citizen from his homeland'.[94] The right of abode is a constitutional right and the term 'peace, order and good government' specifies a power 'intended to enable the proper governance of the territory, at least among other things for the benefit of the people inhabiting it. A constitution which exiles a territory's inhabitants is a contradiction in terms'.[95]

Bancoult (No. 2) is an unusual case, not least because of the importance of history in the judgments. The case raises questions about imperial powers long after the end of empire and is awash with all but forgotten bits of imperial jurisprudence. Indeed, the division between majority and

[90] *Council for Civil Service Unions v Minister for the Civil Service* [1985] AC 374 (the *GCHQ* case).

[91] *Bancoult (No. 2)* [50] (Lord Hoffmann).

[92] *Bancoult (No. 2)* [109] (Lord Rodger).

[93] *Bancoult (No. 2)* [130] (Lord Carswell). Lord Carswell and Lord Rodger also ruled that the Colonial Laws Validity Act 1865, 28 and 29 Vict., c. 63, precluded judicial review, on the ground that Parliament in 1865 would simply not have contemplated the possibility of an Order in Council legislating for a colony as being open to challenge in an English court on principles of judicial review.

[94] *Bancoult (No. 2)* [70] (Lord Bingham).

[95] *Bancoult (No. 2)* [151] (Lord Mance).

minority can be understood as a disagreement over how to approach these historical questions. The minority judges were dismayed about what they saw as the majority's refusal to recast historical jurisprudence in light of today's norms. The case also directly implicates prerogative power, a form so encased in history that it has been seen as something of a constitutional anachronism since Blackstone's time. But *Bancoult* is also a liminal case and as such very much about the present. Secrecy, security, power politics – all with an international dimension – play central roles. The prerogative itself has long been associated with this sphere of activity, often seeming to lie at the limits of legality – and especially of the jurisdiction of the courts. However, since at least the 1980s, the judiciary has been waging a fairly consistent campaign to bring prerogative within the ambit of 'normal' judicial review.[96] This trend is consistent with the post-war hostility to claims of exceptional power, a sentiment certainly given voice in human rights conventions.[97] The courts have gradually rolled back the 'excluded categories'[98] of state action falling under the prerogative,[99] so much so that it has become all but impossible to escape the jurisdiction of the court by hiding behind the prerogative form. *Bancoult* is itself part of this trend – after all, the case closed another loophole relating to prerogative *legislation.*

These developments unquestionably count as rule-of-law gains against prerogative (reason of state). But the story is not quite as linear (or Whiggish) as it first appears. The prerogative might now be classified as a normal sub-statutory source of power for the purposes of judicial review, but in practice courts still tend to review the prerogative with caution.[100] More often than not – and *Bancoult (No. 2)* is a very good example – a decision that a particular aspect of the prerogative is now subject to

[96] *Council of Civil Service Unions v Minister for the Civil Service* [1985] AC 374 (*GCHQ* case).

[97] In relation to the European Convention on Human Rights 1950, consider (a) the requirement in Article 15 to derogate from certain articles of the Convention in situation of 'public emergency threatening the life of the nation' (*Lawless v Ireland* (1961) 1 EHRR 15) and (b) the more general stipulation in relation to qualified rights that to even possibly count as a legitimate interference with a right, the relevant decision or action must have been authorized by law: e.g., *Malone v United Kingdom* (1984) 7 EHRR 14.

[98] *GCHQ* case, at 418 (Lord Roskill).

[99] *R v Secretary of State for the Home Department, ex p Bentley* [1994] QB 349 (review of prerogative of mercy).

[100] For a more elaborate version of this argument see Thomas Poole, 'Judicial Review at the Margins: Law, Power, and Prerogative' (2010) 60 *University of Toronto Law Journal* 81. See also Mark D. Walters, 'The Law behind the Conventions of the Constitution: Reassessing the Prorogation Debate' (2011) 5 *Journal of Parliamentary and Political Law* 131, 135–137.

normal principles of judicial review is accompanied by a final ruling in the government's favour.[101] As such, the law relating to the prerogative can be seen as an only partially resolved struggle with the past, with the prerogative form still retaining some of its 'singular and eccentrical' character.[102] Sometimes, as in *Bancoult (No. 2)*, the musty quality of the prerogative helps shroud the arcane mysteries of state in a form that still manages to be only semi-pervious to norms of legality.

Developments within the law relating to prerogative give a more detailed and intricate example of the dynamics of reason of state and rule of law described in more general terms in this book. The empire of law advances through the normalization of aberrant forms of power and authority. The prerogative is enclosed ever more closely in a surrounding belt of law and, in that process, ancient meets modern and is (at least partially) revised. Called upon to take stock, update and revise in this way, judges have the opportunity to make explicit what has previously been implicit or obscured. This process is unquestionably an advance, certainly from the perspective of the rule of law, not least because it serves to clarify, however imperfectly, the relationship between constitutional principle and governmental practice as it operates at the margins of legitimate state action. But just because an area becomes more amenable to judicial oversight it does not necessarily follow that the underlying problem is solved. The juridical situation might be clearer, but what was a hard case remains a hard case, the reason of state questions it raises still likely to prove difficult to resolve.

Trade

Commerce is such a pervasive feature of the modern world that it is hard to imagine that it was once a questionable activity that fell within the sphere of the king's prerogative.[103] The unpredictable exercise of that royal trading monopoly was a significant factor in the instability of the Stuart constitution,[104] and the success of the post-1689 regime owed much to its

[101] See, e.g., *R v Secretary of State for Foreign and Commonwealth Affairs, ex parte Everett* [1988] EWCA Civ 7; *R v Secretary of State for Foreign and Commonwealth Affairs, ex parte Rees Mogg* [1993] EWHC 4 (Admin); *Ex parte Molyneaux* [1986] 1 WLR 331. In the *GCHQ* case too the applicants lost.

[102] Blackstone, *Commentaries* I.VII, 232.

[103] See, e.g., *East India Company v Sandys* (1683), discussed in Chapter 5.

[104] Robert Brenner, *Merchants and Revolution: Commercial Change, Political Conflict, and London's Overseas Traders, 1550–1653* (London: Verso, 2003).

capacity to regularize this zone of activity.[105] Even today, the constitutional dimensions of trade and trade politics are sometimes visible, occasionally vividly so as in recent examples of emergency legislation granting exceptional powers to executives and central banks after the global economic collapse of 2007–2008.[106] Our focus here is the specific case of *R (Corner House Research) v Director of the Serious Fraud Office*.[107] The case arose from a Serious Fraud Office investigation into allegations that British Aerospace had bribed Saudi Arabian officials while negotiating a sale of aircraft. The Saudi government asked for the investigation to be halted, issuing what Lord Bingham described in the case as an 'ugly threat' that if it were not it would result in 'Saudi Arabia withdrawing its cooperation with the UK in countering terrorism'.[108] After considering the views of the British ambassador to Saudi Arabia, the Prime Minister, the Foreign Secretary and the Defence Secretary, the Director of the SFO stopped the investigation, a decision challenged in court by an NGO, Corner House. The House of Lords held that the risk to British lives and national security was a relevant consideration in the exercise of the Director's discretion, and that it was lawful for the Director to defer to the government on the nature of the risk.

Reason of state pervades the judgement. Lord Bingham referred to a 'personal minute' from the Prime Minister to the Attorney General (the SFO Director's superior) noting that 'higher considerations were at stake'.[109] The withdrawal of Saudi security cooperation meant that there would be 'a real threat to British lives'.[110] The judges were content to categorize the case accordingly, as something that was 'wholly exceptional'.[111] The case is not about prerogative in the strict sense – it deals with an exercise of statutory discretion – but it breathes the same rarified air as cases like *Bancoult*. There is a concentration of decision-making power in a handful of individuals and a related personalization of those

[105] Steve Pincus, 'From Holy Cause to Economic Interest: The Study of Population and the Invention of the State' in Alan Houston and Steve Pincus (eds.), *A Nation Transformed: England after the Restoration* (Cambridge: Cambridge University Press, 2001).

[106] See, e.g., Julia Black, 'Paradoxes and Failures: New Governance Techniques and the Financial Crisis' (2012) 75 *Modern Law Review* 1037; Posner and Vermeule, *The Executive Unbound*, 37–41; Teubner, 'A Constitutional Moment?'; Mark Aronson, 'The Great Depression, This Depression and Administrative Law' (2009) 37 *Federal Law Review* 165.

[107] [2008] UKHL 60. [108] [2008] UKHL 60 [41] and [20].

[109] [2008] UKHL 60 [17] and [18].

[110] [2008] UKHL 60 [20]. [111] [2008] UKHL 60 [40].

decision-makers. The judgments explore the machinations of an inner circle, including the Prime Minister, various ambassadors and the most senior law officers in the country. There is also the use of a standard reason of state vocabulary – interest, exception, risk, necessity. *Corner House* is transparent in the way that *Bancoult* was cluttered – its central claim that considerations of (state) interest should take priority over the normal course of justice (rule of law) is particularly clear. That claim the Law Lords accept, agreeing that a trade-off between interest and justice was probably necessary in this instance and also that it was really up to others to decide this.[112] But they do so not without a little hand-wringing about man's fallen state: 'I would wish that the world were a better place where honest and conscientious public servants were not put in impossible situations such as this.'[113]

Critics are quick to point out the naivety of the Law Lords' belief that *Corner House* was and would remain a 'wholly exceptional' case. They observe that on the contrary something like a *Corner House* doctrine has emerged: the argument 'that threats by another state to UK security form an important policy consideration which public authorities are entitled to take into consideration in their decision making, has seen further service in the current security climate'.[114] That is, *Corner House* shows how making threats against UK security can work. If true, this provides an excellent example of the risks a court runs when deciding cases in this area. From the analytical perspective, *Corner House* might be seen as in a very particular sense a true case of the 'exception'. No change in the law was being requested, just a suspension of the operation of the law on reason of state grounds. However, it remains the case that the court is asked to review that suspension. As such, it is consistent with the general observations of this chapter, which sees some second-best value in having judicial explication of at the very least the minimal reasons why the matter is

112 [2008] UKHL 60 [23]: 'In cases touching on foreign relations and national security the duty of decision on the merits lay with the Government, and the courts were obliged to maintain the boundary between their role and that of the Government.' See also *Secretary of State for the Home Department v Rehman* [2001] UKHL 47 [63].

113 [2001] UKHL 47 [57].

114 Murray, 'Out of the Shadows', 219, referring to *Lord Carlile v Secretary of State for the Home Department* [2012] EWHC 617 (Admin). See also Adam Tomkins, 'National Security and the Due Process of Law' (2011) 64 *Current Legal Problems* 215. The issue of security arrangements was also central to argument in R (*Binyam Mohamed) v Secretary of State for Foreign and Commonwealth Affairs* [2010] EWCA Civ 65, although there the court took rather a different line. But see *R (Omar) v Secretary of State for Foreign and Commonwealth Affairs* [2012] EWCA Civ 118.

political and thus for the executive. The trade-off between interest (reason of state) and justice (rule of law) is clear. We have spoken of the benefits that accrue from the advance of the rule of law. But these gains can have a cost. The more the belt of law tightens around decision-makers and the more frequently 'reason of state' decisions come to court, the more judges will be required either to make or approve trade-offs of this sort. As 'exceptional' cases become more common, the second reason that the Law Lords gave in *Corner House* – that it is really up to others to decide this question – looks increasingly less convincing. Not getting judicial hands dirty becomes an unviable strategy.

Diplomacy

Diplomacy can be seen as a 'standing' or normalized reason of state practice. It unquestionably forms part of the basic tasks of government. It is an area certainly not devoid of or sparse with law but is on the contrary structured and conditioned by established bodies of domestic and international law.[115] But it is also liminal, operating in the space between the ordinary and internal, to which constitutional principles might be said to attach in a relatively uncomplicated way, and the exceptional and external, which always remain at least somewhat outside the grasp of those ordinary principles. Seen in these terms, diplomacy provides a particularly good example of the complexities of interaction over time between reason of state and rule of law. It also provides a particularly illuminating setting for evaluating claims for the extension of human rights and the rule of law into all areas of governmental practice.

Recent cases arising from the turbulent international situation that existed after the 9/11 terrorist attacks have raised the question of the amenability of diplomatic matters to judicial review. In one sense, then, this area provides another example of the trend already noted towards infiltrating what were previously no-go zones with rule-of-law principles. *R (Abbasi) v Secretary of State for Foreign and Commonwealth Affairs* concerned a British national captured by US forces in Afghanistan. In January 2002, he was transported to Guantanamo Bay in Cuba, a naval base on territory held by the United States on long lease pursuant to a

[115] Gerry Simpson, 'International Law in Diplomatic History' in James Crawford and Martti Koskenniemi (eds.), *Cambridge Companion to International Law* (Cambridge: Cambridge University Press, 2012); Tom Farer, 'Diplomacy and International Law' in Andrew Cooper, Jorge Hein and Ramesh Thakur (eds.), *The Oxford Handbook of Modern Diplomacy* (Oxford: Oxford University Press, 2013).

treaty with Cuba. By the time his case reached the British courts he had been held captive for eight months without access to a court or any other form of tribunal or even to a lawyer. His mother brought a case on his behalf contending that one of his fundamental human rights, the right not to be arbitrarily detained, was being infringed. She asked the court to compel the Foreign Office to make representations on his behalf to the US government or to take other appropriate action or at least to give an explanation as to why this has not been done. The situation had an additional layer of complexity since at the time US courts had shown no willingness to exercise supervisory control of activities in Guantanamo Bay, opening up the charge that they were operating a legal black hole, a criticism to which some senior British judges had already lent their voice.[116]

In *Abbasi*, Lord Phillips described the US detention policy as 'objectionable', a position emboldened by the criticism made outside the court. But the court faced a formidable line of authority supporting the government's case that decisions taken by the executive in its dealings with foreign states regarding the protection of British citizens abroad are non-justiciable.[117] Even the judges in the *GCHQ* case, which opened the door to the review of the exercise of prerogative functions, had said that the foreign affairs prerogative remained out of bounds. Despite this body of precedent, the court managed to carve out a justiciable interest that it was in principle capable of protecting. It identified a 'normal expectation of every citizen' that 'if subjected abroad to a violation of a fundamental right, the British Government will not simply wash their hands of the matter and abandon him to his fate'.[118] *Abbasi* can be read, then, as a particularly creative example of the trend towards judicialization, the rolling back of at least the stronger claims made on behalf of prerogative.

But what remedy did this juridically novel approach deliver? In principle, the court was willing to impose a (weak) duty on government to 'consider' making representations to the US authorities. The court was clear, though, that the decision about whether to make any representations in a particular case, and if so in what form, was 'left entirely to the discretion of the Secretary of State' and that the judgement did not in any substantial way make incursions into the foreign policy prerogative. 'The Secretary of State must be free to give full weight to foreign policy considerations,

[116] Johan Steyn, 'Guantanamo Bay: The Legal Black Hole' (2004) 53 *International and Comparative Law Quarterly* 1.

[117] See, e.g., *British Airways v Laker Airways* [1985] AC 58.

[118] *R (Abbasi) v Secretary of State for Foreign and Commonwealth Affairs* [2002] EWCA Civ 1598, [98].

which are not justiciable.'[119] In practice, the court issued no such order. Satisfied that it had made clear its 'deep concern' with US indefinite detention policy, the court denied the applicant's claim to relief essentially on the ground that the Foreign Office had already considered Mr Abbasi's request for assistance, thereby fulfilling the obligation that the court might otherwise have imposed. But, in addition, the court said that it would not be appropriate to order the Secretary of State to make any specific representations to the United States, even where fundamental rights were being breached. Such an order, particularly coming at a 'delicate time', it said, 'would have an impact on the conduct of foreign policy'.[120]

So what does this decision amount to? Uncharitably interpreted, the case can be interpreted as a particularly inept example of judicial politics. The court was eager to criticize US practice in this area, but incapable of going beyond that criticism to identify a remedy or order that had even the strength of a declaration, traditionally the weakest weapon in the judicial arsenal. Rather more charitably, we might view the judgment as a sincere attempt on the part of the court to enter a complex zone where the ordinary law – understood here as the principles applied by the courts in domestic judicial review – had not previously applied. Even on this reading, though, the case indicates that diplomacy and foreign affairs is at best only partially amenable to ordinary legal principles. We can certainly imagine and might even welcome juridical developments that extend the scope of judicial supervision of activities that fall within this zone.[121] But even if a court thought itself able to issue an order to government in relation to such matters, there is little means of enforcing it. Foreign affairs and diplomacy are destined to remain at best a partially juridified practice.

Emergency

We finish with the seminal English case of the human rights era, *A v Secretary of State for the Home Department* – the *Belmarsh* case.[122] The

[119] *Abbasi* [99].

[120] *Abbasi* [107]. Parallel cases in other jurisdictions include *Hicks v Ruddock* [2007] FCA 299 (Federal Court of Australia); *Smith v Canada* [2010] 1 FCR 3 (Federal Court of Canada); *Kaunda v President of the Republic* of South Africa (2005) South African Law Reports 235.

[121] See, e.g., *R (Al Rawi) v Secretary of State for Foreign and Commonwealth Affairs* [2006] EWCA Civ 1279; *Rahmatullah v Secretary of State for Foreign and Commonwealth Affairs* [2012] UKSC 48.

[122] *A v Secretary of State for the Home Department* [2004] UKHL 56.

case ruled that a key part of the government's post-9/11 terrorism policy violated fundamental rights. It was brought by a number of foreign nationals who were detained without charge or trial as suspected terrorists under provisions of the Anti-Terrorism, Crime and Security Act 2001. The case addressed two issues. The first was whether the government's derogation from the European Convention in respect of the detention measures was lawful. Article 15 ECHR provides for a state to derogate from certain obligations in time of 'war or other public emergency threatening the life of the nation'. The government invoked this power in order to derogate from Article 5 (the right to liberty) in respect of the power to detain within the Act. The second issue was whether the statutory provisions under which the claimants had been detained were strictly necessary in order to deal with the emergency, as prescribed by Article 15. The claimants argued that the measures in question were disproportionate and discriminatory, and hence unlawful.

By an eight-to-one majority, the Law Lords quashed the derogation order and issued a declaration under the Human Rights Act 1998 to the effect that the detention provision in the 2001 Act was incompatible with the ECHR. The majority held that, while the decision whether there was 'public emergency threatening the life of the nation' was one only the government could take, the detention provision was not 'strictly required' by that emergency: it was disproportionate and discriminatory and hence unlawful. One of the judges who formed the majority, Lord Hoffmann, would have held the derogation order unlawful on the first ground that there was no 'war or other public emergency threatening the life of the nation' within the meaning of Article 15.

The case involves a collision between the rule of law and reason of state of a type that has become very familiar over the past decade or so. As such, many of its features are not surprising – the dramatic and normatively freighted scenario involving claims of liminal legality, questions involving the acceptability of differential treatment of the foreigner or legal 'other', the need to wrestle with the past in the juridical construction of the present. The irritant capacity of reason of state pressing judges to reassess and restate constitutional fundamentals is very much in evidence. Lord Hoffmann's short judgment provides perhaps the clearest example. While overwrought and overwritten – an unfortunate outburst of Anglo-Saxon parochialism, one commentator called it[123] – it

[123] David Dyzenhaus, 'An Unfortunate Outburst of Anglo-Saxon Parochialism' (2005) 68 *Modern Law Review* 673.

nonetheless attempts openly and boldly to update the stock of constitutional principle so that it fits the heightened normative expectations of the human rights age.

So much for the representative aspects of the *Belmarsh* case: what about its more distinctive features? One new dimension of the current generation of reason of state cases is how they take place under the shadow of international legal norms that give juridical shape and political ballast to the rule of law. The *Belmarsh* case simply doesn't make sense absent that background.[124] European human rights jurisprudence shaped the government's terrorism strategy, since the earlier *Chahal* case outlawed the simple strategy of deporting non-nationals suspected of terrorist involvement where there was real risk that they would suffer torture or inhuman and degrading treatment as a result.[125] The *Belmarsh* court proceeded along a reasoning process structured by the ECHR – derogation, 'public emergency', proportionality and discrimination. And its decision was reliant on the existing jurisprudence of the European Court of Human Rights on emergencies.[126] In turn, the Strasbourg Court later approved the *Belmarsh* decision.[127] Commentators agree that the path taken after 9/11 would almost certainly have been different but for the involvement of the Strasbourg Court.[128] More generally, these multi-layered legal dynamics can be seen as characteristic of the current stage of reason of state.[129]

The *Belmarsh* case continues to have a ripple effect on British constitutional politics,[130] not just within the security and terrorism context. Its most

[124] Sangeeta Shah, 'The UK's Anti-Terror Legislation and the House of Lords: The First Skirmish' (2005) 5 *Human Rights Law Review* 403.

[125] *Chahal v United Kingdom* (1996) 23 EHRR 413. For critical analysis of the influence of *Chahal* in this area of law and policy see David Campbell, 'The Threat of Terror and the Plausibility of Positivism' [2009] *Public Law* 501.

[126] See, e.g., *Lawless v Ireland*, 3 Eur. Ct. HR (ser. A) (1960–1961); *Brogan and Others v United Kingdom*, 145-B Eur. Ct. HR (ser. A) (1988); *Brannigan & McBride v United Kingdom*, 258 Eur. Ct. HR (ser. A) (1993); *Aksoy v Turkey*, 23 Eur. HR Rep. 553 (1996); *Sakik v Turkey*, 26 ECHR 662 (1998); *Demir v Turkey* (1998) ECHR 88.

[127] *A v United Kingdom* [2009] ECHR 301.

[128] See, e.g., Adam Tomkins, 'National Security and the Role of the Court: A Changed Landscape?' (2010) 126 *Law Quarterly Review* 534; K. D. Ewing, *Bonfire of the Liberties: New Labour, Human Rights, and the Rule of Law* (Oxford: Oxford University Press, 2010).

[129] See, e.g., Gearty, *Liberty and Security*, Chapter 3.

[130] One particularly significant consequence of the decision was that the government began to argue that the court was obstructing the policy necessary to protect the nation from terrorist attack and, more broadly, most of the major political parties took a position against the Human Rights Act 1998 (or at least the way it was being applied in the terrorism context and certain other policy areas), and some questioned the United Kingdom's

direct consequence was the government's decision to replace the policy of internment with a control order regime.[131] That system of control, while not significantly more liberal than the one it replaced, is certainly more juridified – and to that extent more 'normal' – than its predecessor, not least because it involves judges in the process of control whereas the system it replaced sought to exclude judicial supervision. Unsurprisingly, the judges find their new role within an abnormal legal framework difficult.[132] The first control order cases to reach the House of Lords found the Law Lords in particularly confused mood.[133] The resulting lack of clarity necessitated an intervention from the Strasbourg Court[134] and a subsequent (and rather tetchy) clarificatory judgment from Britain's highest court.[135]

Another area of legal action relates to the government's revival of its strategy of deporting non-nationals suspected of involvement in terrorism, working through the framework established in *Chahal*, through the use of 'memoranda of understanding' with receiving states.[136] But a more general feature of the recent cases is secrecy, which now operates almost

participation within the ECHR system. See Prime Minister Tony Blair's the 'rules of the game are changing' speech, delivered a month after the 7/7 London bombings: 5 Aug. 2005. For analysis see Ian Loader, 'The Cultural Lives of Security and Rights' in B. Goold and L. Lazarus (eds.), *Security and Human Rights* (Oxford: Hart Publishing, 2007).

131 Prevention of Terrorism Act 2005. For commentary see Clive Walker, 'Keeping Control of Terrorists without Losing Control of Constitutionalism' (2007) 59 *Stanford Law Review* 1395. Control orders were subsequently replaced by 'TPIM' notices under the Terrorism Prevention and Investigation Measures Act 2011. TPIMs contain more by way of rule of law protections than control orders – less onerous restrictions; a 'reasonable belief' rather than 'suspicion' threshold; a two-year limit compared with control orders which were open-ended.

132 Gavin Phillipson and Helen Fenwick, 'Covert Derogations and Judicial Deference: Redefining Liberty and Due Process Rights in Couterterrorism Law and Beyond' (2011) 56 *McGill Law Journal* 863; Conor Gearty, *Can Human Rights Survive?* (Cambridge: Cambridge University Press, 2005), Chapter 4.

133 *Secretary of State for the Home Department v JJ* [2007] UKHL 45; *Secretary of State for the Home Department v MB* [2007] UKHL 46; *Secretary of State for the Home Department v E* [2007] UKHL 47. See also Thomas Poole, 'Courts and Conditions of Uncertainty in Times of Crisis' [2008] *Public Law* 234.

134 *A v UK*. Another stimulus to judges deciding cases in this area is unquestionably the extremely important and influential decision of the European Court of Justice in *Kadi and Al Barakaat International Foundation v Council and Commission* [2008] ECR I-6351.

135 *Secretary of State for the Home Department v AF (No. 3)* [2009] UKHL 28.

136 On the Deportation with Assurances scheme, see *RB (Algeria) v Sec of State for the Home Dept* [2009] UKHL 10; *Othman (Abu Qatada) v United Kingdom* [2012] ECHR 56; *W (Algeria) and BB (Algeria) v Secretary of State for the Home Department* [2012] UKSC 8. On asset freezing see *Mohammed Jabar Ahmed* [2010] UKSC 2, where the international law dimensions so important in the context are manifest.

as a second front in the post-9/11 national security debate. In a sense, this is nothing new. After all, secrecy has always been a central aspect of reason of state politics – *arcana imperii* and all that. But the specific argument about the role of special advocates in control order cases – who are not allowed to interact with those subject to control orders on whose part they argue in court – has spilt over into a wider debate about the suitability of secret justice ('closed material proceedings') in cases where national security is at stake.[137] Once again, the arguments about the legitimacy of particular exceptions have been extended into more general (and so apparently more 'normal') exceptional practices. The key 'normalizing' measure is the Justice and Security Act 2013, which requires courts to consider using closed material proceedings where there is a risk that sensitive material would be disclosed in the course of the proceedings.[138] The effect of using a Closed Material Procedure (CMP) is to allow the court to consider sensitive material without it being disclosed to the other party in the case.

Lawyers and other commentators are critical of these developments, seeing them as at odds with basic rule-of-law guarantees. An inconvenient truth, however, is that developments of this sort are a natural consequence of *Belmarsh* and similar cases. There exists an internal relationship between human rights law, on one hand, and exceptionalism and secrecy, on the other. *Belmarsh* and its progeny show the effects of rights-based litigation in the context of government drive to increase security. First, rights judicialize. They make it more likely that cases come to court, and once there put pressure on the court to take seriously the liberty interests implicated. Second, rights either contain strict minimum standards or else generate them through litigation. The precise dynamics depend on your analysis of the way rights jurisprudence develops, but that question need not delay us here.[139] The effect of this is that rights-based public law is less fluid and also probably less ambiguous in its outcomes than the classic judicial review tests of legality, procedural fairness and unreasonableness. Third, the spiralling litigation since *Belmarsh* shows how these

[137] See, e.g., *Binyam Mohamed*; *Al Rawi v The Security Service* [2011] UKSC 34; See also *Tariq v Home Office* [2011] UKSC 35; *Bank Mellat v Her Majesty's Treasury (No. 1)* [2013] UKSC 38; *Bank Mellat v Her Majesty's Treasure (No. 2)* [2013] UKSC 39.

[138] Justice and Security Act 2013, Part II, s. 6.

[139] For contrasting perspectives on this question see Kai Möller, 'Proportionality and Rights Inflation' and Grégoire Webber, 'On the Loss of Rights', both in Grant Huscroft, Bradley W. Miller and Grégoire Webber (eds.), *Proportionality and the Rule of Law: Rights, Justification, Reasoning* (Oxford: Oxford University Press, 2014).

situations should be read as ongoing or sequential scenarios. The government that loses an important case on rights and security is not necessarily going to throw in the towel. It is just as likely to look for other ways of securing its objectives. In the post-*Belmarsh* scenario this includes both the move towards more secrecy and towards deportation.[140] The ensuing cases are themselves subject to the first and second points – judicialization and strict minima – as well as the decisions in previous cases.

Reason of state in our time

The cases examined in the last section are significant in their own right. But their inclusion here is designed to reinforce the contention that reason of state provides an important and useful category of analysis. Reason of state offers a conceptually and historically rich framework in which to capture and make sense of themes that connect and animate what can otherwise appear diverse cases or scenarios. But even if we accept this contention, it may not be enough to see off the Rawlsian challenge. We can interpret that challenge in the following way. Granted reason of state is a feature of the recent jurisprudence, perhaps an increasingly important one. But so what? This might just be an indication of the imperfections of the current constitution. We should really be working towards a constitution in which reason of state as such plays no part, save in war or real emergency.

One problem with this argument is that it misses or misreads so much of importance. As such, it is seriously deficient if it aspires to provide a normative map of constitution politics. Like the Marxist who thinks the state will wither away after the Revolution, this type of liberal hopes that reason of state will disappear with liberalism's triumph. But as I tried to show earlier, the issues that now arise are to a significant extent the *consequence* of a move towards liberal constitutionalism, given certain facts about the modern world. More liberalism does not eradicate reason of state, although it may channel it and even to a degree transform it. Reason of state concerns resurface perhaps in a different – and often more

[140] There has also been a shift towards exclusion from the UK of individuals who have gone overseas allegedly to take part in violent conflicts or who would represent a threat to the UK on return. Strategically, this negates the need to 'gist' the evidence for the decision where there is no Art. 5 ECHR liberty interest at stake. It correlates with a decline in the use of TPIMs and control orders, and is linked to Chapter 2 of the Counter-Terrorism and Security Act 2015 which allows for 'temporary exclusion orders' and 'managed return'.

juridical – form. A study of the cases helps to confirm this impression. Reason of state is a gathering trend rather than a diminishing one, a trend that is consonant with a hardening of the constitutional politics of rights and risk. So, even if a state were to model itself on pure Rawlsian principles it would continue to face reason of state questions. Unless it cuts itself off from the world – an impossible manoeuvre for such a state[141] – it would still have to engage with other polities, including less perfectly liberal and illiberal states. But what is diplomacy, as I argued in relation to the *Abbasi* case, if it is not a 'standing' or normalized reason of state practice to which pure liberal principles can only at most partially apply?

Note that the rise in reason of state in the modern liberal state is not simply a result of supposedly activist courts or the activities of litigation-minded NGOs. The causes are structural, the point when stripped of its dyspepsia being essentially the one that we saw Oakeshott make in the previous chapter. Like it or not – and Oakeshott did not – the modern state is a concept made of two practices of association that are at variance with each other. The state is a framework of rules (*societas*) but it is also an actor, a manager of forces and populations (*universitas*). The post-war constitution certainly reinforced the *societas* side of the state, bolstering the normative state at the expense of the prerogative.[142] But it did not by any means eradicate the state's *universitas* features. (Oakeshott would accept that it probably couldn't.) In fact, some of the *universitas* dimensions of the state were *increased* after the war. 'The post-war state across Europe was a "social state"', Tony Judt writes, 'with implicit (and often constitutionally explicit) responsibility for the well-being of its citizens.' As such, it aimed to match Mill's prescription that the criterion of good government is (ordered) progress.[143] 'It had an obligation to provide not only the institutions and services necessary for a well-regulated, safe and prosperous land, but also to improve the condition of the population.'[144]

Judt's analysis of the ambitions of the post-war constitution is instructive. For what is at issue in modern reason of state cases is a competition

[141] And one that Rawls himself, of course, rejected: see his *Law of Peoples* (Cambridge, MA: Harvard University Press, 2001).

[142] The conceptual structure relates to Ernst Fraenkel's *The Dual State: A Contribution to the Theory of Dictatorship* (New York: Oxford University Press, trans E. A. Shills, 1941), discussed in Chapter 7.

[143] J. S. Mill, 'Considerations on Representative Government' in Mill, *On Liberty and Other Essays* (Oxford: Oxford University Press, ed. John Gray, 1991), 218–222.

[144] Judt, *Postwar*, 77.

between two understandings of what constitutes the health and well-being of the people – or *salus populi* – or rather of which understanding ought to apply (more) in a given situation. We start with the proposition that the state exists for the well-being of its people – the principle which acts, as it were, as the *Grundnorm* of the concept of the post-war constitution. But how is so capacious a responsibility to be actualized? Well, in the first instance, through the conceptual and practical structures of the post-war *Rechtsstaat*, at the heart of which is inscribed the idea that the state is a thoroughly legal construction. The potential arbitrariness of state power is reduced formally through the legal construction of the state. Officials are entitled to exercise only those powers that law prescribes and in the manner that law allows. But arbitrariness is also reduced informally through democratic constraints that require officials to justify policies in terms of common considerations. Both sets of constraints are enforced through a battery of checking and deliberative mechanisms and institutions – Parliament, the courts, public inquiries, the press, even public protest – designed to impose a regime of transparency and deliberation on decision-makers. With reference to Hobbes and his fashioning of the state on the model of the Judge,[145] we might call this the state acting in the persona of *iudex*, as purveyor of justice or arbitrator.[146]

However, the health and well-being of a population may also require in some instances that these constitutional and democratic constraints are bypassed or truncated. The argument can be made on paternalist grounds. That was the basis of the historic claim made on behalf of the royal prerogative.[147] But in the modern era it tends to be made as an ancillary of the first principle of state noted above, that is, the idea of *salus populi* given a liberal gloss. Well-being is in general best served through a government structured through laws and ordered so as to act in the public interest and

[145] *Leviathan* – see chapter 10, pp. 32–33.

[146] The idea of the state as being the function of the personality or personalities it adopts – or the functions it performs – is a familiar one in political and constitutional theory. The origins lie in the classical theatre, the Latin 'persona', evolved from the Greek *prosōpon*, which originally signified a mask worn by an actor upon the stage. But its use as a political idea can be traced back to Hobbes on personation (*Leviathan*, chapter 16) and, through him, to Cicero's translation of the idea of personality from theatre to the tribunal. See Runciman, *Pluralism and the Personality of the State*, chapter 11.

[147] See, e.g., Robert Filmer, *Patriarcha* (Cambridge: Cambridge University Press, ed. Johann P. Somerville, 1991), 43: 'the laws in many cases give the king a prerogative above common persons'; 129: 'No man holds any lands but under a condition to defend the realm. And upon the selfsame ground also the king's prerogative is raised, as being a preeminence in cases of necessity above and before the law of property, or inheritance.'

non-arbitrarily in respect of individuals and groups within the population. But that order will be compromised if it is not made secure. In fact, the more we value the existing constitutional order, the greater the incentive to protect it. And if we really value what we have, then protection cannot be, as Hayek argued, reserved for war or serious emergency. The speed, variety and insidious nature of the potential threats to the constitutional order are such as to require significant and ongoing attention from designated state agencies. Unfortunately, the question about whether and to what extent to use 'exceptional' legal and political channels cannot be judged on a case-by-case basis through normal democratic and constitutional processes. There is certainly scope for wider institutional and popular input when framing the legal landscape in which these exceptional agencies operate, especially at so-called constitutional moments. But when it comes to deciding how to proceed in particular cases, about when and to what extent 'normal' constitutional and democratic conditions apply, logically it can be a matter only for those state agencies that have been granted the capacity to work within the exceptional category. This means above all the executive, which inhabits a nodal point between both the normal and the exceptional constitutional structure. With what is I hope a very faint echo of Carl Schmitt, we can call this the state acting in the persona of *custos*, that is, as guardian or protector.[148]

Some contemporary liberals make it too easy for themselves by denying almost outright the validity of the second conception. In doing so they overlook the fact that at least on its best formulation it derives from the same foundation as the first, namely, a liberal and constitutionalist understanding of *salus populi*. The importance of the modern rendering of reason of state as a juridical concept lies in its potential to mediate between these two personas of state. It accepts the existence of an exceptional domain that is necessarily part of the stable ordering of the state. In so doing it recognizes the state in its persona of *custos*. To this extent it is a descendant of older traditions of *raison d'état* and *Staatsraison*. But the emphasis on the *reason* of reason of state that modern constitutionalism requires allows us to insist that even in these more exceptional contexts the basic reasoning and justification obligations on those who exercise state power are not obviated. In so doing it recognizes the state in

[148] Carl Schmitt, 'The Guardian of the Constitution' in Lars Vinx (ed.), *The Guardian of the Constitution: Hans Kelsen and Carl Schmitt on the Limits of Constitutional Law* (Cambridge: Cambridge University Press, 2015). Note that holding out this model as one of two dominant conceptions of reason of state does not commit me to a thoroughly unmodern doctrine of the real group personality of the state.

its persona of *iudex*. The difficulty with reason of state matters, and what makes them when translated into legal claims such hard cases, relates precisely to the all but intractable nature of the conceptual and practical difficulty of trying to navigate between these two different positions.

What does the modern idea of reason of state entail in practice? The main fear from the perspective of the liberal constitution is that the state as *custos* will cannibalize the normative state, an indicator of which would be the declension of *reason* of state into princely prerogative or *raison d'état*, now no doubt run through bureaucracies but in the interests of a governing elite. So the old question resurfaces: *quis custodiet ipsos custodes*? David Hume wrote that a wise man proportions his belief to the evidence. The more improbable something seems, the more proof is required. 'Suppose, for instance, that the fact, which the testimony endeavours to establish, partakes of the extraordinary and the marvellous; in that case, the evidence, resulting from the testimony, admits of a diminution, greater or less, in proportion as the fact is more or less unusual.'[149] Exceptional claims, in other words, require exceptional evidence. This can mean two rather different things. It can mean, as in Hume's original argument about miracles, that claims that appear implausible or abnormal need very strong evidence to support them. But it can also mean that abnormal claims require a procedure for testing them that is equally at variance from the norm.

Both meanings are relevant when considering the practice of modern reason of state. The starting point must be that reason of state arguments are exceptional claims and should be subject to exceptional scrutiny. This position generates two principles. The first is that reason of state should be subject to the most rigorous scrutiny possible, using the normal formal (legal) and informal (democratic) constraints whenever possible. But it also entails that where this is not possible second-best mechanisms are used to provide the best scrutiny possible in the circumstances.[150] To halt the declension from modern reason of state properly so called to a bureaucratic *raison d'état*, we need to generate or reinforce existing strategies of the kind described by Christian List and Philip Pettit in their recent study of group agency.[151] To function well, they argue, a group agent like the state must form true rather than false beliefs about the world (the

[149] David Hume, *An Enquiry Concerning Human Understanding* (Cambridge: Cambridge University Press, ed. Stephen Buckle, 2007), 10.8, p. 99.

[150] For an analysis and defence of second-best mechanisms in the constitutional context see Adrian Vermeule, *Judging under Uncertainty: An Institutional Theory of Legal Interpretation* (Cambridge, MA: Harvard University Press, 2006).

[151] Christian List and Philip Pettit, *Group Agency: The Possibility, Design, and Status of Corporate Agents* (Oxford: Oxford University Press, 2011).

'epistemic desideratum'). It should be able to cope with its members' tendencies to act strategically and self-interestedly when the opportunity arises (the 'incentive-compatibility desideratum'). And it should be organized in such a way as to respect its members' rights and freedoms (the 'control desideratum').

The first and third (epistemic and control) requirements are especially important for our purposes. Three principles of organizational design may be beneficial in helping the group agent fulfil the epistemic requirement, which the authors call democratization, decomposition and decentralization.[152] Democratization is the application of the 'many minds' principle – the idea that many minds are typically better than one or a few at reaching accurate decisions[153] – to the question of group agency; decomposition the idea that there may be gains from splitting a larger judgemental task into several smaller ones such as making judgements on certain relevant premises; and decentralization relates to the 'division of cognitive labour' – dividing a large task among several subgroups each with a different skill set or specialism. Now, of course, the modern state does not operate in the image of the prince and his Privy Council. So strategies of democratization, decomposition and decentralization already occur to an extent *inside* the executive.[154] Even so, the democratization argument pushes towards greater institutional involvement in reason of state matters. Such a move widens the number of 'minds' that are brought to bear on those questions and brings greater transparency, both of which are usually thought to translate into epistemic gains. (Although unusually complicated trade-offs exist between secrecy and transparency in the reason of state context that may affect an otherwise straightforward equation,[155] on which more shortly.)

The decomposition and decentralization principles pull in a similar direction. We are often told how tough it is to arrive at judgements on reason of state matters. But the tougher the problem, the more valuable the disaggregation of judgement and the division of cognitive labour should be. We accept this idea readily in other contexts. Indeed, one reason we

[152] *Group Agency*, 87.

[153] For elaboration in the constitutional context see Cass R. Sunstein, *A Constitution of Many Minds: Why the Founding Document Doesn't Mean What it Meant Before* (Princeton: Princeton University Press, 2009).

[154] A point effectively brought out in Posner and Vermeule, *The Executive Unbound*. See also the same authors' *Terror in the Balance: Security, Liberty, and the Courts* (New York: Oxford University Press, 2007).

[155] A parallel can be drawn here with the inter-war debate on the virtues or otherwise of 'secret diplomacy': Black, *History of Diplomacy*, Chapter 6.

have a hierarchy of courts – often multi-member especially nearer the apex – staffed by adjudicators expert in law and supported by strong norms of judicial independence is because we see value in disaggregating complex social and moral questions and from involving different types of decision-makers in resolving them.[156] It is difficult to see why the hard cases that arise under the umbrella of reason of state should be immune from these techniques.[157] The legislature has special strengths when it comes to transparency and deliberation.[158] The court brings different virtues into play. First, it is capable of giving special attention to the impact of a policy on individual rights and interests.[159] Second, as a reviewing body that reacts to the petitions of litigants as and when they arise, the timing of its input is often quite different from that of other institutions.[160] Judicial review in the area of reason of state is almost certainly less adept at judging risk than, say, specialist agencies reporting to the executive.[161] But it can nonetheless be justified on the basis that it performs more effectively than competing institutions[162] a role in formulating strategy on reason of state matters that is consistent with the state's duty to provide security for its citizens in a way that does not infringe basic freedoms.

The control requirement is equally important. Controlling a group agent so that its individual members retain certain 'spheres of control' is a particularly problematic endeavour. The requirements for a group agent to act as an agent,[163] List and Pettit show, are incompatible with the maintenance of a sphere of control (in a strong sense) for individual members of the group.[164] This is particularly problematic in what is an

156 Indeed, one might press the point further and argue that disaggregation is a standard, perhaps even *the* standard, technique in legal argument and judgement-giving.

157 But see, e.g., Hirschl, 'The Judicialization of Mega-Politics and the Rise of Political Courts', which criticizes the trend towards a 'third level of judicialization' in which courts increasingly attempt to settle 'core political controversies that define the boundaries of the collective or cut through the heart of entire nations' (at p. 98).

158 Waldron, *Law and Disagreement*.

159 See, e.g., T. R. S. Allan, *The Sovereignty of Law: Freedom, Constitution, and Common Law* (Oxford: Oxford University Press, 2013), Chapter 8.

160 David Dyzenhaus, *The Constitution of Law: Legality in a Time of Emergency* (Cambridge: Cambridge University Press, 2006).

161 Compare the unconvincing case made on behalf of the courts as more able risk managers in David Feldman, 'Human Rights, Terrorism and Risk: The Roles of Politicians and Judges' [2006] *Public Law* 364.

162 Such as the Independent Reviewer of Terrorism Legislation in Britain, for instance.

163 Specifically, the 'robust rationality requirement'.

164 See also Franz Dietrich and Christian List, 'Judgment Aggregation without Full Rationality' (2008) 31 *Social Choice and Welfare* 15, building on Amartya Sen, 'The Impossibility of a Peretian Liberal' (1970) 78 *Journal of Political Economy* 152.

effectively non-voluntary group agent like the state. In practice, democratic constitutions seek to reduce arbitrary state action through a familiar battery of techniques, including the separation and sharing of powers among different authorities, as described above. The control requirement enjoins the state to make itself contestable by its citizens, individually and collectively, by providing 'means for holding government accountable against the standard of mutually acceptable reasons that can be generated and sustained in popular deliberation'. This is necessarily an inexact operation – aligning state action to members' attitudes while ensuring that they retain rights and freedom calls for 'a dynamic, continuing exercise of identifying and reconciling individual spheres of control'.[165] The task involves making continual adjustments and compromises not just vertically, as between the state and its citizens (individually and collectively), but also horizontally among or across citizens. My attitude (e.g., on security matters) may vary according to what strategy the government adopts in relation to other citizens or groups of citizens (e.g., suspected terrorists).

Let us bring these observations down to earth by applying them to at least one of our case studies. In *Belmarsh*, the court was called upon to decide whether a new terrorism policy accorded with the public laws that generate the authority (agency) of the state. The public manner of deliberation can be seen as a transparency gain in that it enabled a fuller understanding of the trade-offs at stake between liberty and security – all the more so given that the area had previously been seen as something of a legal black hole, in relation to which judicial oversight was restricted.[166] The questions the court asked itself related to but were distinct from the questions addressed by other institutions. The court drilled down on the impact that the policy had on the rights and freedoms of those subject to it with a view to deciding whether a permissible reason of state had been shown such as would justify what otherwise amounted to the infringement of basic constitutional guarantees.[167] The judgment thus fits the idea of the division of cognitive labour. It also reflects the control desideratum

[165] *Group Agency*, 148–149.

[166] In fact, more was arguably at stake. First, the basic orientation of the British constitutional landscape after the passing of the Human Rights Act 1998. Second, the idea that post-9/11 and -7/7, the rules of the (political, constitutional, legal) game were changing, as Prime Minister Tony Blair expressed in a famous speech (5 Aug. 2005).

[167] The additional dimension – and added importance – of *Belmarsh* stems from the fact that these foundational principles were arguably new, in that they had been introduced or restated (depending on your point of view) by the Human Rights Act 1998.

in that its concern was the protection of individuals[168] from arbitrary state action. Moreover, its outcome matches the understanding of control being an ongoing or 'dynamic and continuing' affair. The case resulted in what amounts to a call (through a declaration of incompatibility) for the government to recalibrate its reason of state argument and readjust the relationship between security and liberty in its terrorism policy.

Modern reason of state and the regression of sentiments

So far, we have a fairly rich but still insufficiently dynamic model of reason of state as a category capable of managing claims made by the state in its persona of *custos* when they clash with the requirements of the state understood as *iudex*. But there are two complicating factors. The first is that in practice much of the argument over reason of state takes place in what might be called the realm of the second best.[169] An ideal-typical scenario might involve a clean decision on the exception followed later by an equally clean reversion to the constitutional *status quo ante* after the emergency is over – the *Belmarsh* situation as understood by Lord Hoffmann perhaps, or the stereotypical model of dictatorship in the Roman Republic.[170] But things in political life do not come so neatly packaged, especially where reason of state is concerned. Far more typical are 'second best' scenarios in which a series of trade-offs take place between reason of state and the rule of law, a state of affairs that creates a lack of clarity about what precisely now constitutes norm and exception – what one might call the problem of the 'embedded exception'.

Since these situations still present juridically as exceptional carve-outs from the normal juridical structure of the state, justified on exceptional grounds, the requirement that exceptional claims be subject to exceptional proof stands. (In fact, one might plausibly argue that it applies with greater force given the capacity of the embedded exception to alter what

168 This is a somewhat problematic feature of the case. Since the aspect of the government's policy at issue impacted only on non-nationals, some argue that the rights and freedoms of the individual members of the relevant group (the British state) were not at issue. The case is made forcefully by Campbell, 'The Threat of Terror and the Plausibility of Positivism'. For a contrasting perspective see David Cole, *Enemy Aliens: Double Standards and Constitutional Freedoms* (New York: The New Press, 2003).

169 Vermeule, *Judging under Uncertainty*; 'Hume's Second Best Constitutionalism' (2003) 70 *Chicago Law Review* 421.

170 See, e.g., John Ferejohn and Pasquale Pasquino, 'The Law of the Exception: A Typology of Emergency Powers' (2004) 2 *International Journal of Constitutional Law* 210.

we consider the juridically normal.) It is in this context that the second version of Hume's dictum comes into its own – the idea that abnormal claims may require a procedure that is at variance from the norm. The initial decision on the exception is usually only the starting point. It may well be the case that institutions should look to create compensatory processes that are capable of realizing, although perhaps to an imperfect extent, the epistemic, incentive-compatibility and control objectives.

Consider in this light the series of cases decided after *Belmarsh*. We saw earlier how these became more intricate and involved as government and court engaged in a step-by-step contestation on a number of legal fronts. Now, the cases were not always consistent or clear.[171] So much so that the Law Lords let themselves be brought back into line by the European Court of Human Rights after their earlier decisions had caused confusion in the lower courts. But we can still model the cases in a stylized way as examples of the way in which the second Humean principle might work in practice. The result looks something like this. We (the court) have decided that you (the government) cannot have non-national terrorist suspects interned without trial (*Belmarsh*). But you *can* have control orders, so long as they do not infringe the right to liberty (*JJ*, *E*). If you absolutely cannot allow lawyers to act for terrorist suspects in the normal way for security reasons, then employ special advocates subject to restrictions on communications with the suspect whose interest they are charged to protect (*Chahal*, *MB*). And you must try to ensure that the special advocate arrangement works as closely as possible to the ideal of the lawyer-client relationship, ensuring in particular that the suspect knows the substance of the case against them (*AF (No. 3)*; *Tariq*). If you absolutely cannot have open court proceedings, then hold parts of those proceedings *in camera* – but no more than is strictly necessary (*Al Rawi*; *Bank Mellat*; the new cases on the Justice and Security Act cases).[172] If you have to deport non-national terrorist suspects, you can only do so to problematic receiving countries once there is a sufficiently strong and believable memorandum of understanding in place (*RB*; *Abu Qatada*; *W*).[173]

Admittedly, the fit between the model and post-*Belmarsh* reality is less than perfect. Arguably, one problem may have been that the courts in these cases did not stick strictly enough to our second Humean principle.

171 Tomkins, 'National Security and the Role of the Court'.

172 See, e.g., *CF v Ministry of Defence* [2014] EWHC 3171; *R (Ignaoua) v Secretary of State for the Home Department* [2013] EWCA Civ 1498; *CF v Ministry of Defence* [2014] EWHC 3171.

173 For an excellent summary by the former president of the Supreme Court see Nicholas Phillips, 'Closed Material', *London Review of Books*, 17 Apr. 2014.

If so, it serves as a reminder that this second principle (that abnormal situations may require abnormal techniques of oversight) works properly only if it operates in tandem with the first principle (that exceptional claims require very strong evidence). Although it can be hard to do so in practice, exceptional claims within an embedded exception scenario ought to remain exceptional claims. We should not be too harsh on the courts. These are extremely hard cases and their task of resolving them is not made any easier by the uncertainty that persists over the deep structure of the British constitution.[174] In particular we have not quite made up our minds whether Parliament should be understood in Austinian terms as an ultimate and unconstrained lawgiver or whether its authority should be understood in Burkean terms as a competent and supreme declarer of law whose judgement is ultimately circumscribed by a new kind of natural law.[175]

The second complication picks up on a wider point about constitutions and political order. We saw in earlier chapters how writers influenced by Hume, including Smith and Burke, tended to see law as a central part of a far greater moral and social enterprise. For Burke, society was a 'dense medium', a characteristic of which was the never entirely penetrable atmosphere of real-life relations.[176] A constitution relatedly was a 'system of opinion and sentiment' whose central feature was continuity across time.[177] Law on this account is both absolutely vital for a society's moral health and stability, while at the same time fragile in that it can have no beneficial integrative effect if divorced from public opinion and popular sentiment. The topic – in eighteenth-century terms, of law's relation to the progress of moral sentiments – has again risen to prominence,[178] no doubt

174 See, e.g., *Jackson v Attorney General* [2005] UKHL 56; *AXA General Insurance v The Lord Advocate* [2011] UKSC 46. For analysis see, e.g., Vernon Bogdanor, *The New British Constitution* (Oxford: Hart Publishing, 2009).

175 'Thoughts on the Cause of the Present Discontents', 169: 'We do not make laws. No; we do not contend for this power. We only declare law; and, as we are a tribunal both competent and supreme, what we declare to be law becomes law, although it should not have been so before.'

176 'Letter to a Member of the National Assembly', quoted in David Bromwich, *The Intellectual Life of Edmund Burke: From the Sublime and Beautiful to American Independence* (Cambridge, MA: Harvard University Press, 2014), 5.

177 Burke famously hymned the ancestral constitution in these terms as 'a partnership not only between those who are living, but between those who are living, those who are dead, and those who are to be born': *Reflections on the Revolution in France* (New Haven: Yale University Press, ed. Frank M. Turner, 2003), 82.

178 Indeed, Ronald Dworkin's theory of 'law as integrity' can be said to incorporate these Burkean cross-generational sentiments. See *Law's Empire* (London: Fontana, 1986).

due in large measure to the increasing demands placed on public law as an integrative mechanism.[179] A key finding within that body of scholarship really just reiterates the observations of Enlightenment authors. The following observation is representative: 'One claim that can be made with some conviction is that neither the technical brilliance of its design nor its efficacy as law offers much guidance on a constitution's integrative capacity. That quality rests not on a constitution's status as law but on its symbolic power. Its integrative capacity is a product of political culture.'[180]

Reason of state is a pre-eminent terrain of the regression of sentiments. Burke was always alive to this possibility. Indeed, as we saw in an earlier chapter, it lay at the heart of his critique of the impact of corrupt government in India on the British constitution and of the corrosive nature of the French Revolution on the European legal order. Early in his political career, long before the events of 1789 and before his engagement with Indian affairs, he wrote this on the subject of constitutional decay:

> When the people conceive that laws, and tribunals, and even popular assemblies, are perverted from the ends of their institution, they find in those names of degenerated establishments only new motives to discontent. Those bodies, which, when full of life and beauty, lay in their arms, and were their joy and comfort, when dead and putrid, become but the more loathsome from remembrance of former endearments. A sullen gloom, and furious disorder, prevail by fits: the nation loses its relish for peace and prosperity, as it did in that season of fullness which opened our troubles in the time of Charles the First.[181]

This passage contains a warning to governing institutions that they are all in it together. There is little to be gained in the long run from throwing mud at each other since they are not playing a zero-sum game. There is no likely winner in such a contest, as animosity between institutions is just as likely to engender a loss of respect for and attachment to the institutions of state as a whole. The pertinence of such a warning in the current political climate is apparent.[182]

179 See, e.g., Dieter Grimm, 'Integration by Constitution' (2005) 3 *International Journal of Constitutional Law* 193.

180 Martin Loughlin, 'The Constitutional Imagination' (2015) 78 *Modern Law Review* 1.

181 Edmund Burke, 'Thoughts on the Cause of the Present Discontents' in *Pre-Revolutionary Writings* (Cambridge: Cambridge University Press, ed. Ian Harris, 1993), 153.

182 A point recognized by the President of the Supreme Court, Lord Neuberger. In a series of interviews picking up on a tendency among politicians to criticize the courts and particular decisions that they make, he said: 'If we start attacking each other in public when each group was honestly trying to do its job, even if we don't agree with the way they're doing it, it does no credit either to the minister who's attacking or to the judge who is

But the passage is also and more broadly an eloquent reminder that a constitution is more than a bundle of norms. In Robert Cover's terms, a legal tradition is part and parcel of a complex normative world and includes 'not only a *corpus juris*, but also a language and a mythos – narratives in which the *corpus juris* is located by those whose wills act upon it'.[183] One might be tempted to apply Cover's analysis to the reason of state context by saying that nomos equates to the law that governs the modern state understood as *iudex*, whereas narrative tacks towards the community and identity claims that inform the state as *custos*. While there may be something in this characterization, it is nonetheless too simple. It is probably more accurate to think of *both* personas of state as comprising nomos and narrative – this at least is what the analysis in this book would suggest. Each may be said to have its own constitutive histories (narrative) as well as its own juridical and justificatory structure (nomos).

If this is right, then the current constitution of reason of state is a product of an iterative process involving the catalytically imaginative interplay of norm and exception. A corollary of this point is that the relationship between norm and exception that characterizes reason of state is not uniform across time and place. It is a mistake, Hans Lindahl argues, to imagine a pristine domain of the normal, unmediated by law, and which the norm simply follows, as constitutional normality is always to a greater or lesser degree the outcome of a process of (constitutional) normalization. What counts as the normal 'is never only *pre*-reflexive, such that norms would merely "follow" normality', but 'also always *post*-reflexive, in the sense of a normality that has come about and become consolidated as a result of the reiterated qualification and enforcement of legal behaviour. Normality is always already "contaminated" by a normativity that has been imposed on it.'[184] The Baroque dance between norm and exception from the *Belmarsh* case onwards is a good example of these dynamics in miniature. It is hard to say, after all, that either the norm or the exception is understood in precisely the same way as it was before. Indeed, we might go further and argue that the *Belmarsh* ruling itself helped to constitute a vision of what counted as constitutionally normal pre-*Belmarsh*.

being attacked. It's bad for both of us and I don't see what the benefit is.' (*Daily Telegraph*, 4 Mar. 2013).

[183] Robert Cover, 'Nomos and Narrative' in Martha Minnow, Michael Ryan and Austin Sarat (eds.), *Narrative, Violence, and the Law: The Essays of Robert Cover* (Ann Arbor: University of Michigan Press, 1995), 101.

[184] Hans Lindahl, in Dyzenhaus and Poole, *Law, Liberty and State*. See also Lindahl, *Fault Lines of Globalizaton: Legal Order and the Politics of A-Legality* (Oxford: Oxford University Press, 2013).

Similar dynamics are present on a much larger scale in the history of the constitution of empire, aspects of which formed a major part of this book. Here again we see the extended interplay between norm and exception. Consider the Hastings impeachment, a seminal moment in this story, where law, convention, ideology and interest collided with great force. While Hastings walked free, the trial was at least suggestive of legal limits to imperial rule. This in turn made it possible to claim that law had trumped prerogative and order at least notionally imposed on a state of exception. As Nicholas Dirks argues, the trial thus produced 'the conditions not just for empire's success but also for its transformation into a patriotic enterprise by allowing Burke a platform on which to make clear that empire was a sacred responsibility. Empire was no longer the province of unprincipled pirates, but rather an affair of state answerable to the nation.'[185] We can read back into that engagement the subsequent normalization of what was a previously liminal or potentially exceptional situation – a territorial and authoritarian empire – a situation that our own time would in turn judge to be exceptional.

Conclusion

Reason of state cannot be eliminated altogether or reserved for moments of real emergency. But it can be given greater legal specification and channelled through normal constitutional processes. That was the strategy that Hobbes in his own way and the republicans in theirs proposed. It was what the 1688 Settlement managed (in time) to achieve, as Hume showed, folding prerogative into a parliamentary constitution. Smith and Burke worried about how global trade and empire might unsettle the fragile balance that resulted between freedom and state power. And Mill subsumed it all under the head of 'Progress' and attempted to work out an institutional strategy for reconciling mass politics and liberty. Containing few absolute or non-negotiable elements, this way of proceeding belongs to the world of the second best. It rests on little more in the end than an institutional willingness to listen to reason – reason being understood not as an appeal to a transcendental standard but as immanent and unadorned,

[185] Nicholas B. Dirks, *The Scandal of Empire: India and the Creation of Imperial Britain* (Cambridge, MA: Harvard University Press, 2006), 125. See also James Epstein, *Scandal of Colonial Rule: Power and Subversion in the British Atlantic during the Age of Revolution* (Cambridge: Cambridge University Press, 2012), 72: 'Through the excoriation of Hastings and his coadjutors in Burke's theatre of the criminal sublime, empire could be put right and saved from itself, and Britain restored to national virtue.'

pertaining to the structure of deliberation. It is precisely the sort of approach that Schmitt detested.

The post-1945 constitution added clarity at the level of basic legal structure and a stronger sense of the legal limits on legitimate state authority, now often elaborated and sometimes enforced beyond the state. This is not just a consequence of the Moderns' love of written legal texts. It also stems from the fact that we had lost our way so badly that we were forced to write down what should have been self-evident. Human rights fit very neatly with the strategy of taming reason of state by subjecting it to the structures and rhythms of ordinary law and politics. Rights not only provide our main vocabulary for describing the limits of authority. They also aspire to engender a particular style of juridical and political conversation. 'The fundamental moral commitment entailed by rights', Michael Ignatieff has observed, 'is not to respect, and certainly not to worship. It is to deliberation.'[186] A central contribution of the post-war constitution was to reinforce the old republican idea that secrecy and closed conversations almost inevitably lead to the dominance of private interests, while with open deliberation among diverse institutions there is at least the chance of public-interested decision-making.

Rights also drive up the number of reason of state cases that reach the courts – all the more so in a political climate which prizes personal security so highly and thinks in terms of catastrophe and risk. There are difficulties with such a move. But on balance it represents an important dimension of the post-war constitution's strategy for realizing the epistemic, incentive-compatibility and control objectives. In the face of such trends, conservatives often end up despairing about the modern condition and, although sometimes having the best lines, lead to little more than a poetic dead end. Dogmatic liberals offer a make-believe world inhabited only by the pure. The position I have sketched in this chapter may not appeal to perfectionists or dreamers. But the study of constitutions is not a matter of clean lines and final solutions. I am happy to keep Hume company in the republic of the second best.

This book is about reason of state, but it has also been about the British constitution. In this respect, this and the previous chapter have a slightly different focus from others in the book. Whereas earlier chapters concentrated on the development of the constitution against the background of British imperialism, the final two chapters have had a wider frame, connecting developments in British public law to wider European and global

[186] Ignatieff, *Human Rights as Politics and Idolatry*, 84.

legal and political trends at and after the end of empire. This change in focus is as revealing as it was necessary. As we come closer to the present, it becomes increasingly hard to discuss British public law as though it were an island story. For better or worse, it becomes a story of a constitutional order like many others, albeit one with a peculiarly rich and particularly influential tradition. Some might see the internationalizing and 'normalizing' trends discussed in this chapter as symptoms of the downward spiral in the nation's fortunes. This is a picture of Britain defanged, they would say. Britain internationalized. Britain stripped of sovereignty and majesty. Britain hollowed out.

An alternative reading is available, though, and it is one that I prefer. If what I said earlier about the constitution comprising both nomos and narrative is true, then it is a mistake to think in terms of selling out or giving up. A better way to think about it is to focus on the creative use of traditions, including traditions of which we are no longer proud, to reinvent and reimagine ourselves constitutionally now and into the future. David Armitage wrote, in a phrase I quoted earlier in the book, that the British saw their empire as protestant, commercial, maritime and free. Well, both nomos and narrative have seen plenty of change since then. But it does not seem too much of a stretch to rework Armitage's phrase to describe the ideology of the British constitution in its present incarnation, at least as I have presented it here, as individual, commercial, international and free.

INDEX

Page numbers with 'n' are notes.

Lightning Source UK Ltd.
Milton Keynes UK
UKHW020822091022
410176UK00011B/106

9 781107 461741